INFRASTRUCTURE ENGINEERING AND MANAGEMENT

INFRASTRUCTURE ENGINEERING AND MANAGEMENT

NEIL S. GRIGG

A Wiley-Interscience Publication

JOHN WILEY & SONS

New York   Chichester   Brisbane   Toronto   Singapore

Library of Congress Cataloging in Publication Data:

Grigg, Neil S.
  Infrastructure engineering and management.
  "A Wiley-Interscience publication."

  Bibliography: p.
  1. Municipal engineering.   2. Public works.
  3. Infrastructure (Economics) I. Title.

TD159.3.G75 1988   363.6   87-22993
ISBN 0-471-84974-X

ACKNOWLEDGMENTS

Abundant food is in the fallow ground of the poor, But it is swept away by injustice.
(*Proverbs* 13:23 NASB)

Solving the problems of infrastructure is linked closely with the objective of improving life for humans. The benefits brought by effective infrastructure systems are sometimes swept away by "injustice" in the absence of effective engineering and management. The noble objective of providing the services needed is sometimes obscured when we think about the nitty-gritty of infrastructure systems: potholes, sewage, soil and water, and garbage collection. Generally the professionals who care for these matters are called "public works managers," and there are many capable ones out there who serve well. This book is dedicated to them.

I would like to express appreciation to the public works managers and engineers who have influenced my work in this field. They are too numerous to list. I would like to mention, however, the fine work of the American Public Works Association in providing a focal point for communication, training, the exchange of ideas, and the inspiration provided to our public works leadership. I have enjoyed and profited from my participation with them.

The National Science Foundation funded a small project in 1982 which enabled me to start on this infrastructure work, and I would like to express appreciation for this support. The objective was to identify the interdisciplinary research needs indicated by the infrastructure "crisis." The details of this work are reported in Chapter 11.

I would also like to express appreciation to the city of Fort Collins, Colorado, first for being so well managed, and second for providing data and information which has been used extensively in the book to illustrate technical points and methods.

The problems of infrastructure are closely connected with those of cities. Providing physical facilities will not by itself improve living conditions, but it is a start. I did not feel I could go into the social problems of cities in the book, but these words from a hymn begin to describe the situation:

Proudly rise our modern cities,
Stately buildings, row on row;
Yet their windows, blank, unfeeling,
Stare on canyoned streets below,
Where the lonely drift unnoticed
In the city's ebb and flow,
Lost to purpose and to meaning,
Scarcely caring where they go.

(Words from *God, Who Stretched the Spangled Heavens*, used with permission from Hope Publishing Company, Carol Stream, Ill.)

PREFACE

The problems of infrastructure naturally attract the attention of engineers and public managers. Their imaginations are quickly captured by the messy management problems to be solved and the large sums of money involved, and by the high level of policy and political content of the subject. All together the infrastructure area constitutes an important problem to be solved.

This book is about the engineering and management techniques that can help solve the problems. It strives to provide a focus on the combined management and technical aspects of the problem in an integrated way from the perspective of the engineer/manager, but understandable to the lay person. The philosophy of the book is simple: good management and the absence of corruption lead to effective infrastructure and basic public services; these provide the means for an acceptable quality of life for human beings.

The book began about 1970 with the notes for a course I taught at the University of Denver called "urban engineering," essentially a course on public works management and urban planning. Later, at Colorado State University, I changed the name to "urban systems engineering." In 1986 I changed the name again to "infrastructure engineering and management." The book has a wide intended audience: students of civil engineering, construction management, public administration, and associated fields which may lead to careers in public works or city management; engineer/managers already in the public sector; consulting engineers and management consultants; and those working in the broad policy or research fields relating to infrastructure.

I use the material in this book for a one-semester course at the master's degree level. It is also appropriate for upper-level undergraduates. The proportion of students from developing countries is usually near half in the course, and so the material is meant to illustrate basic principals that will apply to their problems as well as to U.S. conditions. This would seem a challenge due to the political content of much of the material, but I have found that students from the United States and from developing countries have the same need with regard to this material: to learn to analyze and apply basic principles of management to find solutions to difficult and unstructured problems facing infrastructure managers, and to communicate the results of their analysis effectively. With these targets in mind, the problem of aiming the course at the two groups was solved.

Since the material is so new to most of the students who have taken the course, and since the problems involved are for the most part unstructured, I have taken the case study approach to illustrate the principles involved. This comes in the form of a series of exercises that require analysis and writing. The reader who is not a formal student may benefit from reading and trying these exercises, at least briefly. They are meant to illustrate basic skills needed by public works managers, with applications to the most important problems of infrastructure management: analysis, written communication, economic and financial analysis, problem solving and planning, business organization and strategy, management skills, and use of quantitative techniques of analysis.

As the material is presented in a practical form, it has been necessary to present data and illustrations throughout the book. The city of Fort Collins, Colorado, has made a convenient source for illustrations, and their municipal management data have been used extensively. I am thankful that the management techniques used by the city are up to date and innovative, and they constitute a good example for other cities and management organizations.

NEIL S. GRIGG

Fort Collins, Colorado
October 1987

CONTENTS

INFRASTRUCTURE ENGINEERING AND MANAGEMENT

CHAPTER ONE

INFRASTRUCTURE MANAGEMENT AND ENGINEERING

Since the condition of the nation's infrastructure began to attract media attention about 1980, there have been articles and monographs written about it. This book is intended to make a contribution by systematically outlining the management strategies and elements necessary to begin to solve the problems.

In all human societies the quality of life depends first on the physical infrastructure that provides for basic necessities such as shelter, water, waste disposal, and transportation. The planning, management, and engineering of the infrastructure necessary to provide these necessities is one of the most important historical responsibilities of engineers and managers. The early days of science and technology were devoted to finding better ways to provide this infrastructure and related improvements to life. Maintaining and improving this infrastructure now constitutes a formidable challenge since important decisions are made in a political environment. Success in managing infrastructure requires special talents and dedication exercised in an interdisciplinary environment by engineers, managers, and policymakers.

"Infrastructure" refers to the physical systems that provide transportation, water, buildings, and other public facilities that are needed to meet basic human social and economic needs. These facilities are needed by people regardless of their level of economic development. When infrastructure is not present or does not work properly, it is impossible to provide basic services such as food distribution, shelter, medical care, and safe drinking water. Maintaining infrastructure is a constant and expensive process which often is neglected in favor of more attractive political goals.

The basis for public provision of infrastructure facilities goes back in history, at least to the time of Socrates. His theories included the belief that in order to function at all, a person needs the facilities and arrangements available from community, security, institutions, and economic goods, and that these can only be available when individuals support the concept of community and the responsibilities that it entails (1). Chief among these responsibilities is the provision of infrastructure and the services it provides.

Infrastructure needs attracted much attention in the United States and elsewhere when it became clear that increasing demands on facilities and past neglect have created enormous capital investment needs. This news is not all bad, of course, since fixing the problems will offer substantial business opportunities. In fact, the renovation market has become a substantial and attractive one for engineering and construction companies. *ENR* magazine reported in 1986 that the building renovation market alone had reached $68 billion per year, and to that can be added military maintenance, industrial plant retrofit, and the four highway "R's": resurfacing, reconstruction, rehabilitation, and restoration (2). According to *ENR* this renovation work particularly attracts specialty contractors, many of whom specialize in electrical and mechanical work.

In developing countries, enormous problems are faced as the countries grapple with how to provide adequate infrastructure for exploding urban populations in the face of a debt crisis and other problems. Whereas the infrastructure problem in the United States and Europe is still, in most cases, a matter of levels of services provided, it is an urgent matter of public health and survival in developing countries.

This book is about the engineering and management techniques that can help solve the problems. The book focuses on the combined management and technical aspects of the management problem in an integrated way from the perspective of the technical person, but understandable to the lay person.

Although a number of aspects of the "infrastructure crisis" can be debated, many agree that the technologies and funds to take care of the situation can be made available if good management techniques are employed. This is a matter of providing the funds from resources available to the governing body, however scarce. If it is apparent that adequate funds are not available, then it is management's responsibility either to find the funds or to make the system work with less. This is a tall order, but it is what infrastructure management is all about.

To repeat, it is the business of public works engineers and managers, in both the public and private sectors, to solve the infrastructure problem. The complexity of the problem and the skills they must bring to bear are the subject of this book.

1.1 DEFINITION OF INFRASTRUCTURE

The word "infrastructure" is not even found in some dictionaries. To some who have heard the word, it has only a generic meaning: the general inner structure of something. The term is becoming increasingly associated with public works and the physical facilities of cities and nations. In public management and in investment banking it is readily understood to be synonymous with physical facilities. Such a long word is resented by some, and if it is used, they pass it off as "a 14-letter word that doesn't mean anything, nothing but the latest buzzword out of Washington." It may be a new word, but it is the bread and butter of millions working in the construction and related industries, and seems to be here to stay.

For the purposes of this book the term will be taken to mean those physical facilities that are sometimes called "public works." Tarr, in writing about infrastructure history, refers to public works as the "sinews" of cities (3). Public works have been defined elsewhere by the American Public Works Association (APWA) as follows (4):

> Public Works are the physical structures and facilities that are developed or acquired by public agencies to house governmental functions and provide water, power, waste disposal, transportation, and similar services to facilitate the achievement of common social and economic objectives.

APWA goes on to list 18 categories of public works and environmental facilities that are included in this definition. Some of the categories are quite general and not directly related to infrastructure facilities, so the following list of 12 categories is taken on a selective basis from APWA's list. It omits some generalized categories of public administration concerns, but includes all the categories of physical facilities listed.

1. Water supply systems, including dams, reservoirs, transmission, treatment, and distribution facilities.
2. Wastewater management systems, including collection, treatment, disposal, and reuse systems.
3. Solid-waste management facilities.
4. Transportation facilities, including highway, rail, and airports. This includes all of the lighting, signing, and control facilities as well.
5. Public transit systems.
6. Electric systems, including production and distribution.
7. Natural gas facilities.
8. Flood control, drainage, and irrigation facilities.
9. Waterways and navigation facilities.
10. Public buildings such as schools, hospitals, police stations, and fire facilities.
11. Public housing facilities.
12. Parks, playgrounds, and recreational facilities, including stadiums.

A briefer list would be potentially more workable. The following list consists of six categories. They are intended to cluster together by industry and professional interest group.

1. Roads group (roads, streets, and bridges)
2. Transportation services group (transit, rail, ports, and airports)
3. Water group (water, wastewater, all water systems, including waterways)
4. Waste management group (solid-waste management systems)
5. Buildings and outdoor sports group
6. Energy production and distribution group (electric and gas)

Not all of the facility types will be analyzed in this book. Most of the recent studies which make up the basic source material for this book concentrate on transportation and water facilities, broadly defined. These will be used throughout the book to illustrate principles which also apply to the other categories of facilities. Occasionally other types of facilities will be used as illustrations. Infrastructure managers are aware that once certain basic principles are learned, they can be applied to other types of facilities as well. This is why we can find retired military officers in public works management positions and public administrators moving from management positions in one category of infrastructure to another.

1.2 HISTORICAL BACKGROUND OF INFRASTRUCTURE

The development of infrastructure in any region of the world closely parallels the historical development of the area involved. In the United States, infrastructure development patterns reflect the different phases of national development: the early agricultural society, the emerging nation, the Civil War, the industrial revolution, the advent of the automobile, the Great Depression, World War II and the postwar urban explosion, the suburbanization and road-building era, and the shift to the information society. In Europe the infrastructure patterns in large cities reflect the early history of Europe as well as wartime difficulties. In the less developed countries some have never benefited from high-quality infrastructure; others struggle to maintain facilities put into place in colonial times.

Tarr provides an excellent discussion of the phases of development of infrastructure in the United States. His classification includes the development of urban networks and walking cities, a period of foundations, 1790–1855; the construction of the core infrastructure in central cities, 1855–1910; the domination of the automobile and enlargement of the federal role, 1910–1955; and the rise of the outer city and recent trends, 1955–1982 (3).

One might wonder how it came to be that we neglected our infrastructure. A historical perspective helps to understand the sequence of events, as it is clear from the influence of large historical forces that infrastructure cannot always be one of the top national priorities. These historical forces are discussed in the next sections, and from them one can draw conclusions about the causes of current problems with inadequate finance and deferred maintenance, as well as the way the public works management profession evolved.

In the early period of infrastructure development beginning in the eighteenth century, the United States was just becoming an urban nation. We have to remember that in the period of the American Revolution there were few urban centers, and even the great metropolitan areas such as New York had small populations at the time. By 1800 New York City had a population of only 60,000. The western part of the United States was unexplored, and the South was almost entirely rural. Thus infrastructure development before about 1800 was essentially nonexistent. However, some of the technologies that emerged in the United States later, such as road building, were already in practice in Europe.

In the nineteenth century there were great developmental moves in the United States. Infrastructure construction began with arrangements between the three levels of government and the private sector that were born out of necessity. Economic development was the driving force behind construction. An example of this is the beginning of the canal-building era, with the opening of the Erie Canal in 1825. This was also a great period of railroad construction. In urban areas there was no definite organization for handling services, and needs were met on an ad hoc basis, often with volunteer groups stepping forward when needed. Cities gradually developed the service orientation we are familiar with today. They were reluctant to form operating departments and to incur debt to initiate and operate services. This accounts for the haphazard public-private development of infrastructure in the early periods of the nation's history.

Street construction in the nineteenth century was the most obvious infrastructure development. Cobblestone was in frequent use, but its disadvantages of noise, fragility, and difficulty in cleaning made it unsatisfactory and led to a search for better methods. It was not until the beginning of the automobile era, however, that modern asphalt and concrete pavements began to be used. In effect, all of the roadways we have in the United States were built since about 1900, and the part that carries most of the traffic, the interstate highway system, was built after 1956.

Water supply systems were initiated in the nineteenth century due to the drive for improved living conditions and the need to protect public health in the increasingly crowded neighborhoods in the cities. The first city to construct a large-scale municipal water system was Philadelphia, which initiated its system in 1798 as a result of a yellow fever epidemic. Other large U.S. cities such as New York and Boston were following this lead by the mid-nineteenth century. There was a mixture of public and private development of systems, with the balance remaining until well into the twentieth century when the shift to public ownership become more apparent. Today there remain some private water companies, and the concept is returning to favor with less initiative on the part of the federal government to subsidize public services of all kinds. The resulting emphasis on "privatization" is discussed in Chapter 7.

Wastewater systems had their beginning with the advent of in-house water supply systems, which made the former cesspool and privy vault arrangement overloaded. After moving water supplies into the house, it became a necessity to provide for a wastewater system. The presence of storm drains in some cities provided convenient receptacles for waterborne wastes, and with the invention of the water closet, the form of the present wastewater system we have was set. The waterborne nature of the system was not set, however, without considerable debate and study of alternatives. It was the discovery of the water seal for building drains that finally made in-house plumbing socially acceptable, since before the use of the seals the odor problem was considerable.

The industrial revolution created many new problems and opportunities for infrastructure systems. New technological developments such as electricity, steam plants, the automobile, and mass production changed society and created not only a demand but an imperative for infrastructure systems to meet the needs of the day. The automobile changed the form of cities and roads forever, and even today with our shift to a communications society the automobile is still the basis for much of the demand on infrastructure systems.

In the United States the rising standard of living accounted for the demand for infrastructure. The availability of single-family housing, particularly after World War II, required significant increases in facilities to serve the needs for water, energy, and transportation. The increasing availability of family cars, with explosive growth between 1910 and 1930, required streets and road systems beyond previous expectations.

Management organizations rose to meet the needs for infrastructure development and management. With the rise in suburban development, there was a vast increase in the number of special-purpose districts for the development and management of infrastructure facilities. Central cities grew to meet the special districts, and their growth was halted by the end of the 1960s.

In the early days of the development of cities there was no professional cadre of engineer-managers to meet the needs of infrastructure development, and decisions were made by citizen governing boards. As the need for foreign engineers ended and the engineering profession grew in the United States, civil engineers began to take on the full role of administrative and technical management of infrastructure systems. By the early part of the twentieth century the shape of the professions that were to manage infrastructure had taken form.

Civil engineering had been represented by the American Society of Civil Engineers, already a force by 1900. There was, however, a need for societies to represent the special infrastructure challenges faced by management of public works agencies. The American Society of Municipal Improvements (ASMI) was formed in 1894 with the first meeting in Buffalo. A split occurred in 1897 with the formation of the now-defunct League of American Municipalities. This split led the ASMI to focus on technical matters rather than broader management questions. An initiative to form the Association for Standardizing Paving Specifications led to a merger with the ASMI in 1913. The name of ASMI was changed to the American Society of Municipal Engineers (AME) in 1930.

Another organization, the International Association of Street and Sanitation Officials, operated parallel with AME. Changing its name in 1925 to the International Association of Public Works Officials (IAPWO), this organization worked with the International City Management Association (ICMA) to develop systems for financial and administrative management of cities. They produced a text entitled *Municipal Public Works Management* in the mid-1930s. This text might be considered the forerunner of the green book series of the ICMA on public works management. In 1935 AME and IAPWO formed a joint secretariat and asked Donald C. Stone to become the executive director of the joint organization. In that same year, the two organizations finally merged and created the American Public Works Association (5).

New challenges for the development of infrastructure include coping with the next economic phase: the postindustrial information society. This can bring some dramatic shifts in the demand and management needs for infrastructure, and the shape of the changes is not yet known. Maintaining an already extensive infrastructure will be a formidable financial challenge that the nation has not yet solved. Resource depletion may raise the cost of some cheap materials such as those used in road building, and continuing revelations about other common construction materials, such as asbestos, will bring other changes. Infrastructure managers will have to adapt to a more complex society with different infrastructure demands and waste products to manage. Emergency procedures grow more complex all the time with the interdependence of society. The Chernobyl nuclear plant disaster near Kiev in the Soviet Union received considerable attention as this book was being written, emphasizing the interdependence of all societies on infrastructure. Finally, the trade-offs between transportation and communications and the move toward an automated society will drastically affect the nature of infrastructure management.

These new challenges will drastically affect the demands on management for the remainder of this century. Meeting these challenges is the subject which we turn to now.

1.3. PURPOSE OF THE BOOK

Developing an effective management approach is the only long-term way to handle a problem as large as an infrastructure with a replacement value of trillions of dollars. This book is devoted to this question: What are the skills needed to manage infrastructure, and how should they be applied? The book is intended to be interdisciplinary. The need for an interdisciplinary approach was put well by Donald Stone (4). In advocating new educational strategies for public works administrators, he stated:

> Engineering capability alone is insufficient for these multidimensional purposes. Engineering and other specialized skills must be complemented by public affairs and managerial competences. These include capacity to deal with the gamut of social, economic, environmental and political factors inherent in planning, policy resolution and program implementation. Practitioners are needed who can integrate public works systems and subsystems into urban and national development programs.

Because of the importance of management and policy skills, this book is organized according to management subjects rather than by category of infrastructure. This recognizes that some of the key skills needed by the engineer are precisely those relating to management.

The tasks of management are sometimes taken to be planning, organizing, directing, and controlling. For engineers working on infrastructure these correspond to planning, designing, constructing, and operating. These terms overersimplify the question, however, since there is more to infrastructure management than just getting the facilities planned, built, and operated. There is a high level of dependence on finance, on project management, and, increasingly, on the use of computers for management. The application of these topics to operation and maintenance of facilities is especially important. The chapters of this book follow these topics. We begin with the characteristics of critical categories of infrastructure, and then go to engineering and management techniques associated with programming and budgeting, finance, project management, operation and maintenance, decision support systems, organization of agencies, political aspects, and future issues. Emphasis is on the general principles that apply to all categories of infrastructure.

1.4. THE INFRASTRUCTURE "CRISIS"

For persons working in public works, the beginning of the 1980s was characterized by media attention to a perceived infrastructure "crisis." In 1981 a pair of writers named Pat Choate and Susan Walter took a collection of federal reports on facility needs and wove them into a booklet entitled "America in Ruins: Beyond the Public Works Pork Barrel" (6). Their purpose was to make recommendations for improving public works investment and management. They made recommendations for creating a national capital budget, for improving management accountability, and for clarifying responsibilities.

The media picked up on the infrastructure theme, and by 1982 there were several national cover stories on the subject. *Newsweek* had a cover story on August 2, 1982, entitled "The Decaying of America" (7). *U.S. News & World Report* followed on September 27 with a story entitled "To Rebuild America: $2,500,000,000,000 Job" (8). In these and many other publications, the high figures of $2 trillion to $3 trillion estimated to be the price tag of infrastructure needs came from taking all of the categories and adding together needs estimates. The needs in transportation alone, taken over a 20-year period, amount to $1 trillion to $2 trillion, depending on the estimates used.

The Congressional Budget Office took a look at the problem in 1983 and reported needs for federal expenditures amounting to $28 billion per year under current program structures. The categories considered were highways, public transit, wastewater treatment, water resources, air traffic control, airports, and water supply. Total needs for these categories (federal and nonfederal) were given as some $53 billion per year, a figure that could be interpreted to be of the same order of magnitude as 20-year estimates of, say $2 trillion for all categories (9).

A review of the infrastructure studies would not be complete without mentioning studies by the University of Colorado for the Joint Economic Committee (10) and by the National Council on Public Works Improvement (11). "Hard Choices," a study for the Joint Economic Committee, made recommendations in four areas: the need for a national infrastructure "fund," the need for a coordinated national needs assessment, the need for a review of technical standards, and the reevaluation of statutory and administrative rules that govern the use of assistance programs. The study's estimates of needs, in billions of dollars, for the period 1983–2000 were as follows:

	Needs	Resources	Shortfall
Highways and bridges	720	455	265
Other transportation	178	90	88
Water supply and distribution	96	55	41
Wastewater collection treatment	163	114	49
Totals	1157	714	443

These estimates are seen to be in the same range as the others. If other categories are added, especially buildings, energy, and other water needs, the estimates will approach the $2 trillion–$3 trillion range for a 20-year time period.

Regardless of the estimate used, it is clear that substantial demands will be made on the treasuries at all three levels of government, and for this reason, the general subject of how to finance infrastructure has taken a front row seat in most debates.

The National Council on Public Works Improvement was established by the Public Works Improvement Act of 1984 (PL 98-501). It oversees the infrastructure problem area, and is preparing a series of reports as this book is being written. The first one was released in the fall of 1986, discussing three subjects: decision-making issues, technological issues, and economic and finance issues. These themes are familiar and recur throughout this book, as they are the most important dimensions of the infrastructure problem area.

The report regards decision making as involving all three levels of government. It discusses the roles of the government and the private sector, as well as management and decision-making practices. The report recommends that the government and the private sector work together, with a focus on the following: improving decision-making tools; recruiting, training, and supporting public works managers to meet new challenges; revising regulations and standards; and finding ways to encourage technological advances, apply new knowledge, prevent and resolve disputes, and improve means of intergovernmental cooperation and coordination.

Under technological issues the council found that there are opportunities in both the software and hardware areas. Many of the possible advances are said to be in the computer and telecommunications areas. In the case of financial and economic areas, both the problem of finding the adequate finances and the question of economic impacts of infrastructure are covered.

To this writer an infrastructure bill of $1 trillion spread over 20 years does not look so large. A 20-year infrastructure bill of $1 trillion would amount to about $200 per year per capita. That is not much compared with the total wealth of the country. According to a Department of Commerce study reported in U.S. *News & World Report*, the total wealth of the United States is some $12.5 trillion (12). For a population of 250 million, that comes to about $50,000 per capita. Most of the wealth is in structures, equipment, housing, and land. Since infrastructure is the facility basis for the wealth, certainly more than $200 per year per capita, or 0.4 percent of the wealth, could be devoted to upgrading and replacing infrastructure.

Numbers reporting the extent of the infrastructure problem are rather academic until the specific categories and conditions are specified. One report had a needs estimate in the range of $8–10 trillion (13). This is close to the estimates of the total of the national wealth. On further examination this report includes about $2.4 trillion for manufacturing plants, $2.8 trillion for electric generating plants, and $3.8 trillion for the construction of new cities. These are additional categories beyond those mentioned in most of the media articles; otherwise the estimates are about the same as in the other publications. The variance in these figures illustrates the point that how large the problem is depends mostly on how you look at it.

Whatever our impression of the infrastructure crisis, one message is clear: it is a large problem and requires the best management skills we can give it.

1.5. URBAN COMPLEXITIES OF THE INFRASTRUCTURE CRISIS

Whatever our impression of the overall infrastructure crisis, it is clear that much of it is bound up in the urban nature of the problems. Cities are not easy to manage, and the interdependent economic–social–physical nature of the urban system exacerbates the problem. In Chapter 3 some data about the urban "system" are presented to show this interdependent relationship and the linkages involved.

All we have to do to gain some insight into the urban nature of the problems and the great complexity that must be solved is to look at a few cases, and they abound. In this regard, two cities that receive attention constantly are New York and Chicago.

New York is a city that seems almost unmanageable at times. From massive power outages to social problems such as crime on the subways, the city's problems are huge in scale. New York City even went bankrupt in the 1970s, with the state having a difficult time reviving it due to the vast sums involved.

Recently one seasoned observer, a former New York City housing commissioner, concluded that the quality of life in the city has declined along with the civic spirit which is so important in being a great city (14). The observer states that the quality of life in cities is due to more than how well public authorities patch streets or supply water; it is due to those intangible factors that involve the spirit. The primary problem is caused by the failure of public and private agencies to deal with the vast increase of people on welfare—this problem affects everything else the city tries to do.

The subways present a good example of the kinds of problem New York has to grapple with. The subways are plagued with brightly painted graffiti, litter, crime, and pollution. A recent issue of the *Wall Street Journal* carried an interesting article about how difficult it is to solve some of the problems of providing this basic service, transit, in New York. This article, about a subway tunnel on Manhattan's East Side, is reprinted with permission from the *Journal* as an appendix to this chapter. The purpose of reprinting it is to provide a vivid case study of the complexity and difficulty of solving some urban infrastructure problems (15).

The current estimated cost of the tunnel, originally estimated at $154 million, is now $800 million. At the time the article had been written (1985), the tunnel had been under construction for 16 years. It is now said to be going nowhere. It is not viewed as an important leg in the metro subway transportation system which tranports millions of passengers daily. One plan would only have the tunnel transporting 220 passengers during rush hour, but some advocate completion anyway. Problems include bad maintenance, corruption, delays, inflated costs, bad communication, and others. The problems are interesting to study since they show what can go wrong in infrastructure projects, particularly those in urban areas.

The problems in New York have attracted attention for years. The city was even the setting for a disaster prediction in a social forecasting book, *The Coming Dark Age*. The book, which is intended to be taken seriously but reads like science fiction, is about the breakdown of large-scale systems, including infrastructure systems (16). In the book New York is the subject of a chapter entitled "The Death of New York." The story goes this way. On a Friday night there is a heavy snowstorm that impedes traffic, as it often does in New York. Airline controllers are unable to get relief. They get tired, and one makes a mistake—an airliner hits a key electrical facility, and this causes a large-scale blackout. The snow continues, people abandon their cars, food gets scarce, riots begin, people are killed, fires are accidentally begun by people cooking and trying to get warm, disease spreads, etc. This is Vacca's vision of what could happen in a city like New York. Let's hope that the infrastructure is more redundant than that!

Chicago is another well-known urban area with a vast infrastructure to manage. A recent *Business Week* article had an alarming title, "Chicago: The City That Works Doesn't Anymore" (17). According to this account, which was during the administration of Mayor Jane Byrne, a number of difficult problems plagued the city. These included deficits in the transit systems and schools that totaled $200 million in 1982; a tax base that was dwindling; turmoil in the city leadership, with rapid turnover of financial managers; and a falling population. These problems came at a time when the infrastructure capital needs in the city were estimated at $3.3 billion. One of these infrastructure problem areas was the giant Tunnel and Reservoir project (TARP), a controversial project that attracted investigative reporting from the CBS news show "60 Minutes." Obviously, infrastructure investments in Chicago have competition for capital, and this is a city that faces some uphill battles for effective government.

These short examples provide insight into the unique urban complexities that face the infrastructure manager. Suggested solutions for these problems are discussed throughout this book.

1.6. A MANAGEMENT SYSTEM FOR INFRASTRUCTURE

Managing an aggregation of large-scale systems called "infrastructure" is too complex to be reduced to a system. In reviewing the elements of public works management, however, there are certain "systemic" elements that enter into the equation for success.

In formulating these elements it becomes clear that they are the same as they would be for managing any complex enterprise: they are the skills involved in organizational, operational, and personnel management. They must be exercised in the framework of management tasks: planning, organizing, directing, and controlling. Table 1.1 illustrates these tasks, along with some of the management systems elements that are necessary to be successful in managing infrastructure.

The public works manager needs to have a good organizational structure, with good managers and workers at every level. All of the elements of organization have to work well: communications, personnel matters, motivation, working space, and the rest.

In operations the mission of the organization needs to be clear. Planning must be effective, and engineers and managers need to be competent and well

TABLE 1.1. Management System Elements

Planning	Organizing	Directing	Controlling
Effective planning/ programming, and budgeting	Effective organizational structure	Leadership and decision making	Maintenance management system
Ongoing program evaluation	Workable decision support systems		Effective operations[a] management
			Quality control

[a]Operations include operation of the physical systems as well as the organizational system that delivers services.

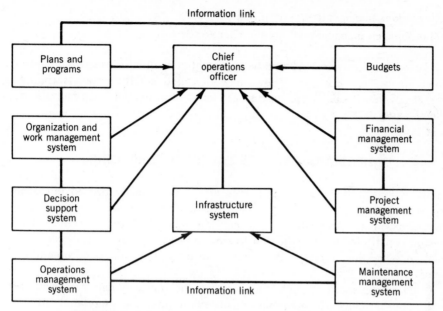

FIGURE 1.1. Infrastructure management system, with subsystems.

trained. It is essential that no corruption be tolerated in the organization. Excellence in contracting and supervising the work of contractors is required. Operations and management need to be well planned and executed.

In addition to these expected requirements the public works manager needs a high level of leadership and political skills to succeed in the demanding environment of infrastructure management. These are discussed in Chapter 10.

The general topics covered in this book make up an infrastructure management "system." They can be used to look at how well an individual organization is doing in putting together modern-management approaches. Figure 1.1 shows the concept of the different management systems discussed in the book, all interrelating to form an overall infrastructure management system. Perhaps this conceptual formulation can serve as a guide for the manager.

The eight subsystems that are included on the figure are:

- Plans and programs (Chapter 3)
- Organization and work management system (Chapters 4 and 9)
- Decision support system (Chapter 4)
- Capital and operating budgets (Chapter 5)
- Financial management system (Chapter 6)
- Projects control or management system (Chapter 8)

- Operations management system (Chapter 9)
- Maintenance management system (Chapter 9)

Each of the subsystems should be represented in all infrastructure organizations. The first test is whether they can be identified; and the second is whether they are working well. This forms the basis for a self-evaluation for organizational effectiveness.

1.7. MANAGING CAPITAL AND OPERATIONS

In discussions of the infrastructure crisis, attention is usually focused on raising and managing capital. The emphasis in this book is on managing operations, as well as on managing the capital once the infrastructure is installed. This section constitutes an introduction to this subject. As you work through the book, it is helpful to look at the concepts of managing capital and operations jointly.

Good management of capital facilities (facilities management) and good operating performance (the operations management problem) are related through planning and maintenance, since the capital facility durability and ultimate cost depend on how well planning and maintenance are carried out. Without effective maintenance, operations cannot be successful.

One way to characterize this relationship is by the following table, which shows the area of management concern, the staff of the organization involved, and the financing vehicle employed:

Management Concern	Staff Involved	Financing
Facilities adequacy		
New facilities	Planning/Engineering	Capital budget
Existing facilities	O&M	Operating budget
Operating effectiveness	O&M	Operating budget

Due to financial constraints there is today considerable interest in making existing facilities last longer and operate better. This is the natural outcome of disillusion with poor operation of capital-intensive projects, such as in the wastewater treatment program.

The need to focus on making existing facilities work better is illustrated by the creation of the REMR Research program announced by the U.S. Army Corps of Engineers in 1983. (REMR stands for repair, evaluation, maintenance, and rehabilitation.) The objective of the program was stated in the first newsletter of the program: ". . . to identify, develop, and apply effective and affordable technology for maintaining, and where possible, extending the service life of existing civil works projects" (18).

The need to focus on making existing facilities work better is illustrated by the creation of the REMR Research program announced by the U.S. Army Corps of Engineers in 1983. (REMR stands for repair, evaluation, maintenance, and rehabilitation. The objective of the program was stated in the first newsletter of the program: ". . . to identify, develop, and apply effective and affordable technology for maintaining, and where possible, extending the service life of existing civil works projects" (18).

The REMR program is mirrored in the general concerns of infrastructure managers with other slogans. For example, there are the four R's of the highway program (resurfacing, reconstruction, rehabilitation, and restoration) and the general three R's of the infrastructure problem (repair, rehabilitation, and replacement).

These principles of facilities management may seem elementary to experienced managers, but it is surprising how many engineers involved in public works have not dealt with the important questions of operations and maintenance and with the "Rs" as a management tool. The use of the capital and operating budgets and the operation of an effective maintenance program are absolutely essential to success in facilities management.

The cost of capital and operations is the critical factor that needs most attention in providing good management. Cost factors will be discussed in Chapter 6, which covers financial management. However, the concept of "needs" is introduced at this time, since it is a key concept in understanding the infrastructure "crisis."

In operating facilities the two categories of finances, capital and operating, are normally met from two different sources: the capital budget, often based on borrowing, and the annual operating budget, usually based on fees collected or on taxes. The total cost of these two budgets, including debt service, represents the cost of providing a particular service. Maintenance and depreciation have been neglected in many infrastructure systems, since they are easy to defer from one political administration and budget year to another. As a result there is normally considerable uncapitalized depreciation and deferred maintenance in most infrastructure systems. In this sense the term "uncapitalized" means that funds are not collected in an account to pay for the depreciation when it occurs. When this finally becomes too great to ignore, it can be handled with bonds, renovation, and other approaches that are initiated by a current political administration. Current ratepayers are thus paying for past use and neglect of facilities. The ideal way to manage is to collect enough funds to pay for depreciation and the "R's" on an ongoing basis, but this is often not palatable politically.

In describing this widely recognized problem, and the resulting statement of "needs," several financial concepts are in use. First, the "replacement value of facilities" refers to the current cost of providing the facilities if they had to be completely replaced. The concept of "book value" would be some kind of depreciated value of facilities, and the accuracy of the values would depend on whether a true depreciation rate is used or whether a convenient accounting value is used. Since we normally do not know the rate of depreciation of infrastructure facilities, the book value usually is just an accounting value. There is a controversy in the water supply field in regard to these concepts. Managers are in favor of calculating depreciation on the basis of current cost accounting, since this provides funds through the rate base to repair and replace facilities on the basis of current, or today's costs. Much of the practice of accounting is based, however, on historical cost accounting, which means that costs for the "R's" do not recognize added amounts for inflation.

The concept of "needs" is the important one from the standpoint of management planning, and has turned out to be a difficult concept to deal with. "Needs" refers to the total of deferred maintenance, depreciation, and projected demand for new facilities. Since we do not normally know the rate of depreciation for most infrastructure facilities, and since deferred maintenance is also difficult to estimate, the backlog part of the needs is seldom known with much accuracy. With regard to future demands for facilities, even more unknowns exist.

Future demands depend on population projections, on standards for construction and performance of facilities, and on technological trends. For example, the future needs for a certain roadway network will depend on transportation demands caused by urban growth in an area, on the standards for construction (such as 55 mph versus 70 mph), and on trends affecting the mixture of autos and mass transit, as well as possible shifts in demand from increases in work at home that could reduce some of the needs for travel.

The subject of identifying needs has received much attention from researchers and from policy studies. As an addition to the "Hard Choices" report, Cuciti has prepared a needs-assessment manual for use as a guide to preparing needs estimates (19). In this handbook Marshall Kaplan, who directed the "Hard Choices" study, makes the case for improving the needs-assessment process. He states that we must have better needs assessments if we are to do a better job of building capacity. Problems are due to the lack of agreed-upon standards, inadequate attention to changing prices, the absence of solid growth data, and the absence of decent definitions and relevant inventories. Cuciti's outline for the needs-assessment planning process includes the following steps:

- Determine the scope of the analysis: geographic area, types of infrastructure, time frame, and participants in the process.
- Inventory existing infrastructure.
- Assess condition of existing infrastructure.
- Identify past trends in condition, service levels, and other factors responsible for trends.
- Forecast future patterns of growth.
- Estimate capital investment needs, including rehabilitation, reconstruction, and new facilities to handle growth.
- Identify levels of revenue available.
- Consider ways of dealing with the possible shortfalls in revenue.

This will appear to the seasoned planner as a rather traditional outline of a planning study; the author goes on the present some interesting data on innovations in preparing these studies.

1.8. NEW DIRECTIONS NEEDED IN CAPITAL MANAGEMENT

Finally, in the way of introduction, some recent studies of the infrastructure needs are reviewed due to their relevance to the subject of this book. The Urban Institute, an urban policy and management research institute in Washington, has devoted considerable attention to the infrastructure problem since it began to receive attention a few years ago. This resulted in a series of reports entitled "Guides to Managing Urban Capital Series." Considerable research went into the compilation of these volumes, and they provide a starting point for the examination of some of the key subjects we examine in this book. They will be reviewed briefly in this section (20–25).

The studies are comprehensive in presenting an inventory of current management practices in some 40 operating agencies, particularly those with responsibility for roads, bridges, and water and wastewater systems. In addition, surveys were conducted of a random sample of 35 cities to determine priority-setting procedures, a sample of 62 local governments to determine the condition and performance levels of facilities, and 33 members of the urban consortium to determine methods to finance capital budgets and maintenance plans.

The results of the studies are presented in the form of three basic strategies and 30 "ideas." These are presented here to stimulate thinking about the details ahead in the book:

Strategy 1: Better Identify Capital Needs and Priorities

1. Establish a facility condition assessment process to obtain on a regular basis information of major facilities within the jurisdiction.
2. Create and maintain a comprehensive inventory of facilities.
3. Encourage interagency cooperation to undertake joint maintenance work and joint inventory.
4. Start small and develop your inventory system as demand for it becomes clearer.
5. Encourage agencies and central staff to evaluate a variety of maintenance strategies.
6. Encourage operating agencies to reduce their dependence on crisis maintenance and on automatic maintenance without need.
7. Periodically scrutinize maintenance rules of thumb, such as repair or replacement cycles.
8. Resurrect preventive maintenance as a major maintenance strategy.

9. When the need for a facility is in question, consider abandonment or turn-over to the private sector.

10. Require agencies to identify instances of deferral of planned maintenance activities; identify reasons for the deferral, and provide an estimate of the consequences of the deferral.

11. Require that each major maintenance decision by an agency be backed by an economic comparison of alternatives.

12. Be sure that agencies consider life-cycle costs when deciding on maintenance actions.

13. Require that major new, replacement, or rehabilitated facilities be designed for maintainability.

14. Require that all capital budget proposal submissions include backup information on the potential effects of each proposal on service quality.

15. Incorporate a more formal, systematic way to consider new maintenance technology when examining maintenance options.

16. Require a systematic process for reviewing capital proposals.

17. Require that information on capital proposals be provided according to a preselected set of evaluation criteria so that the proposals can be more easily compared.

18. Require that all requests for capital improvements identify impacts on the operating budgets.

Strategy 2: Build Community Support for Facility Maintenance Needs

19. Initiate a joint public-private investigation of the jurisdiction's facilities and need for future action.

20. Involve citizen representatives in various parts of the capital facility project review and selection process.

21. Use the evidence provided on proposals to help market those proposals—such as evidence that a proposal will improve service quality or reduce future costs.

22. Encourage operating agency heads to improve their communications about the capital budget with central, administrative, and elected officials.

Strategy 3: Identify Financing Options

23. Estimate the local "capital financing gap."

24. Make aggressive use of the pricing system to finance capital investments.

25. Make full use of revenue bonds for capital financing.

26. Modify local institutional arrangements, if necessary, to achieve full application of user pricing, for example, by use of enterprise funds or independent authorities.

27. Dedicate specific tax revenues to capital investment or capital maintenance to provide a more stable source of financing.

28. Look for new ways to cooperate with the private sector and the business community in capital provision and capital financing.

29. Finance capital facilities in part or in whole by requiring private developers to install such facilities.

30. Use the same public-private cooperative efforts that are used for capital financing to gain support for capital bond issues.

These "ideas" can be recognized as similar to other concepts advanced throughout the book. One place they appear in particular is in Appendix B, which provides a "self-test" for organizations to use to see if their planning, budgeting, and capital management strategies are good. You may want to examine that appendix to take the test. A suggested procedure for taking the test appears in the exercises at the end of Chapter 3.

EXERCISE: LITERATURE FAMILIARIZATION AND PROBLEM IDENTIFICATION

Now you are familiar with the character and size of the infrastructure problem. It is important to be familiar with the literature and professional journals in the field. In this exercise you should seek out and study articles and papers about a particular infrastructure problem that interests you.

The objective of the assignment is to help you find the literature where infrastructure problems are described. This consists of construction trade magazines such as *ENR* and *Public Works* and the journals of the professional associations serving the different parts of the infrastructure sector. In large measure the media of infrastructure are trade journals, published free or at low cost to provide an outlet for advertising to the design and construction professionals who specify and purchase construction and operational components.

In the first part of the exercise you should identify one or more infrastructure sectors (such as street construction, water supply, wastewater, solid waste) and find the answers to the following questions:

1. What is the main trade or professional association serving this sector?

2. What are the main two journals or magazines you should read to keep up to date with this infrastructure management sector?

3. What are the main issues for this category of infrastructure? What problems confront it at the present time?

In the second part of the exercise you should take note that many different infrastructure problems have common threads: inadequate infrastructure development, insufficient funds, inadequate maintenance, and political problems. By reviewing the magazines and journals of the different infrastructure categories, you will find many case histories of infrastructure problems. One, a difficult transit problem, is described in the appendix to this chapter.

For the second part of the exercise you should prepare a brief written paper, no more than two pages in length. It should be a "problem identification" exercise. Later we will see that problem identification is the first step in the overall planning process. Your paper should describe the following:

1. Nature of the problem
2. Cost of the solution, both total cost and cost per capita
3. Barriers to the solution (technical, political, or whatever)
4. The process needed to solve the problem
5. The way the solution will be financed
6. The agency responsible for solving the problem
7. The reference

The problem you select can relate to any part of the physical infrastructure, and be a general problem or one confined to a particular city or region. If you have a problem you are familiar with from your city or another region that is of interest, that would be particularly appropriate. You may address the same problem in a later exercise in Chapter 3, concerned with policy analysis.

REFERENCES

1. Kolenda, Konstantin, "Moral philosophy in the core curriculum: The bipolarity of morality," *Assembly Magazine*, U.S. Military Academy, West Point, 1984.
2. "Renovation grows as a specialty," *ENR*, August 28, 1986.
3. Tarr, Joel A., "The evolution of the urban infrastructure in the nineteenth and twentieth centuries," in *Perspectives on Urban Infrastructure*, Royce Hanson, ed., National Academy Press, Washington D.C., 1984.
4. Stone, Donald C., Professional Education in Public Works/Environmental Engineering and Administration, American Public Works Association, Chicago, 1974.
5. Armstrong, Ellis L., History of Public Works in the United States: 1776–1976, American Public Works Association, Chicago, 1976.
6. Choate, Pat, and Susan Walter, America in Ruins: Beyond the Public Works Pork Barrel, Council of State Planning Agencies, Washington, D.C., 1981.
7. "The decaying of America," *Newsweek*, August 2, 1982.
8. "To rebuild America: $2,500,000,000,000 job," *U.S. News & World Report*, September 27, 1982.

9. Congressional Budget Office, Public Works Infrastructure: Policy Considerations for the 1980's, Washington, D.C., April 1983.

10. University of Colorado at Denver, Hard Choices: A report on the Increasing Gap between America's Infrastructure Needs and Our Ability to Pay for Them, Denver, February 1984.

11. National Council on Public Works Improvement, The Nation's Public Works: Defining the Context, Washington, D.C., October 1986.

12. "How much is US worth? $12.5 trillion, and we're getting richer," *U.S. News & World Report*, September 5, 1983.

13. Freeman, Richard, The Scope of the Infrastructure Deficit: How Much Is Needed Where, EIR Special Report, August 21, 1984.

14. Starr, Roger, *The Rise and Fall of New York*, Basic Books, 1985.

15. Penn, Stanley, "How a subway project in New York has led to doubt and dismay," *Wall Street Journal*, October 25, 1985.

16. Vacca, Roberto, *The Coming Dark Age*, Doubleday, Garden City, N.Y., 1973.

17. "Chicago: The city that works doesn't anymore," *Business Week*, November 23, 1981.

18. "The REMR Research Program," *REMR Bulletin*, January 1984, Vicksburg, Miss..

19. Cuciti, Peggy, *Planning for Infrastructure: A Handbook for State and Local Officials*, University of Colorado at Denver, 1985.

20. Hatry, Harry P., and George E. Peterson, Guides to Managing Urban Capital: A Summary, Vol. 1, Urban Institute, Washington, D.C., 1984.

21. Godwin, Stephen R., and George E. Peterson, Guide to Assessing Capital Stock Condition, Vol. 2, Urban Institute, Washington, D.C., 1984.

22. Peterson, George E., Mary J. Miller, Stephen R. Godwin, and Carol Shapiro, Guide to Benchmarks of Urban Capital Condition, Vol. 3, Urban Institute, Washington, D.C., 1984.

23. Hatry, Harry P., and Bruce G. Steinthal, Guide to Selecting Maintenance Strategies for Capital Facilities, Vol. 4, Urban Institute, Washington D.C., 1984.

24. Hatry, Harry P., Annie P. Millar, and James H. Evans, Guide to Setting Priorities for Capital Investment, Vol. 5, Urban Institute, Washington, D.C., 1984.

25. Peterson, George E., Rita Bamberger, Nancy Humphrey, and Kenneth M. Shell, Guide to Financing the Capital Budget and Maintenance Plan, Vol. 6, Urban Institute, Washington D.C., 1984.

APPENDIX

The *Wall Street Journal* article, reprinted as an appendix to Chapter 1 illustrates the complexity of making infrastructure systems work well. The reader is encouraged to read the article as a case study of the political, financial, and technical aspects of infrastructure systems management.

Tunnel Vision.

How a Subway Project In New York Has Led To Doubt and Dismay

Structure's Cost Has Soared, But Role Has Narrowed; Now Nine Years Overdue

---

Maintenance Called a Disaster

By STANLEY PENN

Staff Reporter of THE WALL STREET JOURNAL.

NEW YORK—It was 1969. In Vietnam, a war raged. In Georgia, a farmer named Jimmy Carter grew peanuts in comfortable obscurity. In New York, construction began for a new subway tunnel on Manhattan's East Side.

By the mid-1970s, the digging and blasting had reached lawyer Lawrence Bonaguidi's brownstone on East 63rd, one of the city's most fashionable streets. "It went on from 7 in the morning till midnight," he recalls. "The walls shook. It was almost like slow torture."

Today, 16 years after the tunnel began, the Vietnam war is a painful memory. Jimmy Carter is an ex-president. Mr. Bonaguidi has long since moved to quieter precincts.

But the three-mile subway tunnel is still abuilding. Its cost, at first projected at $154 million, has swollen to $800 million, much of it federal funds. The date of completion, at first scheduled for 1976, is still in doubt. And when the tunnel is finished—if it is finished—it may carry only 220 rush-hour passengers a day, less than a trainful, between their jobs in Manhattan and their homes in the borough of Queens across the East River.

'How Not to Spend'

"My God!" says New York Sen. Alfonse D'Amato. "Where was the supervision? Where were the studies to justify expenditure of such sums? This tunnel is an example of how not to spend federal dollars."

Conceived in an era of free-flowing public largess and executed during the lean years of New York's fiscal retrenchment, the tunnel was the keystone of a subway expansion that was whittled down until the tunnel's only purpose—to relieve rush-hour subway and surface-train congestion in and out of Queens—lay out of reach. All the same, the tunnel acquired a weird momentum of its own.

Despite swelling costs, construction has doggedly proceeded. But instead of connecting to existing subway express lines as planned, the tunnel ends abruptly in a bleak Queens neighborhood of warehouses, gas stations and a public housing project, and connects with nothing.

'Going Nowhere'

"You ended up with no program and a tunnel going nowhere," says John P. Keith, president of the Regional Plan Association, a nonprofit civic group. Ralph L. Stanley, head of the federal Urban Mass Transportation Administration, says New York state's Metropolitan Transportation Authority (MTA) never bothered asking a "simple" question: "How many riders will benefit from the investment?" Instead, he asserts, "the attitude was, the money's there, why not spend it?"

In part, the story does seem one of extravagant carelessness in the spending of public money and in the maintenance of public property. Federal officials have raised doubts about the tunnel's structural integrity, while state officials are investigating suspicions of fraud, including the possibility that some contractors who did the work engaged in bid-rigging. A spokesman for Sanford Russell, inspector general of the MTA, whose office reports to Gov. Mario Cuomo and the state legislature, says work documents submitted by major contractors have been subpoenaed.

Aside from questions of integrity—structural and otherwise—vital equipment

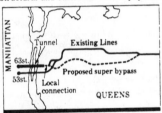

has so deteriorated from premature installation and sloppy maintenance that the tunnel will have to be fixed even before its opening. Any hope that it would finally be completed this year was dashed last spring when David Gunn, president of the New York City Transit Authority (TA), inspected the tunnel and found it in disrepair.

Mr. Gunn says some equipment was only half-built or severely damaged by corrosion. In the tunnel's signal room, which contains electrical traffic-switching equipment, "the whole roof was leaking badly, and the floor had six inches of water," he says. Mr. Gunn plans to announce next month when the tunnel will be ready for service and what it will cost to repair and replace damaged equipment.

Robert F. Wagner Jr., an MTA board member, also inspected the tunnel. "There were stalactites hanging from the ceiling," he says. "Unbelievable amounts of water. The pumps were not where they should be."

The tunnel is the creation of the TA, which serves more than five million subway and bus riders daily, and its parent, the MTA, which also operates train lines. Although it is common practice to employ an outside engineering firm to supervise a construction project of this size, the TA chose instead to itself design and oversee

Please Turn to Page 18, Column 1

Tunnel Vision: How Subway Project Led To Doubts, Dismay

Continued From First Page

construction of the tunnel. Dozens of outside contractors performed the work. The TA's engineering department did the overseeing. That included the job of making sure that contractors maintained the tunnel equipment they installed.

As work progressed, that job became harder to keep up with. In late 1983, after considering hiring an outside contractor to perform the maintenance—not just oversee it but actually do it—the TA decided to turn this task over to its own operating department. The operating department, after inspecting the tunnel, refused the assignment just then. "They concluded," says Michael Ascher, the TA's chief engineer since June, "that a great deal of work had to be performed before they would accept responsibility for the equipment. That's where the [maintenance] program fell apart."

With the operating department declining the task, maintenance continued to be the function of a hard-pressed engineering department overseeing the contractors. Mr. Gunn, who became TA president in early 1984, inspected the tunnel this past spring. He found that little if anything was being done to protect the tunnel and its equipment. According to Constantine Sidamon-Eristoff, an MTA board member, Mr. Gunn reported to the board, "We've got a disaster on our hands."

Mr. Gunn says the TA engineering department lacked the necessary "management tools" to build the tunnel. "We were missing some key elements in all areas," he says. The department was so inept, he adds, that it even "had things built in the wrong sequence." A federal source familiar with the project contends that track, for example, should have been installed last, to prevent it from rusting. Instead, it was laid in the 1970s, years before subway wheels would actually touch it, and it has rusted.

George Zeigler, the TA's chief engineer until his retirement this year, says such criticisms are exaggerated. "Some of the electricity boxes and fixtures did rust," he says, "but it was extremely minor." He insists that contractors did maintain tunnel equipment. "They were under warranty, and we wouldn't let them off," he says. He concedes that some fans designed to dry up moisture weren't operating when they should have been. "In hindsight," he adds, the engineering department should have insisted on an outside maintenance contractor, "but the operating people said, 'We can do it cheaper.'" That was before the operating people decided not to take the assignment after all.

Evidence of possible fraud in the tunnel's construction may surface in the pending criminal trial of Raymond Donovan, a former secretary of labor in the Reagan administration. Last year, a Bronx grand jury indicted him for larceny and falsification of business records while he was executive vice president of Schiavone Construction Co. in Secaucus, N.J., before joining the cabinet.

Joint ventures headed by Schiavone received the biggest share of the tunnel's construction contracts, $395 million worth. The district attorney for New York City's borough of the Bronx contends that Mr. Donovan and former business associates defrauded the TA of $7.4 million by overstating payments to a subcontractor. Mr. Donovan and other defendants deny any wrongdoing. A trial date hasn't been set.

Sen. D'Amato says that the Senate Appropriations subcommittee on transportation, of which he is a member, will hold a hearing regarding the tunnel Nov. 2. He has asked U.S. Attorneys Raymond Dearie of Brooklyn and Rudolph Giuliani of Manhattan to investigate possible misconduct in the tunnel's construction. "We agreed to take a look and are doing so," Mr. Dearie says. "There are certain aspects that invite a certain amount of scrutiny."

Meanwhile, questions have also arisen about the quality of construction materials in the tunnel. In an internal memo dated this Sept. 12, James L. Benson, a regional manager for the U.S. Department of Transportation, warned of "deficiencies" in some concrete and questioned the "structural integrity" of a section of the tunnel. But a preliminary report last month by consultants hired by the TA found only "minor" water leaks in the tunnel and attributed cracks in the concrete to "normal shrinkage" and "thermal stress."

The tunnel was conceived in the late 1960s as a critical element in an MTA plan to add 30 miles of new subway routes, much of it in fast-growing Queens. "That was a very different era, a world of unlimited resources," says Richard Ravitch, a former MTA chairman. Money from a 1967 state transportation bond issue, along with city funds, helped get the project started. But the federal government financed the rest, eventually paying out a total of $580 million in a series of grants authorized by the Urban Mass Transit Act.

William J. Ronan, the MTA's chairman from 1965 to 1974, was a prime booster of new routes. "When I left," he says, "we had a [partly built] tunnel. We had a commitment from the federal government. We had state money. I figured everything was secured."

Critics say, however, that the MTA planners greatly underestimated the time and money it would take to build the tunnel. "Experienced engineers were bypassed," says Edward Regan, New York state comptroller. "Their thinking was never taken into account."

From the outset, red tape created lengthy delays. Carol Bellamy, New York City council president and a former MTA board member, says a 1978 study showed that up to 17 federal, state and city agencies had to grant approval before TA construction money could be spent. And typically, she says, when TA projects bog down, middle managers are "afraid to squawk, to tell the guys at the top that things aren't moving along."

In 1975, the fiscal crisis that brought New York City to the brink of bankruptcy also scuttled the subway expansion. The city's mayor then, Abraham Beame, with the authority he had under a 1974 amendment to the mass-transit act, used some of the federal funds earmarked for tunnel construction to pay the TA's operating expenses—and stave off an unpopular subway-fare increase. "I was fighting to get federal funds to help keep down the fare," Mr. Beame says.

Then the city's priorities changed. Austerity required a new emphasis on patching the existing subway system, which had been crumbling even as workmen blasted the new tunnel. Officials accordingly abandoned an ambitious plan to build a Long Island Railroad station on Manhattan's East Side and use the lower, or foundation, level of the tunnel to carry some of that line's commuter trains.

Though the lower level now would carry no passengers, its construction continued. It was needed, transit officials say, to support the upper level. Building the lower level, a federal source says, consumed more than $100 million in federal aid.

But the TA failed to maintain the lower level, says its current president, Mr. Gunn, who found six or seven feet of water standing in it during his first inspection. "There was no assessment of what physically had to be done to stabilize it," he says. "Instead, they finished up the concrete structure and walked away."

Eventually, the subway expansion shrank from 30 miles to only two projects, one of them the tunnel, totaling 5.5 miles. Though the tunnel survived, its original rationale has disappeared. The budget cutters had scrapped a $900 million "super bypass" to link the tunnel with express subway lines in Queens. Without the bypass, there was no good way to divert passengers from the congested lines that already existed.

By 1979, transit officials themselves were heatedly debating whether the tunnel should be finished or junked. "We found that it was more expensive to terminate the existing contracts than to complete it," says Mr. Ravitch, who became the MTA's chairman that year. John D. Simpson, then the TA's president, says that if the project were abandoned, the state might have been forced to reimburse the federal government for its spending on it.

(Appendix continues on p. 24)

What was the federal government doing all this time? Mr. Stanley, the urban transit chief, says the agency was "passive" in its dealings with the MTA, at least before he took charge in late 1983. "Someone should have questioned the grant requests when they came in," he says.

Last July, Mr. Stanley forbade the TA to spend $31 million of a remaining federal grant until the TA's outside consultants complete their study of the tunnel.

If the tunnel ever goes into service, TA officials face the task of coaxing more than a handful of rush-hour passengers to use it; a current estimate is that 220 rush-hour commuters will use the tunnel as now designed. One plan being considered is to deposit Manhattan-bound bus riders at the Queens end of the tunnel, so that they can complete the last leg of their trip by subway. This would rid Manhattan streets of some bus traffic but would seem unlikely to please Queens commuters accustomed to uninterrupted bus rides.

A more likely alternative is a 520-foot extension to the tunnel, linking it to existing local subway lines in Queens. This extension, called the "local connection" to differentiate it from the super bypass planned originally, would increase tunnel ridership to 16,500 during rush hour—a vast improvement over 220 but not enough, critics say, to greatly reduce current subway crowding. (Rush-hour traffic under the super-bypass plan was projected at 36,-500 riders.)

Construction of the local connection, even if begun today, wouldn't be completed until 1993 at the earliest—a quarter-century after work on the tunnel began. As for the cost, transit officials say they have no idea where the needed $245 million, which includes the purchase of subway cars, would come from.

CHAPTER TWO

INFRASTRUCTURE SYSTEMS

Infrastructure systems have similar characteristics. It is not uncommon to find an infrastructure manager who has learned on one system, say electric power, and transfers management skills to another area, such as the management of a water utility. The skills needed, essentially those of public administration as it deals with technological areas, are those discussed in the previous chapter concerned with the infrastructure management system. Systems must be planned, financed, constructed, operated, and maintained. Unless all of these engineering and management functions are properly fulfilled, either the systems will not fully meet the intended need, or they will cost too much. The management challenge is to provide the capital facilities needed, and then to operate and maintain them effectively.

Regardless of the management skill available, managers must understand the unique features of the systems they manage. Although diverse kinds of public works facilities have common characteristics and management needs, they have unique operating characteristics, interest groups, and technological features. The purpose of this chapter is to present some of the most important of these unique features for the six infrastructure groups identified in Chapter 1. For the sake of convenience, the groups are repeated here:

1. Roads group (roads, streets, and bridges)
2. Transportation services group (transit, rail, ports, and airports)
3. Water group (water, wastewater, all water systems, including waterways)
4. Waste management group (solid-waste management systems)
5. Buildings and outdoor sports group
6. Energy production and distribution group (electric and gas)

In this chapter these infrastructure groups are discussed with emphasis on management-oriented information such as service provided, systems configuration and components, dimensions and performance standards of systems, management organizations and structure, cost of service, regulatory arrangements, causes of deterioration and obsolescence of facilities, data needed for management, important interest groups, and main issues confronting each category of infrastructure.

The first two categories of infrastructure deal with transportation. This is the largest of all the infrastructure "need" areas and consists of a complex set of systems interwoven throughout the nation's economy. Pikarsky states that a "social contract" has been in place in the United States for 40 years, whereby personal mobility in urban areas has been emphasized. Under the "contract" the public sector built roads and subsidized the operation of public transit. The private sector provided parking facilities or located near public transit, while the private citizen assumed responsibility for either paying the subsidized transit fare or buying an auto (1). He goes on to state that the following problems are reducing the public sector's capability to perform its part of the bargain: financial problems of the transit industry, shortage of funds needed to maintain the road network, and increasing difficulty of all levels of government to finance the system.

Formidable difficulties must be faced in renegotiating the social contract described by Pikarsky. They are problems of the transit industry, which will be described later in this chapter. Chief among these is the unionization of the industry, which is heavily dependent on labor. Then there is the high cost of owning and operating automobiles. This includes the cost of new cars in the United States, not to mention the cost of repairs and insurance. The future will be one of adjustment in transportation, both in the United States and in other developed and developing countries. The discussions that follow are snapshots of the transportation situation today, with recognition that it will change in the future. These changes are important to infrastructure managers, since the financial and social stakes are so high. The final chapter in the book also discusses some of the trade-offs we must examine.

2.1. ROADS GROUPS: ROADS, STREETS, AND BRIDGES

Roads, streets, and bridges make up the essential fabric of the nation's transportation system. Roads and streets account for a substantial part of all public works expenditures, and their 20-year needs for the future, amounting to about $2 trillion, form the largest part of the needs list that makes up the infrastructure "crisis." The economic and social impact of the transportation of people and goods over this system is a substantial share of the nation's total domestic product, which stands at nearly $4 trillion in 1986. Roads have been a major economic factor since the emergence of the automobile for personal transportation and the truck for shipping in the early part of the twentieth century.

The United States has some 3.9 million miles of roads. The 20 percent, or 820,000 miles, of them that make up the federal-aid system carry approximately 80 percent of the traffic. The full breakdown of the mileage is as follows (1982 figures) (2):

Urban mileage	641,000
State control	103,000
Local control	536,000
Rural mileage (% surfaced 85.7)	3,226,000
State control	825,000
Local control	2,140,000
Federal control	261,000
Federal-aid highway system	
Primary	298,000
Interstate	42,000
Urban	134,000
Secondary	402,000
Total mileage all categories	3,866,000

The classification of local streets normally includes local, collector, arterial, and expressway/freeway categories. Mileages for these classifications would be included in the previous list.

Bridges constitute an important part of the roadway network. The federal-aid system also includes about 260,000 bridges, or 1 bridge for every 3 to 4 miles of highway. The remainder of the roadway network includes some 314,000 bridges. Bridge design and construction is an especially important part of highway engineering due both to the cost of construction and to safety considerations. Bridges carry the roadway over either another roadway or a stream. Culverts carry out the same general function as bridges. Normally bridge design is the primary province of structural engineers, with important inputs from hydraulic engineers concerned with extreme flows and with erosion damage.

The levels of service of the different categories of roadway vary considerably, particularly those not included in the federal-aid system which conforms to federal standards developed over the years by the Federal Highway Administration and its predecessor organizations, most notably the Bureau of Public Roads. The non-federal-aid system carries about 20 percent of the traffic, but this traffic is often of life or death importance to local residents.

Levels of service are basically determined by design characteristics and by road condition. Some of the most important design characteristics include capacity, vertical and horizontal alignment, and cross section.

The concept of capacity of the roadway has been developed to measure its ability to move traffic. For freeways, the capacity is 2000 passenger cars per hour per lane; and for a two-lane road with two-way traffic, it is 1000 cars per hour per lane. The capacity of the latter is reduced due to the difficulty in passing and to other obstructions related to access. The guidebook for capacity is the *Highway Capacity Manual* published by the Highway Research Board, now the Transportation Research Board (3).

Capacity is related to the quality of service through the concept of service levels. These are commonly designated as A through F as follows: A is free flow; B is stable flow; C is stable flow (more restrictions); D is approach to unstable flow; E is volumes near capacity; and F is forced flow. The reader can refer to texts on highway engineering and planning for more detailed descriptions of these categories.

Depending on the general density of vehicles on the roadway and the mean speed of travel, there is a trend of volume/capacity ratio that is shown generally by Figure 2.1. In the figure the maximum *V/C* ratio is shown to occur before the time that the roadway becomes saturated, and there exists a saturation where the ratio becomes zero, indicating the density at which a traffic jam occurs.

Vertical and horizontal alignment allows for important operating parameters such as sight distance and design speed. The alignment also determines much of the cost and location constraints of the roadway.

The cross section of the roadway is an important factor in its cost, structural strength, durability, service level, safety, and drainage. Cross-sectional standards have evolved over the years through experience to allow for the use of different materials for base and surface courses, for adequate pavement drainage, and for the safe operation of vehicles under all traffic conditions. Typical cross sections for two-lane and interstate highways are shown in Figure 2.2. City streets would have different cross sections, allowing for the functions of drainage, bike lanes, scenic strips, and other urban considerations.

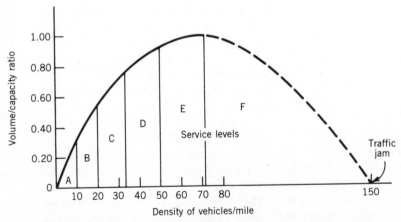

FIGURE 2.1. Relationship of levels of service to V/C ratio and vehicle density.

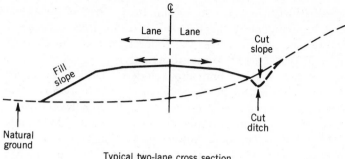

Typical two-lane cross section.

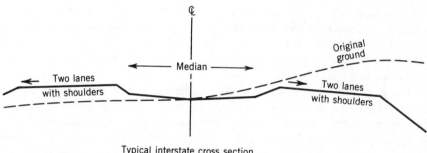

Typical interstate cross section

FIGURE 2.2. Typical cross sections of two-lane and interstate highways.

Roadways have been built with a combination of standards which determine, for the most part, the cost and level of performance. These standards have been based in recent years to a large extent on research completed to support the planning and design of the interstate system, which represents the highest level of service attainable on a practical basis. Typical values for the interstate system include a design speed of 70 mph, maximum grade of 3 percent, total width of roadway and median of about 160 feet, total right of way of from 250 to 500 feet, and full design for bridges, acceleration lanes, exits, and access ramps. Oglesby (3) includes the following in his discussion of important design-standard categories: design speed, lane width, number of lanes, shoulder design, medians, frontage roads, cut or fill slopes, guard rails, right-of-way widths, fencing, cross slopes, minimum and maximum grades, vertical curves over crests and sags, alignment design, superelevation, and horizontal alignment. These are not by any means all of the critical design areas of roadways, but they illustrate some of the complexity of roadway design.

The management organizations that govern roadways fall under the general guidance of the Federal Highway Administration (FHWA), part of the Department of Transportation (DOT). FHWA is the successor organization to the Bureau

of Public Roads (BPR), which was formed in 1918 as part of the Department
of Agriculture. The name of FHWA dates to 1970 after BPR was absorbed into
DOT (which was formed in 1967). The federal presence also includes the
National Highway Traffic Safety Administration (NHTSA) and the Urban Mass
Transit Administration (UMTA), both also included in DOT. State departments
of transportation have most of the operational responsibility for construction
and maintenance of federal-aid and state roads. Local road networks are normally
administered by city and county governments. In some cases highway authorities,
such as the New Jersey Turnpike Authority, administer special portions of
roadway. Professionals working in transportation can look to the American
Association of State Highway and Transportation Officals (AASHTO) as their
association for the development of certain standards, guidelines, and helpful
publications. Another useful organization is the Transportation Research Board
(TRB), a nonprofit agency operating under the National Academy of Sciences.
TRB also administers the National Cooperative Highway Research Program
(NCHRP), which allocates research funds for projects selected by AASHTO.
Two other influential associations are the Institute of Traffic Engineers and the
American Road Builders Association.

The high economic stakes of road building are evident in the number of
trade and interest groups that cluster around it. A 1987 symposium on pavement
maintenance, for example, drew a large number of participating associations
on the planning team, including the Highway Users Federation, International
Public Works Federation, TRB, AASHTO, National Association of County
Engineers, International Road Federation, APWA, National Asphalt Pavement
Association, American Concrete Pavement Association, Portland Cement Asso-
ciation, Asphalt Recycling and Reclaiming Association, Concrete Sawing and
Drilling Association, Asphalt Emulsions Manufacturers Association, International
Grooving and Grinding Association, International Slurry Seal Association, Asphalt
Institute, and European Asphalt Pavement Association. These groups are all
mentioned in a trade publication that organized the symposium (4).

The regulatory structure of the highway and road part of the transportation
industry is fragmented. Since most of the costs are paid from taxes, the financing
of the service is determined politically, rather than by ratepayers. The most
notable exception is the toll road system, which is concentrated for the most
part in the East. Traffic safety is regulated by NHTSA and by state and local
law-enforcement officials.

The cost of highways and roads is highly variable since so many items are
involved. The construction and reconstruction of the interstate system dominates
the cost picture, and construction contracts are normally in the tens of millions
of dollars with per mile costs exceeding $1 million and going much higher in
special conditions. Some examples of construction contracts taken from various
reports in the mid-1980s are as follows: 4.7 miles of interstate with two bridges,
$7.4 million; 1.2 miles of highway reconstruction in Wyoming, $2.24 million;
realignment of 3.8 miles of state road with dual bridges, $9.99 million; an 8-
span bridge in Maine, $13.88 million; 3.9 miles of reconstruction in heavy

traffic, $24.18 million; 1.04 miles of 2-lane road in Utah, with one bridge, $2.7 million; 3000 feet of urban expressway including 5 bridges and 4000 feet of railroad relocation, $23 million; and 6.4 miles of reconstruction of interstate, $14.01 million. These figures are typical of those appearing in construction journals.

Roadways are subject to substantial wear and deterioration. The causes are use, abuse, and weathering. The roadways require surface maintenance, snow and ice control, and roadside, shoulder, and drainage maintenance. Bridge maintenance is an especially important need since the safety of bridges is always of concern.

Roadway surfaces have a life cycle as shown in Figure 2.3, where the initial period of life is characterized by a rather constant level of condition and the latter period is characterized by rapid deterioration. Maintenance and repair strategies, to be discussed in more detail later, should be planned to take advantage of this relationship, and in fact, pavement management is becoming a science that is based on the curve shown.

Road repair and the highway four R's take up large chunks of the highway dollar. The Congressional Budget Office (CBO) estimated in 1982 that the annual *federal* needs would be roughly $13.1 billion per year through 1990 (5). Considering the state and local needs as well, it is relatively easy to extrapolate these figures to the range of at least $1 trillion for a 20-year planning period, and then the CBO figures can be reconciled with some of the large estimates quoted in Chapter 1. Taken at a state level, some of the figures look larger. Colorado, for example, cited a 15-year need of $11 billion in 1986. This figure would consist of $2 billion of rebuilding or resurfacing, $3.4 billion of additional lanes, $800 million of safety measures on primary and secondary roads, $2.4 billion of new roads, $107 million of bridge work, $498 million of interstate-completion work, and $460 million in interchange work (6). The report cited $5.5 billion shortfall in funds available to complete the work.

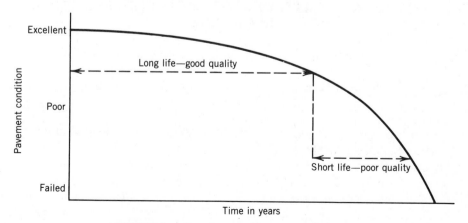

FIGURE 2.3. Life-cycle curve for pavement condition.

Bridge deterioration is an especially serious matter relating to safety. In 1967 a suspension bridge in West Virginia collapsed due to structural fatigue, taking 46 lives. Following this a national program of bridge inspection and replacement has been undertaken. The result of this inspection program is a better determination of the condition of bridges than we had in the past. This is a form of *condition assessment*, which is an essential part of public works management and which will be discussed in more detail in Chapter 9.

Bridge rehabilitation has received much attention in the past few years, and states are beginning to develop new and innovative methods to repair and rehabilitate them. The rating system for bridges provides a clue to how much work is needed. A 1983 FHWA report to Congress stated that almost half the nation's bridges were obsolete or structurally deficient. In North Carolina the figure was more than 70 percent, and in Arizona it was only 5 percent (7). A survey of the activities under way in the states at about the same time uncovered considerable activity, spurred by the Surface Transportation Assistance Act. The bridge work has produced considerable innovation for mixing old and new methods of repair. Methods range from inexpensive ways of reinforcing structures to the introduction of cathodic protection to arrest the corrosion of reinforcing bars (8).

We got a glimpse of some of the critical technological issues facing highways in 1984. A task force of the Transportation Research Board developed a plan for strategic research in transportation (9). The issues that were identified are as follows: developing improved practices for using asphalt, improving long-term pavement performance, improving the cost-effectiveness of maintenance, protecting bridge decks, improving the use of cement and concrete, and controlling snow and ice chemically. These needs, especially those concerned with maintenance procedures, are directly related to the material presented in the following chapters.

2.2. TRANSPORTATION SERVICES GROUP: TRANSIT, RAIL, PORTS, AND AIRPORTS

After roads, highways, and bridges, there remain considerable infrastructure facilities that support transportation services for people, vehicles, and goods. In this category we include transit, rail, port, and airport facilities. With rising energy costs these are obviously important to the movement both of people and of goods.

There are common characteristics that distinguish these categories of infrastructure facilities. One of these characteristics is the fact that transit, rail, port, and airport facilities are of strategic importance to national governments and receive considerable attention and public investments due to their linkage with economic and social development and national defense. The categories are diverse enough, however, to prevent making too many generalizations about them. In effect, each must deal with its own industries, unique financing and development needs, and interest groups.

Transit

As far as urban infrastructure is concerned, transit has received the most recent attention due to the agony many local governments are feeling about how to pay for it, first with regard to capital investments, then with concern about operating deficits. The concern with operating deficits has produced another problem: deferred maintenance. On the one hand, transit is necessary to provide alternatives to the private automobile and to make sure that citizens of all income categories can afford to be mobile. On the other hand, transit is difficult to plan, finance, and operate economically.

The transit dilemma continues to plague planners since transit ridership declined from 9 percent of all work-related travel in 1970 to 6 percent in 1980. Cars carrying only one driver constituted 64 percent of such travel in 1980, with vans and carpools making up about 20 percent. These percentages are based on Department of Transportation data.

Transit includes all modes such as buses, light rail, and subway. In large cities such as New York, where automobiles are either unaffordable or not convenient, transit takes on great importance. In other cities people seem to prefer the convenience of the private automobile where possible. Due to congestion, air pollution, and cost, transit is becoming more important in most cities, however, and this is causing a demand for new capacity at the same time that ridership is difficult to attract.

The capital facilities of transit are related to highway facilities when transit travels along the same routes as other passenger vehicles. Vehicles and support structures such as garages form the other part of the transit capital facilities network. Buses, for example, are the nucleus of many transit companies, and constitute one of the main calls on capital. The Congressional Budget Office estimates the annual capital needs for bus rehabilitation and replacement in the United States to be $610 million. For comparison, the annual cost for rail rolling stock replacement and modernization is $500 million (5). Similar figures are estimated for maintenance facilities and track systems. The total needs estimated by CBO for bus and rail transit system are between $3.6 and $5.5 billion per year, including repair, modernization, and replacement as well as additional capacity.

The dimensions of the bus industry in the United States are reported annually by the American Bus Association and printed in *Metro* magazine. In 1985 there were some 3588 bus companies, 20,200 buses in operation, 43,100 employees, and total revenues generated of $1879 million, with expenses totaling $1814 million. These statistics are for all classes of carriers, both local and intercity (10). The revenues include considerable subsidies. As reported later in Chapter 9 for a typical bus company, the Regional Transportation District of Denver, the fare box only accounts for about $18.5 million in revenue out of about $126 million total. The remainder comes mostly from a sales tax and from subsidies.

The structure of the transit industry continues to evolve. Before 1940 many private transit companies were in operation. With the rise of private automobile travel after the war, and the resulting urbanization, transit ridership declined by about 65 percent from 1945 to 1965, and many private transit companies failed. This set the stage for the first federal intervention in 1963 with a small program to enable local governments to take over ailing companies. Now, after over 20 years of active federal participation, the tide is, beginning to turn back toward the private sector. While most of the activity is still in government hands, there are increased opportunities for private operators. Annual operating deficits nationally are in the range of $5 billion, and only 40 percent of operating budgets are covered by revenues. This creates new opportunities either for the development of new services by the private sector or for privatization (11).

In recent years the federal government has been active in transit through the Urban Mass Transportation Administration, part of the Department of Tranportation. UMTA has provided grants both to help finance new systems and to acquire equipment, as well as to subsidize operating deficits. In the tight financial times of the 1980s the amounts available through UMTA have come under increasing scrutiny.

In 1982 the federal government allocated 1 cent of a 5 cent gas tax surcharge for mass transit. This created a surge in demand for new systems, and by 1984 there were some $19 billion in requests for new rail systems, far more than the federal government could allocate. In addition, the requests for additions to existing systems, such as those in Washington, D.C., and San Francisco, were substantial.

Costs for rail systems have been high. The Metro system in Washington, D.C., for example was originally estimated to be $2.5 billion. Now, UMTA puts the total expected cost at $12 billion. The operating deficit is expected to hit $200 million for 1986. The operating cost is $6.94 for each mile of train travel with passengers. In spite of these financial problems, there are many good sides to Metro, such as the safety record, the relative absence of crime, and the development it has spurred (12).

On the other side of the picture the subway in Hong Kong is reported to be doing very well. It has all the advantages: a captive constituency without many cars, government-owned land, favorable topography, and effective management. These factors go together to make a transit system with relatively few problems and a model for others (12).

Continuing evolution in the transit industry will see further structural changes. Bus companies depend on labor for 70 percent of the operation, and negotiations with labor are critical to continued success. Just as this was written the announcement was made that the old-line Greyhound Corporation had been sold, ending 73 years in the U.S. bus operations business. The sale came after the 7500 employees of the corporation rejected a contract through their union, the Amalgamated Transit Union (13). In the case of urban rail, the industry has been struggling for years. *Metro* magazine reports that the U.S. market is the largest in the world, and that every railcar builder in the world bids on every order that comes out. The railcar industry is said to be in decline due to the absence of government support, the competition from foreign manufacturers, increasing insurance rates, and other economic factors (14). Bus purchases have been falling since the mid-1970s.

Urban transit is especially important in developing countries that lack the access to private automobiles that is available in the developed countries. Large cities in developing countries (LDC's) typically devote some 15–25 percent of their budgets to transit. In Calcutta, India, investment in transport from 1972 to 1978 amounted to $50 million per year, an amount equivalent to 48 percent of all available investment. The critical nature of transport in a city of that kind should be obvious (15). In a recent World Bank report about transit options the following were suggested for the LDCs to consider: buses, at $40,000–$150,000 each, with operating costs of 2–8 U.S. cents per passenger-kilometer; light rail with moderate capital costs and operating costs of 3–10 U.S. cents per passenger-kilometer; rapid rail, with capital costs in the range of $30 million–$100 million per kilometer and total costs of some 15–25 U.S. cents per passenger-kilometer; and suburban rail with costs of $6 million–$10 million per kilometer and operating costs of 8–15 cents per passenger-kilometer (16). Obviously these costs are just approximate, but they reveal that the transit choices in LDCs are generically the same as in the United States, but with different cultural and economic factors.

Rail

The rail system is the United States is largely owned by private companies, but there has been government intervention through various means such as subsidies and regulation in the last 20 to 30 years. Two of the most visible of these moves have been the creation of the National Railroad Passenger Corporation (Amtrak) in 1970 and the formation of the Consolidated Rail Corporation (Conrail) in 1973. Both of these efforts were intended to provide government assistance to maintain adequate rail service for passengers and freight in critical parts of the United States at the same time that private companies were having increasing difficulties due to falling demand and competition from other modes of transportation.

As a regulated private industry, rail is continually making adjustments to structural changes in the economy. A view of the situation with regard to Amtrak's operations was reported in the *Wall Street Journal* in October 1986 (17). According to the article, Amtrak's long-haul trains were subsidizing the heavily used Northeast Corridor (NEC) due to underreporting of fixed costs in the NEC. The long-haul trains produced 55–60 percent of the system revenues on 20 percent of the passenger traffic, while the NEC, in attempts to compete with air shuttles, produced 25–30 percent of the revenues on half the riders. The writer's conclusion is that the long-haul trains are a viable service, but NEC needs to reexamine its accounting procedures and look for ways to cut the operating deficit.

Ports

The nation's port system is of strategic importance for military and economic reasons. Many large and smaller cities rely on their port traffic as generators of business activity. There is competition among port cities to improve their facilities and attract business. Ports require facilities for berthing of ships, loading and unloading, and transporting goods inland. These facilities can represent enormous infrastructure investments and management problems. The port at Newport News, Virginia, for example, handles large quantities of coal for export from eastern coal fields. The rail network leading into the port facility must handle substantial traffic. The loading and unloading facilities must have capacity to handle large fluctuations in demand. The harbor area must be maintained at sufficient depths, and environmental protection must be assured. Most of the infrastructure management work at ports is done through public management agencies, such as port authorities. An example of such an authority is the Port of New York Authority. The Congressional Budget Office estimated in 1983 that the total "water resources needs" of ports and harbors for the next 31 years was $1.7 billion (5). When all public expenditure needs for all facilities are taken into account, however, the total will be much higher.

Airports

Infrastructure development needs for airports constitute a very visible problem due to the growth of air travel, especially with airline deregulation as it proceeded in the 1980s. CBO includes needs for both air traffic control and airport development in their 1983 study (5). The needs for air traffic control, about $10.7 billion, would be due to modernization of aging electronic equipment. The needs for airports, some $15.3 billion in federal costs alone for a 10-year period, would cover expansion, equipment, facilities, and airport operational facilities.

The United States has approximately 15,000 landing places, but only 3159 of these are publically owned, open for general use, and equipped with at least one paved and lighted runway. About 90 percent of the nation's passenger traffic comes through 66 of these airports, approximately 2 percent of the total. Airport congestion is a major problem, worse than deferred maintenance at airports. In 1980 the airlines spent an extra $1 billion in crew time and fuel and delayed airline passengers some 60 million hours. This problem has become worse later in the 1980s with the fare cutting and competition that spurred additional travel.

The financing problems with airports do not seem to be as severe as with other categories of infrastructure. For one thing, alternative ways exist to collect revenue from users (ticket taxes, landing fees, concessions, and other use charges). For another many underused airports could be called upon to take some of the load from the most congested areas. CBO's policy analysis of airport development recommends further study of these as ways to alleviate the current problems with congestion.

The economic implications of airport development are clear. Hub airline service is critical to the growth and development of major cities. Examples can be seen by studying the development of cities such as Atlanta, Chicago, Denver, Dallas, and Los Angeles. In the 1980s Denver is struggling with the problem of developing a new airport, with a projected cost of about $3 billion. The development of the new airport was the number-one economic development priority of the new governor in 1986, Roy Romer, even though the state government was confronted by many economic problems associated with the mining, tourism, and agricultural industries.

The world's airports face many problems in addition to infrastructure and congestion. In the 1980s the hijacking problem illustrates the span of problems airport managers must deal with. Not only do the facilities need to accommodate high volumes of passengers, aircraft, and surface traffic, but the security must be tight enough to avoid hazard to passengers from hijackers. The years ahead will focus on airport management even more.

2.3. WATER GROUP: WATER, WASTEWATER, ALL WATER SYSTEMS, INCLUDING WATERWAYS

The water component of infrastructure systems includes facilities for water supplies, wastewater management, flood control and stormwater, and all control facilities that deal with large hydraulic systems, including dams and reservoirs, groundwater systems, waterways, and irrigation facilities. It is a large and complex part of the overall infrastructure network.

The services provided by water facilities extend into all parts of economic and social life. Moreover, flood-related hazards are the principal cause of damages to life and property from all natural hazards. Thus, proper management of water facilities is an essential part of all aspects of social and economic life.

The first category of water infrastructure is the most important human need: drinking water. It is normally furnished by urban water supply systems, which in the United States provide about 150 gallons per capita per day to consumers, including domestic, commercial, and industrial. Much of the industrial water in the United States is self-supplied. Figure 2.4 shows a typical urban water balance, including a category for "unaccounted-for water," a common problem afflicting urban water managers.

Urban water supply systems include sources of supply, treatment facilities, and distribution systems (Figure 2.5). The distribution systems have a public part, from the treatment plant to the meter, and a private part, the in-house or in-plant component. These are important distinctions since the different parts of the system are different cost centers, and often fall under different management authorities.

Urban water supply systems are sized to provide the average per capita needs that are unique to each area, depending on the mix of housing types and industry, as well as climatic and cultural factors. Normally, the per capita figure must be augmented to account for peak demands and for the likelihood of prolonged drought. Also, in-system storage must be provided. Fire flows must be available on demand, and this factor is important in the setting of fire insurance rates. This aspect of service, along with the general level of public

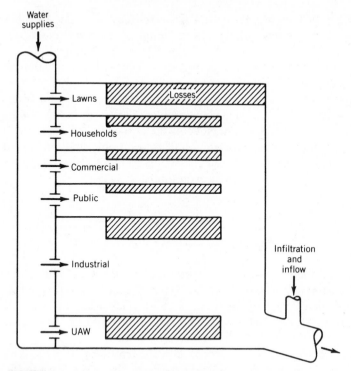

FIGURE 2.4. Metropolitan water balance showing unaccounted-for water.

confidence in a system, is important for the economic development of a community.

Wastewater systems have received more attention since the passage of the Clean Water Act in 1972. This act has mandated improved treatment of wastewater for all dischargers, and has resulted in more complex treatment of wastewater, as well as more attention to the operation and maintenance of all parts of

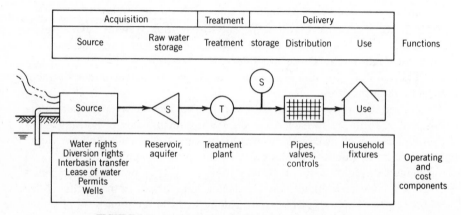

FIGURE 2.5. Configuration of urban water supply system.

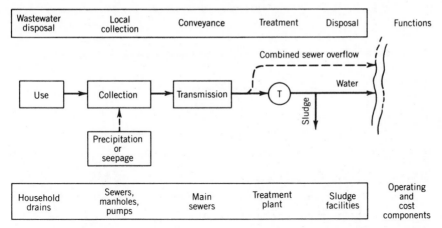

FIGURE 2.6. Configuration of urban wastewater management system.

systems. The service provided by these wastewater systems is twofold: to remove the wastewater from dwellings and businesses, and to provide for pollution control by proper treatment of the wastewater. Unfortunately, people are far more interested in the first aspect of the service, and not so interested in the second. This accounts for the recent emphasis in the United States on subsidies for wastewater management but not for water supply.

The configuration of wastewater systems begins with the collection system (Figure 2.6). Again, there is a private part and a public part, corresponding to the parts of the systems on either side of the property line. The effluent from the collection system is transported through main sewers and outfall sewers to the treatment plant, which can be at the primary, secondary, or advanced levels. The treatment plant provides for treatment of the wastewater and the resulting sludge. Wastewater treatment has become the most complex and expensive part of wastewater management.

Stormwater is another form of wastewater that must be handled through a collection, transport, and disposal system. The configuration of stormwater systems is shown in Figure 2.7. Although there has been considerable discussion of the need for treatment of stormwater, there seems to be little prospect that systems for treatment will become fact in the near future. The interface between stormwater and wastewater systems is the combined sewer system, which provides for the transport of both wastewater (dry-weather flow) and combined storm and wastewater (wet-weather flow). Combined sewer systems are prevalent in the large cities of the United States and constitute a management problem for the treatment of effluents in wet weather to avoid pollution episodes caused by overflows.

The management of water systems is mostly done in the public sector. There are about 50,000 community water systems providing for the management of water supply, slightly fewer wastewater management systems, and stormwater organizations in most cities and towns. Numerous special-purpose districts

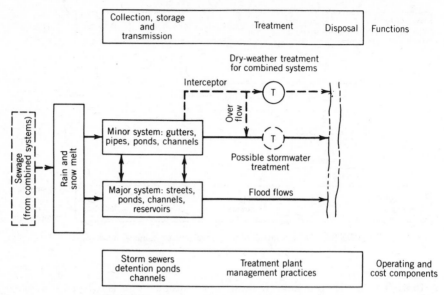

FIGURE 2.7. Configuration of urban stormwater system.

provide these services as well. Private water companies are actively providing some service, mostly in the East, but there is little private-sector involvement in operation of wastewater facilities.

Regulation of both drinking water and wastewater has been mostly by federal actions. The Public Health Service, in conjunction with county health departments, had been regulating drinking water standards since the early part of the century, but it has only been in recent years that any serious attention has been given to strong regulatory measures. Serious attention began with the passage of the Safe Drinking Water Act in 1974. This act requires the determination of maximum contaminant levels (MCLs) for substances that can affect health adversely. By 1985, EPA had determined these MCLs for coliform bacteria, turbidity, six pesticides, nine heavy metals, trihalomethanes, and radiation (18). In addition to these regulated substances, there is a great deal of public concern over synthetic organic substances, with considerable news coverage of discoveries of these contaminants in water supplies.

Wastewater has been mostly regulated by the Clean Water Act, both in the federal version and in the implementing acts passed by the states. Basically, this act regulates both effluents and the quality of water in the streams. This is done through the issuance of discharge permits that are stringent enough to ensure that in-stream water quality remains good enough to maintain the intended uses of the streams, whether it be for drinking water, industrial water uses, fishing, or recreation. There has been considerable controversy over the implementation of the Clean Water Act, due to its cost and due to the difficulty in setting some of the standards, with the concomitant cost implications to local governments and to industry.

Stormwater has not been regulated up to this date. In the 1960s there were implications that stormwater contamination was a principal cause of the quality problems in a number of U.S. streams, and there were many studies and threats of regulation, including a requirement for universal treatment of stormwater; however, these threats subsided when studies failed to show definite links of stormwater to generalized stream pollution, and when the impracticality of stormwater treatment was recognized due to the substantial cost. There is, at this time, a threat to require discharge permits for storm sewers, and local governments are resisting this potential requirement as they perceive it may be the first step toward greater bureaucratic control over storm sewers, without commensurate public benefits.

Combined sewers are regulated by the Clean Water Act, but not many treatment plants have been constructed to deal with full quantities of wet-weather flows due to the lack of appropriated funds. Some municipalities have, however, taken steps to introduce control programs that use storage and other management mechanisms for dealing with the problem.

Operational techniques for water and wastewater systems have been concentrated on treatment plants. More attention has been given to water supply plants, but with attention given to improving the investments under the construction grants provision of the Clean Water Act, the late 1970s and early 1980s saw greater attention given to wastewater also. Little attention has been given to how stormwater systems can be operated better.

The management of large hydraulic systems has received substantial attention in recent years due to large-scale and difficult problems such as the decline of the Ogallala aquifer, the high cost of the Tennessee-Tombigbee waterway, the rise of the Great Salt Lake, and the movement of water from the north to the south in California. These are examples of large-scale problems that involve massive infrastructure systems, but that are difficult to solve due to political factors.

Maintenance problems of water systems have received greater attention in the last few years than in previous years. The problems of water distribution systems and wastewater collections systems are particularly difficult since they are out of sight, constructed with uneven quality, and subjected to environmental conditions of all kinds. It is anyone's guess what the expected lifetimes of such systems are, and more attention needs to be given to evaluating these lifetimes in order to develop better management strategies.

Interest groups abound in the water field since it is so fragmented. The American Water Works Association, headquartered in Denver, is a group that is concerned with drinking water. AWWA has become more active in recent years, and its programs and publications are beginning to center on some of the overall water management questions, as well as on drinking water. The Water Pollution Control Federation has been the main representative of the wastewater community. Although WPCF has its own set of publications and a successful annual conference, it has not been as active as AWWA in promoting research and an overall approach to water management. There is no principal interest group for stormwater, but the American Public Works Association claims as members many of the city engineers and public works administrators who are responsible for stormwater and flood management. APWA also gives attention to the management aspects of water supply and wastewater.

The main issue in water management today seems to be financial. There is a movement toward greater local responsibility for overall water management, with the removal of federal subsidies. This will force greater attention to basic fundamentals of good management, such as identification or maintenance needs and the recovery of full costs from users. Another important issue is the need to deal with toxic substances in wastewater and in water supplies. This issue has not been an overwhelming constraint so far, but is a difficult one to deal with from the standpoint of both cost and technological difficulty.

Not much is known about the generalized true cost of water, either capital or operating costs. Any estimate of the cost of replacement requires that the lifetime of the item be known, and these lives are not known in general in water systems. There is little regulation of local water and wastewater rates, resulting in the lack of an experience base for comparing costs from one water utility to another. This results in widespread variation of costs and the lack of generally accepted rate levels.

The cost of water service is a summation of the capital, operations, and maintenance costs. Water supply acquisition represents the cost of developing a water supply, buying water rights, or leasing wholesale water, or the extra cost of going long distances to find water supplies. Treatment costs are necessary to furnish the treatment plants and the associated equipment needed. Water distribution and wastewater collection systems include the distributed pipe systems and all of the necessary support. All of the capital costs for these facilities add about $2000 per capita. The costs for operations and maintenance seem to be in the range of $100–$150 per capita.

The cost of water and wastewater service will be an important consumer issue in the future, and it needs the careful attention of the industry. With the willingness to pay fair and full charges, the public can assist in solving national water problems such as safe drinking water, environmental protection, deterioration of infrastructure, and the alleviation of drought shortages.

Irrigation systems constitute another large component of water infrastructure. These systems are heavily concentrated in the western United States and in Asia/Near East regions, as well as in certain arid and semiarid parts of Africa and Latin America. Some data on operation of these systems are given in Chapter 9 in the section on operations.

2.4. WASTE MANAGEMENT GROUP: SOLID-WASTE MANAGEMENT SYSTEMS

Solid-waste management is one of the difficult problems of infrastructure since people really don't want to deal with waste—they just want to get rid of it. This is referred to by one writer as the "Not in my backyard" concept (19).

Beginning with the ignoble name of garbage disposal, the field has evolved to today's concern with hazardous wastes.

Most solid waste, say 90 percent, is land-filled using traditional technologies. Although this has been an improvement over the open-dump or open-burning approaches of a few decades ago, there are two basic problems with landfills: disposal agencies are running out of space, and groundwater sometimes becomes contaminated. These problems are resulting in a focus on new approaches, such as reemphasis on recycling and waste-to-energy plants.

The infrastructure service elements associated with solid waste are storage, collection, transfer, processing, and disposal. Collection has traditionally been one of the greatest cost factors, accounting for some 80 percent of the total cost. This may be changing with the new stringency in disposal regulations, however. In any event, both collection and disposal are major problem areas for the infrastructure manager.

Collection is a distributed, difficult-to-control problem involving the cooperation of citizens and a high labor content. Efforts have been made to automate the service as much as possible with various techniques to reduce the labor requirements. A typical approach is for the collection agency to supply easy-to-roll containers for curbside pickup such that even older citizens can place their own waste on the curb. Even with continuing labor problems, the problems of collection have abated in the last few years as collection agencies have improved their management approaches. Privatization is a common practice for collection, an arrangement that removes the problem from the direct attention of the public works manager.

Disposal is the chief problem of the 1980s, with considerable attention given to the alternatives to the landfill. Waste management has become a "growth industry" with many different aspects to deal with. The American Society of Testing and Materials has presented a list of common waste management terms which includes the following: ash, bulky waste, combustible waste, domestic waste, food waste, hazardous waste, industrial waste, infectious waste, litter, municipal solid waste, noncombustible waste, residential waste, refuse, rubbish, rubble, sludge, street reuse, toxic waste, white goods, and yard waste (19). The variety of these terms illustrates the confusion and complexity that has entered this field.

After various solid-waste management acts, the regulation of the field has now moved to the Resource Conservation and Recovery Act of 1975 (RCRA), which provides stringent regulations for the handling and disposal of solid wastes. Numerous other laws also govern disposal of solid wastes, especially those dealing with hazardous wastes. Examples are the Hazardous Materials Transportation Act and Superfund (CERCLA).

Solving the disposal problem has become a major new business area, with attention from large waste management, construction, and equipment companies. *Fortune* magazine published an analysis in 1985 with an appropriate title, "The Sweet Smell of Profits from Trash" (20). They predicted that capital investment could be $20 billion in the next 20 years, with some 75 incinerators coming on line with annual revenues of about $4 billion. These new plants would use a technology called *mass burning*. Examples of such plants, which originated in Europe, are those in operation in Pinellas County, Florida, and in Baltimore, Maryland. These approaches would seek to avoid the problems of the failed plants which sought to use recycling and incineration in the 1970s.

Costs of such plants are significant. Five plants to serve the five boroughs of New York would cost about $1.5 billion. Operating costs of a 2250-ton-per-day plant in Westchester County, New York, are reported at $60 per ton. This compares favorably with landfill disposal costs, which have risen rapidly in the 1980s from practically nothing to the range of $50 to $100 per ton for some expensive locations such as Philadelphia (21). Buchholz states that construction costs of waste-to-energy plants range from $55,000 to $105,000 per ton of daily capacity. With about 63,000 daily tons of capacity currently under construction in 1986, the total capital involved is $1.84 billion (22). The projected total number of plants to be completed by the year 2000 is placed at about 210, with daily capacity of some 205,000 tons. The cost involved would be some $18.4 billion. This capacity would amount to approximately 75 million tons yearly, about 45 percent of the tonnage generated in 1986 in the United States.

2.5. BUILDINGS AND OUTDOOR SPORTS GROUP

The category of public buildings appears on some lists of infrastructure needs, and there is no doubt that public buildings are essential to the effective functioning of public systems. Buildings, however, constitute a very diverse infrastructure category, since they belong to many different categories of services.

In public works management, buildings have come under the responsibility of departments of "buildings and grounds," or the "physical plant." These terms, while descriptive enough, may be giving way to more functional terms such as "facilities management." Indeed, buildings, along with associated facilities, are a generic category of infrastructure whose needs for operation and maintenance are similar to the other categories of facilities. In the United States the total value of all buildings consists of some $3.1 trillion for structures (which would include structures other than buildings also) and another $2.7 trillion for housing out of a national total "wealth" of about $12.5 trillion. This is according to the Department of Commerce study that was cited in Chapter 1. The diversity of these buildings is wide, and generalizations are difficult to make, of course.

The needs for buildings reported in the infrastructure needs studies of the early 1980s were spotty in terms of categories reported. For example, in Choate and Walter's book cited in Chapter 1, categories of buildings that were mentioned included educational facilities, hospitals, industrial buildings, military facilities, and redevelopment housing. In the National League of Cities report, four categories of public structures were included: public buildings (fire stations, police stations, municipal garages, city halls, and jails), community social-service facilities, public school buildings, and public hospitals and clinics (23). In the report by the Associated General Contractors, the types of buildings listed were hospitals, prisons, post offices, educational facilities, and housing (24).

Regardless of the categories used, the management of buildings as components of infrastructure is an important responsibility. "Facilities management," a new umbrella term describing total management of building space, is receiving more attention from the architect-engineer community. *ENR* magazine ran a cover story on the increased attention in 1985 (25). Facilities management was described as the discipline of planning, designing, constructing, and managing space. This means that the same functions are necessary as will be found in other infrastructure facilities.

In fact, the advent of "smart" buildings is a move toward the same kind of computerized management of information and facilities that will be useful in the other categories of infrastructure. The Honeywell Corporation has analyzed the needs for managing buildings and is now promoting a concept called the "integrated building." This concept would consist of a linking of building management, information management, and telecommunications. According to Honeywell, this system would offer (26):

- Energy-saving control of climate and lighting
- Security
- Fire protection
- Centralized data processing
- Distributed workstations
- Word processing
- Networks that let computers communicate with each other
- Electronic mail
- Teleconferencing
- Transmission of voice and data between offices, buildings, and cities

The linkage between the three systems would include the following allocation of subsystems:

- Building management system
    Temperature control
    Energy management
    Security surveillance
    Fire management
    Lighting control
    Maintenance scheduling
- Telecommunications system
    Digital PABX
    Voice data transmission

    Least-cost long distance routing

    Message reporting

• Information management system

    Data processing

    Word processing

    Management reports

    Accounting reports

These concepts are interesting to compare with the concepts contained in Chapter 4, which describe the emerging decision support systems for all kinds of facilities.

Public housing is one of the responsibilities of public administrators with programs in other categories of infrastructure. Public housing is a challenge in all countries that deal with it. Stories of needed demolition of housing projects in the United States, as well as failures in other countries, are easy to find. The television program "60 Minutes" reported in 1986 on a success in St. Louis that involved tenant organizations—essentially people talking responsibility for their own problems. It showed that public housing projects can be successfully operated if the right principles are followed.

In developing countries the problem of furnishing shelter is a matter of life and death. Financing the shelter is the main problem. The World Bank gives priority to finding successful methods that lead to access to housing. Barriers include the general shortage of capital, lack of trunk infrastructure, land administration, rent control, and poor planning (27). It is interesting that the United States has been able to do so well in furnishing housing and other building space with its entrepreneurial atmosphere, while other countries with regulated economies have had difficulty. Still, access to housing in the United States needs to be improved for the poor—this is one of the social problems associated with infrastructure management.

Financing housing is a problem across the United States, and the federal government, as well as some states, has developed housing finance agencies. The main ones at the federal level are the FHA and the VA; and at the state level, there are numerous housing finance agencies, such as the New York State Housing Finance Agency which has provided over $7 billion in loans since 1960. In addition to housing, this state agency provides financing for public buildings such as schools, day care centers, and health facilities.

The Department of Housing and Urban Development was active in the late 1960s and in the 1970s with programs designed to enhance housing. Generally the programs were not successful due to institutional problems. The new cities program and the "Operation Breakthrough" program to cut the cost of housing are examples. The new cities that had loans guaranteed did not make it, and the cost of housing was kept high not because of lack of technological progress, but because of codes and standards and political issues.

In the 1980s the Reagan administration has moved further to take the government out of the housing business. The administration has tried to eliminate the Center for Building Technology, part of the National Bureau of Standards. This agency has had the strong support of the engineering community, and has resisted elimination. The focus of the programs of the agency shows the research directions needed for buildings: advanced construction materials, components, and systems; automation; structural engineering; earthquake hazard reduction; building physics; and the associated work on fire research.

The importance of preventing disasters in buildings is an obvious need in research and in management. The Mexico City earthquake in 1986 taught valuable lessons. The quake registered 8.1 on the Richter scale, with a 7.5 aftershock. This was the strongest quake ever measured in soft soil. Engineers were surprised at the resilience of the buildings: in the zone of high damage only 1.5 percent of them received severe damage. There were, however, a large number of dramatic collapses of tall buildings. Interestingly, little damage was reported to the subway system, a result some attribute to the design which used rubber tire rather than rail (28).

Interest groups for buildings are too numerous to list. Such organizations as the National Homebuilders, the American Institute of Architects, the engineering associations involved in civil and mechanical engineering, and all of the construction industry associations are keenly interested in the health of the nation's buildings and their renewal.

2.6. ENERGY PRODUCTION AND DISTRIBUTION GROUP: ELECTRIC AND GAS

Electric Power Systems

The nation's electric power systems are an important part of the infrastructure. They, like water systems, have production, transmission, and distribution facilities, and they constitute an important call on capital resources with large capital investments to make and maintain. The electric business has evolved over many years to its position today, with complex relationships between the private sector, the government, and the consumer. The availability and the cost of electricity are important factors in industrial competitiveness and strategy. Power plant emissions are an important source of pollutants of concern to both air and water resources. Coal-fired plants are one of the chief contributors of sulfur dioxide to the atmosphere, and a suspected culprit in the acid rain controversy which continues to rage. The electric industry is the most capital-intensive in the United States, accounting for one-fifth of all new industrial construction, one-third of all corporate financing, and half of all common stock issuance among industrial companies. Electric utilities account for one-third of all primary energy demand (29).

The industry is composed of some 3000 companies that serve some 92 million households and business operations. Four basic types of organizations are involved: investor-owned utilities; public systems owned by the federal government; public systems owned by states, municipalities, or utility districts; and co-operatives. The largest investor-owned utilities are familar names: Pacific Gas and Electric, Commonwealth Edison, Southern Company, and American Electric Power. Federal systems revolve around six agencies that market power: the Bureau of Reclamation, the Tennessee Valley Authority, and the Bonneville, Alaska, Southwestern, Southeastern Power Administrations.

The size of the electric power industry reflects its importance. In 1982 the total sales were reported to be $140 billion, with a distribution of some 96 million customers being 76.1 percent private, 10.6 percent rural co-op, and 13.4 percent local public. Total sales of electricity were about 2,058,479 million kilowatt-hours (29). Capital investments of the entire industry were about $40 billion in 1982. Operating and maintenance costs for electric power generation have grown significantly in recent years due to factors such as environmental regulations. In 1982 they stood at $24.7 billion for investor-owned utilities. Figures reported were 2.98 mills/kilowatt-hour for fossil plants and 5.98 mills/kilowatt-hour for nuclear plants in 1980 (29).

One estimate put the capital needs of electric generating plants at $2.795 trillion (30). The estimate assumes that the United States will have to intensify its electrification by a per capita factor of 2.5 to meet the needs of future society. This will require the construction of 1795 gigawatts of energy, with the estimator assuming that 1000 of these will come from nuclear and 795 from hydro, coal, oil, and gas plants. This seems an unlikely scenario at the present, given the problems of the nuclear industry. The estimate apparently did not include the needs for distribution system renovation.

The situation in Colorado is typical, with the investor-owned utility, Public Service Company of Colorado, serving the major metropolitan area of Denver and outlying areas. Fort Collins went into the power business itself in 1935, as did some other municipalities in the state. The story of this transition is interesting, with local leaders playing the key role in the decisions and actions that led to "independence" and the establishment of the light and power department, as it was called in 1935. At the time, electrification was viewed as a good thing to be encouraged, both by the Roosevelt administration and by local promoters. Rates averaged 3.7 cents per kilowatt-hour for the average user, and the power superintendent used the slogan: "Electricity is cheap: use it freely" (31).

In the case of cooperatives the Rural Electrification Administration (REA) provides low-interest loans to cooperatives and has helped to electrify rural America since the 1930s. There are 965 distribution cooperatives in 46 states, some serving dense surburban areas and some serving rural areas with sparse populations. Many of these borrowed money at the 2 percent rate that was available from 1945 to 1972. The rate has recently been 5 percent, with the government paying a subsidy of about 1–2 percent. This has led the Reagan administration to attempt to dismantle the agency, an initiative which has been fiercely resisted. A typical cooperative is very dependent both on subsidized loans and on low-cost federal power. The Y-W Cooperative in eastern Colorado, for example, has a $40 million investment which will require on the order of $120 million over the next 20 years for replacement. The Y-W also buys low-cost hydropower from the Western Area Power Administration. Since the Reagan administration threatened to close the REA and sell the federal power administration, this cooperative, located in distressed farm country, is threatened (32).

Regulation in the electric power industry is generally split between the federal role, mostly centered in the Federal Energy Regulatory Commission (FERC), and the state role, which operates through public utility commissions to regulate the investor-owned utilities. The 1980s have seen a number of pressing issues before the commissions: nuclear problems, defaults, rate issues, and efficiency standards.

The problems with the nuclear industry have centered on safety and cost. The problems with the Three Mile Island meltdown and then the Chernobyl disaster alerted the public to the dangers of nuclear power. The lower margins of safety in operation and the critical nature of the training, monitoring, decision making, and operational management of the nuclear industry, as compared with the conventional power industry, make nuclear power a unique problem with an uncertain future. Regarding cost, the safety problems with operation, along with other concerns, have greatly increased the cost both of construction and of operation. In 1986, for example, TVA, long known for its effective operation, was in the news due to shutdowns and difficulties in operation of existing plants.

Some still believe in the future of nuclear plants. As recently as 1984 *ENR*'s "man of the year" was cited for the construction of Florida Power & Light's St. Lucie unit two plant. It was guided to construction in 6 years, a record. The 802-megawatt plant had a cost of $1.4 billion. The construction lead times of other plants had stretched from 96 to 144 months, so the 72-month performance was notable (33). This proved that construction costs of nuclear plants could still be managed.

In spite of the problems of the nuclear industry, no utilities have gone under as a result of the cost overruns. The default of the Washington Public Power Supply System over nuclear power was the largest default of public bonds in the nation's history, but the company is still in operation. One utility, Gulf States Utilities, had a $4.2 billion plant with problems in 1986, and it was questionable whether the utility could make it. It was counting on rate hikes to pay for the plant, but the increases were not granted. The year 1987 will be a pivotal one for this utility, and it is possible it could be the first one to go bankrupt (34).

In fact, it is possible that electric rates could begin to come down in general, rather than continue the rise that has outstripped inflation for some 20 years. Data Resources Incorporated predicted a 4.7 percent decrease in the cost of electricity in 1986, a fall that can be attributed to fuel cost savings and lower interest rates. Considerable refinancing is occurring in this capital-intensive industry (35).

One of the forces causing downward rate pressure is the push by regulatory commissions to implement efficiency standards in electric utilities. With the end in sight of the long rise in rates, utilities will not be able to count on automatic increases any more. Regulatory commissions are imposing standards for operational efficiency of plants on the utilities. This has the objective of replacing the discipline of the competitive environment (36).

Another of the regulatory trends on the horizon is the recent move by Commonwealth Edison to split its power operation into two parts; one would move to federal regulation and the other remain under state control. The federal part would be the nuclear plants, which would be transferred to a new subsidiary. As the federal government is responsible for the regulation of wholesale power, this part would move out from the control of the state. This is significant due to the industry restructuring it implies, if the pattern holds with other companies as well (37).

Cogeneration could be another important trend for electric utilities. It refers to the simultaneous generation of power along with other industrial processes. The Public Utilities Regulatory Policies Act of 1978 (PURPA) required utilities to buy cogenerated power. While it was not a large factor until recently, it is now equivalent to some 2–3 percent of the nation's power. In California, the cogeneration either in place or planned is equivalent to the output of 18 nuclear plants (38).

Electric plants are subject to the same deterioration and obsolescence as manufacturing plants. The General Electric Company believes that renovation can be the source of new business for it. It states in its ads that at least 20 percent of the nation's plants will be 30 years old or more by 1990, with life expectancies of 40 years. General Electric believes that the plants can be renovated at a cost of $250 per kilowatt, while new construction would cost $2000 per kilowatt. It is likely that this kind of innovation in infrastructure management can eventually reduce the total cost of all of the infrastructure categories.

Some of the key interest groups for the electric power industry are the Edison Electric Institute, the American Public Power Association, and the Electric Power Research Institute.

Gas Systems

The production, transmission, and distribution of the nation's natural gas resources is an important part of the infrastructure problem. Like electricity, gas is more often associated with the energy industry, and not thought of as an important part of the infrastructure problem area. It has, however, many features in common with water, especially in the pipeline area.

The three parts of the industry—production, transmission, and distribution—are handled differently. In this sense, the gas industry is, for the most part, not well integrated. Even within the distinct sectors, notable differences arise from the pressures of regulation. For example, there are differences between the regulatory treatment given to interstate versus intrastate transmission companies and differences in treatment among different categories of producers (39).

Most of the attention in the gas industry is given to large economic issues such as gas shortages and rate regulation. This leaves the condition of the transmission and distribution infrastructure largely out of the public eye. These facilities, however, are critical to the health of the gas industry and to the cost and availability of energy, and need the same kind of care and attention as other categories of infrastructure.

Gas supplies about one-fourth (26.8 percent in 1981) of all U.S. energy uses. For comparison, oil supplies 43.4 percent, coal 21.7 percent, hydropower 4.0 percent, nuclear plants 3.9 percent, and other sources 0.2 percent (39). Gas is of special interest as a source since it is the largest domestically supplied component of national energy supplies (34.1 percent versus 29.2 percent for coal and 27.9 percent for oil in 1981).

Gas is normally of concern to public works managers as another type of underground pipeline and a possible source of safety hazards. Management of facilities is the concern of the mostly private and regulated companies. This difference in economic organization is one of the reasons for the general lack of communication between the water and wastewater industries and the gas industry.

The largest production companies tend to be the same ones that are involved in the production of oil: Exxon, Texaco, Standard Oil of Indiana, and Mobil. The largest transmission companies are familiar names such as El Paso Natural Gas Company, Columbia Gas Transmission Corporation, Tennessee Gas Transmission Company, and the Natural Gas Pipeline Company. Large distribution companies include Southern California Gas Company, Pacific Gas and Electric Company, InterNorth Incorporated, and Consolidated Gas Supply Corporation.

Technology in the gas industry has evolved continuously since its beginning in the nineteenth century. In 1930 pipelines were limited to about 20 inches with pressures up to 500 psi; however, by 1980 the sizes have increased to 42 inches with pressures exceeding 1000 psi, and technology exists for pipes up to 56 inches with pressures up to 2000 psi.

Interest groups for gas include the American Gas Association and the Gas Research Institute, started in 1978. With the lack of integration in the industry, there is an important need for interest groups to represent the production, transmission, and distribution interests. In this sense, the gas industry is also similar to the fragmented water industry.

EXERCISE: COSTING MUNICIPAL SERVICES

In planning it is often useful to make approximate cost estimates. In this exercise you should determine the approximate cost of a bundle of municipal services. The calculations involved should be very approximate, with only enough detail to give you an idea of the magnitudes involved.

This exercise will get you thinking about costing of services. Without the data you need, it will be difficult to complete in detail.

Make a rough plan for a hypothetical town of 100,000 inhabitants, and estimate the cost for the water supply system. The following components should be included:

Source of supply
Treatment plant
Distribution system

Your estimate should include the capital and operating expenses. After presenting them, you should prepare an amortization schedule for repaying the capital expenses at 12 percent over 30 years. Add your capital expenses to the operating expenses, and calculate what the monthly bill should be for a home with three inhabitants.

Can you make this estimate? The data are scarce, but that illustrates the difficulty of obtaining data at an early stage of reconnaissance of projects. Do you have enough understanding of cost estimating to know how to begin the analysis and to find the data? Do you have enough information on the per capita quantities involved?

REFERENCES

1. Pikarsky, Milton, and Christine Johnson, "Transportation in transition," *APWA Reporter*, January 1983.
2. U.S. Department of the Census, *Statistical Abstract of the United States*, 1985.
3. Oglesby, Clarkson H., *Highway Engineering*, Wiley, New York, 1975.
4. Roads and Bridges, Pavement Maintenance Symposium to Foster Technology Transfer, November 1986.
5. Congressional Budget Office, Public Works Infrastructure: Policy Considerations for the 1990's, Washington, D.C., 1982.
6. Udevitz, Norm, "State highway system a wreck," *Denver Post*, February 16, 1986.
7. "North Carolina bridges get a rough rating," *USA Today*, December 8, 1983.
8. "A new era in bridge-rebuilding," *ENR*, January 5, 1984.
9. Transportation Research Board, Strategic Transportation Research Study: Highways, Washington, D.C., 1984.
10. Metro, *Transit Industry Statistics, Annual 1986–87 Fact Book*.
11. Conte, Christopher, "Resurgence of private participation in urban mass transit stirs debate," *Wall Street Journal*, November 27, 1984.
12. "Mass transit: The expensive dream," *Business Week*, August 27, 1984.
13. Rose, Frederick, "Greyhound to sell US bus operations for $350 million to group of investors," *Wall Street Journal*, December 24, 1986.
14. "Survey shows railcar market changes," *Metro*, May/June 1985.

15. Armstrong-Wright, Alan, "Urban transport in LDC's," *Finance and Development*, September 1986.

16. "Urban transport: Policies and priorities, *Urban Edge*, May 1986.

17. Selden, Andrew C., "Sidetracked in the Northeast Corridor," *Wall Street Journal*, October 24, 1986.

18. Miller, Jeffrey G., "Safe Drinking Water Act," in *Environmental Law Handbook*, Government Institutes Inc., Rockville, Md., 1985.

19. Cristofano, Sam M., and William S. Foster, Management of Local Public Works, International City Management Association, Washington, D.C., 1986.

20. Leinster, Colin, "The sweet smell of profits from trash," *Fortune*, April 1, 1985.

21. Morrin, David, and Neil Seldman, "New ways to keep a lid on America's garbage problem," *Wall Street Journal*, April 15, 1986.

22. Buchholz, John D., "Waste-to-energy: Analyzing the market," *World Wastes*, June 1986.

23. National League of Cities, Capital Budgeting and Infrastructure in American Cities: An Initial Assessment, April 1983, Washington, D.C.

24. "Contractors put USA's repair bill at $3 trillion," *USA Today*, June 7, 1983.

25. "Hot new market lures AE players to cutting edge, *ENR*, April 4, 1985.

26. Honeywell Technalysis, The Integrated Building, 1985 promotional brochure, New York.

27. "Housing finance: An urban priority," *Urban Edge*, October 1986.

28. "Learning lessons from the rubble of Mexico City," *ENR*, September 4, 1986.

29. Fenn, Scott, *America's Electric Utilities: Under Siege and in Transition*, Praeger, New York, 1984.

30. Freeman, Richard, The Scope of the Infrastructure Deficit: How Much Is Needed Where? Economic Information Report, August 21, 1984.

31. City of Fort Collins, Light and Power Utility, Partners in Power: A History of the Light and Power Utility, 1985.

32. Nyberg, Bartell, "Dimming of REA lights fire," *Denver Post*, April 21, 1986.

33. "Man of the year," *ENR*, February 9, 1984.

34. "Time may be running out for Gulf States Utilities," *Business Week*, November 17, 1986.

35. "The rush to plug into lower electricity rates," *Business Week*, April 28, 1986.

36. Paul, Bill, "States tighten rules for electric utilities," *Wall Street Journal*, November 13, 1986.

37. Richards, Bill, "Utility's proposal seen as step toward deregulation," *Wall Street Journal*, December 22, 1986.

38. Richards, Bill, "Cogenerated power irritates utilities," *Wall Street Journal*, October 23, 1985.

39. Tussing, Arlon R., and Connie C. Barlow, *The Natural Gas Industry: Evolution, Structure and Economics*, Ballinger, Cambridge, Mass., 1984.

CHAPTER THREE

PLANNING INFRASTRUCTURE SYSTEMS

The problems that made up the infrastructure "crisis" in the early 1980s seem to fall into three general categories: finance, planning and management, and technology. In the planning and management area, the most important problem was insufficient emphasis on *preparing* to manage infrastructure better. This is a problem affecting both facilities and operations, and it manifests itself in actions such as keeping records of maintenance needs so that budget actions can be planned. In this broad problem area of planning and management, the beginning point of doing better is to have an effective planning program in place; that is the subject of this chapter.

Planning is the first task of management; it is followed by *organizing* (Chapter 4 and others) and then *controlling* (Chapter 9 and others). Managers understand that if plans are faulty or missing, operational control will not be effective; still, planning is such a general concept that not many managers have a full understanding of it.

Planning is a ubiquitous task; it is needed everywhere in the organization at the same time, constantly and in the future. Every phase of management must be planned, including construction and development of facilities as well as arrangements for long-term operations.

Some of the most important categories of plans for infrastructure managers are capital development plans, financing plans, organizational development plans, and plans for the improvement of operations. Of these categories, the one normally receiving the most emphasis in infrastructure work, due to its capital intensity, is capital development planning, for it is here that new facilities are planned and developed. This category also includes the development of needs estimates for the three R's relating to existing facilities: repair, rehabilitation, and replacement. In discussions of the national infrastructure problem, "capital planning" is usually the main topic covered (1).

As will be pointed out in this chapter, the jargon of planning can be an obstacle to the development of a clear vision of how to implement it. To remove some of this confusion, plans can be organized into five categories:

1. A master linking or integrated plan (sometimes called the "comprehensive general plan")
2. Master plans for the development of each service or type of facility
3. Needs assessments tied to the budgeting process
4. Plans to develop the infrastructure organization
5. Plans to improve operations and services

Everyone acknowledges the importance of planning, but there are differences in ideas of how to go about it. This chapter describes some of the most useful and important procedures and techniques. There is so much to learn about planning that it cannot all be put into one chapter, or, in fact, learned from a book. Planning requires a lot of experience in the operating environment. This chapter is distinguished from other written material about planning, however, by its deliberate avoidance of emphasis on mathematical techniques, and its preference for practical aspects of planning that face the infrastructure manager.

One of the reasons for the complexity of infrastructure is that there are so many different classification schemes of plans needed. This includes policy plans, master plans, development plans, site plans, and many other categories. These are placed into a classification system in the next section. Planning does not have to be such a complex subject when the manager understands the exact tasks facing the infrastructure organization.

Planning is linked to facilities development and operation and to the financial management of an enterprise. Thus in Chapter 5 we discuss planning as it relates to the budget process, and in this chapter we discuss the general aspects of planning. In the budget process the planning-programming-budgeting (PPB) use of planning enters the picture. This is the point where facilities planning links with budgeting. The planning required is the same. The application varies, and talented management is able to use effective planning for facilities, operations, and financial planning. Program evaluation is also related to planning and budgeting; it is discussed in the last section of this chapter.

The linkage between facilities, operations, and financial planning lies in the information system, or the decision support system (DSS). This is discussed in Chapter 4, which covers the organizational and informational aspects of infrastructure management. In effect, since planning is a rather unstructured responsibility of management, it is not always clear who should be doing the planning; this means that communications through an effective DSS is especially important to the success of planning.

3.1. THE INTERACTIVE ASPECTS OF INFRASTRUCTURE SYSTEMS

One of the main challenges in planning infrastructure systems is to consider how everything affects everything else, the linkages and the impacts. The world is increasingly complex, and this includes its subsystems. Infrastructure planning needs to be interdisciplinary and "multisectoral," meaning that the different sectors of the economy need to be involved in the planning efforts. This reality is the reason that we have seen recent legislation that calls for impact assessments of different kinds, especially impact on the environment. There is also social impact, economic impact, and financial impact. Impact assessments are simple ways to consider the interactive nature of infrastructure systems.

If planning is too "global," it cannot be effective. On the other hand, if it is too specific and directed at single-purpose missions, it cannot succeed either, for it will become the victim of opposing political forces. In planning, it is best to approach the problem at the appropriate level of global concerns with full consideration of impacts and external effects, but still to concentrate specifically on the problem at hand. One chorus that planners are accustomed to hearing is the one from operating managers who say, "Enough of this studying, let's get some action." This is a frustration with planning that does not lead anywhere, often as a result of wrapping too much into the planning process. On the other hand, action without the right planning is even more counterproductive, leading to wasted resources and other problems.

Basically, infrastructure supports a complex socioeconomic system, represented in Figure 3.1, illustrating the reliance of the social system on the economic system, the economic system on the infrastructure, and the infrastructure on the natural environment. This simple diagram must be expanded greatly to show all of the different categories of infrastructure, industries in the economy, and levels of government involved in infrastructure management. The correctness of the concept, however—that the infrastructure is necessary to support society—is seldom in dispute. Debates are usually over how much, what kind, where, when, and who pays. This is related to the observation made in Chapter 1 about Socrates' theory of the need for humans to recognize the importance of community in providing the means of life; it shows in the diagram that infrastructure is a foundation of economic and social life. It is also clear from

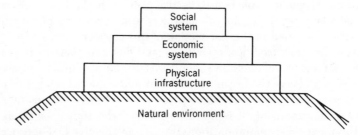

FIGURE 3.1. Relationship of infrastructure to socioeconomic systems and environment.

the psychological theories of human needs that infrastructure meets basic human needs, and enables the higher-order needs, such as cultural development and education, to take place.

The simple diagram presented in Figure 3.1 can be made much more complex. In the literature of urban systems, or regional economic systems, there are models that seek to show the entire interaction of a socioeconomic region. One of these is contained in a study by the International Programme on Man and the Biosphere of the United Nations (2). The diagram seeking to represent the urban system is complex, as shown in Figure 3.2. Interestingly, infrastructure is only assigned a rather minor role in this diagram, which seeks to portray the environment and the social system prominently.

However complex the situation, it is not possible to deal with infrastructure management without some idea of the interactions involved. For this reason we need a conceptual model of how infrastructure categories relate to one another. From Figure 3.1 it is easy to see that all of our most important social and economic activities depend on infrastructure, and it is also true that many interdependencies are built into our infrastructure systems themselves, such as between water and wastewater, transportation and waste management (air pollution), and buildings and energy.

It is also possible that infrastructure categories can impact each other in the construction phase. Construction activities are greatly impacted, for example, after a natural disaster, like a flood, when everything has to be rebuilt at once and there is a shortage of inputs. In the Denver area there is currently some concern about how all the construction activity envisioned in the years ahead might affect the supply of building materials (3). The projects envisioned are the new Stapleton Airport at $3 billion, the new Two Forks Reservoir at $500 million, the Rocky Mountain Arsenal groundwater cleanup at $500 million to $2 billion, the Lowry landfill cleanup at $20 million to $40 million, the metro area transit system at $2 billion, the Denver convention center at $100 million to $150 million, and Platte Valley Development at unknown cost. The cost of all of this potential activity is at least $6 billion, and in addition to the cost of materials, the region will have to worry about how to finance everything.

The basic purpose of infrastructure can be inferred from Figure 3.3, which illustrates flows of goods and labor in an economic system. Industry supplies goods and services to the public, which pays with dollars in return. The public furnishes labor to business, which pays wages in return. These wages enable the public to buy the goods and services produced by business. To live and produce the goods and services, business and the public need natural resources and energy. This economic diagram illustrates the points in the economic support system where infrastructure is necessary.

These points include furnishing the transportation to deliver goods and services, creating the systems to deliver water and energy to business and to the public and to handle waste products, and providing the buildings to house the economic and social activities. A way to classify all of these activities is shown in the following table:

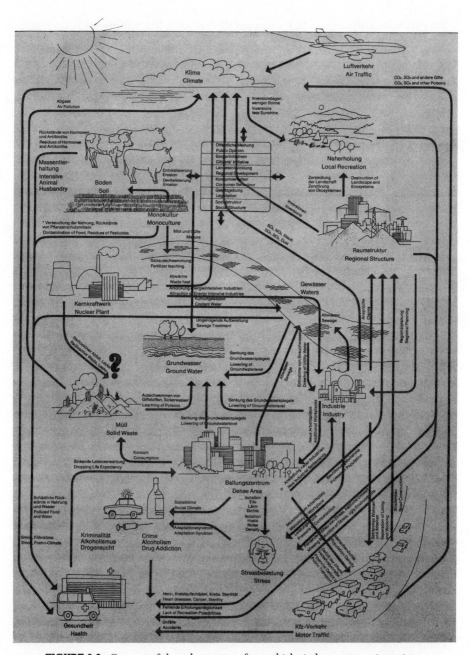

FIGURE 3.2. Concept of the urban system from a biological-ecosystem viewpoint.

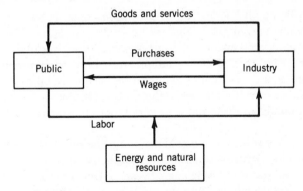

FIGURE 3.3. Economic system supported by infrastructure.

Socioeconomic Facilities	Linkage Facilities	Energy and Environmental Facilities
Factories	Transportation	Water systems
Public buildings	Communications	Wastewater systems
		Solid-waste systems
		Stormwater systems
		Energy systems
		Environmental management

In fact, the systems shown all support each other and in turn depend on each other. Planning must take this interdependency into account.

The importance of infrastructure to economic development is easy to appreciate. A study of Sao Paulo, Brazil, one of the world's "super cities" with an expected population of 24 million by the year 2000, showed that the availability of public services, especially electricity and telecommunication links, was among the chief priorities of firms making decisions about where to locate (4). The availability of these services make business operations less expensive and raise the attractiveness of business sites. These location decisions then determine employment and growth, and enable the improvement of life in the community.

These interactions among infrastructure categories and among infrastructure development and regional economics can be seen in modeling studies which are carried out to aid in planning. There are many different kinds of models, mostly those run on computers, which purport to simulate one process or another. Some are useful; some are just blue-sky academic exercises. Modeling is discussed later in the chapter in the section covering special studies in planning.

The interaction that must be considered in infrastructure planning is widely appreciated in development planning, especially in regions where much of the investment is by development banks such as the World Bank or the Inter-

American Development Bank. These institutions have highly sophisticated planning methodologies in place. One recent study of integrated development planning that highlighted experiences in Latin America advocated an approach with three steps: diagnosis, strategy, and projects. In developing this approach the investigators found that "comprehensive regional development planning," or trying to relate everything to everything else, did not work. By the same token, just compiling projects did not work; some intermediate process was needed (5).

In spite of the difficulties in regional planning, the process is necessary, and it sometimes works. A recent analysis by a journalist in Denver resulted in a conclusion that read this way: "weighing 20 years of Denver planning, remarkable goals met" (6). By "weighing," the writer cited the following goals that had been impacted: to enhance Denver's potential as a continental city; to minimize effects of geographic isolation by improving transportation and communication systems; to preserve Denver's historical Western image; to preserve the natural advantages of Denver's climate; to encourage development of a sound industrial base; to reduce friction, inefficiency, and duplication in metropolitan government; and to eliminate all blight; to strengthen Denver's excellence in man-made works and activities; to provide a safe, rapid, and economic system for transporting people and goods; to promote specific character and identity for functional areas such as downtown; to preserve and improve the environment of all areas of the city; and to provide properly located and well-designed public facilities. These are goals that had been stated in a comprehensive plan for the city in 1965, and in the writer's judgment, many had been favorably impacted. Planning was given credit for some of the progress.

3.2. LAND USE, GROWTH AND DEVELOPMENT, AND INFRASTRUCTURE DEMANDS

Land use and growth and development drive the demand for infrastructure. There will be one set of infrastructure problems in an area with rapid growth and another in an old, declining area. For these reasons the person who intends to manage infrastructure should know something about land-use management. Not only is land-use management a "planning" subject, but "planners" are typically charged with land-use studies, reviews, and regulatory proceedings. Typically an urban area will have some kind of zoning or land-use board, and the staff will be from the planning department.

The next section discusses the principles of planning, one of which is the need for "comprehensive" infrastructure planning, along with some sort of overall plan for land use. There is no such thing, of course, as having absolute land-use planning and control in a free society such as the United States. Land-use decisions are made by independent economic persons. For this reason there needs to be some regulation in the public interest, and much of infrastructure planning revolves around the land-use decisions that come from this regulatory process.

The process requires a developer and the regulatory agency. The developer makes proposals, and the agency decides if the proposals can be accommodated within some structure of public interest. Zoning is the most obvious vehicle for regulation, but it is a static concept, subject to many exceptions and variances.

In an ideal world, we would begin with a master land-use plan for a "planning area" around an urban area. When proposals come in, they would be evaluated for consistency with the land-use plan. If consistent, they would be granted. If not, they would be disapproved. The developer would pay the fair share of development fees, and everything would work well.

In practice things are not nearly so simple. We may have a concept for land use, but there are too many changes to stick to any kind of static plan. For this reason the whole field of "growth management" has arisen, along with its own field of experts and gurus. Even though it is beyond the scope of this book to discuss detailed growth management, it is briefly discussed next in order to place it in proper perspective in terms of its influence on infrastructure planning and management.

Growth management cannot be neglected; there must be some process to accommodate new development. Cities that ignore it do so at their peril. Houston, for example, is well known as a city that has no zoning. The result of its rapid growth, from 1 million in 1965 to 1.6 million in 1980, was considerable congestion and other urban problems. Developers severed major arterials and prevented adequate crosstown transportation from being maintained, with the result that Houston has only 9.6 miles of limited-access arterials per 100 square miles, compared with 25 for Los Angeles and 32 for New York. This results in a "need" of $17.4 billion for arterials and other transportation construction by the year 1997 (7).

There are many methods of growth management, including those with emphasis on infrastructure. A publication of the American Society of Planning Officials recently gave a list of them (8). Notable methods listed were public acquisition, public improvements (infrastructure), environmental controls, development rights transfer, restrictive covenants, zoning techniques, conventional subdivision regulations, regulations for permanent population control, zoning and subdivision controls relating to off-site facilities, exactions and other requirements, tax and fee systems, annexation, official mapping, capital programming, a plan to be followed, geographic restraints, numerical restraints or quota systems, and other techniques.

The city of Fort Collins, Colorado, has considered all these techniques and arrived at a system called the "land-use guidance system." This system relies on up-front negotiations between the city and developers to arrive at planned unit developments that contribute to the city's goals (9).

The system is basically a "points" approach, where developers may accumulate points by complying with the city's goals, and favorable development decisions result from high point achievement. Developments are judged against a number of criteria, beginning with the following: neighborhood compatibility, plans and policies, public facilities and safety, resource protection, environmental standards, and site design. Infrastructure questions in the system revolve around the city's philosophy that growth must pay its own way. This translates into questions such as the following:

• Will the project's completion not generate a traffic volume which exceeds the future capacity of the external street system as defined by the city?
• Is the development served by utilities with adequate capacity or have arrangements been made for extension and augmentation for the following services: water supply, sanitary sewer, electricity, natural gas, storm drainage?
• Does the project comply with all design standards, requirements, and specifications for the following services or have variances been granted: water supply, sanitary sewer, electricity, natural gas, storm drainage, flood hazard areas, telephone, streets/pedestrian, irrigation companies, mass transit, fire protection, cable television, walks/bikeways?

The land-use guidance system is not perfect, but it has received high marks from developers and growth management advocates alike, and it seems to have the ingredients of a negotiated system that works.

The realities of growth management require attention from planners to make it work. After the political and policy aspects of land-use decisions are settled, then there is still room for effective planning for infrastructure management.

3.3. PLANNING PROCESSES AND FUNDAMENTALS

Planning is fundamentally a simple concept. It is aimed at finding ways to get where you want to go, at making decisions about what to do. Underlying all planning procedures and processes is this fundamental characteristic of planning. Confusion about planning arises due to all the jargon that surrounds it and all the buzzwords it attracts.

Planning is, in general, the act of making a plan, and a plan is a guide for action. The plan tells you what to do. If management is what managers do, the plan then is what tells managers what to do, and planning takes its proper place as the first task of management. Planning is a requirement for problem solving, and problem solving requires decision making; thus planning, problem solving, and decision making follow the same general "process."

In fact, there is a generalized planning process that many people seem to sense intuitively. It consists of defining goals, developing alternative solutions, picking the best one, and putting it into action. Organized and successful people seem to have this process implanted naturally in their brains, a sort of biological "ROM," or "read-only memory" in computer jargon. This process is called, in addition to the "planning process," the "problem-solving process," the "engineering method," and some other terms. It seems that everyone wants to take credit for this logical and necessary process. In the final analysis, problem solving is a basic human activity, as basic as the process of thinking, and these methods have evolved to explain the process of thinking.

Planning is important in managing organizations of all kinds, but in many public organizations little of it is done. In private organizations few can survive without some kind of planning. How can this neglect of planning be overcome? Most likely, it can be overcome through a better understanding of why and how planning is important in solving management problems. Problem solving is the underlying reason for planning (and management), and the manager needs to understand the process of problem solving in order to have a direct approach to handling difficult issues.

When managers plan, it is to solve problems. When "planners" plan, there is the risk that the result will be plans that "stay on the shelf." A basic premise of successful planning is that the managers, the movers and shakers, must be involved in planning. In this way implementation is more likely. Here again the purpose and use of planning exercises must motivate the planning efforts.

There are different phases and objectives of planning, leading to many types of planning with confusing descriptions, such as strategic planning, master planning, policy planning, and so forth. Planning applications for infrastructure fit on a four-dimensional matrix to describe; thus they cannot all be shown on just one diagram. One dimension is the stages of management: planning, organizing, design, and operation. Another is the subdivisions of the organization. A third dimension is the levels within each of the subdivisions of the organization. The fourth is the different types of infrastructure categories. Everything has to be planned, and that includes the physical capital facilities as well as the operating systems. To grasp this view of planning, we must look at planning as a continuous responsibility of the entire organization.

The dimensions of plan types can be shown on an individual diagram for each category of infrastructure, such as water supply, road maintenance and operations, and electric power. This illustration would show the function, stage, and level of the planning required. This allows each part of the organization to establish which plan is its responsibility. This establishment of responsibility is closely related to the establishment of information support requirements, and to the maintenance of data bases and routine studies to support decision making.

Once the decision support system is established, and the data bases delineated, the routine preparation of plans can be assigned readily. This is discussed in the next chapter under decision support systems.

Planning involves studying what to do; it enables us to carefully consider our options. Decision making is deciding what to do, a discrete act, one that cannot be avoided by managers. Implementing is making the decision work, and it often is the most time-consuming and difficult part of solving problems. The entire process begins with planning.

The planning process includes several very important steps, as shown in Figure 3.4. Identifying the problem is the first step, and it cannot be skipped. This means to filter through all the conflicting reports, some without sufficient data and biased, to determine what the root of the difficulty is. Some organizations need to hire management consultants to achieve this level of understanding.

FIGURE 3.4. Planning process.

In Chapter 9 the technique of "diagnostic analysis" is explained as a vehicle to identify problems better.

The second step, goal-setting, while a key feature of the planning process, is very complex due to the different value sets of the many actors involved in managing public organizations. This can lead to extreme frustration for managers who are not ready for the challenge of managing the public organization. Goals cannot be neatly defined by planners in a vacuum; they have to be determined in a political process. Sometimes it is not possible to determine goals without an election; issues supported by the candidates with the most votes are the ones favored.

Formulating the alternative solutions is the creative step of planning. This step in planning can never be turned over to computers since creativity extends beyond mere enumeration of obvious alternatives. There are technical alternatives, financial alternatives, organizational alternatives, and management alternatives.

The evaluation of alternatives is a scientific process involving systems analysis, economics, impact analysis, and political awareness. This is the stage where computers can be most useful to find cost-benefit ratios, financial payouts, and impacts of alternatives. The selection of a preferred alternative needs to be a dynamic process in infrastructure; since implementation is such a challenge in the public arena, the decisionmaker needs to be flexible and ready to shift to different alternatives when the need arises.

Selection of preferred alternatives involves developing a way to rank and present the alternatives to the decision maker, but it is not the decision making itself. That is a discrete step reserved for the decision maker and is not really part of the planning process. Planning can go on for a long time without reaching a decision, especially in the case of complex infrastructure facilities that require permits from multiple authorities and the settlement of court cases.

To even discuss such a broad subject as planning, we need classification schemes. The first one deals with the organization chart. Each of the centers of responsibility must plan. For example, organizing the finance function requires planning. Operating the capital plant requires an operational plan, and this element is the same as planning the operational systems.

The next classification of planning is by facility type of the systems being planned, such as water, transportation, or solid waste. Each of these categories has unique features that require expert attention for success in planning.

Table 3.1 gives some of the classifications of planning, placed in perspective with regard to time horizon, or stage of planning; jurisdiction; systems planned; and planning results, or purpose of planning.

TABLE 3.1. Examples of Types of Planning

Stage of Planning	Jurisdiction of Planning
Policy planning	Areawide planning
Needs assessment	Urban planning
Strategic planning	Organizational planning
Implementation planning	Division of unit planning
Systems Planned	*Planning Results*
Water facilities planning	Master planning
Transportation planning	Preliminary design
Solid-waste planning	Action planning
Building planning	Program planning

You will recognize that "strategic planning" is a current buzzword which is meant to incorporate everything relating to long-range planning, and "implementation planning" is another faddish term meaning the planning necessary to get the job done. If you are thinking about building a house, the strategic planning is all of the dreaming and pencil sketches that precede the implementation planning, which is the final stage of discussions with the architect and the decisions that just precede the design drawings.

Some of the most common kinds of planning arising in infrastructure are policy planning, program planning, master planning, action planning, and preliminary design planning. The spans of these categories of planning are shown in Figure 3.5.

Relating these types of planning to those mentioned at the beginning of the chapter—capital development plans, financing plans, organizational development

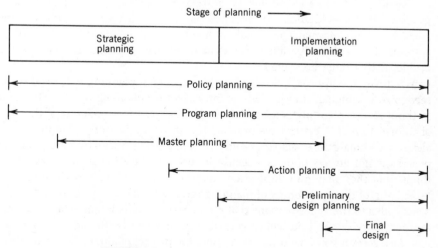

FIGURE 3.5. Stages and classifications of planning.

plans, and plans for the improvement of operations—we see that policy planning, program planning, master planning, action planning, and preliminary design are types of plans needed to prepare capital development, finance, organizational development, and improved operations. The five categories of plans that are most necessary also fit into these categories. Recall that these were a master linking or integrated plan (master planning); master plans for the development of each service or type of facility (also a form of master planning, more detailed); needs assessments tied to the budgeting process (one of the stages of planning, also a special type of capital plan); plans to develop the infrastructure organization (organizational development planning, can be action planning to make organization more effective); and plans to improve operations and services (also a form of action planning, depending on the phase).

Policy planning means developing the overall policies that will govern entire programs and approaches. An example would be to study the need to subsidize infrastructure to improve the chances for economic development.

Program planning must be done for each service category such as transportation, water, or waste management. Since services have capital and operating components, program planning must include both these aspects of a service.

Master planning, a term not much in vogue right now, still is necessary. For each facility category there must be a master plan that specifies where the facilities will go and at what time in order that rational overall facility planning can take place.

Implementation planning can include processes such as action planning and preliminary design. Action planning is a special breed of planning that enables the action agency to decide how to move to solve problems. Preliminary design is the stage between pure planning and construction or final implementation. Sometimes it can be quite detailed.

Classifying planning requirements illustrates the artistic, rather than scientific planning. Planning strategies for organizations are all different, but with common characteristics. The manager needs to develop a unique approach that will be appropriate for the situation at hand in his or her organization and for the problems that must be solved.

Whatever the approach adopted, some aspects of planning will need to be recognized. Vaughan, in his study of infrastructure planning needs, cited four to think about: planning is a continuous process; the management of the flow of information is a central element in the planning process; planning is an alchemist's amalgam of sciences and art; and setting up a strategic planning process is not always popular because it requires busy managers to do three things that they may find unpleasant: set aside time, think, and write (1).

In spite of the uniqueness of planning requirements, it is important to have a clear idea of the types of plans that are necessary to maintain. The plans that are necessary depend on where you sit. In other words, the agency manager will see a certain set of necessary plans, and the project planner will see another. This is a result of the different requirements of the different parts and levels of the organization. This differing perspective of planning is the subject of the next two sections.

Manager's Viewpoint

From the manager's point of view, plans are needed to make the organization succeed. That is to say, the capital development plans, financing plans, organizational development plans, and plans for the improvement of operations should be done in a way that will be useful to management. On the face of it this seems obvious, but to many it is not. The "seat of the pants" manager will not appreciate the need for planning, and the planner may not appreciate the "results" orientation of the manager.

The capital development plans will begin with an overall view of the existing and projected demand for infrastructure. In this we recognize that the ultimate determination of demand for infrastructure is from population growth, land use, and economic activity.

The next necessary step is to have a clear idea of who is responsible for what part of the infrastructure, and to assign the responsibility for each part of the planning. This means the transportation department has responsibility for the traffic planning, the water supply department for water distribution, and the other logical departments for their parts. Conflicts can arise between departments and within the line and staff components of departments when clear responsibilities are not delineated.

For capital development, responsible agencies must maintain at a minimum three related categories of plans: comprehensive general plans; master plans for each facility type; and an inventory of facilities and needs, including a needs assessment for each category of facility. All of these plans should be "dynamic," meaning they should be revised from time to time when needed.

The comprehensive general plan goes by different names. Basically it is the umbrella plan for all related infrastructure facilities and related items. Sometimes it is referred to as the "master plan" for the community, but this term is misleading since communities or areas do not grow and develop according to some master scheme, but according to the collective actions of different actors. For this reason, planners have backed away from reliance on static and rigid documents and guidelines, in favor of more flexible and realistic approaches. These are still controversial. One system, that in use in Fort Collins, Colorado, has been discussed earlier in this chapter. As mentioned before, this city has adopted a land-use guidance system, a flexible approach to land-use planning which allows the community to adapt to changing economic patterns. This is an important element in the overall approach to planning of infrastructure, since it is the land-use pattern that ultimately determines the demand for infrastructure systems.

Whatever the approach used, the concept of the comprehensive general plan is what links all the rest of the planning together, and in that sense, it remains necessary. It may not consist of one "plan," but a comprehensive planning process needs to be in place. You can consult the literature of organizations such as the American Society of Planning Officials (ASPO), the American Institute of Planners (AIP), and the International City Management Association (ICMA) for more information on this subject. In particular, ICMA has texts on planning, one of which is cited in Reference 10.

The next logical step in planning is to have a master plan for each facility category. This means one master plan for streets, one for water lines, one for wastewater, and one each for the other infrastructure categories. Actually it is the sum of these that becomes the comprehensive plan for the community. A master plan for a facility category, such as streets, can then be used to lead to the capital program and then the budget. The master plan would be the least firm of these instruments, changing when necessary. This step in planning is critical, however, so that the later program and budget can be guided by a plan. This is the real essence of the planning-programming-budgeting approach to management, which will be discussed in Chapter 5 under budgeting. The concept is illustrated in Figure 3.6, and discussed in Chapter 5.

Needs assessment is also used for programming and budgeting. This is one of the most important components in infrastructure planning and management since it assesses the needs in the area of the three R's (repair, rehabilitation, and replacement) as well as the need for new facilities. This is one of the most important and most neglected parts of planning for infrastructure. Needs assessment is a current evaluation of the total needs for development and maintenance of a particular category of infrastructure. An example would be the needs for improvement and maintenance of a roadway network within a certain area. The needs assessment process is the part of the planning-programming-budgeting process that leads to a workable definition of "needs" as distinct from "wishes" or some other expression of demand for facilities. This is important because the needs statements must be credible, or they will be ignored. Opinions that are not based on objective data are not worth much, even when they are somewhat informed. This is an important issue for public works managers to understand.

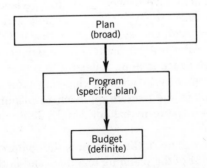

FIGURE 3.6. Planning-programming-budgeting.

When the national infrastructure "crisis" was receiving so much attention, it became clear that one of the reasons for lack of interest in the problem and lack of credibility in estimates of needs was the complexity of the problem and lack of data base for estimating needs. Our capability to make credible needs estimates is still primitive.

One of the reasons for the difficulty in making needs estimates is their high policy content. Some of the questions that require answers before needs can be estimated are political questions, either they have not been answered or the answers keep changing. An example of this would be a question about future growth assumptions. Will it be the policy of the community to attract growth or not?

Needs estimates attracted considerable attention in the national focus on the infrastructure problem. According to a symposium sponsored by the National Academy of Sciences the information needed to prepare an estimate should include performance criteria, economic analysis, future analysis, and evaluation of standards (11). In many studies of infrastructure planning processes, we find general references to the fact that we need to consider economic and future scenarios, but little specific guidance about how to deal with these matters. The truth is that they are difficult to deal with. That is the subject of the next section.

Needs assessments are part of both the maintenance management and capital improvement processes. In effect, it is the needs assessment that links these two processes together. The needs assessment process involves an inventory, a condition assessment, and an identification of desired levels of improvement and maintenance. These must be viewed in the light of present and expected future conditions. The process identifies deficiencies and evaluates alternative programs and projects to produce a needs report and selected programs and projects.

While we have a general understanding and a valid framework for needs assessments, many improvements are needed in the process. Many decision makers have seen so many poorly done needs assessments and plans that they consider a needs assessment as hardly more than a "wish list." This is a debilitating problem for public works managers, one that needs attention to improve the management of all kinds of public facilities.

Project Planner's Viewpoint

From the point of view of the planner, whether an in-house planner or a consultant, the task of planning itself is important, not only the management implications of the results. The planner will be concerned about the resources available and the technical skills needed for planning. Also important is how to report the results of planning for maximum impact on the decision maker. The challenge is to have plans that are technically correct, and effective in communicating recommendations.

Although the different types of infrastructure require different approaches to planning, all have common characteristics when it comes to the purposes of planning. For example, in a United Nations report about water planning, it is pointed out that the purposes of preparing reports are to report on the status of work, to present an inventory of needs or resources, to report on the possibilities for expansion or development, or to make specific recommendations for project development or financing. These purposes would be the same whether the service was water, transportation, or facilities development (12).

In this approach to water planning, the reports (and the plans) have a certain hierarchy: basin reports, project reports, and definite plan reports. A basin report is essentially the report for development possibilities for a certain area. In the case of transportation the equivalent area might be a roadway district or a county. In the case of another service it might be a service district. Water planning is more complex than some other services since water uses are so interdependent.

A project report is an investigation of the feasibility of a specific project, and can range from shallow reconnaissance studies to full feasibility reports.

The definite plan report, according to the UN, is the final and full report containing everything necessary to construct and implement a project. It would include the following:

- Full construction plans
    Final locations
    Designs, estimates, specifications
    Construction schedules
- Operating plans and agreements
    Integrated operation plans
    Operating agreements
    Operation and maintenance guidelines
- Repayment plans

Sorenson, in an article about how to prepare reports for project financing, also covers the types of reports submitted. His classification system includes two types of reports: the appraisal report, which leads to other studies, and the definite project report, which is intended to justify a particular project. He stresses the importance of making reports effective. This is to be done by answering three questions: why do this project, why do it now, and why do it this way? He recommends preparing reports in three parts. The first, most general, part is for the financiers and decision makers. The second is for the general engineering audience, and the third, essentially a technical appendix, contains all of the technical details (13).

Many elements are common to infrastructure plans in the different sectors. The project planner will do well to study methods of preparing plans in different fields, as well as technical communications methods to ensure maximum effectiveness in having the plan implemented.

3.4. PLANNING STUDIES

Planning studies include population projections, economic studies, and land-use studies. Modeling is used in all of these in some cases. In its "green book" on urban planning, the International City Management Association lists these as the three main categories of generalized studies, meant to support the specific studies of program categories such as transportation, water, and other facilities (14).

Population Studies

In most books when the subject of population studies is mentioned, if it is mentioned, there are references to various methods such as straight-line projections, curve fitting, cohort studies, and simulation. Then there is either a cursory discussion of some of these methods or a statement that making population projections is a specialized field and must be left to experts. Population forecasting is a field filled with land mines, and even specialists are apt to stumble unless enough qualifying statements are included with the forecast. Whenever we have a situation such as this, it is important to realize that the situation is not merely complex. No one really knows what will happen, and therefore the population cannot really be predicted. This is not necessarily bad news; it simply means we need to plan for alternatives.

The unreliability of population forecasting is recognized by forecasters as well. The media often contain reports of shifts in population trends and errors in forecasting. A recent report, for example, was entitled, "Why Demographers Are Wrong Almost as Often as Economists" (15). The author of the article claims that demographers missed or underestimated the following important events relating to population: postwar baby boom, baby bust, surge of women in workplace, sudden drop in death rates, exodus to sunbelt, and others. Another article mentioned the difficulty the Census Bureau has in measuring seasonal migration. Another article explains the large differences in estimates as being due to differences in methods.

There are two basic components to population change in an area, natural increase or decrease, and migration. Both components are difficult to forecast, especially migration, and the longer the range of the forecast, the more difficult the task.

At the national level, there can be some assurance that percentage growth rates will be somewhat stable for a brief period. For example, if we study the population of the United States for the decade of the 1970s, we see that the percentage increase every year was between 0.9 percent and 1.3 percent. This is a reasonably stable growth record, as far as we can tell given the difficulty in making accurate estimates and counts of population.

If, however, we look at the separate states, we see tremendous variations due to migration. In 1980, for example, Florida had an annual growth rate of around 4 percent, while New York was essentially static. Urban areas would expect even greater variations, perhaps even sustained growth rates of 5–10 percent per year.

The effects of sustained rates like those on planning can be severe, especially since boom is sometimes followed by bust, such as in the case of oil- or mining-fueled growth. What is at issue is the effect of compounding and exponential growth.

Basically the formula that gives population in some future year $P(t)$ is:

$$P(t) = P_0(1 + G)^n$$

where P_0 is the population in the base year and G is the annual growth rate. The effects of compounding over a planning period can be dramatic, as can be seen from some hypothetical figures. Consider a community with a base population in 1980 of 100,000. Projecting the population with four alternative growth rates yields the following figures:

Year	No Growth	1%	3%	5%
1980 (base)	100,000	100,000	100,000	100,000
1985	100,000	105,100	115,930	127,630
1990	100,000	110,460	134,390	162,890
2000	100,000	122,020	180,610	265,330
2010	100,000	134,780	242,730	432,200
2020	100,000	148,890	326,200	704,000
2030	100,000	164,460	438,390	1,146,740

The figures reveal enormous differences in the eventual characters of the areas involved, the result of compounding. This, however, is what we face when we try to project population. Annual growth rates do not, of course, remain constant. They vary from year to year. The constant rates in the preceding table are shown plotted in Figure 3.7. The actual growth of a certain area would be a composite of different rates.

To add to the uncertainty provided by compounding, consider the effect on population of changes in the economic, social, and political spheres. Any of these can change dramatically in a planning period of from 20 to 50 years. Remember that in the United States a 50-year planning period extending from 1915 to 1965 would include two world wars, the depression, the New Deal, the Korean war, the beginning of the Vietnam war, and the advent of new ages of automobiles, television, and many other technological changes. These changes are all in the memories of many people still alive today.

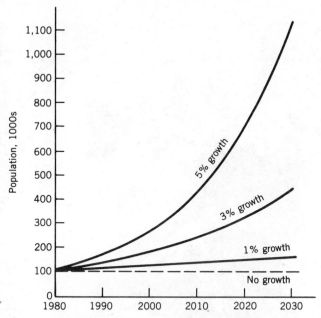

FIGURE 3.7. Plot of different growth rates.

Three examples of changes that are happening right before our eyes might be as follows. As an economic change, consider the price of oil. As a social change, consider shifts in family structure and numbers of working women. And as a political change, consider the interest in controlling growth that we see in many communities. Obviously with these kinds of change being probable, it is not easy to contemplate making population projections for long periods. Still, however, we must make projections for the purpose of rational planning.

The hazards in making long-term population forecasts should be clear. What is also clear, however, is that some areas of the world have large, uncontrolled urban growth under way. Providing adequate infrastructure for this growth is a major, perhaps impossible, task in some places. There will emerge certain supercities, with populations in excess of 20 million in the cases of Mexico City and Sao Paulo. A map showing the location of some of these supercities is presented as Figure 3.8.

No particular technique for population studies is recommended here. The one recommended in Reference 14 is called the *cohort survival method of population* dynamics. A "cohort" is a class of population, and these classes are then followed through the years, including childbearing times, to determine the trends in population they will cause. This approach, of course, cannot determine migration patterns, and is thus more suited to areas large enough to factor out the effects of migration.

Cohort survival is the kind of technique that lends itself to digital simulation, and there are many possibilities for using computer models to have on-line simulations of different population and economic scenarios. However, their

The rise of the cities

By the year 2000 half the world will live in cities, according to the 1986 'State of World Population' Report from the UN Fund for Population Activities.

This map shows what are predicted to be the top 12 urban areas by the year 2000.

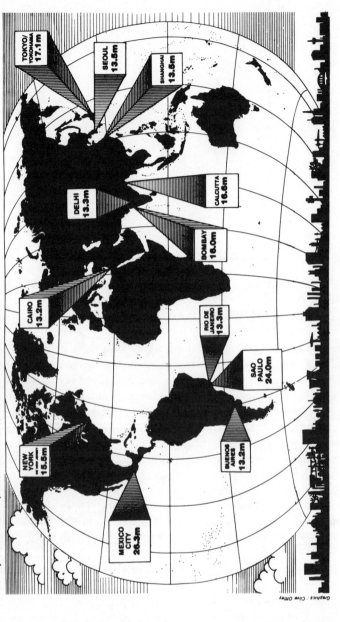

TOKYO/YOKOHAMA 17.1m

SEOUL 13.5m

SHANGHAI 13.5m

DELHI 13.3m

CALCUTTA 16.6m

BOMBAY 16.0m

CAIRO 13.2m

RIO DE JANEIRO 13.3m

SAO PAULO 24.0m

NEW YORK 15.5m

BUENOS AIRES 13.2m

MEXICO CITY 26.3m

Graphics : Clive Offley

FIGURE 3.8. Location of "supercities."

74

validity is apt to be short-lived due to the assumptions necessary and the unknowns.

A useful approach to population projections is to acknowledge from the beginning of the study period the need to look at alternative scenarios in planning; then the population scenarios become alternatives and not cast in concrete. The "official" forecast of the planning agency can be viewed as one possible outcome, but the infrastructure planning can also provide for the possibility of different outcomes. There are always risks in planning, especially when resources must be committed, but these can be minimized in the commitment of the resources.

As an example of population projection techniques, let's look at the practice in the Denver metropolitan area where quite a number of local governments are involved in infrastructure planning and management. The regional council of governments, DRCOG, has been making regional forecasts of population and employment for years. The process is based on areawide studies of population shifts and employment, with the overall population distributed to the subareas by making assumptions about the distribution of growth.

In its most recent annual report, DRCOG presents an illustrative graph showing the components of population change from 1960 to 1984, along with the regional population forecast. These are shown in Figure 3.9 (16).

DRCOG reports that a new method is being used to "project more accurately population and employment growth within subareas of the region, based on analysis of growth factors that determine the pattern of growth . . . the new

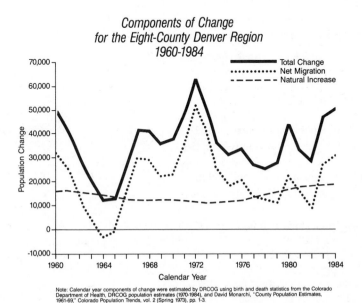

Note: Calendar year components of change were estimated by DRCOG using birth and death statistics from the Colorado Department of Health, DRCOG population estimates (1970-1984), and David Monarchi, "County Population Estimates, 1961-69," Colorado Population Trends, vol. 2 (Spring 1973), pp. 1-3.

FIGURE 3.9. Components of population change in Denver.

method distributes projected growth by taking into account competitive forces in terms of both residential and non-residential development" (17).

DRCOG took into consideration a number of regional factors that will influence growth patterns. It used the regional wastewater plan, the year 2000 transportation plan, assumptions about the development of a new airport, and existing trends in water supply development. Needless to say, there are many possible outcomes with all of these factors.

Recognizing the need to look at alternative outcomes, local planners encouraged DRCOG to adopt one set of "official" projections but also to examine the impacts of alternative scenarios. As a result of this general feeling, a new policy has been adopted where DRCOG recognizes and reinforces an analytical approach that directs that alternative forecasts be used in subarea studies.

As another example of methods in use, consider a technique to project population for the purpose of wastewater treatment grants. The North Carolina Division of Environmental Management uses basically a ratio-extrapolation method, with the controlling element being the historical and projected county population. Tables 3.2 and 3.3 give the results of two examples for wastewater treatment planning for small areas. Even though the methods are simple, they are certainly as good as more complex methods that have little basis in the data available. The basic source of the county estimates in the examples is Reference 18.

Economic data can be used to improve short-term ideas of what is going on in an area. Examples include building permits, new jobs, and other economic data. That is the subject of the next section.

TABLE 3.2. Population Projection for a Small Town

Town of Taylorsville (Alexander County)
    1970 population (from Bureau of Census) = 1231
    1980 population (from Bureau of Census) = 1103
Calculations 1990–2010:

$$\frac{1970 \text{ population of town}}{1970 \text{ population of county}} \quad \frac{1231}{19,466} = 0.0632$$

$$\frac{1980 \text{ population of town}}{1980 \text{ population of county}} \quad \frac{1103}{24,999} = 0.0440$$

Projection factor = (0.0632 + 0.0440) /2 = 0.0536
(Town population in year 19XX = projected county population in year 19XX
    multiplied by 0.0536)
    1990 = 28,521* (0.0536) = 1528
    2000 = 31,183* (0.0536) = 1671
    2010 = 33,402* (0.0536) = 1790

* 1982 Bureau of Economic Analysis Projection.

TABLE 3.3. Population Projection for a Planning Area

Alexander County 201 Facility Planning Area
  Estimated 1970 planning area population (from Bureau of Census) = 8786
  Estimated 1980 planning area population (from Bureau of Census) = 11,230
Calculations 1990–2010:

$$\frac{1970 \text{ population of planning area}}{1970 \text{ population of county}} \quad \frac{8786}{19,466} = 0.451$$

$$\frac{1980 \text{ population of planning area}}{1980 \text{ population of county}} \quad \frac{11,230}{24,999} = 0.449$$

Projection factor = (0.451 + 0.449) /2 = 0.450
(Planning area population in year 19XX = projected planning area population
  in year 19XX multiplied by 0.450)
  1990 = 28,521* (0.450) = 12,834
  2000 = 31,183* (0.450) = 14,032
  3010 = 33,402* (0.450) = 15,030

* 1982 Bureau of Economic Analysis Projection.

Economic Studies

Economic studies can help to predict conditions that attract population growth and thus can cause a need for more infrastructure. Economics is very difficult to predict, especially in local areas. As an example of this, consider what happened to Houston in the mid-1980s as a result of the unpredictable fall in oil prices. Houston had been undergoing a boom, leading to the construction of much downtown office space, residential housing, and, of course, infrastructure to support them. With the fall in oil prices, some firms began to have financial difficulties, others cut back on exploration, and the whole urban area went into economic decline. This had a drastic effect on infrastructure, but it could not have been anticipated.

In economic studies it is necessary to have a basic understanding of the link between jobs and growth. This interest in economic development is fundamental to an understanding of urban economics, and it relates to population prediction also.

Jobs support people. A wage earner who heads a family supports several people. This means there is a ratio between number of jobs and total population. Jobs can be classified as basic, or export jobs, and nonbasic, or service jobs. An example of an export job is a manufacturing position. An example of a service job is a local bus driver. Without export jobs there would be little need for service jobs. Therefore a ratio exists between export jobs in a community or area and all other parameters of population, including service jobs and total population.

The technique for carrying out economic studies of an urban area using these simple facts is the *economic base technique* (14). Certainly it has limitations, but its concepts illustrate the essential relationships between export jobs and total population in urban areas.

Land-Use and Growth Studies

Modelers have been fascinated with land-use modeling as a challenge—and with good reason, since it is clear that being able to predict land use leads to many financial advantages, as well as being able to predict the need for infrastructure. An ideal land-use model would be able to take existing land-use patterns in a region, add expected economic forces, and predict the patterns that will emerge in the future. In practice, of course, this is not possible to do in any but the most general context, since land-use changes are made by individual entrepreneurs, but model attempts have been made. In a recent study six categories of them were reported: conventional multiple regression equations, interdependent regression equations, the Lowry model and its derivatives, dynamic land-use models, judgmental models, and systems of models (19).

It is difficult to bend an instance where land-use models realistically projected future conditions. However, there is no doubt that they can be used to explain what has happened after the fact.

Modeling of all types can be used to get more sophisticated about estimates involving population, land-use, and economic shifts in an urban area. Modeling does not necessarily produce estimates that are more accurate than those produced without models, but it does enable the planner to examine many alternatives quickly.

Modeling and Systems Analysis

Two management tools that have promised much but have not yet lived up to their potential for infrastructure planning and management are systems analysis and modeling. Actually, modeling is a subset of systems analysis.

Systems analysis means different things to different people. Some take it to mean the analysis of entire systems at one time, rather than components, and others take it to mean the use of some sort of mathematical model to aid in making decisions. Of course, the systems analyst in data processing organizations is a computer systems person; this is a different meaning.

Here we use the term "systems analysis" to mean the analysis of systems together, such as infrastructure systems. In the light of this interpretation, many managers are practicing systems analysis, even if they are not using computer modeling for their analyses. With this philosophy we can infer that the use of systems analysis is necessary for effective infrastructure management. However, the use of sophisticated mathematical modeling is not always necessary for effective management.

There are so many different types of models that the term "model" should be used only as a general descriptor. The simplest distinction is one that classifies models according to whether they simulate some sort of system (simulation models), or whether they have been developed to indicate best decisions (optimization models), or whether they are really software developed for a certain purpose (such as project management).

A simulation model is the basic or generic type of model. Examples would include water distribution system operation, route scheduling for transportation, solid-waste collection studies, traffic flow prediction, and financial forecasting. Land-use forecasting models also appear in planning, but these are among the least reliable of all model categories.

A simulation model type with potential for management is the one based on the *systems dynamics technique* developed at MIT by Professor Jay Forrester. This technique was originally developed to simulate corporations, and was later extended to municipalities (urban dynamics) and to larger global systems (world dynamics and limits to growth) (20). This modeling technique is a basic approach to modeling economic systems of all kinds, and its principles seem to be applicable in many cases to today's spreadsheet capabilities.

Forrester's urban dynamics model simulated three basic subsystems of the city: business, housing, and labor. These three were shown to be very interdependent. The infrastructure-related categories, business and housing, would drive demands for diverse kinds of infrastructure. There would be many other ways the models could be structured.

The modeling technique has been applied to the operation of a water supply utility, and it seems to simulate quite well the financial and water stocks of the utility (21). The model of the urban water supply system had four subsystems: population and business which drove the demand for water and the revenue forecasts, the water stocks subsystem that showed the supply and availability of water, the facility subsystem that showed the quantity and condition of capital facilities, and the water rates subsystem that allowed planning for revenues and adjusting charges.

It was later found that the same model can be put together quite nicely on a spreadsheet, and it becomes a rather sophisticated financial and facilities planning model. More complex models can be understood better, however, with the conceptual depiction shown on the Forrester diagrams.

Impact models are a whole category of simulation models that have application in infrastructure management. They show the interdependence of one account, financial, social, or environmental, on another, growth and development. While impact models are controversial, they do allow some study of the interdependencies of categories of infrastructure.

3.5. POLICY ANALYSIS IN INFRASTRUCTURE

Of all types of planning, policy analysis is one of the most important in today's complex world. Policy analysis is concerned with finding the right policies; in effect, it is the part of planning concerned with steering big decisions correctly. All kinds of organizations, but especially public organizations, need good policy analysis.

Policy planning is well embedded in the literature of public administration, but has not found its way into engineering planning literature very much. The reason is that it is mostly a concern of managers. However, infrastructure managers are quite often engineers by background training, and need exposure to this planning technique. The concept of *analysis*, however, is a part of the engineering toolbox. When we recognize the importance of analysis to engineering problem solving, then the concept of policy analysis is easier to appreciate.

The term "analysis" means to divide something into its component parts; it is the opposite of "synthesis," which means to combine the parts into one. Thus we find many uses of the term "analysis": mathematical analysis, chemical analysis, engineering analysis, and, now, policy analysis. The process of synthesis is also necessary in infrastructure management due to the many divergent considerations and opinions that must be synthesized to reach decisions.

Basically, policy analysis is the application of the problem-solving process to finding the best policies to implement. To do this requires breaking the problem addressed and the possible policies into their separate elements. Policies are basically courses of action in relation to particular issues. In a legal sense they have a position in the hierarchy of rules and regulations. A company "policy" is a rule lacking the force of law but still an important guideline. The field of social science has a large subdivision called the "policy sciences," generally being those concerned with government and public matters.

In the case of infrastructure, however, the field of policy analysis generally means the analysis that is done to find lines of action for broad issues. Should the water supply be found independently or in concert with a regional agency? Should the solid-waste utility be privatized? How should the capital program be financed? What strategies should be employed to solve the community's mass transit problems? These are examples of matters that require policy analysis.

The International City Management Association has issued a guidebook on policy analysis in local government (22). In this guidebook, policy analysis is presented as a systems approach to decision making. There are four essential features according to the author: the systems approach, the use of the scientific method, the use of mixed teams (interdisciplinary approach), and an action orientation. In this sense, policy analysis might be thought of as a variation of systems analysis. Since systems analysis is so close to planning, then policy analysis is seen as closely related to policy planning, one of the categories of planning presented earlier.

The essence of policy analysis, when all of the background material is stripped away, is to find the best policies. Following this line, the steps in the planning process should be used to explore alternatives. The problem should be identified, the goals set, the alternative policies identified and evaluated, and the best courses of action selected and recommended.

This outline of steps in policy analysis represents a good outline also for a policy analysis report:

- Statement of the problem
- Diagnosis of the problem including its components
- Purposes, goals, missions, and objectives to be achieved
- Alternative policies to achieve the goals
- Evaluation using all the appropriate tools of analysis
- Recommendation of policy to be adopted

3.6. EVALUATION OF INFRASTRUCTURE MANAGEMENT PROGRAMS

In school everyone gets a dose of evaluation. After a course is taken, the evaluation comes out in the form of a grade for the term. Grades are not easy to give, or sometimes to receive, but they are considered a necessary part of the educational process.

In the same way, evaluation needs to be applied to public management programs. The effectiveness of services needs to be assessed after the fact so that appropriate adjustments can be made. This is part of the planning and problem-solving process; if evaluation is valid, then improvements can be made the next time around. The role of evaluation is shown in Figure 3.4 earlier in this chapter.

This brief discussion of program evaluation is included in this chapter on planning because of the need to link planning and budgeting. Quite often management auditing and program evaluation will be placed in the same office as budget. The federal government is an example of this; it has the Office of Management and Budget, the General Accounting Office, and the Congressional Budget Office, all of which do considerable program evaluation as well as budgeting. In Chapter 5, which presents budgeting techniques, the concept of planning, programming, and budgeting systems will be presented. That kind of planning is planning for the budget, but it needs to connect to the kind of planning discussed in this chapter also. Recall that the main kinds of planning stressed in this chapter are a master linking or integrated plan (sometimes called the "comprehensive general plan"), master plans for the development of each service or type of facility, needs assessments tied to the budgeting process, plans to develop the infrastructure organization, and plans to improve operations and services. All of these categories can have implications for the budget process, and all will need evaluation. The same kinds of skills needed for planning are used for program evaluation.

Unfortunately, evaluation is difficult to carry out effectively. Quantitative methods are available, methods that are based on those of economics, operations research, and "scientific management" as it has evolved from industrial roots.

However, these methods have not been widely adopted in the infrastructure management field since valid measurement is difficult.

The essence of program evaluation is measurement of the effectiveness of programs. It is a form of performance auditing, a concept that fits with financial auditing as described in Chapter 6, which covers financial management. Performance auditing means a check on how the operation is doing. Auditing performance is discussed in Chapter 9, and measures of effectiveness for some infrastructure categories are given in Appendix A.

The concept of productivity is usually introduced in any discussion of performance evaluation, since it is a given that high levels of productivity are desired. Productivity means the quality of being productive, or in other words, gaining a product from the investment of land, labor, and capital in whatever enterprise is being considered. Productivity is generally measured in the same way as efficiency: by a ratio of output to input. This topic is also discussed in Chapter 9.

Effectiveness means doing the right thing efficiently. Efficiency by itself is not enough to evaluate an enterprise, since it does not require the test that the right goals are being pursued. Thus the bottom line of productivity and program evaluation is to make sure that the operation is performing effectively.

To evaluate effectiveness of an operation, measures of effectiveness are needed. In the private sector effectiveness can be evaluated by determining how well the product is being received by the market. This can be accomplished by determining whether there is a need for the product and whether the one offered is considered to be worthwhile as compared with the competition. In the public sector the need for the service is sometimes difficult to establish, and there is usually no competition to allow the evaluation of the quality of the product.

Effectiveness measures for infrastructure services allow the analyst to consider their use in program evaluation and related planning. However, the use of these effectiveness measures is still largely untested in the real world arena.

In an Urban Institute report, Hatry lists 11 types of performance measures (23). By using combinations of these, various approaches can be developed. The ones listed are:

- Cost
- Work load accomplished
- Effectiveness/quality
- Efficiency/productivity
- Ratios of cost to work load
- Efficiency/effectiveness
- Resource utilization
- Productivity indexes
- Pseudomeasures

• Cost-benefit ratios
• Comprehensive performance evaluation

Some of these may seem the same, and it may seem a little like splitting hairs to distinguish among the categories; but in the serious study of evaluation practices, there are many ways to carry out the exercises.

The last of these categories, comprehensive performance evaluation, deserves a second look. The reason is that simple quantitative measures often do not do the job in complex administrative and management settings. Consequently, a comprehensive approach is called for. It should be designed to be appropriate for the particular setting involved. An example of a comprehensive approach is the one recommended by the Government Finance Research Center and Peat, Marwick and Mitchell for evaluating the performance of wastewater utility operations (24). This method, following a more general approach for analyzing complex operations, is described in more detail in Reference 25. The technique is also discussed later in Chapter 9 in the section on how diagnostic analysis applies to operations.

It is appropriate to end this chapter on planning with a discussion of program evaluation. Plans are fine; but in the final analysis there needs to be a check on how well the organization has done. In the private sector, the marketplace will ultimately do this for you; in the public sector, formal evaluation procedures are needed.

EXERCISES

1. For the infrastructure service you deal with, are you able to show how it affects economic development in your local area? Prepare arguments for more investment in these facilities as they are needed to support economic development. If you had to make these arguments to a governing board, do you think they would be received favorably?

2. We presented a planning process in this chapter (see Figure 3.4). For your infrastructure category, test the general process against your daily working and planning needs. Do you believe the process is adequate? If not, can you sketch out an improved process to meet your needs?

3. We presented ideas for main categories of planning needed (master linking or integrated plan, master plans for the development of each service or type of facility, needs assessments tied to the budgeting process, plans to develop the infrastructure organization, and plans to improve operations and services). For your operation make a list of how your current planning effort meets the needs for these plans. Answer how your needs assessment is tied to the budget process. Do you believe this connection is formal enough?

4. Prepare a simple population forecasting model for your area with both natural increase and migration components. The model can be of

the form

$$P(t + 1) = P(t) \cdot (1 + i + m)$$

where $P(t)$ is the population in year t, i is the annual net rate of natural increase, and m is the annual net rate of migration. Using a convenient computational framework (such as a spreadsheet of a simple BASIC program, or even a calculator), show the variation of total population for a 20-year period for the following scenarios. Let P_0 be 100,000:

Year	Scenario 1		Scenario 2	
	i	m	i	m
1–5	2%	3%	1%	1.5%
6–10	1.5%	2%	1%	1%
11–15	1%	1%	1%	0.75%
16–20	0.75%	0.75%	1%	0

Note the differences in the final population figures with these different annual rates. You may want to exercise your "model" with more assumptions of growth rates.

5. In scenario 1 in Exercise 4, consider that the community of 100,000 has 15,000 jobs in the export category. Using the principle of the export base technique, determine how many export jobs you would expect the community to have by the year when the population was 125,000. Do you believe this estimate would be valid?

6. Does the infrastructure system you work with lend itself to simulation modeling? What different kinds of such models are available? Are they useful in managing the system? In anticipation of the day when the models are improved, can you identify data that you should be collecting now for later use in the models?

7. In this chapter you had a brief introduction to policy analysis. Basically it is an analysis procedure that seeks the best policy from the competing alternatives. In this exercise you should analyze an infrastructure problem you have already identified (such as in Chapter 1) or you are familiar with. Make an analysis that answers the questions that follow. Your analysis should be of the detail and quality that you would turn in to your supervisor, knowing that he or she might use your report just as you prepared it to present to the top management from the city or management district that is involved.

These are the questions to be answered (some of them will be the same as in the Chapter 1 exercise, but this time you are expected to answer them in more detail and with more insight):

• What is the infrastructure problem to be solved?
• What management agency is involved?

- What procedures should be involved to find a solution? (Draw a flow diagram showing the process you envision.)
- What are some of the alternative policies that might be followed to find a solution?
- What evaluation procedure must be followed to find the best course of action?
- Which are the constituencies that must be considered in finding a solution?
- What avenues of finance are available for the solution?
- What would be a reasonable cost for the solution, both total and per capita basis?
- On the basis of what you know about the problem, what would you suggest as policies and plans to be adopted and by whom?

8. Can you design a program evaluation scheme? For the same infrastructure problem that you used to answer the previous question, design a procedure for performing a management audit of the program. How would you divide the tasks? How would you collect data? Do you believe this would be useful to the management of the facility program?

9. Appendix B presents a self-test for assessing, planning, selecting, and controlling physical capital. In this exercise you can complete a self-test for a hypothetical organization that has physical capital to manage and care for. The purpose of the exercise is for you to note which practices, as described in the test questions, constitute good management of capital. Rather than see how well your organization does, you should concentrate on noting which practices give the highest point scores. The practices that do are based on observations of organizations that are most effective in managing capital.

Formulate your response in two steps. In the first you should describe in general terms the hypothetical organization you have in mind. You may work for an organization you can use as an example. In the second step you should "take" the test for the organization in the best way you can, and then analyze the results.

For the first part, you may choose an organization that takes care of water supply, wastewater, irrigation, power, drainage and flood control, solid-waste management, streets, or public transit. Give some thought to the kind of organization you would be interested in, as you may be able to use this exercise for practical purposes. For the organization show the following:

1. Name and purpose
2. Organization chart
3. Amount of capital such as pipeline, treatment plants, vehicles, etc. (not necessary to go into too much detail)

For the second part take the test and just report on the results. How could the organization improve in its capital management according to this test?

REFERENCES

1. Vaughan, Roger J., and Robert Pollard, Rebuilding America: Planning and Managing Public Works in the 1980's, Council of State Planning Agencies, Washington, D.C., 1984.
2. Vester, Frederic, Urban Systems in Crisis, UNESCO, 1976.
3. Delsohn, Gary, "Planners to seek concrete facts: Rounding up materials for projects a worry," *Denver Post*, April 17, 1986.
4. "Growth of cities linked to level of economic development," *Urban Edge*, World Bank, Washington, August/September 1986.
5. Organization of American States, Integrated Regional Development Planning: Guidelines and Case Experiences from OAS Experiences, Washington, D.C., 1984.
6. Hornby, Bill, "Weighing 20 years of Denver planning, remarkable goals met," *Denver Post*, January 20, 1986.
7. Reinhold, Robert, "Houston uses pause in growth to battle woes of bloom," *News and Observer*, Raleigh, N.C., September 3, 1984.
8. Gleeson, Michael E., et al., Urban Growth Management Systems, American Society of Planning Officials, Chicago, 1974.
9. City of Fort Collins, Land Development Guidance System for Planned Unit Developments, Planning and Development Department, 1987 (maintained current with updates).
10. Slater, David C., Management of Local Planning, International City Management Association, Washington, D.C., 1984.
11. O'Day, D. Kelly, and Lance A. Neumann, "Assessing infrastructure needs: The state of the art," in *Perspectives on Urban Infrastructure*, National Academy Press, Washington, D.C., 1984.
12. Economic Commission for Asia and the Far East, *Manual of Standards and Criteria for Planning Water Resources Projects*, United Nations, New York, 1984.
13. Sorenson, Kenneth, "Preparing effective reports for project financing," *Consulting Engineer*, April 1963.
14. Goodman, William L., ed., Principles and Practices of Urban Planning, International City Management Association, Washington, D.C., 1968.
15. Otten, Alan L., "Why demographers are wrong almost as often as economists," *Wall Street Journal*, January 29, 1985.
16. Denver Regional Council of Governments, Annual Report, 1986.
17. Denver Regional Council of Governments, DRCOG Notes, March 1986.
18. Regional Economic Analysis Division, County-Level Projections of Economic Activity and Population, North Carolina, 1985–2040, Department of Commerce, Washington, December 1982.
19. Dajani, Jarir S., and Leonard Ortolano, eds., Methods of Forecasting the Reciprocal Impacts of Infrastructure Development and Land Use, Stanford University, Department of Engineering, June 1979.
20. Forrester, Jay, *Urban Dynamics*, MIT Press, Cambridge, Mass., 1969.
21. Grigg, Neil S., and Maurice C. Bryson, "Interactive simulation for water system dynamics," *Journal of the Urban Planning and Development Division*, May 1975.

22. Kraemer, Kenneth L., Policy Analysis in Local Government, International City Management Association, Washington, 1973.
23. Hatry, Harry P., "Performance measurement principles and techniques: An overview for local government," *Public Productivity Review*, December 1980.
24. Government Finance Research Center and Peat, Marwick and Mitchell, *Wastewater Utility Management Manual*, prepared for the EPA, July 1981.
25. Grigg, Neil S., *Urban Water Infrastructure: Planning, Management and Operations*, Wiley, New York, 1986.

CHAPTER FOUR

ORGANIZATION, COMMUNICATION, AND DECISION SUPPORT SYSTEMS

Since infrastructure organizations are normally in the public sector, the management challenges are formidable. This is not a matter of any shortage of competency in management; it is a function of built-in public-sector problems. For example, reorganization of a public agency requires considerable political and bureaucratic effort, more than in most private-sector organizations of comparable size and complexity.

Organizing is a basic task of management, and its importance must be recognized. While having the right kind of organization is not a sufficient condition for success, it is necessary. The adage that it is people and not organizations that get things done is certainly true, but people are not able to work effectively without proper organization, management, and leadership. Nothing is worse than disorganization in trying to raise the productivity or performance of an organization.

There is no such thing as a perfect organization. The effectiveness of organizations is due to the work of individuals in them, and since people change, a structure that is effective with one set of workers may lose effectiveness when the workers or the leaders do.

Organizational theory is a social science, taught in both business and psychology classes. It is really a branch of industrial psychology, of interest to both businesspeople and to psychologists. It considers the interaction of organizational structure, people, and psychology.

The first organizational task is the design of a properly structured working group to carry out the purpose of the organization. Organizational theory begins with the definition of the purpose of the organization, and the important structural components of the organization begin with those that enable it to survive, and then to prosper. That is, the bones and muscle of the organization are those units that enable it to carry out its direct mission. This part of the organization is normally assigned the task of "operations" which are intended to achieve the basic mission and meet the basic purpose of the organization. Chapter 9 provides illustrations of how the operations of an organization can be identified and organized.

After the structure is worked out, it is necessary to staff the organization. This means to identify the kinds and levels of skills necessary to make it work smoothly. Job titles, position descriptions, and work plans for each position are required. The objectives and the design of the work for each job should be set in a hierarchical fashion that enables each worker to meet his or her needs through achievement of the job objectives, which, in turn, will lead to achievement of the organizational objectives. This system has various names. In Chapter 9, the term "work management system" is used, which applies to portions of this system. "Scientific management," as it has evolved since about 1900, focuses on this part of industrial management.

Designing work by breaking it into tasks is the first step of work planning. This creative process is very important in achieving maximum productivity. The successful achievement of the tasks to be performed by an organization is the key to success in the operation of any program, and task assignment follows the organizational form. Tasks must be broken down clearly according to functions within the organization, and the proper organization of tasks can go a long way toward avoidance of duplication and confusion in the organization. The linkage between planning, program development, and the assignment of tasks is the key to success in task assignment.

Communication is one of the most important aspects of the functioning of organizations. This applies both to the internal working of the organization and to its relationship with outside constituencies, one of the most critical elements of public organizational effectiveness. Communication within organizations is changing rapidly due to the proliferation of computers and communications software, such as networking, word processing, electronic mail, and similar developments. In fact, the ability to communicate better in organizations is leading to a shakeout of middle management in some organizations. This is occurring since one of the main jobs of middle management has been to communicate between strategic levels of management and workers/operators.

Throughout this book reference is made to the military model for operations that is referred to as C^3I. This stands for command, control, communications, and intelligence. You will note many recurrences of this concept in describing organizational theory, operations, decision support systems, and the importance of data management.

Now that computers and automated information systems have become such an important part of management, it is essential that organizational forms and methods adapt themselves to the computer age. The answers to how this will be done are not yet clear, but changes are evident. All of the current debate over the effectiveness of the automatic factory and office automation is oriented to this question.

This chapter presents the principles of organizational theory, with special attention to infrastructure organizations. This will include the structure of organizations, the basic principles of management in organizations, and the ways that communciation can be adapted to the realities of the computer age. The intent in this chapter is not to repeat the material to be found in basic organizational theory texts, but to interpret that material in the light of the unique requirements of infrastructure organizations. The presentation is intended to be brief and to the point.

4.1. PURPOSE AND FUNCTIONING OF ORGANIZATIONS: GENERAL MODEL

The structure of organizations flows from their purpose. This also applies to the design of subparts of the basic organization—that they are rationally designed to clearly communicate the purpose to those working within and to the external constituencies of the organization. This is especially important to outside groups and constituencies of public organizations subject to political control. If the parts of the organization are difficult to explain, something is wrong with the concepts.

The general functioning of the organization can be seen from Figure 4.1, where the overall organization has a structure, leadership, and subdivisions of responsibility. Responsibility and accountability generally flow upward from the lower to the higher units in the organization, but there is some flow of responsibility of management to workers, especially for things such as safety, job security, leadership, and effective management. In other words, even though some say responsibility cannot be delegated, it can be shared. It is *ultimate* responsibility that cannot be delegated.

The organization will be subdivided into logical subunits, perhaps with bureaucratic titles such as "department," "division," "section," "branch," "unit," and so forth. The names of these depend on the local practice. Each management unit needs a director or manager, and the individual positions within the organization need job descriptions. It is in this disaggregation of the main organization, and in the design of the jobs, that the organizational design is carried out.

Each layer of the organization, all the way from the top to the lowest level, needs plans for work. Plans include mission statements, goals, objectives, and work plans. The accountability function is based on these plans where evaluation is according to how well the plans were carried out. The essence of work planning and management systems lies in this part of organizational considerations. Work planning and management systems have various names. Some organizations have none at all; others have well-developed and often bureaucratic programs.

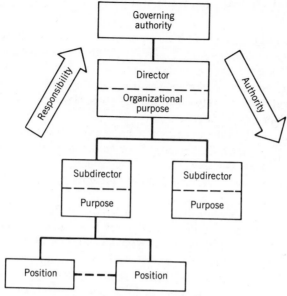

FIGURE 4.1. General organizational model.

Organizations have two necessary elements: line and staff. The line part of the organization is that part that does the direct work of the mission. This is, in effect, the operations part of the organization. In a solid-waste collection unit, for example, the line organization would collect the waste. The staff provides the support for the line operation, as much as is needed, but no more, since staff represents "overhead." Examples of staff activities are financial management, administrative support, logistics, and planning. In the army, functions are designated as G-1, G-2, G-3, and G-4 at the general staff level. At lower levels these are S-1, S-2, S-3, and S-4 staff functions, and they refer to general administration, intelligence, planning, and supply/logistics. These are the generic staff functions needed by almost any organization. Some functions, such as engineering, must be added for infrastructure organizations.

In all organizations, workers and managers are always engaged in either of two basic activities: doing or deciding what to do. This is a basic distinction of the levels of the organization, the extent to which either doing or deciding is going on. This is the other main characteristic of organizations, the level. There are essentially three levels of workers in organizations: executive, middle management, and worker. These position levels are known by different titles. For example, in a water organization, the titles used will be director, manager, and operator. The fourth level in organizations is the policy level. It is always necessary to provide a covering of authority over the management. These four levels, including policy, can be seen in Figure 4.1.

4.2. STRUCTURE AND PRINCIPLES OF ORGANIZATIONS

The starting point for describing organizations is to define them as either line-and-staff or matrix organizations. Figure 4.1 is an example of a line-and-staff organization. Other variations of these such as "functional organizations" or "programmatic organizations" also appear. It is important not to become confused over the different titles given to organizations, since classification schemes often confuse more than they clarify.

Sheeran suggests that developing sound organizational structures will release the capabilities of employees and managers for maximum individual performance, minimize the need for realignments and reorganizations, serve as a solid foundation for professional development, and promote effective performance of the organization (1).

Most public works organizations are variations of the basic line-and-staff organization with individual differences that can be explained by personal preferences of management and by the historical development of the organizations. Organizations grow incrementally, and the present form of one can usually be explained by the collection of past incremental changes. Typical public works organizations are described in some detail in the "green book" about public works (2). There are many details of public works organizations to study, such as functions, governmental authorities and legal arrangements, and organizational structure. A full discussion of these is beyond the scope of this book, but these details are readily found in texts such as Reference 2.

Although there are many variations of public works organizations, there are generic characteristics that enable rapid understanding of them according to principles. Anyone who has served in the military recognizes the line-and-staff organization as similar to a basic rifle company. The company is managed by a commander, who has a small staff consisting of the executive officer, the first sergeant, the staff clerk, the supply sergeant, and the training officer. It is divided into platoons which serve as the line operating units. These are further subdivided into squads and then into individual positions. The lower you get on the chart, the more the position or unit is devoted to pure fighting rather than staff work. This time-tested structure has much to teach us about the bare-bones form of the line-and-staff organization. The "purpose" of the unit is combat; thus the important position is that of the individual fighter. Everything else supports this position. This is similar to operations in infrastructure organizations. The purpose of an electric utility is to produce and distribute power. Other functions, such as to provide scenic facilities, are secondary and peripheral.

The need for coordination and communication within complex organizations has created a search for better forms that facilitate communication and break down barriers. Variations of the basic line-and-staff organization are usually intended to facilitate and improve communication, one of the most important challenges to organizational effectiveness. The matrix organization is an example. The matrix concept can also be seen from the fact that each employee may have two or more reporting points. Figure 4.2 illustrates this concept, and the split reporting that it reveals illustrates one of the disadvantages of the matrix organization concept, that is, that it violates the principle of unity of command.

Knowledge of the principles for structuring organizations has evolved during the last century with contributions mainly from management scientists such as Frederick Taylor and Henri Fayol (3, 4). Modern writers and observers of organizational structure begin by citing their ideas and observations; then they search for more complex forms of organizations that escape the difficulties of rigid ones. These more complex arrangements often do not work.

The basic principles of organizational structure are not hard and fast, but they do provide a basis for beginning the task of organization.

Perhaps the first one should be the principle of *unity of command*. This recognizes the truthfulness of the biblical admonition, that "no man can serve two masters." While the real world is full of cases where we must divide our loyalties (such as between family and career), the principle is still valid. In organizational design it means that each manager or worker should report, as far as possible, to only one supervisor.

A corollary to this principle is the *span-of-control* principle, which holds that each supervisor should be responsible for no more than a fixed number of persons. The number seven is often used, but opinions vary on this. Since one of the main functions of supervision is to exchange and transmit information, the span-of-control principle is very sensitive to communication technologies, and with computers becoming more common the span-of-control guideline may allow for more workers to be supervised. This would mean a reduction in the number of middle managers needed for any organization, and we are currently seeing just such a generalized reduction across industry.

Another important principle is that the structure of the organization should be *goal oriented*, or structured according to the basic mission. The structure should reflect the purpose of the organization, the reason for its existence. Units of the organization should be adapted to achieve the objectives of its

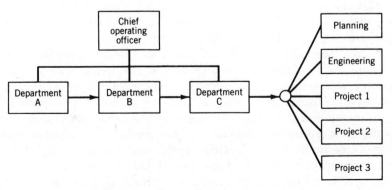

FIGURE 4.2. The matrix organization concept.

strategic plan. Units which have no clear identification with the basic mission become candidates for abolishment.

Another basic principle of the organization is that it should be *consistently structured* and ordered. This means that the geometric layout ought to be balanced, the nomenclature should be consistent (this is where bureaucracy unavoidably seeps in), and the assignment of functions should be homogeneous, or grouped in like clusters. This principle aids in the understanding and clarity of the organization and the avoidance of misunderstandings and confusion.

Finally, related to effectiveness, the organization should be *lean*. This means that there is no excess clutter, no unnecessary staff, no excessive layers of middle management, no confusion in reporting lines, no duplication of effort or competing units (unless that is designed into the organization), and no artificial barriers to communication within the organization.

Although these principles will not guarantee an effective organization, they will provide the means by which an organization can become effective. Anytime these principles are violated, the manager needs to have good reasons for violating them, or the structure set up will engender difficulties.

4.3. PRINCIPLES OF MANAGEMENT IN ORGANIZATIONS

In spite of the uniqueness of organizations, there is a unifying principle behind every effective organization with an operating mission: the path of communications, control, command, and intelligence should be straight and unencumbered by too many levels of supervision or staff. In effect, this is a result of the principles of unity of command and leanness, that the reporting lines for each unit ought to be direct and uncluttered. These terms, "communications," "control," "command," and "intelligence," are the basis for the military concept C^3I and are stressed since they provide the manager with simple concepts that enable a rapid check on how well the organization is operating. They are used in Chapter 9 as the basis for an operations management model.

The effectiveness of organizations depends on complex behavioral factors more than the structure of the organization itself. This is noted in the "green book," where the authors state that no organization can be more effective than its key employees, and that organizational form does not remain fixed for long periods since there arise needs for reorganization. Modern industrial psychology is rich with studies of factors such as motivation, the design of work, influence and power, communications, decision processes, performance evaluation, and numerous other management concerns that seek to explain these phenomena, and you are referred to texts such as Reference 5 for further discussion of these.

Managers in government organizations are familiar with organizational and work management systems such as job classification, position descriptions, work plans, management by objectives, and salary schedules, but these are only the beginning of the set of techniques necessary to make an organization effective.

The design and the development of the organization are of fundamental importance in setting it up for effectiveness in the age of computers. For this reason the essential organizational factors normally considered by management are outlined next, followed by a discussion of how they relate to communications and how they must adapt to the use of computers and information technology.

After the structure of the organization is set, the individual jobs must be designed and established. The jobs, if successfully carried out, will lead to successful accomplishment of the overall work of the organization and to the achievement of the organizational mission. Again, it is the performance and effectiveness of the key employees in these jobs that determine success. This has been pointed out in research by the development assistance project, WASH (Water and Sanitation for Health), where it was found that effective sanitation institutions in Third World countries needed effective leadership and autonomy (6).

The design and evaluation of the work in individual jobs must be planned and performed according to a fixed cycle, say, annually. This is the essence of the approaches known collectively as *management by objectives.* The objectives for an individual job or for a unit led by an individual manager should be negotiated and set by discussion and definite planning. This can be done more often than annually, but the cycle for pay increases and other incentives is annual due to budgeting constraints. This rigidly set frequency is the kind of public-sector problem that is difficult to overcome when trying to improve management.

After objectives are set, then tasks can be assigned. This is one of the most important jobs of managers at all levels, to assign tasks carefully and effectively. In many bureaucracies there is jealousy and conflict over the lack of assignment or the misassignment of tasks. When effective management is absent in infrastructure organizations, the problem is often confused assignments. Certainly confused assignments would doom any football team! In some developing countries where employees have the reputation among some for laziness, the problem is not laziness; it is lack of motivation due to inadequate task assignment and other management problems.

After the plans are made and the tasks are assigned, we enter the period of performance where coaching and motivating by supervisors is in order. This is one of the most neglected parts of management. Managers stay in their offices and do not get out and about to be with workers. The coaching and motivating phase needs attention in every organization.

Evaluation is necessary for everyone. Even the chief executive of an organization is subject to evaluation by a level of authority, the board of directors. Even though the directors may not be able to evaluate the executive's work from the base of personal capability, they can evaluate by results. The stockholders then are to make their evaluation known to the directors by how profitable the company is. This same principle of accountability is present in public infrastructure organizations; the only difference is how the "profitability" is measured, and

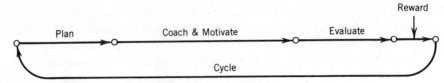

FIGURE 4.3. The work-supervision cycle.

how the oversight-responsible group chooses to exercise responsibility. The concept of performance measurement in infrastructure organizations is discussed in Chapter 9 in the section on operations management systems.

Evaluation is followed by rewards, increases in pay, promotion, and recognition. Then it is time to set new goals. This cycle of planning, coaching, and evaluating is a simple one but overlooked in many organizations. Figure 4.3 illustrates the cycle.

4.4. COMMUNICATION WITHIN ORGANIZATIONS

In recent years the behavioral aspects of organizations have received more attention than pure structural considerations. This is an important trend since the human aspects of organizations are normally the determinants of success or failure, rather than the pure organizational form. During the 1980s the success of the Japanese in business has been one of the main factors leading to an examination of how organizations really function and how well the workers perform. Organizational innovations such as the "quality circle" have grown more popular due to this attention.

Of course, organizational effectiveness has been recognized as an important part of business and industrial concerns for many years, and there is a wealth of literature on the subject. Much of it deals with communication since the presence or absence of effective communication within organizations is enough by itself to ensure success or failure. Much of the research into organizational theory is concerned with communication.

Coordination is also a key requirement of organizational effectiveness, part of the C^3I model along with communications. In C^3I we have the four critical functions of the organization: command, which ensures control; communications to ensure coordination; and intelligence to gather information. In modern public works organizations the emphasis will increasingly be on the communications and intelligence, both being functions of the success of implementing computers in management. Figure 4.4 emphasizes the concept of C^3I.

The climate for communications within organizations is especially important since if the communications are healthy, workers and managers will be more likely to be satisfied with the status quo and to produce at a productive level. On the other hand, if communications break down, there is a built-in potential for trouble.

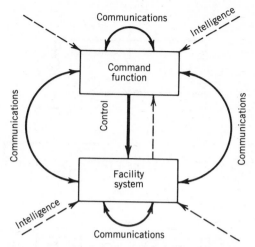

FIGURE 4.4. Concept of command, control, communications, intelligence.

The distribution of power in an organization can be traced by knowing something about communications patterns. Figure 4.5 illustrates a simple organization that looks straightforward on first glance, but when the frequency of communications is graphed as shown in part b, then the real power and activity of different positions is clear. In this hypothetical case the power of a certain staff position, S2, is illustrated.

The importance of a political figure being able to communicate well has been illustrated superbly by Ronald Reagan, who has picked up the nickname of the "great communicator" from the press. "His skill in communications has been largely responsible for some of his success in the presidency. In the case of the troubles that arose during 1986 in his foreign policy, it is clear, however, that his communications outside the administration were where his reputation was gained, rather than communications within his administration and with Congress.

If the public works manager desires to learn about communication and finds a book on the subject, he or she will be confronted with a heavy dose of psychology and behavioral science. This is natural since communications is a matter of human behavior. A full presentation of this material is beyond the scope of this book; however, we can look at some of the main points here and see how they apply to infrastructure systems.

Many texts on communications present a "model" of communications with a sender, receiver, channel for communications and various filters, sources of "noise," and other elements of the model. One model has some especially useful elements to explain why communications in organizations are often not successful. It explains the flow of communications in terms of the social climate and the need-value motivational frameworks of the communicators. This model is appealing since it explains some of the difficulties found in organizations (7).

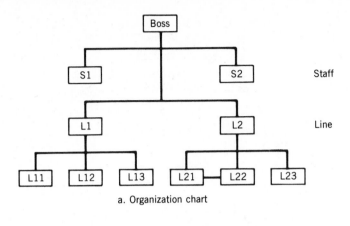

a. Organization chart

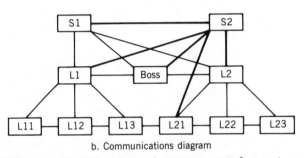

b. Communications diagram

FIGURE 4.5. Organization chart with communications frequencies noted.

The social climate is explained by the *open system* or *closed system* within which communication takes place. The characteristics of the the open system are mutual trust, open relationships, concern for well-being, and emotional security. The closed system features lack of trust, distant relationships, little concern for well-being, and low emotional security. The need-value framework of each individual is characterized by *overt* and *covert* factors. The overt factors are personality, gestures, facial expressions, tone of voice, and physical health. The covert factors are experience, attitudes, beliefs, opinions, motivations, mental health, semantic differences, and interpretations.

This model seems to contain considerable food for thought about organizational health or the lack of it, and you may be able to relate some of the organizations in your experience with the model. Of course, it is not easy to overcome some of the difficulties described; it may take enlightened leadership and a lot of struggle. If there are fundamental difficulties in an organization causing lack of trust, for example, it may be necessary to remove these before conditions

Communication within organizations begins with individual communication. The relationships on an organizational chart among peers, workers and supervisors, and different levels of managers all involve individual communications. These communications take many forms, including electronic, but they cannot all be subsumed in some "automatic office."

Success in individual communications involves considerable skill. Psychological techniques such as transactional analysis have been developed to improve communications, and there are many self-help books on the topic. Effective managers will naturally be interested in improving their skills in communications.

Important communication skills include listening, questioning, using good leadership styles, and dealing with communication problems. In the case of listening, for example, there are certain dos and don'ts that automatically will help in communication. Positive factors include showing interest and understanding, identifying and analyzing the problem from a neutral viewpoint, helping persons to solve their own problems, and avoiding evaluation of another person's position. Negative factors are illustrated by the opposite: arguing, interrupting, judging and evaluating, jumping to conclusions, and backing the other person into a corner.

It is important that both spoken and written communications be effective within an organization. Spoken communications often save time and can be interpreted more clearly with the ability to question, interpret, and clarify. Written communications can be saved for reference, shared with others, and amplified to build successively on the original communication.

Skill in written communication is especially necessary for effective organizational performance in complex situations such as infrastructure problem solving. The infrastructure manager must master the use of written communications such as memos, letters, reports, analyses, proposals, and public information releases. Unfortunately, a number of graduate engineers have low levels of skill in written communication due to lack of exposure to and lack of practice in this kind of communication. This is not the standard accusation that engineers are not able to communicate; indeed, many are skilled communicators. The problem is simply that the engineers have not been exposed to communication requirements. After a few years of work in organizations, skill in written communication greatly increases.

One of the fruits of effective communication is coordination of operations. The word "coordination" implies its necessity: it means to harmonize, and everyone can recognize instantly that the organization that is not harmonious will not function effectively.

Problems of coordination can impair an infrastructure organization in many ways. These include poor intraorganizational coordination, lack of contacts between persons working on similar projects, conflict between sections of organizations, and problems with the public. The director of an infrastructure organization should, of course, make sure that all actions are fully coordinated with the higher management and the governing board.

Sheeran (1) discusses a number of ways to improve coordination in organizations. These include use of committees, frequent staff meetings, clarification of coordination responsibilities, appointment of assistants and deputies with responsibility for coordination, use of job descriptions to pinpoint coordination responsibilities, encouragement of cross-communication through healthy organizational climate, and use of special project-oriented organizational units (matrix approach).

Communication and coordination in organizations are intended to make them work better. With the advent of so much computer power today, the emphasis is on greater use of computers and information systems. We turn now to this subject: how to use computers to enhance the management of infrastructure. This will be the next area of emphasis in organizational development. With improved decision support systems, including the development of management information systems, communication within organizations will improve, and organizations will become more effective.

4.5. DECISION SUPPORT SYSTEMS IN ORGANIZATIONS

Managers know that computers are valuable in managing organizations, and that the more complex the undertaking, the more the computer is needed. In the future the character of work, including infrastructure management organization, will be permanently changed at all levels by the computer, and we need to plan for the changes. This evolution in the use of computers has been going on since they were first developed, but the applications keep changing. In the 1940s when the first UNIVAC went on-line, it was not practical for use in many organizations. By the 1950s we started to see the use of the term "ADP" to refer to automated data processing (processing some of the numerical data, such as payroll, using the computer). By the late 1960s managers were beginning to think about the total use of information for management in organizations, and the term "management information system" (MIS) came into use. This term is still applicable, but some are advocating its replacement with the broader term "decision support system" (DSS) to refer to the use of information to support decisions in an overall way. It is the DSS concept that is presented here, but the MIS concept is embedded within it.

Actually, uses for the computer in organizations seem to cluster in three categories: office automation, decision support, and automatic control of operations. Office automation is much the same in most organizations, and there are many applications for word processing, spreadsheet analysis, data-base management, and communications, the main features of office automation. Decision support systems imply the use of office automation to develop and concentrate decision information where it is needed. Communications refers to electronic mail, networking, and all the features of telecommunications where computers are involved.

More efficiency in office operations will not by itself solve most management problems. A recent book on the transformation of work in the computer age addresses this with the observation that the speeding up of work is not the main aim in using computers; the aim is to use them to simplify the organization, serve the customer better, and make the team and the individual worker more effective (8). This observation is one of the reasons that computers have come on the scene gradually, with a lot of overpromising in the way they can be used to improve management.

The principal future challenge will be to handle the unstructured management problem, for which flowcharts and logic are not applicable. The routine tasks will be handled well by computers; and so in effect, work is pushed up in the organization chart, and the workers who were performing routine work will have to do their bosses' jobs in order to continue their growth. The way to make management more productive is to measure the "value added" by each function. In infrastructure organizations there are both structured and unstructured management problems. Most operator-level problems are structured, and lend themselves to computerization. Many white-collar jobs are unstructured, such as jobs in planning, and cannot be computerized until the tasks are understood better.

In searching for the model of how computers will impact the generalized organization of the future, we need to look for the evolving concepts for organizational structure and the use of information for management and decision making, one of the most important tasks of the manager. This is where the concept of the decision support system enters.

We use the term "decision support system" to refer to the use of computers to develop and display information to improve decisions. "Decision support" implies, however, more than just the processing of data; it includes *analysis*, some using computer models which actually add value to the raw data. In other words, the DSS is the system that organizes the processing, analysis, and delivery of information that is necessary for decision making. The value added to the decision information is a measure of the value of the work done by the white-collar workers who process the data and do the analyses that are required. The value can be measured in some cases, but since the work is mostly unstructured, measurement is almost never attempted.

The main points of the DSS are shown in Figure 4.6, which illustrates the flow of requests for decision support from the decision maker to the support staff. There are two main activities in the DSS, managing data and studying alternatives, and these are the activities that convert data or "information" into "knowledge" that is useful in the decision-making process. The role of the DSS is thus, to bring the data together with the studies, using models if necessary, to produce the decision support. If it is successful it will bring to bear all categories of information as needed, including raw data, model studies, judgment, and analysis results.

How is the DSS different from the traditional staff activity to make recommendations to the boss? It isn't different; it is just a way to organize the concepts better and arrange to handle information more effectively through the use of computers.

In organizations both the management of data and decision making cluster around the organizational form. Before the computer, when data bases could be less formal, every department would have its own files, and both information

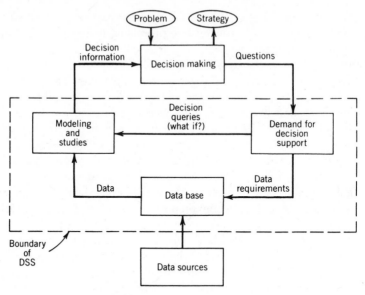

FIGURE 4.6. Decision support system.

management and decision making were very customized, and more expensive than necessary in some white-collar organizations. This, however, is a vestige of the past, and although we often desire to retain comfortable old patterns, the need today in infrastructure organizations is to maximize the sharing of data and to make decisions that affect the public "in the open." If managed properly, these can work toward improved organizational structures and database management.

Decision Making in Organizations

Decision making is one of the most important activities in management; some would say the most important. It is distributed throughout all levels and parts of organizations, many with dissimilar functions but with needs for the same information.

There are several ways to classify decisions according to the stage of management or the level of detail. One model that seems especially useful considers the level of management (executive, management, worker), the stage of management (planning, organizing, controlling), and the function/subfunction (water supply/distribution, transportation/traffic control, energy/distribution).

Some refer to decisions as political, management, or operating, but this classification is another variation of the preceding scheme. The political level is subsumed in the policy level of decision making which oversees the executive manager. It is true that managers get into some political questions at other levels, but this political content should be minimized, and in any case, it comes with the job.

The linkage between decision making and problem solving is that decisions are made to solve problems. This is the essence of the process, as shown in Figure 4.7: a problem arises, the problem-solving process is entered, and a decision is made. If the problem is not clear, we study it to make it clear, or to give it structure. If the problem is complex, we decompose it into subproblems to arrive at a problem structure we can deal with. There appears to be no really "unstructured problem"; the essence is the complexity. It seems that any problem can be made structured with enough analysis and decomposition.

Decisions have different "content" also, as Korbitz points out when he refers to the factual and the value content of decisions (9). This is a useful distinction since one would suppose that the factual content of decisions would be relatively nonnegotiable, whereas the value content would require trade-offs and political analysis. These distinctions would also be typical of policy versus operating decisions. According to Korbitz, the operating decision, as opposed to the policy decision, would be subject to more definable rules, usually on a shorter time span; would be more repetitive, simpler, and less risky and uncertain, and would be based more on knowledge of operational data.

The difference between structured and unstructured problems explains the need to have competent management at the top to deal with new and unstructured situations. These problems often require more experience, judgment, and analysis than routine structured problems. Dealing with them is one of the principal challenges in all societal problem areas, including infrastructure. The reason that office automation alone does not result in greater advances is that many of the problems faced in business and government are unstructured.

The importance of good decision making lies in its link with action. It is only after a decision is made that action is possible. Management studies that look at effective organizations have concluded that a bias toward action is one of the characteristics of success, and a corollary might be that effective decision making will also be present.

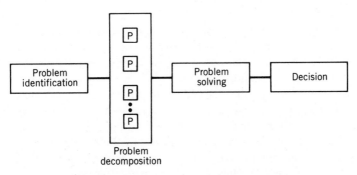

FIGURE 4.7. Problem solving and decision making.

Decision making in organizations, and the need for information to support decisions, is linked to the specific tasks or activities of the organization. An example of this can be seen in a recent study for the U.S. Army Corps of Engineers that developed recommendations for an integrated information system for the office of the Chief of Engineers (10). In this study the researchers sought to link the business of the office to the information flows and data bases. More than 80 data bases were identified. The researchers were using a process developed by the IBM Corporation for business system planning, which begins with a definition of the business that is engaged in. Next is a delineation of the business processes to be followed, independent of the position on the organization chart. These are related to clusters of data systems, called "data classes," which are mutually exclusive and independent of the organizational structure. The matrix that relates the business processes to the data classes is called the "information architecture" of the organization. This matrix identifies the key decision points of the organization and relates them to the information collected and utilized (11).

Although decisions refer to all levels in an organization, the most strategically important ones take place at the upper levels of the organization. This is normally "white-collar" work, and the most important challenge to improving productivity today in organizations is to improve the decision making and the use of time by managers. The challenge is summed up in the books and articles that are appearing about "white-collar productivity." The reason this is difficult is the lack of structure of the work. Overcoming this problem requires continuous efforts to evaluate the important tasks of the organization and structure the work.

Computers and Expert Systems

The rise of new concepts of using computers to think and help make decisions suggests that they will be able to assume more and more human tasks. Although it is clear that there is no danger of computers replacing humans completely, there are some very interesting parallels between automatic control systems, expert systems, artificial intelligence, and human decision making, especially the "automatic" human decision making that we take for granted. The human brain and set of neural processes are much more complex than computers, and there is no chance of computers taking over any time soon. There will, however, be increases in the use of computers to take over structured work. One of the vehicles for this is the "expert system."

An expert system consists of facts and "heuristics"; heuristics means rules of thumb and know-how, such as that which is widely used in operating water systems. There are three parts of the expert system: a knowledge base of facts and heuristics, an inference procedure to use the knowledge base for problem solving, and a working memory. There is an evolving research field called "knowledge engineering," which is used to prime the expert systems. Experts are interviewed to extract from them what they know about a particular problem. Artificial intelligence may seem too futuristic for a book about managing infrastructure, but the concept of using a computer to think and to help operate and make decisions will probably be attractive to most, and that is what the trend is all about. Expert systems continue to make inroads, but in simple and highly structured work. The day this sentence was written, for example, an article in the business news suggested that expert systems could be used to evaluate loan applications for banks. This is an example of structured work, or, at least, work that follows fairly rigid rules.

Computer companies have been eager to find ways to classify information uses in business to make computer systems useful in managing information. Five processes seem to have emerged as being useful in office automation and as compiled into today's integrated software: word processing, spreadsheet analysis, data-base management, graphics, and communications. Other processes are in use, but those five seem to be the most frequently needed.

Such integrated software is ideal to support the decision-support-system processes needed in all organizations, including those that manage infrastructure.

Data-Base Management

Data bases are mostly organized around the working units of the organization, beginning with the file drawers of each manager or supervisor and proceeding up to large central files. A "management information system" would refer to a coordinated arrangement of many of these, with the capability to access them when information is needed for management. The technology for developing and using the MIS is still in its infancy. The other aspect of the DSS, adding value to the data through modeling and analysis, is further away than effective data-base management.

The data base builds on a hierarchy of information, beginning with the bit, or basic binary digital unit, and proceeding through the byte, the field, the record, the file, and the data base. Before the computer we were used to thinking about files in drawers, with the records in the files, and when the computer "IBM card" came, the concept of a field of information became known as that which would go on one card. Now that cards are not used as much as they used to be, we have a new set of concepts. The ultimate result, the data base, can simply be thought of as a related set of files.

In a book on urban water infrastructure systems, the natural data bases for water management are listed, and are reproduced here. These will interface nicely with the other data bases needed to manage infrastructure (12).

1. A geographic-based system inventory data base
2. A condition index data base
3. A system water balance data base
4. A data base for real-time system studies and management

5. Data management systems for operating treatment plants and generating environmental information

6. Various analysis and design data bases

7. A financial data base

The first and most important might be the data base for locating and inventorying the components of the systems themselves. An example of this kind of data base might be the effort that has been reported for Houston called "METROCOM." This data base required over 300 work-years to develop, and contains a continuous planimetric map of some 600 square miles of the city. About 554,000 parcels of property are located and described, and there is location information on water, sanitary and storm sewers, roads, and bridges (13). There are other variations of this kind of data base appearing. One consulting firm has begun to market a lower-cost system with limited graphics capabilities. Called the "Infrastructure Management System," it relies on U.S. Census Bureau maps with information on facilities added by the user organization. The city of St. Paul planned to have such a system on-line in 1985. The city plans to take 2 years to create the data base at a cost of $250,000 excluding hardware (14).

The data base just described for St. Paul is planned to include the capability to add system condition information. This seems really to be a different category of data base—however, one that should be linked with the location and inventory data. The condition data should be linked with the maintenance function, whereas the location and inventory make up a more generalized data base.

These data bases and decision support systems seem to represent the general categories that are evolving. Each organization is unique, and the designs that are forthcoming represent the individual desires of the system developers as well as the nature of the physical systems that are being managed. The impact of commercial firms engaged in developing information systems will also continue to be a significant factor in the evolution of future decision support systems.

As a final word about the evolution of these data bases, it should be pointed out that there is a continuing and increasing cross-fertilization between the different applications of data-base management. The data bases for facilities and building management seem to have many parallel requirements with those for infrastructure, and there are some emerging computer applications for facilities that may apply to infrastructure. *ENR* magazine had a cover story on the evolution of facilities management as a business opportunity area in early 1985 (15). The story pointed out that facilities managers are seeing the following as computer opportunities: access to as-built drawings, space allocation, tenant records, utility information, and long-range planning. These are the same kinds of problems we face with infrastructure, and we will be seeing the same kinds of skills going into the solution of these two parallel problem areas. As buildings become larger and more complex, their management problems will begin to rival infrastructure in scale as well.

Models and Analysis

After data, the next main element of the decision support system is the need to have a capability to study and analyze data. This implies the use of computer models but is not limited to them, as some studies and analysis requirements are simply too complex for the use of models by themselves. In effect, models and studies answer the "what if" questions that are required for decision support. The models and studies follow the organization chart just as the data base. The financial section will require financial models, and the engineering section will require engineering models of different kinds.

What this means is that a certain number of repetitive studies are needed, and the organization's DSS must be structured to provide them. Normally, this is centered on the reporting needs of the organization. If, for example, an organization has a routine need to issue forecasts, such as flooding or electric power consumption, the forecasts needed will be produced by models or studies. For some more subtle decisions the need for studies or models is not so clear, and often has to be determined. In the case of financial studies, for example, it may not be clear how often a rate study will be needed. In some well-managed utilities this is clear, but in others not. The answer to this question, and the resulting organization to carry out the study, is determined by how well management understands the structure of its work.

4.6. A GENERIC INFRASTRUCTURE ORGANIZATION DECISION SUPPORT SYSTEM

Although it is clear that the different infrastructure services need different organizational forms, this section presents information requirements for a "generic" infrastructure organization. This same organization appears in Chapter 9 in the discussion of operational needs. The purpose of presenting it in this chapter is to show the information needs that would lead to the design of a decision support system.

Figure 4.8 shows the organization with the following major units: director's office, operations and maintenance, finance, work management (located in human resources), engineering/facilities planning, and service planning. Each of these units has a need for information for decision support. The information is not all the same or different, but it overlaps quite a bit. Some sort of centralized data base would seem to be called for, but the information needed is enough different to make such an approach impractical. The need is for a practical, but coordinated, approach to the design of a DSS.

To demonstrate the approach needed, an example of the state of the art of applying management information in a water utility will be presented next. The example will then be generalized for the generic organization just shown.

The American Water Works Association (AWWA) has given considerable attention to financial management, but not much to the use of information as

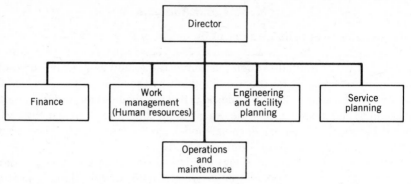

FIGURE 4.8. Generic organizational elements needing information systems.

a management tool (16). In its financial management publications, you can find discussions about how management information is used for the financial management function, but not in a general sense. A discussion of "reporting" given by AWWA spells out management information reports, from the perspective of finance, as follows:

1. Planning reports
   (*Routine*)
   Operating budgets
   Capital expenditures budget
   Financing plan
   Forecasted financial reports
   (*Specialized*)
   Proposed rate changes
   Long-term financing alternatives
   Evaluation of alternative capital investment projects
2. Control reports
   Reports to evaluate the performance of general management
   Monthly operating results, revenue versus expenditures (also, comparison with forecasted values)
   Capital expenditure and status of projects
   Financial condition
3. Information reports
   Long-range demand study
   Trend report
   Relationships between balance sheet items
   Sources of revenue
   Operating revenue and costs on a per unit basis

Water pumpage and usage

External conditions (rainfall, temperature, and population)

Analytical reports (analysis)

These reports show management needs for information for different phases of management, and for different purposes, ranging from pure information to direct control reports, again from a financial viewpoint. The informational reports should ultimately lead to some action also, or there will be no need to maintain them.

This three-way classification of reports forms a valid way to view all types of information needs. These same needs are also present for parts of the organization other than financial management, with the exact needs varying by the dimensions of the organizational chart, that is, organizational unit and level, as well as phase of management. In fact, this classification noted by the accounting viewpoint constitutes a valid overall view of the information needs of the manager, with the needed addition of the perspective of other unit managers.

In the water utility, finances are an overall control mechanism. Operations is a separate activity with general control of the product, that is, water. Facilities provide the physical support for operations, with all maintenance and repair activities being directed toward providing an acceptable quality of facilities support. Planning and engineering provide development support needed by operations and maintenance.

The picture then for a water utility is that the finance information needs currently are the tail that wags the whole operation. This is true for industry in general, however, and the sales of computer hardware and software for financial applications dwarf the rest of the applications, which are not as structured. But what about the future? There will be greater needs for hardware and software packages for operations and maintenance, engineering and planning, and the remainder of the organizations. Next we will look at how the total DSS might evolve with linkages between the functional needs for information in a generic infrastructure organization.

Referring to the "generic" organization in Figure 4.7, we see the line between the director and the operations and maintenance function and the staff work of finance, work management, engineering and facilities planning, and service planning. This makes a total of five places where information should be managed for its eventual use in making decisions.

The nodes of information demands in this generic organization are similar to those referred to by IBM in its information systems planning guide for a utility (11). The categories, given just as an example for a gas utility, are planning, supply of gas, materials/supplies for the organization, property/facilities, gas operations, customer, market, financial, and personnel.

The key questions are: Who should develop and manage the information, and who should use it? Corollary questions are: How are the data input and who inputs the data, and how should the data base be accessed?

Table 4.1 has been developed to show some of the key data bases and key analyses that are generically necessary in an infrastructure organization. The table is not meant to be complete, but it shows the most important information needed in a DSS.

Table 4.1 is self-explanatory. There are three categories of data bases: facilities, operations, and finance. The facilities data base is the primary concern of the operations and maintenance (O&M) staff, but it is also needed by the engineering and facilities planners and the financial management staff. A few observations are apparent here. The facilities data base will contain the inventory and condition information necessary for management maintenance as well as for the preparation of capital needs assessments which are used for budgeting to develop the funds for major repairs, rehabilitation, and replacement.

By the same token the data-base needs for operations and financial management are shown. It follows that the primary responsibility for managing these data bases should be with the main users. In the case of facilities and operations information, this would normally be the operations and maintenance unit. This function could be assigned to engineering and facilities planning for facilities and to service planning for operations. The engineering function normally maintains some information, such as as-built drawings anyway, and would be expected to develop and maintain the geo-data base described earlier.

TABLE 4.1. Data Needs in Infrastructure Organizations

Data Bases	Finance	Work Management	Engineering/ Facilities Planning	Service Planning	O&M
Facilities					
Inventory	X		X	X	X
Condition			X		X
Maintenance history					X
Operations					
Performance history	X	X		X	X
Inputs	X	X			X
Work management	X	X			X
Finance					
Operations accounts	X	X			X
Capital accounts	X		X		X
Budgets	X	X	X	X	X
Recurring Studies					
Responsibilities					
Facility needs			X		
Service needs				X	
Financing	X				
Organizational development		X			
Performance audit		X			X

The recurring studies shown at the bottom of the table refer to the analyses that come up in most infrastructure organizations. Needs assessments have already been described in Chapter 3, and organizational development has been discussed in this chapter. Financing is discussed in Chapters 5 and 6, and performance auditing is discussed in Chapter 9.

This discussion of a generic DSS for an infrastructure organization was not meant to be complete, and will stop at this point. This is a problem area very much still under development. The way to proceed is for each organization to study the generic model and use it as a starting point for an overall look at how information is managed in that organization, and to make sure that there is some integrated plan for the use of information to improve management. This is what was meant by a recent *Business Week* cover story which referred to the rise of the "chief information officer" (CIO) as part of the top-management structure in organizations (17). According to this analysis, the trend to have a CIO has three common features: oversight of all information technology, direct reporting line to CEOs, and concentration on long-term issues, rather than just "number crunching." Perhaps this trend will take hold in infrastructure organizations as well, but only time can tell.

4.7. DECISION SUPPORT SYSTEMS AND WHITE-COLLAR PRODUCTIVITY

There is a close relationship between the DSS and the measurement of productivity, especially white-collar productivity. Blue-collar productivity is easier to measure than white-collar, since there is normally a direct output associated with labor inputs. In infrastructure organizations, the challenge is usually the measurement of both categories, especially as they relate together.

Productivity is explained in some detail in Chapter 9. For the purposes of this discussion, recall that productivity is mainly a measure of the ratio of outputs to inputs, like efficiency. The differences with efficiency measurements are described in Chapter 9.

Blue-collar productivity can be measured directly. For example, a worker on a solid-waste collection crew is associated with the collection of so many tons per day. As another example, a water treatment plant operator can produce so many gallons per day, although this is obviously a different measurement problem due to the fact that demand determines how much is produced, rather than how much the worker produces. If only one operator at a time is needed for the plant, then it is not possible to raise productivity in one plant, unless the operator is assigned other duties along with plant operation, so that the full-time equivalency of the worker applied to water production goes down.

A white-collar worker, on the other hand, is generally involved in some kind of management or staff work, and it is normally not possible to directly measure the productivity. Peter Drucker says, however, that there is a direct way to measure this productivity: use the ratio of the output of the organization and the number of white-collar workers on the payroll (18). This ratio can then be compared with the competition. Other measures, according to Drucker, are the length of time to bring a new product to market, the number of new products brought to market, and the number of support staff and middle managers in the organization. Drucker maintains that all these measures should be improving for a healthy white-collar component of the organization.

While these measures of white-collar productivity in business cannot be directly applied to infrastructure organizations, they can be applied indirectly. Unfortunately no studies are available with comparative statistics so that an organization can compare itself with the "competition." This would be a good service for the associations to perform. Examples would be, for highway departments, numbers of engineers per mile of road and, for electric companies, numbers of engineers per kilowatt of annual power delivered. Instead of measuring new products, measure innovation. This is not easy to do, but there are precedents.

The decision support system can aid in measuring white-collar productivity because the design of an effective DSS requires a good understanding of the work of the organization, including white-collar work. By understanding this work, the flows of decision support can improve, and this will allow the development of a system to identify parameters of white-collar productivity, and begin to measure and control it.

EXERCISES

Three general topics have been covered in this chapter: organizational theory, communications in organizations, and decision support systems. The exercises for this chapter cover two of these subjects, and the third (communications) by inference.

Exercise on Organizational Structure

The design of organizations is an art that follows empirical principles that have been presented in this chapter. Planning for reorganization of existing programs is an especially delicate issue that calls for at least as much understanding as the original design of an organization. In this exercise you can apply your understanding to a simple problem of combining two public works organizations, one responsible for streets and traffic and the other for drainage and flood control.

The two hypothetical organizations are shown in Figure 4.9. In each of them the basic structure is shown, but details of numbers of personnel and specific duties are omitted. Assume that the streets and traffic division has been part of a city government operation and that the drainage and flood control operation is being taken over from a drainage district that is being consolidated with the city government.

The basic functions of the two units are as follows:

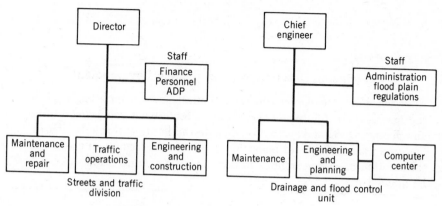

FIGURE 4.9. Two organizations to be merged.

Streets and Traffic Division. Manages the maintenance, repair, and reconstruction of the existing street network and the planning and construction of new streets in the urban growth area. Manages traffic signalization and control. The staff functions included in the self-contained unit are personnel, finance, and automated data processing. The unit receives a subsidy from the general fund of the city, but is responsible for much of its finance through special assessments and other charges.

Drainage and Flood Control Unit. This unit had been initiated due to the need for drainage and flood control in the suburban part of the county. As the sophistication of the city government has grown, the city's drainage needs exceeded the district's service capabilities, and an agreement was reached for the city to assume all the functions. Appropriate intergovernmental agreements for cost sharing have been executed. The maintenance section of the unit is responsible for cleaning and repairing ditches and storm drains, and the engineering and planning unit is responsible for master plans and problem solving as well as the supervision of construction. The unit has a small administrative section responsible for finance, personnel, and purchasing, and a flood plain specialist responsible for maintaining ordinances and land-use information.

Required: The two units are to be consolidated. Prepare an organizational study that addresses the following issues:

1. What should the structure of the new organization be?
2. What functions might be combined to achieve savings?
3. How would the directors and supervisors of the combined units be selected?
4. Prepare a schedule of what activity should occur when, to plan and execute the reorganization.

5. What problems would be expected in the planning and execution stage of the reorganization?

Exercise on Decision Support System Development

After you have developed your hypothetical new organization, analyze the management information needs and design what you believe to be an effective DSS. Make sure you include the location of the data bases, both the responsibility for managing them and the location of users, and the location of responsibilities to carry out the routine studies that will be needed.

REFERENCES

1. Sheeran, F. Burke, Management Essentials for Public Works Administrators, American Public Works Association, Chicago, 1976.
2. Cristofano, Sam M., and William S. Foster, eds., Management of Local Public Works, International City Management Association, Washington, D.C., 1986.
3. Taylor, Frederick W., *The Principles of Scientific Management*, Harper & Brothers, New York, 1911.
4. Fayol, Henri, *Industrial and General Administration*, Pitman, London, 1930.
5. Hampton, David R., C. E. Summer, and R. A. Weber, *Organizational Behavior and the Practice of Management*, Scott, Foresman, Glenview, Ill., 1984.
6. Rosenweig, Fred, Institutions for Management of Water and Sanitation in Developing Countries, AWWA Convention, Denver, 1986.
7. Banovetz, James M., ed., Managing the Modern City, International City Management Association, Washington, D.C., 1971.
8. Strassman, Paul A., *Information Payoff: The Transformation of Work in the Electronic Age*, Free Press, New York, 1985.
9. Korbitz, William E., *Modern Management of Water and Wastewater Utilities*, Garland Press, New York, 1981.
10. Office of the Chief of Engineers, Information Systems Plan, Fort Belvoir, Va., 1984.
11. IBM Corporation, Business Systems Planning: Information Systems Planning Guide, White Plains, N.Y., 1984.
12. Grigg, Neil S., *Urban Water Infrastructure: Planning, Management and Operations*, Wiley, New York, 1986.
13. Hanihan, Francis L., and C. A. Rivera, "METROCOM: An interactive database for managing a modern metropolis," *Journal AWWA*, July 1984.
14. "Consultants join to market municipal mapping service," *ENR*, December 20, 1984.
15. "Computer maze slows managers seeking answers," *ENR*, April 4, 1985.
16. Grinnell, D. J., and R. F. Kochaneck, Water Utility Accounting, American Water Works Association, Denver, 1980.
17. "Management's newest star: Meet the chief information officer," *Business Week*, October 3, 1986.
18. Drucker, Peter F., "How to measure white collar productivity," *Wall Street Journal*, November 26, 1985.

CHAPTER FIVE

THE BUDGET PROCESS FOR MANAGING INFRASTRUCTURE

Engineer-managers stress the importance of financial management in their organizations. There are powerful tools for use in financial management: financial planning, budgeting, accounting, reporting, and auditing. The most important of these financial tools for aiding overall management is budgeting, for it provides the linkage between planning, operating, and controlling. In Chapter 3, as part of our discussion of planning, we showed how planning and budgeting need to mesh for really effective management. Also, in Chapter 4 we showed how information systems are necessary to connect plans, budgets, and operational control mechanisms. In this chapter we show how the budget process can be used to aid in management. In Chapter 6 the principles of financial management itself are presented.

This chapter presents a partial discussion of the principles of budgeting, although not as complete as you would expect to find in a publication on financial management; rather, the objective is to show how budgeting is needed in the improvement of infrastructure management programs. The description is intended to be useful to a manager who is not familiar with budgeting, or to one who would like some information on the broader aspects of budgeting strategies, going beyond the mechanics of filling out the forms.

Actually, budgeting as we know it today has not been around all that long. The concept is credited to the New York Bureau of Municipal Research, which developed today's approaches in the period 1907–1915 in an effort to provide reforms for municipal administration. Of course, budgeting has many legal, historical, social, political, and financial precedents (1,2).

To show how the budget is useful in infrastructure management, we will focus on capital budgeting and operational budgeting. The emphasis in recent years relating to budget implications of infrastructure has been on the management of capital. The operating budget, however, has maintenance implications that must be taken care of if infrastructure is to be properly cared for. There is a natural link between the operating and capital budgets in the maintenance function for infrastructure; if maintenance needs are minor, they should be handled in the operating budget; if they are major, such as major repair, rehabilitation, or replacement, they become capital items.

The topics we will cover in this chapter are the budget "process," management uses of the budget, operating and capital budgeting essentials, budget planning and programming, and the politics of budgeting. These are the essential elements needed to understand the role of budgeting in infrastructure management. These principles will be demonstrated by the case study of budgeting which involves the budget procedures of the Fort Collins city government.

5.1. GENERAL ASPECTS OF BUDGETING

The budget is *much more than just a tool for allocating money*. Planning for the budget, making work programs based on the projected budget, and evaluating what was achieved from the budget are management tasks that revolve around the budget but that are not limited to a narrow definition of financial management; on the other hand, they are keys to the management control of everything the organization does. This is why it is so essential that the infrastructure manager have a good understanding of budgetary and financial management.

A budget is an adopted plan for expenditures and revenues structured to follow the programs and divisions of an organization. After the budget is authorized, it becomes the official plan for the operation of the program for the fiscal year of concern. Before the budget is adopted, it is the "proposed budget."

Later in the chapter, details of an award-winning budget are presented as an example of how the different components are prepared. In order to win the award, there are criteria to be met in the following uses of the budget document: as a policy document, an operations guide, a financial plan, and a communications medium (3).

Budgeting involves many decisions about the policies and directions of the organization. One decision is the level of taxation and charges to the community—or the portion of total community resources that is needed for governmental programs and services. Another is about the emphasis that will be placed in different programs within the governmental structure. Then there are decisions within specific programs of how the money will be allocated to personnel, equipment, contracts, and other categories of expenditures. The budget also states how the revenue will be made available, whether from debt, user charges, or other sources (1).

The most important general categories of budgets are the operating and capital budgets for the organization or program. Developing and administering these budgets is known as the "budget process." The budget process is the overall procedure of planning for, negotiating, presenting, adopting, following, and auditing the budget for the organization or program. It is important for management since the approved budget determines, in effect, what the manager can do. Also the manager is constantly working on budgets; at any given time the manager will be in different parts of the budget process for different fiscal years. This means that planning, negotiating, spending, and auditing will be under way at all times, but with different fiscal years in mind.

From its inception, the budget process has been recognized by financial officers as an important part of management's toolbox, going far beyond fiscal accountability. In recent times new techniques, such as the planning-program-ming-budgeting system (PPBS) and zero-based budgeting (ZBB), have been tried; but due to practical difficulties, these processes have not been widely adopted, and the focus has returned to the overall budget process instead. The manager should, however, understand the goals of the PPBS philosophy so that the best parts can be implemented in the budget process.

This chapter does not contain a full discussion of the origins of PPBS and all of its critiques. The literature on this subject is vast, however, and the reader is referred to shelves on public finance for any additional information needed. A typical study is the critique cited in Reference 4.

5.2. THE BUDGET PROCESS

The "budget process" refers in general to a cycle of planning for, negotiating, and implementing a budget. This is important to managers in all positions since the preparation of the budget will determine the resources they have to operate with, and they should give attention to the budget preparation process whether or not it is their responsibility to prepare the document itself.

Both the operating and the capital budgets should be planned and programmed on multiyear cycles. This requires the appropriate linkages with other manage-ment schedules. The capital budget should be linked with a comprehensive infrastructure planning and needs assessment process. The operating budget should be linked with plans for services, organizational development, and the development of programs. With the federal government withdrawing from subsidies to local governments, local governments will have more future control of multiyear program planning in their hands.

The operating budget must be viewed in a definite cycle. In the year that the budget is spent, the funds that are available are those that were approved during the previous fiscal year. The approval in the previous fiscal year may mean that the planning for those funds took place even earlier. In the budget planning year the organization might be required to submit some estimates of funds needed, say, for a multiyear period. In the budget preparation year, there would be detailed planning, leading up to the approval by the board of directors or governing board of the next year's budget. It is easy to see that in any given year there would be at least three budget years in the manager's life: one for planning, another for approval, and the third for operating.

The budget process and the budget cycle involve definite activities that need to be taken care of at definite times. There is a calendar associated with budgeting that determines what should be done in the way of planning, programming, and budgeting. This determines the sequence of management activities that need to be undertaken for the budget, and disciplines the process.

The sequence is for the budget to be planned well in advance of the budget year, with programming occurring a few years in advance of the budget year (or fiscal year), and for the budget to be used in the budget year for the purposes of management control. In the years before the budget year, the budget is a planning tool. Figure 5.1 shows the general cycle.

Since so much money is involved, the federal budget process attracts far more attention than local budgeting or budgeting by individual infrastructure management organizations. As this is being written, President Reagan has proposed the first trillion dollar budget for the United States, for fiscal year 1988. There are, however, a number of differences between the federal process and those more focused on specific services and operated by different levels of government.

To begin with, the federal process is far more complex and political than other organizational budgeting. There are many more interest groups involved in the federal process, and many more types of programs and budget categories. Decisions about the federal budget have far-reaching impacts on economic health and even on international matters such as the strength of currencies. The federal government has not had a balanced budget in many years, and debt is an instrument of economic policy rather than a financial matter that needs clearing up. The federal government thus borrows to meet its fiscal obligations rather than to pay for some specific service it has authorized. The cycle of the federal budget year is a shown in Figure 5.2.

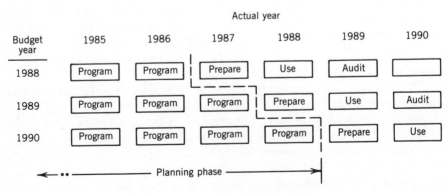

FIGURE 5.1. The general budget cycle.

Calendar Year 1987

Activities	Jan.	Feb.	Mar.	Apr.	May	June	July	Aug.	Sept.	Oct.	Nov.	Dec.
For fiscal year 1988	President's budget to Congress		Budget Committee Hearings	Budget Committee resolutions (April 15)		Appropriation Committee actions				Fiscal year begins (Oct. 1)		
For fiscal year 1989			Preparation of agency budget requests					Agency recommendations to OMB		OMB budget preparation		
For fiscal year 1990			Agency budget planning to prepare budget requests									

FIGURE 5.2. Federal budget cycle.

The federal budget is an example of how complex budgeting can become. The year of budget planning would be an intense one, where agencies battled out the right to even submit budget requests. This process culminates with a review by the Office of Management and Budget of the requests, and often results in fierce battles about whether the budget office can refuse to allow the budget requests to go ahead to the President. All of this culminates with the President's budget message to Congress in early February, which would be in the "budget preparation" year. This is only the beginning of the struggles with Congress, which consume the rest of the time until the beginning of the federal fiscal year on October 1.

5.3. MANAGEMENT USES OF THE BUDGET

Budgets are useful in all phases of management, including planning, organizing, and controlling. As pointed out earlier, the budget document itself is supposed to function, according to the Government Finance Officer's Association, as a policy document, an operations guide, a financial plan, and a communications medium.

The need to link budgeting with planning has been recognized for a long time, and in recent years the effort has become associated with the planning-programming-budgeting system. Although the use of the budget for PPBS-type activities is controversial, its use to aid management in its tasks is long accepted. The control aspect is perhaps the most obvious, and certainly an important application, but the uses for planning and programming are also important. To a certain extent they are built into the budget process.

Planning and programming occur continuously during the budget process. To imply that they do not is to view the budget process too narrowly. One confusing aspect to some is that often the working groups called "planners" are excluded from the budget process due to their separation from decisions of management. The planning that is done through the budget process becomes effective automatically because the planning gets translated into budget actions. This is not true with all categories of studies and reports which are needed to support management; although planners consider those studies and reports important, to some financial planners they are considered as just "informational reports." This is an important distinction, and illustrates why financial managers have so much hidden power; the plans they make end up controlling what the operational managers can do.

Management should use the budget for short- and long-term planning both for operations of the organization and for capital facilities. It is normal to think about capital programs in the long term, but operations should be viewed in the long term as well. This is where planning for services and for operations, as discussed in Chapter 3, fits in.

As the budget year approaches, the use of the budget to implement plans becomes a reality. Attention of management properly becomes focused on individual aspects of the budget since the attention to detail at that stage becomes translated into action programs in the budget year. Budget negotiations get very detailed at that point.

During the budget year the budget is used to control expenditures and to make sure that the different parts of the organization follow the approved plans. By providing the different management levels with budget information and with records of expenditures, management can then control expenditures and stay "within budget." This is the "control" aspect of the budget that is so important to management.

The budget can also be used for evaluating how well the organization did or is doing in delivering cost-effective services. On an ex post facto basis, the actual budget should be used to show how much money went into different categories of program delivery for the purpose of calculating productivity ratios and related management parameters.

5.4. THE OPERATING BUDGET

The operating budget is the primary vehicle for management use of budgeting. It is the instrument where all of the details of expenses and revenues are projected, approved, and reported. Most attention given to budgeting in any organization attaches to the operating budget.

Managing the operating budget is a primary task of the budget officer, who is normally located in the finance office of the organization. The arrangement for this for the city of Fort Collins is shown in its December 1986 ad for a new director of budget (Fort Collins is used as a budget case study later in this chapter):

Director of Budget and Research: Reporting to the Finance Director, this position is responsible for organizing, directing and coordinating the activities of the City's operating budget of $10,000,000. The City maintains a 5-year Capital Improvement Program, and a complete 5-year financial plan. Requires 3–5 years experience in budget planning and administration in a governmental organization. Experience with program performance budgeting preferred. Familiarity with PC and mainframe budget applications, knowledge of economic and revenue analysis, a college degree in Public Administration or a related financial field is required. MPA desirable.

The requirements outlined show some of the priorities that Fort Collins places on budgeting: program performance budgeting, capital improvement programming, and 5-year financial planning. These are all discussed in this chapter.

The resolution to approve the operating budget provides the chief executive of the organization the authorization to spend. In this sense the resolution, as noted by Moak and Hillhouse, is a "positive act" (1). The "negative" side of the budget is its use to constrain spending, this being a control side of management. Managers view one of the most important roles of finance officers to be exactly that: to control spending and provide for responsible financial management.

Moak and Hillhouse list a number of objectives of the annual operating budget (1). These include providing an interdepartmental informational vehicle to aid in planning; requiring the executive branch of the government to produce an estimate of expenditures so that the adequacy of revenues can be checked; providing a means to the different levels of management to evaluate the internal competition for resources; using in-work planning and evaluation; communicating with the policy oversight body the operating objectives for the coming year and making revisions based on signals from that group; providing the information that the annual appropriation ordinance can be based on; providing a basis by which annual plans can be adjusted to conform to appropriations; and providing a basis for financial audit of the enterprise.

These objectives for the annual operating budget reveal its usefulness in the overall financial management of the enterprise, with involvement in the planning, organizing, and controlling phases of management.

The operating budget follows the process already described. It gives the executive branch the opportunity to develop interaction within the agency for the budget process. This is the place where subunit managers have the chance to make their input to budget requests.

The format of the budget document is important to the presentation of the spending requests and remainder of the budget. This format normally contains a budget message of the chief executive, an estimate of revenue, a summary of proposed expenditures, with appropriate comparisons of years past and with other parameters such as cost per capita, any details needed, and appropriate appendixes. Later in the chapter some details of the format of the Fort Collins budget document are given.

5.5. CAPITAL BUDGETING

Capital budgeting is related to operating budgeting, but it is separately tied to capital planning and programming. The requests for capital budget items may appear as capital expenditures in the budget, and in that sense can appear almost as a subset of the operating budget. A better way to view the two, however, is that together the capital and operating budgets make up the annual budget. In some budgets, notably the U.S. federal budget, capital expenditures are not broken out separately. This is a source of considerable discussion for the federal budget, a fact that will be discussed more in this section.

In connection with the infrastructure "crisis" in the United States, the General Accounting Office has prepared several reports on capital budgeting practices. Two are cited in References 5 and 6. In Reference 6, this definition of capital budgeting is given:

It is the way organizations decide to buy, construct, renovate, maintain, control, and dispose of capital assets.

Taken another way, capital budgeting is the procedure for budgeting for capital items having lifetimes longer than, say, 1 year. This is a procedure required in business organizations as well as those organizations managing public infrastructure. A well-known test on engineering economy has a chapter on capital budgeting, with emphasis on the use of interest charges to set priorities (7). A text on financial management has a section on capital budgeting, again with emphasis on business decision making (8). Topics covered in this publication include the time value of money, the cost of capital, the capital budgeting decision, and risk in capital budgeting.

Capital budgeting needs to be related to *capital programming* in the sense that the budget should be programmed in advance by preparing plans, estimates, and studies to justify the budget requests. Actually, there is little difference between the capital budget and the current year of the capital program. A 5-year capital program would show capital expenditures for 5 years in the future, beginning with the next budget year. The items in the first of those years should be the same as the capital requests in the current capital budget.

Figure 5.3 shows the relationship between the comprehensive plan, the capital investment program, and the capital budget (6). The illustration, for public safety facilities, begins with the goals and policies of the plan; goes on to the capital investment program shown in this case for the current budget year and 5 years in the future; and proceeds to the budget year, which illustrates the request for this year. The only entry in the program that is "hard" would be the one for the current year, in that a program would still be considered as provisional until it becomes part of a budget request.

Capital budgeting is essentially taken for granted at the local level and in special districts that are well managed. At the federal level, however, the need for capital budgeting has become a political issue. Almost all the studies coming out of the 1980–1984 period, which featured considerable attention to the infrastructure issue, contained a recommendation about the need for capital budgeting. As an example, the report "Hard Choices" (9) contained this recommendation:

> Congress should mandate the creation of a coordinated national infrastructure needs assessment program and, within the unified budget, require that capital expenditures be presented and highlighted in a clear, comprehensive way.

The justification for this recommendation was as follows:

> No easy, clear way now exists to measure the full extent of federal commitment to infrastructure investment. The federal government, through a variety of investment strategies, provides considerable support for infrastructure development. But it is impossible to determine which approaches are most effective. The Advisory Committee urges Congress to assure that capital expenditures are separated from current operational outlays within the unified federal budget. Congress can then debate and set capital priorities separately and deliberately.

Comprehensive Plan

Public Safety Facilities

Goals

To protect citizens and property from harm caused by fire, criminal activity, and other emergency situations.

To deploy facilities and apparatus so that the Police and Fire Departments will be able to respond quickly to emergency situations anywhere in the city.

Policies

Construct new police and fire facilities in communities not now adquately served.

Replace or consolidate obsolete police and fire facilities.

Build a series of "superstations" on the downtown periphery to meet the special fire protection needs of the MetroCenter area.

Extend sodium vapor lighting to secondary streets and appropriate local streets.

Install sufficient lighting at park and recreation facilities to deter vandalism and promote safety.

Provide modern facilities for the training of fire and police personnel.

Capital Investment Program

FIRE DEPARTMENT	BUDGET 1979	PROGRAM 1980	PROGRAM 1981	PROGRAM 1982	PROGRAM 1983	PROGRAM 1984
Engine Company No. 43 Replacement				1,000,000		
Engine Company No. 47 Replacement					700,000	
Engine Company No. 50 Replacement		1,020,000				
Engine Company No. 53 Replacement						1,200,000
Fire communications and Dispatch System Replacement		1,300,000	1,300,000			
DEPARTMENT OF RECREATION AND PARKS						
Playgrounds-lighting and resurfacing	50,000	50,000	50,000	50,000	50,000	50,000

Capital Budget (1979)

DEPARTMENT OF RECREATION AND PARKS	BUDGET
Playgrounds-lighting and resurfacing	50,000

FIGURE 5.3. Illustration of planning process.

This recommendation has attracted support and opposition. Hofman and Cook, two staff members with a House caucus group, recommend the capital budget (10). They state that the recommendation goes back at least to the Hoover Commission in 1949, and that it has wide support from economists and fiscal analysts. Four years later, in the same forum, Boskin and Ballantine argue opposite cases: one for the capital budget, one against (11). The case for is the same: capital budgeting will not solve all of our capital and infrastructure problems, but it will provide a start to recordkeeping and analysis that is needed to rationally solve the infrastructure problem. The case against is that special interests will have a heyday with a capital budget; that the information needed from a capital budget is already provided by "special analysis D," part of the budget documentation; and that the incentive for all groups would be to have their program classified as an "investment," and hence be placed in the capital budget and not in the operating component of the budget.

5.6. BUDGET PLANNING AND PROGRAMMING

The planning phase of budgeting brings other program and facilities planning into the budget process. For programs, this is part of the need for regular organizational planning. For facilities it means to connect budgeting with capital improvement planning.

It is the planning part of budgeting that is the most important aspect of the planning-programming-budgeting system that has attracted so much attention in management circles. Although PPBS itself has not caught on, the goals of planning and programming are contained in the budget exercises of most successful programs today.

The concept of "program-performance-budgeting," which appeared earlier in the chapter in the ad for a director of budget for the city of Fort Collins, really contains the essence of what was intended for PPBS. The aspects of planning and measuring performance are connected by the planning-budgeting process.

In effect, the way to connect budgeting with the other processes of planning is for the manager to make sure that the planners and managers at the different levels are aware of the need for interaction with the financial staff, and vice versa. If this is accomplished, the benefits of the planning already discussed will be realized in the budget process.

Program budgeting can be implemented in different ways. The following tables are from the Fort Collins 1987 budget; they show how the sewer utilities prepare one set of reports dealing with trunk and collection facilities. Table 5.1 shows the program objectives, staff, and expenses, and Table 5.2 shows the performance measures and analysis.

Programming is a part of budgeting, but different. The fundamental difference between the budget and the program is the level of commitment. The programming of the budget can be thought of really as just planning ahead for the different aspects of budgeting. In that sense, capital "improvements programming" is one of several aspects of budget programming. In most organizations there is no formal approval for the program the way there is for the budget itself. This means that the program is, in effect, a statement of plans to ask for budget authority.

The most visible budget program is the capital improvements program. The relationship of this program to the plans and the budgets was shown in Figure

TABLE 5.1. City of Fort Collins 1987 Budget

Program: Trunk & Collection	*Department: Sewer Utilities*
Fund: 503-Sewer Fund	*Division: Trunk & Collection*

Program Description

Collect the wastewater of our community in a safe and lawful manner so as to protect the environment and public health. Operate and maintain the wastewater collection system including hydrocleaning, television inspection and infiltration control. Locate our facilities for all underground contractors.

Program Objectives

1. To operate and maintain an additional 10 miles of collection system with no increase in budget.
2. To hydroclean 50% of the wastewater collection system.
3. To internally televise 6% of the collection system.

	1985 Actual	1986 Budget	1986 Revised	1987 Proposed
Program Staff				
Permanent	12.5	13.5	13.5	13.5
Seasonal	4	4	4	4
Hourly				
Volunteer	___	___	___	___
Total	16.5	17.5	17.5	17.5
Program Expense				
Personal services	$413,651	$ 416,244	$ 416,244	$ 404,071
Contractual	133,200	62,800	62,924	66,800
Commodities	175,449	76,200	80,179	84,200
Capital outlay	158,375	593,000	593,000	593,000
Transfers/other	0	0	0	0
Total	$880,675	$1,148,244	$1,319,473	$1,148,071

Program Resources
General fund
Program generated revenue
See wastewater engineering,
 planning, and
 administration program

5.3. When budgeted and initiated, the program becomes binding to the extent that the facilities that are initiated will have to be finished. Programs for new operating budget requests have less of an implied commitment, since they can be altered without reversing capital commitments.

The essential features of the links between planning and budgeting have been presented by the GAO (5). The GAO studied the factors that led to success

TABLE 5.2. 1987 Program Performance Budget

Performance Measures	Actual 1985	Budget 1986	Revised 1986	Proposed 1987
Program: Trunk & Collection	*Department: Sewer Utilities*			
Demand				
1. Miles of wastewater line	324	334	334	344
2. Annual wastewater collected (MG)	4,744	4,862	4,862	4,983
3. Customers	20,970	21,610	21,610	22,250
4. Field locations requested	2,486	2,650	2,900	3,100
Workload				
1. Problem calls responded to	103	120	120	120
2. Miles of line hydrocleaned	174.4	167	167	172
3. Miles of line televised	17.7	20.0	20.0	20.6
4. Field locations made	2,486	2,650	2,900	3,100
Productivity				
1. O&M cost p/mi. wastewater line maintained	$1,453	$1,662	$1,675	$1,614
2. O&M cost p/customer	$ 22.44	$ 25.69	$ 25.88	$ 24.95
3. Personnel cost p/locate	$ 11.10	$ 10.28	$ 9.39	$ 9.29
4. Miles of wastewater line p/employee	24.00	24.74	24.74	23.72
Effectiveness				
1. Blockages per mile of line	0.114	0.135	0.135	0.131
2. % Wastewater line hydrocleaned	53.8%	50.0%	50.0%	50.0%
3. % Wastewater lines televised	5.5%	6.0%	6.0%	6.0%
4. Inaccurate field locations made	0	0	0	0

Program Analysis

About 52% of the $1,148,071 budget for this program is for capital expenditures, reflecting the continuing growth of the wastewater collection system. The size of the collection system has increased 10% over the last 5 years with no increase in permanent staff. A 3% growth of the collection system is projected for 1987. In order to maintain existing levels of service, one additional system operator has been included in the 1987 budget. The total 1987 budget has not increased due to this additional position, however, due to reductions in other areas.

in managing infrastructure and to failure. These are listed in Table 5.3. As is evident from the table, the most critical elements in success have to do with how well planning is linked with budgeting.

The three "critical" elements contributing to success should be examined for their relationship to planning. The first is that planning is extensively linked to budgeting. This is done through the formal planning procedure which incorporates planning and programming into budgeting. The key here would be to make sure that planning was taken seriously and not given token treatment.

The second element is to make sure that management is concerned about long-term effects. This would reflect a concern with the organization's capital assets and provide overall mechanisms to make sure they are cared for, as if they were the personal property of the management, and not "government property."

The third element, to incorporate up-to-date information on physical capital into the decision-making process, is covered in the discussion given earlier about having effective decision support systems. This is what an effective decision support system for capital is designed for: to make sure the capital is cared for with a long-term viewpoint.

Appendix B contains a questionnaire that is designed from the elements of success contained in Table 5.3. Take the "self-test" for your own organization, and see how the rating comes out. Perhaps some suggestions will emerge leading to improved planning and budgeting practices.

To summarize planning for the budget, it should be contained in a system that links planning to the eventual budgeting. This is in addition to having effective general planning processes such as those in Chapter 3 in place.

You will be able to get a clearer idea of how this process works in the next section, which presents a case study of local government budgeting with highlights on infrastructure categories.

5.7. CASE STUDY OF BUDGETING: FORT COLLINS, COLORADO

The development of a budget process is part of the "art" of management, and every organization should develop its own approach to the process. To illustrate how this works within an overall framework of budget procedures, this section presents data from the 1986 and 1987 budget exercises of Fort Collins, Colorado (3). The 1986 budget presentation was outstanding, and it won an award from the Government Finance Officer's Association for a "distinguished budget presentation."

The scope of Fort Collins's budget efforts was shown earlier in the ad for a budget director. To repeat some of the key points, ". . . responsible for organizing, directing, and coordinating the activities of the City's operating budget of $10,000,000. The City maintains a 5-year Capital Improvement Program and a complete 5-year financial plan . . . experience in budget planning and administration . . . experience with program performance budgeting. . . . PC and

TABLE 5.3. Elements Contributing to Success and Failure

Elements Found in Successful Organizations	Elements Found in Unsuccessful Organizations
Critical	*Destructive*
Extensively links planning to budgeting.	Does not link planning to budgeting, when planning takes place.
Concerned about long-term effects.	Pays little attention to long-term effects.
Incorporates up-to-date information on physical capital into decision-making process.	Does not consistently feed information on the condition of physical capital into the decision-making process.
Important	*Damaging*
Recognizes the effect of deferred maintenance and minimizes it to the extent possible.	Has limited, if any, controls; misses many financial and work targets.
Protects capital investment funds from being used for operations.	Defers structural maintenance; focuses on cosmetic repairs.
Considers related operations and maintenance costs when making capital budgeting decisions.	Cuts budgets with "closed" eyes.
Considers alternative methods of meeting the objectives of capital investment projects.	*Harmful*
Monitors capital investments and the condition of physical capital.	Lets funding mechanisms drive priorities.
Does not have internal conflicts that disrupt capital budgeting activities.	Sees individual projects as pork barrel.
Sees individual projects as modernization, revitalization, and investment.	Lets special-interest groups get out of control.
Uses funding mechanisms to protect priorities.	
Uses incentives to meet work and financial targets.	
Helpful	
Figures out ways to allocate something for everyone (keeps things even, moves on all fronts).	
Uses categories for decision making that are important to the organization, e.g., productivity items.	
Routinely assesses physical capital and adherence to a maintenance schedule.	

From Reference 5.

mainframe budget applications . . . economic and revenue analysis. . . ." Features to note include operating and budgeting planning process, program performance budgeting, and analysis emphasis.

Appendix D contains a collection of pages from Fort Collins's budget document which will be used to illustrate some of the principles behind the preparation of budgets. This section will be easier to follow and more beneficial if you review Appendix D first. Appendix D is also referred to in the next chapter on financial management.

The city charter requires that:

> on or before the first Monday in September of each year, the City Manager shall submit to the Council a proposed budget for the next ensuing budget year with an explanatory message. The proposed budget shall provide a complete financial plan for each fund of the City and shall include appropriate financial statements for each type of fund.

The character also provides that the budget will then be adopted before the last day of October. The fiscal year will begin on the first of January.

The city manager transmitted the recommended budget to the Fort Collins City Council on August 27, 1985, with the following remaining schedule:

August 28	1986 Budget-in-Brief printed in paper
September 3	Public hearing
September 5	Community meeting, cable TV
September 9	Community meeting
September 10	Council worksession
September 17	Public hearing
September 18	Community meeting
September 24	Council worksession
October 1	Resolution adopting 1986 budget and mill levy
October 15	Second reading of ordinance appropriating 1986 budget and setting mill levy

The intensity of the work going into the budget in this time period is apparent. Before this, the administration had been putting in considerable time getting the budget ready. In preparing the budget presentation, the city departments develop in March of every year 5-year revenue projections and submit them to the city Budget and Research Office, which develops "target budgets" based on projected available resources. Budget proposals are then submitted in May along with policy analyses of matters related to issues requiring decisions before development of the final budget. The departments must stay within their target budgets, and this illustrates the power of the budget office: to decide on how much the departments can request. Any additional requests must be identified as "supplemental requests." Each department meets with the city manager in

May to explain and justify its submittal. In June the Budget and Research Office sends the council a memorandum on issues the council will face, and the council schedules two working sessions to provide the staff with guidance to develop the "recommended budget." That budget is sent to council in late August, as shown in the preceding schedule, and made available to the public. During September two additional council work sessions are scheduled, two public hearings are scheduled, and community meetings are held around the city. When the budget is adopted in October at a formal council session, the final adopted budget is then printed.

Departments are expected to stay within the adopted budgets. There are, however, provisions for increases or decreases in the budget during the budget year. Such changes can occur due to carryover encumbrances, unanticipated revenues, prior-year reserves being used, or budget decreases when economic conditions require.

Control of expenditures is at the fund level, this identifying the "cost centers" of the city. Examples of funds include the general fund; enterprise funds for light and power, water, sewer, and others; special revenue funds such as transportation services, recreation, and community services; and capital improvement funds. Transfers within a fund can be approved by the fund manager, but transfers between funds require action by the Fort Collins City Council. Transfers between capital projects require council approval to maintain control over capital spending. The identification of these funds can be seen in Appendix D.

The use of the budget for management purposes can be illustrated in the themes the manager uses to present the budget to the governing board. Refer to Appendix D for the budget presentation. The city manager's message states that the "budget has been built on the conservative financial and management principles embraced by staff and City Council, and reflects the commitment of both to maintaining necessary services to the City's residents, improving the quality of operation of the City, and keeping expenditures and taxpayer load to a minimum." The message also states that the budget is "a financial plan which provides the necessary resources to respond to needs identified by three basic 'driving forces' within the City." These are Council goals, citizen input, and manager's expertise.

Council goals had been articulated at a retreat in April 1985. This is part of the planning that links to budgeting. The goals included:

• Basic municipal services and infrastructure
• Evolution of the natural resources program
• Air quality protection
• Corridor of open space between adjacent cities
• Railroad issues
• Intergovernmental issues
• Relationships with the university

Citizen input had included the report from a citizen's committee for a recommended capital plan, which formed the basis for the budget's capital plan, and a quality of life survey, which revealed that citizens viewed life in the city, including its infrastructure, as pretty good.

Management considered the numerous uncertainties in formulating the budget strategy. These included uncertainties in the federal budget, tax reform, labor issues such as the Fair Labor Standards Act, and expected tax revenues. The level of inflation, as always, stood as an unknown. To a certain extent this uncertainty is handled through an "inflator provision" which allows for the funding of supplemental requests if the funds are available.

The "budget-in-brief" is presented to show the public the key points of the budget without the laborious work necessary to decipher facts and figures in a full document. Some of the diagrams and figures from it for 1986 and 1987 are given Figures 5.4 to 5.9, which illustrate key concepts. These data are from the "budget-in-brief" prepared by the Fort Collins budget office for the local newspapers.

Figure 5.4 presents the definition of the budget that was provided to the public to explain the budget's concept. The definition shows the concept of the budget, and the explanation of the 5-year projections shows how programming is done. Also furnished to the public is a definition of the concept of performance budgeting. This is, in effect, a PPBS approach. Fort Collins handles PPB in an acceptable way without all of the usual objections about it.

WHAT IS A BUDGET?

A budget is a document used to plan, manage and control the city's expenditures and revenues for the coming year. Financial and management policies are adopted by City Council annually, and form the foundation on which the budget is built.

The 1987 Budget is balanced, as required by the City Charter, and five-year projections of expenditures and revenue ensure sound financing in future years as well.

WHAT IS PROGRAM PERFORMANCE BUDGETING?

The City of Fort Collins recently converted to a new Budget format, known as Program Performance Budgeting. This type of budget is so named because it breaks City services and Departments down into their functional units, or programs. The switch to a program budget allows City Council, and the residents of Fort Collins, to take a closer look at the services which the City provides.

Along with each Department's budget request was submitted a list of performance indicators. Performance indicators are designed to be a statistical measurement of how well a program is achieving its goals and objectives.

By converting to this new format, City Council feels it will be easier to examine programs and services to determine how they can best meet the community's goals and priorities.

FIGURE 5.4. What is a budget?

The 1986 Recommended Budget:

- Continues priority funding for basic services and infrastructure needs
- Utilizes the final year of Revenue Sharing funds for Capital projects and programs of direct benefit to residents
- Provides low income housing assistance
- Provides rebate programs on property taxes, utility bills and sales tax on food
- Initiates a three-year program to reconcile the issue of comparable worth
- **Does not increase taxes**

OVERVIEW

The 1987 Recommended Budget:

- continues priority funding for basic services and infrastructure needs;
- responds to reductions in federal funding;
- utilizes a carry-over of Revenue Sharing for rebate programs and other programs of direct benefit to the residents of Fort Collins;
- places emphasis on City Council's goals and priority programs;
- **DOES NOT INCREASE TAXES OR UTILITY RATES.**

FIGURE 5.5. The 1986 recommended budget.

Figure 5.5 shows the overviews of the 1986 and 1987 budgets. They present a "keyhole" view of the overall budget, with the emphasis placed on the items the council believes to be of most interest to the public. Note that in both years the budget is said to "continue priority funding for basic services and infrastructure needs. . . ." This does not sound too exciting, but after all, it is what the city government does. In the 1986 projections, the council was able to brag that the budget did not increase taxes, and in 1987 that it does not increase taxes or utility rates. Since there were utility rate increases in 1986, these had to be presented in a palatable manner, and this is shown in Figure 5.6. Note that the increases are modest except in storm drainage, where an increase of 15 percent is shown. This reflects changes in the new stormwater utility.

IMPACT

- The average <u>increase</u> in service user's costs, based on 1986 rate adjustments, is projected to be:

AVERAGE MONTHLY UTILITY BILL:

- Light and Power   No Increase
- Transportation Utility   No Increase
- Storm Drainage   13ᶜ
- Sewer   42ᶜ
- Water $1.50

• NO increase in Sales and Use Tax or Property Tax Rates.
• <u>Decrease</u> in residents' costs from:

- Sales Tax on Food Rebate Program
- Property Tax and Utility Charge Rebate Program
- An Affordable Housing Program will construct low-income housing units and provide rental subsidies for qualifying families.

RATE AND FEE ADJUSTMENTS

BENEFITS

Utility Rate Changes:

• Electric	0%	Maintains current service levels and provides for service expansions.
• Transportation	0%	
• Sewer	+4%	
• Water	+9%	
• Storm Drainage	+15%	

User fee increases for parking, golf, cemeteries, Lincoln Center, and recreation.

Recovers operation and maintenance costs in accordance with City financial policies.

Development Fee Changes:
- Parkland   +4.8%
- Street Oversizing:
  - Residential   + 2.4%
  - Commercial   +11.3%
  - Industrial   +33.4%

Increases recovery of the City's costs associated with the development of parks, commercial, and industrial properties.

New Storm Drainage Fees
- Cooper Slough $2500/acre

FIGURE 5.6. Impact, rate, and fee adjustments.

The city likes to emphasize prudent financial operations. Figure 5.7 shows how this is presented, with a historical presentation of budgets for 3 years. Budget impacts are carefully presented.

The capital program is shown along with the regular budget, and this is presented in Figure 5.8 for both 1986 and 1987. Also shown in Figure 5.9 is a special presentation for an improvement district that was included in the 1986

PRUDENT FINANCIAL OPERATIONS

The 1987 Recommended Budget totals $139,905,841, including all internal transfers. Proposed net City expenditures total $103,359,105. The General Fund budget will be $24,123,509. General Fund expenditures represent a decrease from spending levels proposed in the 1986 Adopted Budget.

HISTORICAL COMPARISON

	1985 Actual	1986 Adopted	1987 Proposed
	($'s in millions)		
Operation & Maintenance	$123.2	$119.8	$119.1
Capital	46.4	22.5	15.1
Debt Service	3.3	4.6	5.7
TOTAL	$172.9	$146.9	$139.9

TAXES

THERE ARE NO TAX INCREASES IN THE 1987 RECOMMENDED BUDGET:

In accordance with City Council's goal, tax levies will remain at the same levels as 1986:

- Property Tax Levy will remain at 12.86 mills
- Sales & Use Tax will remain at 2.75 cents

BUDGET IMPACTS

The average increase in service user's costs, based on the 1987 Recommended Budget, is projected to be as follows:

- **NO INCREASE IN UTILITY RATES**
- **NO INCREASE IN PROPERTY TAX OR SALES & USE TAX RATES**
- Minor increases from user fee adjustments for services such as golf, parking, cemeteries, Lincoln Center and Recreation programs.
- **DECREASES** in residents costs from three rebate programs.

The 1987 Recommended Budget reflects City Council's goals of providing quality services in a cost-effective manner, without raising the cost of government to the residents of the city.

FIGURE 5.7. Prudent financial operations.

1986 CAPITAL PROGRAM

The following Capital Projects are included in the 1986 Recommended Budget:

• Water Utility	$6,950,000
• Light and Power	6,494,090
• General City Capital	3,081,510
• Sewer Utility	2,925,000
• Parkland (Neighborhood Parks)	1,374,904
• Storm Drainage	1,341,152
• Conservation Trust	210,000
TOTAL	$22,376,656

1987 CAPITAL IMPROVEMENT PROGRAM

Capital Projects in the 1987 Recommended Budget total $15,146,370 and are divided among various City funds. A listing of how these Capital Projects are dispersed throughout the City and some examples of projects which are included in 1987 follows:

Light & Power Utility - $7,269,489
- Richard's Lake Station
- Linden Lake Station
- Power Equipment + Vehicles
- Subdivision

General City Capital Projects - $2,682,000
- Railroad Crossing Improvements
- Street Rehabilitation
- Sidewalks Improvements
- Recreation Trails West of Taft Hill Road

Storm Drainage Utility - $1,507,698
- Canal Importation Basin Improvements
- Cooper Slough Basin Improvements
- Foothills Basin Improvements
- Spring Creek Basin Improvements

Water Utility - $1,424,000
- Northeast Loop Water Line
- Timberline Water Line
- Treated Water Reservoir
- West Prospect Water Line

Sewer Utility - $1,020,000
- Drake Trunk Relief Sewer System
- Methane Reuse System
- Spring Creek Relief Sewer
- WWTP #2 Improvements

Parkland Fund - $868,183
- New Park Site Acquisition
- Trilby Area Acquisition
- Park Site Equipment and Plantings
- Rossborough Park

Conservation Trust Fund - $375,000
- Open Space Aquisition
- Spring Creek Trail
- Strauss Cabin Trail
- Poudre Trail

FIGURE 5.8. The 1986 capital program.

budget. Two illustrations of the way the budget shows the services provided by public works and streets are also shown.

The entire budget document is too bulky to reproduce here, but if you will refer to Appendix D and review the pages reproduced, you will get a good idea of the portion of the budget that is important to infrastructure management.

Capital Programming

In general, the capital expenditures contained in the budget came from programs of the various departments of the city government. To illustrate the technique of programming, this section presents some aspects of the capital program as prepared by the Department of Public Works (12). This capital program includes the budget year 1986 which is illustrated in Appendix D.

The program states its limitations from the outset: "The Five Year Program shows where the Public Works Department wants to be in five years. It is a flexible document which is updated yearly to reflect actual development and changing conditions. However, the Five Year Program is not an official policy statement of the City Council and, therefore, does not oblige the City to complete these proposed projects" (emphasis added).

The services included are street capital and rehabilitation, storm drainage, facilities, traffic signals, bikeways, water projects, and sewer projects. The

GENERAL IMPROVEMENT DISTRICT #1

General Improvement District #1 was created for the construction and installation of parking facilities and street and sidewalk beautification improvements in conjunction with the 1977 Downtown Redevelopment Project.

The District is financed by property taxes of the district. The mill levy for the District is recommended to continue at 6 mills for 1986.

PUBLIC WORKS

The City engineers, cleans, and maintains 277 miles of streets and bicycle paths, 7 miles of unimproved streets, 240 blocks of alleyways, and installs, operates, and maintains the traffic signal system for 11ᶜ per resident per day.

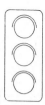

STREETS AND TRAFFIC

The City cleans and maintains streets, bicycle paths, unimproved streets, and alleys. In addition, the City installs, operates, and maintains the traffic signal system. These services are provided at an annual cost of $48.86 per capita.

FIGURE 5.9. General improvement district #1.

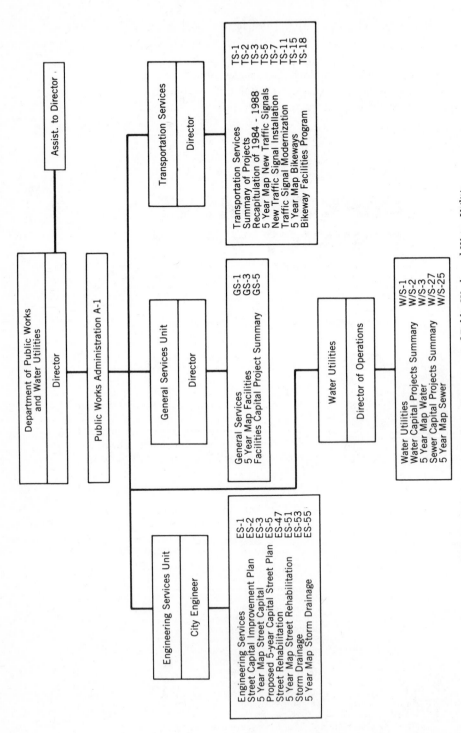

FIGURE 5.10. Organization chart, Department of Public Works and Water Utilities.

program elements are arranged according to the organization chart, reflecting the need to allow individual program managers to plan for the needs in their areas of responsibility. As shown on Figure 5.10, the divisions of the department are engineering services, general services, transportation services, and water utilities.

The specific aspects of the public works departmental organization are discussed in Chapter 4. The chart shown in Figure 5.10 presents only the general aspects of the organization, but this suffices to show where the capital programming is done.

The program elements as reflected in the document are the results of capital improvements planning. To illustrate how the program is displayed, some elements from the street rehabilitation program are reproduced in this section. Table 5.4 presents the introduction to the street capital improvement plan.

Responsibility for the maintenance of this plan is seen, from Figure 5.10, to be with the Engineering Services Unit, along with several other responsibilities.

TABLE 5.4. Street Capital Improvement Plan

The following is a presentation of the Draft Street Capital Improvements Five-Year Program. The plan was developed from the attached page titled "Proposed Street Capital Improvements Projects," which is a listing of proposed projects. The list is not arranged in any specific priority. Projects are added to the list as needs are identified. Projects on the list that are included in the Five-Year Program are denoted with an asterisk.

The second attachment, titled "Five-Year Capital Street Program, 1984–1988," is a presentation of the Draft Five-Year Plan. The estimated costs were broken down into three activity phases; D—design, R—right of way acquisition, and C—construction. The estimated cost column is in 1983 dollars. The costs listed under the program years 1984–1988 are escalated for anticipated inflation by the following factors: design: 5% per year; right of way—7.5% per year; and construction: 12% per year. The last column, Program Total, is a summation of the escalated costs for the Five-Year Program.

The projects included in the Draft Five-Year Program were selected based upon a priority system. The system is a cooperative effort between Engineering Services, Transportation Services and other departments. Factors used to set priorities include traffic congestion, accidents, safety, cost, intra-city and interagency coordination, community impacts, projected growth of the city and current priorities in the 1984 budget. The remaining projects on the proposed project list are considered projects needed within 20 years.

Funding for the 1984 work is approved. Beyond 1984 no funding sources have been identified.

The items on the street capital improvement program are delineated in Table 5.5, which breaks them into "projects." This delineation is necessary to move them into the approval and execution stages.

The program itself is shown in Table 5.6, which illustrates the projects and the times when they are "programmed" for execution.

TABLE 5.5. Proposed Street Capital Improvement Projects

* 1. Mason Street and Howes Street one-way couplet
* 2. Linden Street bridge replacement
* 3. Timberline Road and Prospect Road Intersection
* 4. Timberline Road—Prospect Road to Summitview Drive
* 5. South Lemay Avenue—Horsetooth Road to Harmony Road
  6. Horsetooth Road—College Avenue to Landings Drive
* 7. Drake Road and Taft Hill intersection
* 8. Lincoln Avenue and Mountain Avenue realignment at Riverside Avenue
* 9. Prospect Road and Shields Street intersection
*10. Prospect Road and Taft Hill Road intersection
*11. Prospect Road—Shields Street to Taft Hill Road
*12. Shields Street and Mulberry Street intersection
*13. South College medians—south of Horsetooth Road to Creger Drive
 14. Shields Street—Spring Creek to Swallow Road
*15. Drake Road—BNRR to Shields Street
*16. Shields Street and LaPorte Avenue intersection
*17. Shields Street—Laurel Street to Prospect Road
*18. Drake Road railroad crossing west of Timberline Road
 19. Horsetooth Road—Lemay Avenue to Timberline Road
 20. Horsetooth Road and Shields Street intersection
 21. Elizabeth Street—Taft Hill Road to Kimball Road
 22. LaPorte Avenue—Shields Street to Taft Hill Road
*23. South College medians—Creger Drive to Harmony Road
 24. Lemay Avenue—Lincoln Avenue to Willox Lane
 25. Drake Road—Shields Street to Taft Hill Road
 26. Timberline Road—Harmony Road to Prospect Road
 27. Prospect Road—Timberline Road to the Poudre River
 28. Horsetooth Road—Shields Street to Taft Hill Road
 29. West Mulberry Street 600' west of Tyler Street to city limits
 30. Mulberry Street—Riverside Avenue to Howes Street
 31. Cherry Street—Lyons Street to Franklin Street
 32. Linden Street—Redwood Street realignment at Vine Drive
 33. Shields Street and Harmony Road intersection
*36. Horsetooth Road railroad crossing west of Timberline Road
 37. Mason-Howes one-way couplet—Cherry to College Phase II
 38. Mason-Howes one-way couplet—Laurel & College Phase III
*39. Shields Street/Vine Drive intersection widening
 40. Shields Street—Laurel Street to Vine Drive

* 1984–1988 Five Year Capital Street projects.
Remaining projects are future projects.

TABLE 5.6. Proposed Five Year Capital Street Program 1984–1988 (Costs Shown in Thousands of Dollars)

Project Title	Phase	Estimated Costs	1984	1985	1986	1987	1988	Program Total	Future Costs
Mason & Howes one-way couplet	Design								
	R-O-W								
	Constr	1,701	1,906					1,906	
Linden Street Bridge replacement	Design								
	R-O-W								
	Constr	535	599					599	
Timberline & Prospect intersection	Design								
	R-O-W								
	Constr	1,574	500	1,100				1,600	
Timberline—Prospect to Summitview	Design								
	R-O-W	651		400	379			779	
	Constr	2,419							2,419
South Lemay—Horsetooth to Harmony	Design								
	R-O-W	515		595				595	
	Constr	1,100			1,545			1,545	
Drake & Taft Hill intersection	Design	36		39				39	
	R-O-W	95		110				110	

(Table continues on p. 142)

TABLE 5.6. (Continued)

Project Title	Phase	Estimated Costs	1984	1985	1986	1987	1988	Program Total	Future Costs
Lincoln & Mountain realignment	Constr	459			645			645	
	Design	10		11				11	
	R-O-W	11		13				13	
	Constr	200		251				251	
Prospect & Shields intersection	Design								
	R-O-W								
	Constr	210			295			295	
Prospect & Taft Hill intersection	Design								
	R-O-W	90				120		120	
	Constr	500				787		787	
Prospect Road—Shields to Taft Hill	Design								
	R-O-W								
	Constr	900					1,586	1,586	
Shields & Mulberry intersection	Design	11			13			13	
	R-O-W	25			31			31	
	Constr	105			148			148	
Drake Road—BNRR to Shields	Design	11			13			13	
	R-O-W								
	Constr	930				1,639		1,639	

TABLE 5.7. Financing Expenditures for Linden Street Bridge Replacement

	Prior to 1984	1984	1985	1986	1987	1988	Total
Resources							
Sales tax	$48,966	$175,000					$223,966
Fees							
Grants		424,154					424,154
Contributions-in-aid							
Assessable costs							
Bond proceeds							
Plant investment fees							
Total	$48,966	$599,154					$648,120
Expenditures							
Conceptual design							
Preliminary design							
Final design	$48,966						48,966
R.O.W. land acquisition							
Pre-construction							
Construction		$599,154					$599,154
Contingency							
Total	$48,966	$599,154					$648,120
Operation & Maintenance Costs							
Personal services							
Contractual services	No O&M costs are associated with this project.						
Commodities							
Capital outlay							
Other							
Total							
Comments							

Table 5.7 is a financing/expenditure table for a single project, in this case, the Linden Street Bridge Replacement project. It shows the sources of funds and expenditures.

Other tables and illustrations in the document show the details of the preliminary plans for the projects.

5.8. POLITICS OF BUDGETING

The reader has noticed, no doubt, that in the Fort Collins budget considerable attention has been devoted to the use of the budget document as a communications vehicle. The interaction among the staff, the city council, and the public in determining the budget must be carried on carefully, since budgeting is perhaps the most sensitive act of the governing body, and the most important management tool that management has.

The politics of budgeting is a subject that is of concern to managers at all levels of government, especially those involved in any aspect of infrastructure where so much money is involved. After being in an organization for a few years, the manager becomes aware of the political nature of budgeting, especially in terms of employees and middle managers seeking to achieve status and power within a public organization. This struggle for status and power is the internal competition involved in budgeting. For a larger budget, say, for the U.S. budget, this problem becomes political on a larger scale. Budget process scholars may be interested in studying this subject further, and a good reference would be Reference 13.

This section presents a short view of the politics of budgeting to provoke thought. For a simple view we may look at the politics of budgeting from the standpoints of internal power plays and the aspirations of external constituencies. The internal politics have to do with bureaucrats gaining power, and the external pressures are exerted by interest groups in order to obtain the programs or influence that they seek. External groups have lobbyists working for them, so the level of conflict rises quickly in this aspect of budget politics.

Considerations at the federal level form an outline for our examination of this subject. Wildavsky (13) presents discussions of the following topics, which are presented here as an outline of some of the concerns we should face when discussing budget politics:

- The agency: roles and expectations
- Deciding how much to request
- Deciding how much to spend
- Department versus bureau
- Role of the budget office
- Deciding how much to recommend
- The appropriations committees: roles and perspectives
- Deciding how much to give
- Client groups

For the first subject, the role of the agency, there are often multiple objectives among the managers. Some managers may be appointed; some may be career employees working on the fringes of policy. Each of these groups will have different expectations. The higher a manager goes in the organization, the more responsive that manager must be to the policy goals of the elected or appointed leadership.

Deciding how much to ask for is a tactic that responds to the budget climate and to the objectives of the agency. In the lower level of the organization, managers may feel that they must ask for all they really need, and perhaps more, knowing their requests will be cut. This may not mesh at all with the objectives of the top management.

Deciding how much to spend is the role of the executive leadership in the agency. In infrastructure organizations this is one of the problems encountered with maintaining capital facilities: it is always easy to defer capital items, especially those that are for the long term, or those that have long-term implications but few short-term consequences.

Department versus bureau conflicts have to do with the relative needs of a subunit within a larger department. In the case of Fort Collins, some reorganizations have occurred in the past few years, such as the one combining light and power with water utilities. With these mergers it is possible that a rate increase in electricity, for example, could lead to a decision by the utility manager not to seek one in water. This hypothetical situation would mean that the interests of a bureau (water) would be put behind that of the entire department (not to ask for too many rate increases).

The role of the budget office is a tough one for line managers to deal with. They often lack access to the budget officials and do not appreciate their way of working. Consequently, when decisions are made about how much budget to seek, the line managers may feel that they are ignored. On matters of the agenda, budget officers usually align themselves with their bosses, the top management, and not with the line managers. This illustrates the importance of cooperation among the staff and the line, if the organization is to work well together.

The top leadership, along with the budget office, will decide how much to recommend. The strategy here depends on many factors, and will certainly be different in a local situation than in the far more complex world of federal government politics.

The roles and perspectives of the appropriations committees will be an important factor at the federal level, and to a certain extent, at the state level. This is normally not a factor at the local level, unless the governing board has some sort of budget committee that has to be dealt with.

The policy organization must decide how much to give. It is not entirely free to decide this since it always faces some contraints. The U.S. government is the only level that is normally allowed to go into debt; this adds another layer of complexity to the process, since the budget is so large that it becomes an instrument of national economic policy, and to a certain extent, an important parameter in the welfare of the whole world. At the local level, both the estimate of revenues that can and should be raised and the distribution of monies between services and other needs are policy decisions.

Client groups at the federal level must be dealt with in a sophisticated manner. They range from the elderly who have a great interest in social security, to the environmentalists who will lobby for more money to build wastewater plants. At the local level, the developers will be watching the budget process carefully, especially to determine how much they will be expected to pay for in the way of infrastructure. The development fees in Fort Collins are a part of the expected revenue side of the budget, as shown in Appendix D. The city has a philosophy that "growth must pay its own way." This policy is politically set, and has political implications for how tax burdens are spread in the community.

Budget politics are of great importance to the development and maintenance of infrastructure, and the manager needs to give careful attention to them.

EXERCISES

Learning budgeting should be a case of "learning by doing." The purposes of this chapter have been to familiarize you with the budget process, and to show you how budgeting should be used as a management tool to accomplish other jobs as well as to allocate funds. You can profit from exercises by doing a little thinking, however, and the exercises presented next are intended to aid in that process.

1. Appendix D contains a great deal of budget material from the award-winning Fort Collins 1986 budget. Examine this material in detail. Note the method of presentation and the detail included. Can you find ways the presentation can be improved with regard to the infrastructure material?

2. Appendix D contains some budget material for infrastructure services, notably that dealing with "enterprise funds." You may also have access to your own budget, perhaps in more detail. Select a budget or a service you have data for and answer the following questions. Can you do a productivity analysis based on the budget that shows the portions of the budget devoted to labor, to materials, and to other commodities? What percentage of the budget is devoted to labor? Do you believe this can be reduced? How can automation be used in the future to reduce this cost?

3. For the same budget or data you utilized in Exercise 2, can you identify where the funds are to finance the three R's? Do you believe these funds are adequate, or will this be a case of inadequate attention to repair, rehabilitation, or replacement?

4. Assume that you are working for an organization that is developing a new city. (This is the kind of ideal situation we would all like to work on sometime!) The population will grow from zero to 10,000 in 5 years at a rate of 2000 persons per year. Your task is to prepare a planning-programming-budgeting exercise for the infrastructure of the city, consisting of streets, water, wastewater, and storm drainage. Obviously this is a complex task, so let's look at just the high points. Can you make a sketch of the schedule you would follow? What plans would be needed? When? Can you develop an organization chart for the staff you would need to plan and program these facilities? What studies will be needed? What other data? How would you present the budgets for your needs?

REFERENCES

1. Moak, Lennox L., and Albert M. Hillhouse, Concepts and Practices in Local Government Finance, Municipal Finance Officer's Association, Chicago, 1975.

2. Aronson, J. Richard, and Eli Schwarz, Management Policies in Local Government Finance, International City Management Association, Washington, D.C., 1975.

3. City of Fort Collins, Colorado, 1986 Annual Budget.

4. Meriwitz, Leonard, and Stephen H. Sosnick, The Budget's New Clothes: A Critique of Planning-Programming-Budgeting and Benefit-Cost Analysis, Markham/Rand McNally, Chicago, 1971.

5. U.S. General Accounting Office, Federal Capital Budgeting: A Collection of Haphazard Practices, Washington, D.C., February 26, 1981.

6. U.S. General Accounting Office, Effective Planning and Budgeting Practices Can Help Arrest the Nation's Deteriorating Public Infrastructure, Washington, D.C., November 18, 1982.

7. Grant, Eugene L., and W. G. Grant, Principles of Engineering Economy, Ronald Press, New York, 1970.

8. Block, Stanley B., and G. A. Hirt, Foundations of Financial Management, Irwin Press, Homewood, Ill., 1981.

9. University of Colorado, Hard Choices: A Report on the Increasing Gap between America's Infrastructure Needs and Our Ability to Pay for Them, Report for the Joint Economic Committee of Congress, 1984.

10. Hofman, Steven, and Matthew Cook, "Crumbling America: Put it in the budget," Wall Street Journal, October 7, 1982.

11. Boskin, Michael J., and G. J. Ballantine, "Does Washington need a new set of books? Wall Street Journal, December 2, 1986.

12. City of Fort Collins, Colorado, Department of Public Works and Water Utilities, Five Year Program, 1984–88, dated 1984.

13. Wildavsky, Aaron, The Politics of the Budgetary Process, 4th ed., 1984, Little, Brown, Boston.

CHAPTER SIX

FINANCIAL MANAGEMENT FOR INFRASTRUCTURE

Finance is the most important subject that the high-level infrastructure manager must master. This does not mean to master all the accounting details; it means to be able to obtain the revenues needed and to manage them well. Without the funds to build and maintain the facilities, success is not possible. This is true at all levels and in all divisions of organizations since each job on the organization chart requires a different perspective on financial management due to the differences in the budgets involved and the levels of responsibility. The management tasks at all levels involve planning, programming, budgeting, accounting, cost control, and revenue management. The successful accomplishment of these tasks at all levels of the organization means success at the top as well.

Planning, programming, and budgeting have already been presented in previous chapters. The purpose of this chapter is to present the basic principles of financial management which are required after the budget is developed.

The infrastructure manager must be competent in finance to make the best decisions among all of the technological and management approaches that are necessary and available today. Financial management should not be a foreign subject to the manager, and topics such as revenue sources, debt financing, the bond market, interest rates, inflation, and rate structures must be thoroughly understood. Understanding of tax law is increasingly necessary also, since the options available to the manager may include access to private capital or services, and the tax implications can be an important factor.

It is in the best interests of all managers to make finance an important subject in their continuing self-education. In periods of tight money (and when have you not seen a period of tight money?) managers with financial skills ascend to higher levels of management. This is because their skills are very much in demand in that period. In better times, the same skills are needed to guard against waste and corruption. In reviewing a long career in public administration, one manager concluded that having a firm grasp on the finances is a key to success. Through such understanding, the manager can make the system work.

Even though the managers should learn about finance, certainly they need not become professional finance officers. These officers are ready to provide the help and analytical support needed to manage public enterprises, but in order to fully utilize their talents, managers must be familiar with the questions to ask and the critical points to examine.

While this chapter is written from the general viewpoint of the U.S. infrastructure manager, many of the findings and principles are applicable to managing in developing countries where the financial management still must follow general principles that are valid for the service of concern and that will work within the culture of the individual country. A recent World Bank study evaluated the status of urban finances in a number of large world cities. Those included were Ahmedabad and Bombay, India; Bogota and Cali, Colombia; Kingston, Jamaica; Jakarta, Indonesia; Manila, the Philippines; Nairobi, Kenya; and Tunis, Tunisia. Findings of the study sounded much like those contained in this chapter: pay good attention to finances, avoid bad investments, and rely on user charges wherever possible (1).

To illustrate the positions and functions contained in the typical finance office of a local government, Figure 6.1 is presented. This figure illustrates the functions of budgeting, accounting, auditing, assessments, purchasing, and the treasury. All of these will be discussed in this chapter, with the exception of the treasury function, which is the collection/disbursement area.

The manager can also take advantage of the publications and guidelines of the professional groups that study government finance. The Government Finance Officers' Association (GFOA, formerly the Municipal Finance Officer's Association, MFOA) has especially good publications and services, and its subsidiary unit, the Government Finance Research Center in Washington, is usually right up to date on infrastructure issues. Quite a bit of assistance is also available from the publications of the International City Management Association.

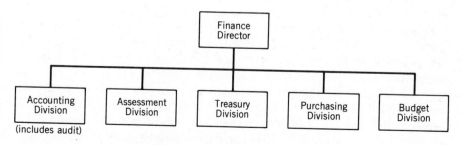

FIGURE 6.1. Divisions of finance office.

How the manager sees financial management depends on his or her position in the organization. The first step in making a financial analysis is to determine the organizational level and the degree of the total enterprise in the analysis. Some complex organizations require separate financial management for the different parts, such as for enterprise funds. Other simpler organizations have all of the finances lumped together into one set of accounts.

Regardless of the position in the organization, financial planning and budgeting are important skills that are necessary before management can even begin. Inadequate budgets are the cause of many infrastructure problems, and the cause for inadequate budgets is inadequate planning and management at all levels. As discussed in detail in the previous chapter, budget plans are statements of what the manager intends to do and how it will be accomplished.

The budgets of an agency display its programs. The operating budget shows the plans to operate and maintain the agency. The capital budget reveals its plans for expansion and renewal. The planning skill of an infrastructure management organization will ultimately be evident in the capital budget. A manager should be able to examine the operating budget, the organization chart, and the job descriptions and tell what will happen during the year. By the same token the performance of the organization should be reviewable by comparing the output of the organization with its potential as revealed by these documents.

The productivity of an organization, public or private, is ultimately measured by financial ratios or the ratio of output to input. The input is ultimately measured from the budget expenditures. Any other kind of systems approach to management will depend on the financial information as well, examples being calculations of benefit-cost ratios or cost allocation formulas. These techniques are discussed in detail in the section on operational management in Chapter 9.

More and more, public works management is going to a self-supporting basis, following what is known as the "enterprise principle." The enterprise principle, a generally understood topic for budget officers, is described in detail in a publication offered by the Government Finance Research Center (2). The general concept is that services should be self-supporting and charged according to the benefits users receive from the services. The use of pricing through user charges is the basis for controlling the allocation of the services and for raising revenue. The equity issue is central to the philosophy that the charging schemes should be fair.

Financial management principles follow the trend toward the enterprise approach, since if the decision is made that a service will be self-supporting, then revenue generation approaches and the financial control function are brought under the control of the manager rather than the political process. The major advantage of the enterprise approach for managers is that they gain the control needed to make decisions and implement innovations in financial management. Still, there is a built-in political component in infrastructure management, and the needs of the local population must be factored into decision making. This is one of the principal issues in the decision of whether to "privatize" a public service, a topic dealt with extensively in the next chapter. Thus the financial management process must consider both political and administrative factors. This is healthy and represents a good balance between bureaucracy and politics alone.

The manager of a self-supporting organization will have the entire organization in mind when considering financial aspects. If the organization is large and complex, it will be divided into subdivisions, each of which is a center of responsibility and maybe a cost center. If it is a cost center, then there will be separate budgeting, control, and financial responsibility for it. Examples of cost centers might be a full water utility, a transportation department or division of a local government, or a project which is determined to be a cost center due to the need for it to break even on the enterprise involved.

For the manager or the analyst the elements of financial management important in infrastructure management are financial analysis and planning, financial control and reporting, revenue management, and cost control. These are the topics of the remainder of the chapter. In the sections to come, several analytical tools that are needed by the manager are discussed. These tools include the cash flow analysis, the use of the income-expense statement, and the evaluation of the balance sheet. These are added to the technique of budgeting which was presented in the last chapter. You are encouraged to make sure you thoroughly understand these techniques.

6.1. FINANCIAL ANALYSIS AND PLANNING

Financial analysis for an entire organization increases in complexity with the complexity of the organization itself. Usually the perspective that is used to illustrate principles is the project or single enterprise. With this perspective it is possible to highlight the different considerations that must be faced in decision making.

Financial analysis and planning involve important steps related to the responsibilities for financial management. According to the Government Finance Research Center these include revenue analysis, cost analysis, institutional analysis, ability-to-pay analysis, secondary impacts analysis, and sensitivity analysis (3). In this sense the analysis is necessary to support continued planning.

It is helpful to relate financial analysis to the generic enterprise of making a profit. Financial planning in the public sector is really the same as in the private sector with the differences in goals highlighted. Obviously it will be more difficult financially when some of the revenues or costs are uncertain and difficult to predict.

The beginning of financial planning has to be the budget process. When discrete enterprises are identified as needed, whether they be programs or projects, then the next step of planning can be taken, to look at the services the program or project will provide, the revenues and costs, and the final determination of whether the venture will succeed and how well. Further discussions of this part of the planning process were presented in Chapter 5.

In Reference 41 the authors propose that financial planning and projections can be presented using "pro forma" or projected financial statements, the income statement, the cash budget, and the balance sheet. Their proposal reveals immediately the importance of financial reporting instruments for use in planning as well as in financial control. The proposal would mean that these instruments are no longer solely the province of the financial officer, where they usually reside in an organization, but also the domain of the manager.

In essence trial accounting instruments are used to show the effects of management actions on the future projections of the financial health of the enterprise. These can be used in either public or private enterprises. In the case of a single enterprise such as a project with revenues, the benefits of this approach can be quickly appreciated, and this approach will be illustrated as an example in this section.

The income statement will provide an estimate of the differences between revenues and expenditures over a period of time, say, 1 year. This may be too long a period to determine whether there will be cash flow difficulties within the period, say, on a monthly basis. The cash budget can be used to determine this. The balance sheet will provide the final illustration of changes in assets and liabilities over the accounting period.

In a public enterprise that must be managed to recover costs and be self-sufficient financially, the cash budget is the most important analysis instrument. The income statement and balance sheet require the use of accounting values such as depreciation and book value, and may be properly the sphere of the professional accountant rather than the manager. For the purpose of the manager the income statement will be a financial control device with the main interest being in cash receipts and cash disbursements, and the balance sheet will mainly be a way to display the debt structure and the cash accounts payable.

The use of the cash budget to examine the performance of an infrastructure enterprise over a period of some 20 years will be illustrated as an example. The year time period is used to hold down the amount of information presented. With a modern spreadsheet analysis, which this is, it will be a simple matter to make the analysis for any time increment, such as monthly.

The example is illustrated in Table 6.1. There ae two basic sets of accounts. In the first the enterprise, say, a solid-waste plant, requires a certain amount of cash for the development of plant and equipment over a period of 5 years. As shown in the table, the total amount of funds needed are about $90 million. These are to be repaid with a loan to be amortized over a 15-year period or sooner, if the revenues are adequate. The interest rate is 10 percent per year, and with $n = 15$ years the capital recovery factor is 0.13147. The payback begins at the beginning of year 6. Interest is accumulated in the loan until the payback begins. Thus the "scheduled loan" increases to a maximum until the beginning

TABLE 6.1. Cash Budget Example (Capital Account Interest = 10%, Term = 15 years; Operating Account Interest = 15%)

| | | | Capital Account | | | | | | Operating Account | | |
(1) Year	(2) Cash Needed	(3) Scheduled Loan	(4) Debt Service	(5) Interest	(6) Principal	(7) Year-end Balance	(8) Revenue	(9) Cost	(10) Annual Balance	(11) Interest	(12) Cumulative Balance
1.00	50.00	50.00		5.00		55.00			0.00	0.00	0.00
2.00	10.00	65.00		6.50		71.50			0.00	0.00	0.00
3.00	10.00	81.50		8.15		89.65	5.00	10.00	-5.00	0.00	-5.00
4.00	10.00	99.65		9.97		109.62	5.00	10.00	-5.00	0.75	-10.75
5.00	10.00	119.62		11.96		131.58	5.00	10.00	-5.00	1.61	-17.36
6.00		131.58	17.30	13.16	4.14	127.44	15.00	5.00	-7.30	2.60	-27.27
7.00		131.58	17.30	12.74	4.56	122.88	15.00	4.00	-6.30	4.09	-37.65
8.00		131.58	17.30	12.29	5.01	117.87	15.00	3.00	-5.30	5.65	-48.60
9.00		131.58	17.30	11.79	5.51	112.36	21.00	3.00	0.70	7.29	-55.19
10.00		131.58	17.30	11.24	6.06	106.29	21.00	3.00	0.70	8.28	-62.77
11.00		131.58	17.30	10.63	6.67	99.62	21.00	3.00	0.70	9.42	-71.48

(Table continues on p. 154)

153

TABLE 6.1. (Continued)

		Capital Account							Operating Account		
(1) Year	(2) Cash Needed	(3) Scheduled Loan	(4) Debt Service	(5) Interest	(6) Principal	(7) Year-end Balance	(8) Revenue	(9) Cost	(10) Annual Balance	(11) Interest	(12) Cumulative Balance
12.00		131.58	17.30	9.96	7.34	92.29	40.00	3.00	19.70	10.72	−62.50
13.00		131.58	17.30	9.23	8.07	84.22	40.00	3.00	19.70	9.38	−52.18
14.00		131.58	17.30	8.42	8.88	75.34	40.00	3.00	19.70	7.83	−40.30
15.00		131.58	17.30	7.53	9.76	65.58	40.00	3.00	19.70	6.05	−26.65
16.00		131.58	17.30	6.56	10.74	54.84	40.00	3.00	19.70	4.00	−10.94
17.00		131.58	17.30	5.48	11.82	43.02	40.00	3.00	19.70	1.64	7.12
18.00		131.58	17.30	4.30	13.00	30.02	40.00	3.00	19.70	0	26.82
19.00		131.58	17.30	3.00	14.30	15.73	40.00	3.00	19.70	0	46.52
20.00		131.58	17.30	1.57	15.73	0.00	40.00	3.00	19.70	0	66.22

Explanation of columns:

(1) = year of project

(2) = cash needed, millions, at beginning of year indicated

(3) = nominal scheduled loan; basis for debt service

(4) = debt service (paid at beginning of year) for interest rate and term indicated

(5) = annual interest

(6) = annual principal paid

(7) = balance remaining at year-end

(8) = annual revenues

(9) = annual costs

(10) = net annual balance = (8)−(9)−(4)

(11) = 15% * (12) of previous year

(12) = (12) of previous year + (10) − (11) (*Note:* positive balance earns no interest for this account)

154

of year 6, and then remains constant for the purpose of calculating debt service until the loan is repaid.

Since debt service will be required from the operating budget before the project revenues are sufficient to handle it, another short-term loan at 15 percent is arranged to pay any deficits. This loan, as shown in columns 8 to 12, is paid on a year-by-year basis. The balance in this short-term account increases until a maximum of $36.73 is owed at the end of year 11. After that, the project revenues begin to take over and the loan is repaid rapidly. Beginning in year 17 there are surplus funds that can either be invested in short-term investments (provided the yield is higher than 10 percent) or be used to repay the original loan. With this stream of revenues the project could be repaid about a year early. If revenues increased somewhat, the loan could be paid much faster. If revenues were slow, it might be necessary to refinance the lower-interest loan, to avoid being stuck with high interest on the short-term loan.

In the Government Finance Research Center publication described earlier (3), the elements of financial planning are said to include revenue analysis, cost analysis, institutional analysis, ability-to-pay analysis, secondary impacts analysis, and sensitivity analysis. These are shown in Figure 6.2.

Revenue analysis would lead to a determination of the revenue sources available and feasible, from both an economic and political basis. This will be covered later in the chapter in a section on revenue management.

Cost analysis would consider the construction costs, the operating and maintenance costs, and other costs such as the cost of regulatory programs and the continuation of planning. Cost analysis is important due to the need to make sure, through value engineering and other techniques, that there is no waste in the system. Cost analysis is also important when the financing study determines the components of cost that can be assigned to different users.

Costs can be classified as direct and indirect. Direct costs are those directly assignable to the provision of a particular service. Examples are wages, equipment, operation and maintenance expenses, depreciation, and capital expenses. Indirect costs are those which are necessary for the delivery of a service but which

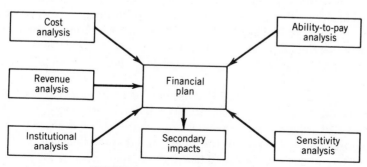

FIGURE 6.2. Inputs to the financial plan.

cannot be attributed directly to the service itself. Examples would include central services such as computer and support services (2).

Institutional analysis is concerned with the ability of existing or planned institutions to manage the program. While this is part of the financial planning study, it borders on the policy area and is certainly of concern to the public and to political leaders as well as to lenders.

Ability-to-pay analysis involves a determination of the capability of the community and its citizens to bear the cost of the service. Here is where financial ratios may help. One example might be a limitation on the debt of a local government as a percentage of, say, the assessed valuation.

Secondary impacts would normally look at three categories: economic, social, and environmental. These also go into a wider category of planning than financial considerations alone.

Sensitivity analysis examines the changes in the outcomes of the analysis that result from changes in the assumptions. Sensitivity analysis is an important technique in all kinds of planning, and is especially applicable to financial planning.

6.2. FINANCIAL CONTROL AND REPORTING

Financial management enables the success of management by providing the funds that are necessary to plan, build, operate, and maintain facilities, and the information and "handles" necessary to control the facilities and the management organization. To accomplish these purposes, two features of financial management deserve attention: the control and the reporting features.

Control is accomplished through accounting and auditing, with its reports, checks, and balances. The reports furnish management with information needed to make adjustments and to report to boards of directors, to customers, and to regulatory agencies.

Accounting is the function of maintaining the information and continuous analysis needed to provide management and outside interests with the facts necessary to make decisions. It is a general term meaning all of the analysis and record keeping necessary in financial management. "Auditing," a term usually included in the more general term "accounting," is the process of examining accounts or making an outside check on the validity of the financial management and the health of the enterprise. Auditing, as a regulatory measure, is generally carried out by accountants other than those who keep the regular accounts.

Utilities and enterprise funds should use the "accrual" method of accounting, according to the National Council for Governmental Accounting (NCGA) (2). This means that expenses and revenues are credited when they occur, rather than when the cash is received or disbursed, and that the financial reports will reflect a picture of the actual financial health at all times, allowing for appropriate adjustments when unexpected events occur.

Accounting follows the use of "funds" in public organizations. Each fund has its own statement, and this procedure differs from that used in commercial accounting. The NCGA suggests eight categories of funds:

1. The general fund, accounting for most of a municipality's operations such as general administration and police
2. Special revenue funds, to collect revenues for specific purposes, such as a tax levy for parks
3. Debt service funds, to provide for the payment of debt
4. Capital project funds, to finance capital projects from a variety of revenue sources
5. Enterprise funds, for the separate enterprises of the organization
6. Trust and agency funds, to account for assets in special circumstances, such as those belonging to others
7. Intergovernmental service funds, to account for intergovernmental transactions of services
8. Special assessment funds, to account for building of facilities constructed using special assessments

The accounting part of management's responsibilities is reflected in reports to management, the public, and investors. Normally the key report is the organization's annual financial report, which contains the overall results of the past year's activities, including operational and fiscal performance. The preparation of an effective annual report can go a long way toward focusing management attention on the results achieved and on the financial health of the organization. This is easily seen in private organizations, where one of the primary goals has been the "bottom line," with the stockholders holding management accountable for profits and share appreciation at the annual stockholders' meeting.

The annual report that is presented to citizens is referred to by some financial managers as a "popular report," with no set format. In the opinion of these managers, the fact that popularized performance information is included along with the financial data detracts from the financial reporting (5). In the water industry, the annual report is recognized as an important part of management's reporting to either stockholders, as in the case of an investor-owned facility, or to citizens, for a public enterprise (6).

AWWA's text states that the annual report should contain the balance sheet, the income statement, the statement of retained earnings, the statement of changes in financial position, and a 5-year summary of operations, accompanied by management's analysis of performance. The preparation of effective annual reports is a work of art, and the manager will do well to learn from those put out by other organizations, in both the private and public sectors.

Public enterprise goals are usually more complex and politically set than profit goals of a private company, and it is not normally as straightforward to report results and financial position. However, the goals of most infrastructure organizations can be quantified in terms of such indicators as vehicles handled, gallons of water delivered, tons of trash handled, and so on, with financial results reported in terms of service delivered as a function of cost. These are performance indicators that might be used in the annual report.

The design and presentation of the annual report require careful attention from management. This is management's annual opportunity to brag about what it has done and how well. Surprisingly some organizations either do not issue annual reports or prepare them hastily and with little care.

The contents of the annual report will normally include messages from the governing board and management and financial statements. The introductory messages can be quite flexible and unique, depending on the needs at the time for the organization.

How financial statements are presented is a decision of the organization's financial management, with guidance from sources of accepted practice in the financial management profession. The National Council for Governmental Accounting has issued guidelines, one of which specifies a comprehensive annual financial report (CAFR) that includes the elements of financial reporting most necessary for management and outside interests. This report would sum up different funds and combine information in a carefully specified manner (2).

The most common financial statements are the balance sheet; the statement of revenues, expenses, and changes in retained earnings (income statement); and the statement of change in financial position. The first two of these are of principal interest to managers. They can be compared with statements of water balances in a reservoir. The statement of revenues, expenses, and changes in retained earnings is like the annual water budget where the report is of inflows, outflows, and change in storage. The balance sheet is like the report of how much water is in the reservoir at the end of the year, along with how much is owed to users and how much is expected from others.

Perhaps the most important financial statement is the income statement, the one that reports revenues, expenses, and changes in retained earnings. In private business this is sometimes called the "profit and loss statement," and reports how well the enterprise did during the last fiscal year. An example of this statement for the Birmingham (Alabama) Water Works Board is presented in Table 6.2. In this case the statement is referred to as "statements of income and earned surplus." It shows revenues, expenses, and earned surplus at the end of each fiscal year.

The balance sheet shows how the finances balance at an instant in time. An example of this statement for the same water organization is shown in Table 6.3. The balance sheet reaches the balance point due to the inclusion of the quantity "earned surplus," which is like "net worth" on an individual's financial statement.

The manager may want to calculate certain financial ratios from the statements. Three ratios commonly used are the coverage ratio, the operating ratio, and the working capital ratio (current ratio). The coverage ratio is the net income of an enterprise divided by the debt service. This ratio could be checked over

TABLE 6.2. Statements of Income and Earned Surplus 1983 and 1982

	1983	1982
Operating Revenues		
Sale of water:		
Residential	$14,174,698	$13,039,648
Commercial	9,077,270	8,162,323
Industrial	1,238,663	1,282,555
Other water utilities	3,453,946	3,008,648
Municipal	294,169	256,015
Public and private fire protection	250,081	241,323
Miscellaneous water sales	105,847	50,588
	28,594,674	26,041,100
Miscellaneous operating revenue	279,073	223,143
Rent from utility properties		
(principally fire hydrants)	741,414	701,663
Miscellaneous	50,415	41,859
	29,665,576	27,007,765
Operating Revenue Deductions		
Operating expenses:		
Water purchased for resale	4,820,349	2,590,804
Source of supply	113,822	91,302
Power and pumping	4,098,458	3,966,389
Purification	1,863,652	1,809,236
Transmission and distribution	3,503,689	3,421,288
Customer accounting and collection	1,502,065	1,421,589
Administrative and general	3,294,927	3,056,063
	19,196,962	16,356,671
Provision for depreciation	3,159,883	3,086,264
Payments in lieu of taxes:		
To the city of Birmingham	498,923	414,849
To other cities	195,526	194,340
	23,051,294	20,052,124
	6,614,282	6,955,641
Other Income, Primarily Interest	1,556,933	1,873,861
	8,171,215	8,829,502
Other Deductions, Primarily Interest	2,684,155	2,969,529
Income before cumulative effect of		
changes in accounting principle	5,487,060	5,859,973
Change in accounting method for		
vacation pay (Note 8)		(347,370)
Net income	$5,487,060	$5,512,603

(Table continues on p. 160)

TABLE 6.2. (Continued)

	1983	1982
Earned surplus beginning of year	$68,843,201	$63,527,030
Net income	5,487,060	5,512,603
Payment to the City of Birmingham General Fund	(264,448)	(196,432)
Earned surplus end of year	$74,065,813	$68,843,201

TABLE 6.3. Balance Sheets for December 31, 1983 and 1982

Assets	1983	1982
Utility Plant		
Utility plant in service	$162,516,628	$159,647,277
Construction work in progress	2,191,732	1,393,129
Utility plant acquisition adjustment	4,730,912	4,730,912
	169,439,272	165,771,318
Less accumulated depreciation	40,538,497	37,809,392
Total utility plant	128,900,775	127,961,926
Trusteed Funds Assets		
Cash on deposit with trustee	3,490,234	1,632,588
Securities and certificates of deposit at lower of cost or market	14,221,342	15,202,468
Interest accrued on securities and certificates of deposit	360,435	364,966
Due from current assets	138,880	131,960
Due from other trusteed funds	2,800,744	3,316,364
Total trusteed funds assets	21,011,635	20,648,346
Current Assets		
Cash and temporary cash investments	1,496,084	1,190,011
Due from trusteed funds	2,155,559	1,617,489
Customers' accounts receivable–net of allowance for doubtful accounts of $112,501 in 1983 ($89,032 in 1982)	2,155,959	1,915,726
Accrued water revenue	1,118,941	941,064
Unbilled State of Alabama contracts	271,431	439,560
Materials and supplies	1,646,099	1,495,657
Prepaid expenses	46,820	57,930
Other		32,512
Total current assets	8,890,893	7,689,949

TABLE 6.3. *(Continued)*

Assets	1983	1982
Other Assets		
Insurance deposit	168,627	118,484
	$158,971,930	$156,418,705

Earned Surplus, Contributed Capital & Liabilities	1983	1982
Earned surplus	$74,065,813	$68,843,201
Contributed capital for construction	20,242,776	19,264,410
Long-term debt	41,330,000	45,677,000
Trusteed Funds Liabilities		
Interest accrued on long-term debt	1,032,102	1,130,321
Due to current assets	2,155,559	1,617,489
Due to other trusteed funds	2,800,744	3,316,364
Total trusteed funds liabilities	5,988,405	6,064,174
Current Liabilities		
Due to trusteed funds	138,880	131,960
Accounts payable, including contract retentions	1,581,982	895,331
General taxes	106,770	229,460
Customers' guarantee deposits	1,415,570	1,287,795
Payments in lieu of taxes	11,281	11,281
Accrued expenses	628,625	472,201
Total current liabilities	3,883,108	3,028,028
Deferred Credits		
Customers' advances for construction	13,190,398	13,102,332
Unbilled State of Alabama contracts	271,430	439,560
Total deferred credits	13,461,828	13,541,892
Contingency		
	$158,971,930	$156,418,705

a period of years to ascertain the stability of an organization's ability to service debt. The operating ratio is the operating revenues divided by the operating expenses. A low ratio would show that the organization is not recovering costs well with direct charges for service. The current ratio is the organization's current assets divided by the current liabilities payable from the current assets. This is a measure of liquidity for private firms, and for these firms a ratio of 2 is a general guideline of adequacy. The public organization may follow a different guideline.

Financial control involves more than accounting. The built-in checks of the organization for control of purchasing, the fixed-assets records, the inventory, and the control of hiring through staff activities all support the management of the financial health of the organization.

One presentation of these approaches used a three-way classification of the financial management responsibilities: liability management, assets management, and fund accounting and management. Both liability and asset management require long- and short-term viewpoints (7). Funds management means that we must have a budget and it must be managed. All of these approaches to financial management must be integrated for a full control system.

Auditing is an important control function due to its independence and objectivity. No matter how careful management is, it cannot be totally objective, and the outside auditor provides this objectivity. Auditing is an important tool for management since it also provides management consulting services to make suggestions of how things can be done better.

One of the busiest accounting offices in the U.S. government is the General Accounting Office, part of the Office of the Comptroller General of the United States. The GAO oversees programs financed with federal money, an enterprise approaching $1 trillion per year in 1986. Naturally it is interested in how well the funds are spent as well as purely in the numbers. For the purpose of extending the traditional financial audit into the broader function of performance evaluation, the GAO has begun to use the term "performance audit," understood to include three elements: financial, economic, and programmatic. The full definition of these three elements by GAO is as follows (8):

Financial and compliance—determines (a) whether financial operations are properly conducted, (b) whether the financial reports of an audited entity are presented fairly, and (c) whether the entity has complied with applicable laws and regulations.

Economic and efficiency—determines whether the entity is managing or utilizing its resources (personnel, property, space, and so forth) in an economical and efficient manner and the causes of any inefficient or uneconomical practices, including inadequacies in management information systems, administrative procedures, or organizational structures.

Program results—determines whether the desired results or benefits are being achieved, whether the objectives established by the legislature or other authorizing body are being met, and whether the agency has considered alternatives which might yield desired results at a lower cost.

Financial control also extends to cost control, another subject of substantial interest to effective managers. Cost control is not so much a matter of accounting or auditing, although those procedures help, as it is a matter of making sure that full value is received for every dollar spent. This is a function of management at all levels, and requires careful attention to the planning and approval of expenditures, as well as postaudits to determine how well the investments in program and equipment have paid off.

6.3. REVENUE MANAGEMENT FOR OPERATING BUDGETS

The operating and capital budgets should be financed from logical sources. Operating funds should come from current revenues, with minimum reliance on subsidies whenever they can be avoided, and with a close connection between the service rendered and the charge imposed. This simple model represents a conservative approach to financing public services which is often partially feasible, but which should not be viewed as an absolute guide, since there are exceptions to every rule.

Subsidies cannot always be avoided, such as in the case of providing vitally needed services when they cannot pay for themselves. The use of subsidies for transit is common, for example, since the fare-box does not pay the full bill. This is illustrated in Chapter 9, where the Regional Transportation District of Denver is highlighted. The federal government has been providing transit operating subsidies on a general basis for a number of years, but this trend seems about to end. Other examples of subsidies are in the construction grants program for wastewater (capital grants) and in the construction and operation of public housing. Of course, the use of subsidies in developing countries is widespread, often providing the difference between life and death. In the case of irrigation systems in developing countries, for example, even though operation is not directly subsidized, it is indirectly subsidized through the allowance of deferred maintenance, with "catch-up" grants and loans for "rehabilitation."

Subsidies are always controversial. One disaster relief consultant even maintains that when natural disasters occur, the government ought not to come in and provide tents and other assistance, but to give the means for the people to build their own shelters. In the case of transit, some maintain that it will only be when the United States discontinues subsidies that real service and an end to the problems with traffic congestion will begin.

Revenue sources that are normally used for the operation of infrastructure systems center on rates and user charges, property taxes, and other taxes. Other revenues are used for capital funding, such as system development charges, bond proceeds, loans, and grants, and they will be discussed in the next section. The use of revenues for operating and capital budgets is discussed separately, although those revenues are often mixed, such as use of current revenues for capital improvements. Also, debt financing has to be serviced from current revenues.

The operating budget has to be renewed each year, and it is logical that it should be financed from recurring revenues. In past years the property tax was used to finance operating budgets in many organizations, but with the "new" emphasis on enterprise budgets, the trend is toward greater reliance on user charges. Again, this depends on the category of infrastructure. Of course, some organizations have never become reliant on tax revenues, but have been self-supporting for a long time.

Rates and user charges allow the implementation of the "user pays" principle. This is easy to see in the case of charges for services such as garbage collection and the delivery of electricity, but it also applies to cases such as a property discharging stormwater into a ditch.

User charges increased in popularity at about the same time that we were seeing various "taxpayer revolts" such as the one that led to Proposition 13 in California in the late 1970s. At the same time, there were other taxpayer initiatives, such as in Massachusetts. In general, these placed limitations on the amount of automatic property taxation that local governments could levy, and led to "creative ways" to raise revenue. The use of user charges is a creative technique in some cases, such as the transportation utility fee that has been proposed in Fort Collins; and in other cases, it is a logical and tested approach to financing. In extreme cases, the use of user charges without tax subsidies for services will make the cost of operation excessive. An example of this is the public library. If the book borrower had to pay a fee of, say, $3 every time a book was taken out, there would be a drop in books borrowed, and the library would probably fold.

The principle of user fees suggests that they provide the opportunity for both economic "efficiency" and economic "equity" in the provision of public services. Efficiency means that there is no waste. The public sees that it gets what it pays for, and it rations its use of the public service accordingly. Not wasting electricity is a clear example of this; most people are careful about its use since the charge is often a significant part of personal budgets. On the other hand, people are apt to waste water, even when it is metered, since the unit cost is lower. This is reflected in the demand curve for the service, the slope of which, or the "elasticity," reflects the willingness of the public to ration in relation to the cost. Figure 6.3 illustrates this concept for a hypothetical service. One way to think about user fees is that they are the price paid for the service, just like in the private marketplace.

There is a well-developed theory for how to set user fees. In the case of electric, gas, and telecommunications utilities the economic literature refers to "utility" economics. The magazine *Public Utilities Fortnightly* discusses issues, and makes good reading for someone interested in this topic. In the case of water, most of the literature is put out by the American Water Works Association. Roads have their own literature, but since the advent of the Interstate Highway Act, there have been fewer toll roads to provide precedents to study. Toll roads may be coming back, however, with the retreat of the government from subsidies.

One publication about setting user charges provided a classification scheme that may be useful (9):

1. Public-utility-type goods:
   Airport facilities
   Water supply

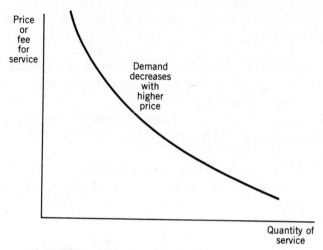

FIGURE 6.3. Demand curve for infrastructure service.

    Electric power

    Gas supply

    Transit services

    Water transport (pipelines)

2. Private goods with important public services:

    Sewerage services

    Trash collection and disposal

    Industrial waste disposal

    Toll roads and bridges

3. Services where public purposes dominate:

    Water effluent control (water quality management)

    Air pollution control

    Highway usage control

In addition, the author discussed numerous other services that did not apply to infrastructure.

The use of user fees may have additional benefits. It has been reported that highways with toll financing have lower maintenance needs by 17 percent (10). Toll financing is not always appropriate, however, for a number of reasons. One reason is that it is expensive to operate toll facilities. The traffic volume must be high enough to justify the collection costs. As a result of these factors, and the domination of the interstate highway program, debt issues for toll roads have fallen dramatically, but the trend may be about to reverse, due to the reduced role of the federal government in financing infrastructure facilities.

There is often opposition to the imposition of user fees. Vaughn lists the following arguments (11):

- Services bring social benefits that cannot be measured and charged for.
- Tax payments for services provide for the redistribution of income to those who cannot afford vital services.
- Public facilities and services attract economic development, and the resulting tax revenues help pay for the services (this is actually the argument used to justify "tax increment financing").
- Dedicating tax revenues to specific services (a form of user charges) reduces flexibility to budget and manage public services in a time of changing priorities.
- A separate approach to managing specific services with dedicated user charges inhibits the coordination of different public services.

Opposition to user charges will certainly appear when they begin to increase. The use of "impact fees," a particular type of user charge which is mostly related to new development, attracts opposition from developers. An example of this occurred in 1986, and will be discussed in the next section, on capital financing.

After analyzing the general aspects of user fees, Vaughn presents five principles for their use:

- They should be levied on the beneficiaries of the services.
- Prices or fees should be set at the marginal or incremental cost of providing the service, not the average cost.
- Peak-load pricing should be used to manage demand.
- Special provisions should be made to ensure adequate access to services for low-income residents where burdens will result from marginal cost pricing.
- User fees should be responsive to inflation and to economic growth.

These are generally accepted principles. Following principles like these, the city of Fort Collins uses user charges extensively to finance both capital and operating needs. For example, the city has instituted a transportation utility fee to provide for the payment of user fees for the roads and streets of the city. The city maintains that the fee is necessary to pay for the cost of maintaining the streets, and bases the fee on the amount of traffic expected to be generated by different categories of land use. The fee has been challenged by churches and other nonprofit organizations, which state that it is just another form of tax. The city has sought to circumvent the taxation issue by reducing the costs to the nonprofit groups.

Fort Collins recently joined a number of other communities in creating a "stormwater utility" which enables the city to collect both operating and capital fees on a monthly basis to improve systems on a basin-by-basin basis. In 1985 these fees were about $2 per month per house, split about evenly between operating and capital charges.

Setting user fees high enough turns out to be an important subject in developing countries that are trying to improve sanitation services. The Pan American Health Organization has been working to improve the situation for 25 years, since donors can only do so much. Morse, writing in the newsletter of the Inter-American Association of Sanitary Engineering, describes the obstacles the organization faces: public mistrust of the government, the assumption that water should be free, and the assumption that increasing the cost of water will fuel inflation. Morse concludes that lending agencies need to get interested in this issue again, that they have neglected it (12).

In spite of the popularity of user charges, tax revenues remain a popular source of finance for infrastructure, particularly for those services where it is difficult to identify the beneficiaries. The major source of tax revenues is the property tax.

The property tax is called an "ad valorem" tax since it is calculated according to the value of the property. Different states have different formulas. The Colorado formula, for example, provided at one time that assessed valuations would be one-third of market values and that taxes would be levied on the assessed values. A management district that had a 10-mill levy for service on some 10,000 properties with an average assessed value of $30,000 each would then collect:

$$\text{Revenue} = 10/1000 \cdot (30{,}000/3) \cdot 10{,}000 = \$1.0 \text{ million}$$

These funds could then be used to help operate the district. This would be a revenue of $100 per property per year.

Colorado reported a total assessed valuation of $19.2 billion in 1986, up 2.7 percent from 1985. The categories of property involved are residential, commercial, industrial, agricultural, natural resources, mines, oil and gas, and vacant land. To demonstrate the specific impact of property tax revenues, Table 6.4 shows values for Fort Collins.

Sometimes other forms of taxes have been used. Income taxes are fairly common as well as sales taxes. Sales taxes are used to finance the operation of the Regional Transportation District in Denver, as discussed in Chapter 9. Normally these "other taxes" would be used on a one-time basis for capital improvements, rather than to finance continued operations of infrastructure. There are always exceptions to every generalization, of course.

Again, to demonstrate the impact of other taxes in a specific case, the collection of sales and use taxes in Fort Collins is listed in Table 6.5. The use tax is a 2.25 percent levy on the storage, use, distribution, or consumption within the city of tangible property purchased outside the city. Also shown are the volumes of other taxes and license fees.

As a further illustration of the sources of revenue for the city of Fort Collins, the data in Appendix D show the sources of revenue for the General Fund. The major share is the ad valorem tax, with significant other sources being permits and licenses, intergovernmental revenues, including payments in lieu

TABLE 6.4. Property Taxes in Fort Collins

The following property tax levies and collections have been reported by the City in the tax years 1976–1981:

Tax Year (1)	Tax Levy (Mills)	Dollar Amount Levied	Collections Amount	Collections %
1976	10.00	1,276,420	1,273,372	99.8
1977	9.10	1,403,588	1,389,525	99.0
1978	9.10	1,651,072	1,643,508	99.5
1979	9.10	1,882,455	1,899,732	100.9 (2)
1980	9.10	2,185,260	2,197,700	100.6
1981	10.70	2,754,290	N/A	N/A

(1) Taxes are collected in following year.
(2) Percentage in excess of 100% reflects primarily the payment of delinquent property taxes from prior years.

Ten Largest Property Taxpayers of the City (1981 Taxes Due in 1982)

Taxpayer	Principal Business	Number of Employees	Total Assessed Valuation (Property in the City)	Total 1980 Property Taxes Paid to the City
Hewlett-Packard	Electronics, calculator components	3,000	$10,889,300	$116,516
Mountain Bell	Telephone utility	500	9,278,900	99,284
Woodward Governor Co.	Governors for diesel engines	817	3,909,100	41,827
NCR Corp.	Micro-electronic circuitry	200	2,695,990	28,847
EverWest	Shopping mall	13	2,316,770	24,789
Public Service Co. of Colo.	Gas utility	147	1,668,160	17,849
First Interstate Bank of Fort Collins	Banking	208	1,194,010	12,744
Teledyne Industries, Inc.	Personal home care products	1,000	1,147,350	12,277
United Bank of Fort Collins	Banking	155	965,110	10,327
Dayton-Hudson Corp. (Target Store)	Retail store	156	784,630	8,395

TABLE 6.4. (Continued)

Present Tax Levy Applicable to Most Properties Located in the City 1980 Taxes Due in 1981 (1)

Governmental Unit	Mill Levy
City of Fort Collins	10.700
Larimer County	20.527
School district R 1	49.880
Northern Colorado water conservancy district	1.000
Poudre Valley hospital district	2.000
	84.107

(1) Portions of the city are subject to additional mill levies due to their location within or outside of special districts as follows:

Governmental Unit	Mill Levy
East Larimer water district	3.743
Fort Collins general improvement district (2)	6.000
Fort Collins–Loveland water district	2.700
South Fort Collins sanitation district	5.059
Poudre Valley fire protection district	8.223
Fort Collins downtown development authority (2)	5.000

(2) Downtown area only.

TABLE 6.5. Sales and Use Tax Collections in Fort Collins

Year	Taxable Retail Sales	Sales Tax (1)	Use Tax	Total Sales and Use Tax
1976	$203,109,931	$4,022,575	$ 439,029	$4,461,604
1977	230,809,390	4,511,760	852,246	5,364,006
1978	278,473,954	5,458,235	1,005,513	6,463,748
1979	336,552,253	6,553,786	1,694,030	8,247,816
1980	375,552,253	7,328,320	1,588,300	8,916,620
1981	414,132,039	8,070,207	1,394,363	9,464,570

(1) Sales tax revenue does not equal precisely 2% of taxable retail sales due to 3% collection charge and other minor accounting adjustments.

(Table continues on p. 170)

TABLE 6.5. (*Continued*)

Tax Collections and License Fees (Exclusive of Sales and Use Taxes)

Year	Licenses and Permits	Specific Ownership Tax	Occupation Taxes	Payments in Lieu of Taxes by City Utilities and Franchise Taxes
1976	$213,137	$ 92,135	$ 57,155	$ 976,071
1977	355,806	106,047	87,148	1,131,019
1978	373,650	197,165	79,472	1,295,958
1979	614,689	169,330	92,752	1,341,379
1980	504,648	186,933	98,461	1,710,648
1981	405,125	204,472	121,959	2,168,527

of taxes from the utilities, and other miscellaneous charges. Of some $9.3 million in General Fund revenue, about $3 million is from the property tax. Sources of revenue for the enterprise funds in the budget show the influence of the user charges.

6.4. REVENUE MANAGEMENT FOR CAPITAL BUDGET FINANCING

Capital financing for infrastructure facilities comes either from current revenues or from debt financing, primarily general obligation or revenue bonds, or from combinations of these sources. Because of difficulties in raising funds from traditional sources, there is considerable attention being given to nontraditional sources such as public-private cooperative ventures and "creative" bond financing. The public-private approach is mostly discussed in the next chapter in the section on privatization. The approach also includes techniques such as developer financing, sometimes called "exactions," and various cooperative ventures, in addition to pure privatization. Creative approaches include techniques such as deep discount/zero coupon bonds, variable-rate bonds, put option bonds, bonds with warrants, mini-bonds, and mini-notes.

When financing is from current revenues, provision must be made to divert the revenues into a capital reserve account, so they can be used when needed. This is also known as "pay-as-you-go" financing. In a recent survey by the International City Management Association, current revenues were shown to be used for capital spending by 73 percent of the respondents (13).

Using current revenues is the easiest way to finance capital, due to the administrative ease involved and the lack of carrying charges. This form of financing is easily understood by the public and politically acceptable. However, current revenues are easy to divert from capital spending when other priorities hit or when crises occur, as they inevitably do. Using debt financing may be more effective, though, due to the equity issues involved in the financing of long-term facilities. Using current revenues means that current ratepayers are paying for the facilities that will be used in the future by others. Debt financing may be more cost-effective due to inflation, uncertainty, and the opportunity to invest revenues elsewhere. If interest rates on debt are low, then it pays to use debt financing to fund construction. If interest rates are high, then current revenues may be a better choice, with the option of borrowing at more favorable terms later.

Debt financing is known as "pay-as-you-use" financing. This arises when the term of the repayment is the same as the life of the facility (an uncertainty since we do not know, in general, the lifetimes of facilities). The amortization of principal and interest in regular payments then means that the facility is fully paid for just as it needs to be replaced.

The use of debt financing is becoming more popular with the increase in attention to the concept of enterprise management. The traditional view is one of the use of general obligation bonds and revenue bonds, but the trends are toward different methods that will adapt to the debt markets of today. In fact the debt market is not nearly as simple as it once was. With the increase in interest rates of the late 1970s, there was a strong move toward "creative financing." Many of those "creative" strategies are not new, but merely different ways to package the same concepts. They can be confusing, however, since so many new terms are in use (14).

Regardless of the trends toward "creative financing," the emphasis seems to be toward an increasing tendency to use revenue-secured debt as the vehicle to obtain capital financing, and away from general obligation bonds. Vaughan reports that revenue debt is now nearly three times general obligation debt (11). This trend seems perfectly consistent with the increasing emphasis on enterprise management. However, as Valente points out, the use of general obligation bonds is more important to infrastructure than that ratio suggests, since revenue bonds are often used for home mortgage lending, industrial development, and quasi-private investment, leaving the general obligation bonds primarily to infrastructure-related purposes. The ICMA survey discussed earlier showed that general obligation bonds were the second most popular form of capital financing, with 59 percent of the respondents using them (13).

General obligation (GO) bonds are backed by the full faith and credit of the organization issuing the debt. The bonds are usually paid off with some source of revenue, but the guarantee is with the taxing power of the entity. Of course, an organization must have taxing power to issue GO bonds. It makes sense to issue GO bonds when the project involved has communitywide benefits, such as municipal buildings, public schools, streets and bridges, and economic development programs.

The trend away from GO bonds can be explained by a number of factors. One reason is the requirement in some places that voters approve the bonds, in some cases with two-thirds approval. This kind of approval is expensive and difficult to secure. Another reason is the tendency to try to assign payment responsibility to the beneficiaries of projects, the "user-pays" principle.

Interestingly, the Northeast is more likely to have local governments using GO bonds, with large, metropolitan areas being more likely to use them than small communities located outside metropolitan areas. The West seems to have stronger traditions of voter approval with less use of GO bonds (13).

Revenue bonds are used when the dedicated revenues of a self-supporting project can be used to pay the bonds off. Revenue bonds can be issued by more entities than are able to issue GO bonds, and are usually viewed as being riskier with correspondingly higher interest rates. Infrastructure services such as water, power, buildings, solid-waste management, parking garages, airports, and other facilities that can be used for a fee are candidates for revenue bond financing.

Since revenue bonds are paid by dedicated revenues, the same concerns that accrue to user charges for services need to be considered. First there is the question of equity. The repayment scheme must take into account the need for all citizens, regardless of their income level, to have a fair access to essential services. Then there is the question of economic development. If charges are too high, or not well distributed, the community's ability to compete may be affected.

The approach to debt financing for managers is to determine how much money is needed and when, and to find the best financing deal. This will require professional advice, of course. Many firms today are vying for the right and business of providing this advice. The repayment of the debt will require funds to be allocated from revenues, usually from the operating budget, to retire the bonds. Preparing for a bond issue is complex and expensive. This is one of the disadvantages of entering the bond market.

The general process of issuing bonds is shown in Figure 6.4. It illustrates the roles of different parties in a bonding arrangement. In this figure the bonds are to be sold to finance a project which provides services to a governmental organization that deals with users of the service, such as water users. The bonds are issued by the "issuer," who goes through the trustee to sell the bonds to the bondholders. The revenues then flow back from the users to the issuer and eventually to the bondholders. There are many variations of this basic plan, of course.

Investment banking firms are active in the infrastructure financing area. Lavish social events are organized by investment bankers to attract municipal officials and others who are empowered to issue bond debt. These events are often held at the conventions of groups such as the Government Finance Officer's Association, the National Association of State Treasurers, the Airport Operator's Council, ICMA, and the International Bridge, Tunnel and Turnpike Association, as well as other infrastructure professional associations.

Touche Ross & Company completed a survey in 1985 of infrastructure financing needs and plans. The company received a 19 percent response out of 5000 questionnaires sent. The conclusion was that GO bonds and federal grants

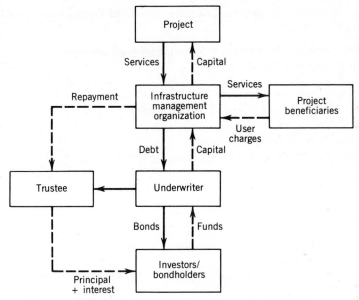

FIGURE 6.4. Flow of activities in bond process.

seemed the best ways to finance facilities, with revenue bonds and special assessments coming in next. Less than 30 percent favored privatization, tax increment financing, infrastructure banks, or other financing means (15). Again the regional difference is there, with the East favoring GO bonds and federal grants, and the West favoring revenue bonds more than GO bonds. While respondents did not favor tax hikes, they seemed to indicate that the hikes may be inevitable. Also, even though the use of privatization and infrastructure banks was not favored by respondents, Touche Ross believes they will be used more in the future.

Debt financing is directly tied to capital budgeting and decision making. This is one of the most important subjects of financial management in all organizations, even the U.S. government. When discussing the topic, it is necessary to consider additional topics such as investments, inflation, interest rates, and currency exchange rates, especially when projects are financed in other than the home countries' currency.

Of course, there is no such thing as a free lunch, and there are limits to the use of debt financing. The statutory limits mentioned earlier apply for a reason, with usual limits of about 10 percent of assessed value. The ratios experienced by Fort Collins in recent years are shown in Table 6.5.

The default of the "Whoops" bonds made many headlines in the 1980s. "Whoops" is the Washington Public Power Supply System (WPPSS), which defaulted on $2.5 billion in municipal bonds in 1983. These had been used to finance nuclear power. With such a large default, many questions are being

TABLE 6.6. City of Fort Collins, Colorado, Assessed Valuation and Debt, December 31, 1981

Estimated actual valuation (estimated, assuming assessed valuation to be 30% of true valuation)	$858,034,300
Assessed valuation	257,410,290
General obligation direct debt	9,595,000
Less portion supported from sources other than property taxes	6,595,000
Net direct debt	3,000,000
Estimated overlapping debt	12,274,415
Net direct and estimated overlapping debt	15,274,415

Permanent population estimate: 64,623

Debt Ratios

Ratio of net direct debt to estimated actual valuation	.35%
Ratio of net direct debt to assessed valuation	1.17%
Net direct debt per capita	$ 46
Ratio of net direct and estimated overlapping debt to estimated actual valuation	1.78%
Ratio of net direct and estimated overlapping debt to assessed valuation	5.93%
Net direct and estimated overlapping debt per capita	$ 236
Estimated actual valuation per capita	$13,278
Assessed valuation per capita	$ 3,983

asked by regulators and the public about the bond process. Some asked by Leigland, author of a book on the default (16), are:

- Why were the bonds characterized as "obligations of the United States"?
- Why did the bonds say "hydro-backed" when they were for a nuclear facility?
- What is the responsibility of the underwriter?
- Why were the bonds rated highly
- Why was the WPPSS pressured to build the facilities?
- If there were staff difficulties, why were they not discovered before all the trouble?

These questions and the default of WPPSS show the limits to which debt financing can go, and offer a caution to both the issuer and the purchaser of high levels of debt instruments.

The use of so many new debt financing terms may confuse you if you are not familiar with financial jargon; for this reason, the following section presents a short glossary of the most frequently encountered terms having to do with the bond market.

DEFINITIONS

Amortization. The process of repaying debt by making periodic payments to the lender or bondholder, with the payment normally including both principal and interest.

Arbitrage. The process of investing funds borrowed from one source in investments yielding higher interest payments.

Assessed Valuation. The taxable value of real property, usually a percentage of the market value.

Bond. The written evidence of debt, with the fixed interest rates, maturity dates, and the amount of the debt.

Bond Anticipation Note (BAN). A note issued in advance of the bonds, usually paid from the proceeds of a bond sale, issued to provide additional flexibility in the management of investments; there are also revenue anticipation notes (RAN) and tax anticipation notes (TAN).

Bonds with Warrants. Bonds sold with warrants that entitle the buyer to purchase additional bonds at a fixed price for a certain period; similar to stock warrants.

Bullet. A form of a term bond where the maturity schedule provides for the payment of all outstanding amounts on the maturity date.

Call. Like prior redemption, an action to pay the principal amount in advance of the maturity date; may involve a penalty provision.

Commercial Paper. Generally unsecured promissory notes, issued for the short term, usually with the purpose of supporting interim capital financing or current operations.

Coupon. Instrument used with bonds which represents the right to a certain amount of interest, usually paid every 6 months.

Debt Limits. Limits imposed by a constitution or other legal instrument on the amount of debt, usually about 10 percent of assessed valuation.

Debt Service. Principal and interest charges on a debt.

Deep Discount. A discount greater than the traditional 1 to 2 percent discount charged.

Discount. Amount by which the selling price of a bond is less than its face value.

Floating-Rate Instruments. Debt instruments that put the risk of changing interest on the investor; examples include flexible-rate general obligation certificates of indebtedness and floating-rate collateralized revenue bonds.

General Obligation Bond. Bond which is secured by the issuer's taxing power.

Mini-bonds. Small bonds with short times to maturity, usually issued by the municipality without an underwriter involved.

Municipal Bonds. Bonds issued by a municipality, the interest on which is tax-exempt; sometimes called "tax-exempt bonds."

Put Option Bonds. Bonds that carry the "put" feature, which entitles the investor to redeem the bond at par value at the end of a specified period.

Rating. The indication of the investment quality of the bond, usually rated by either Standard & Poor's Corporation or Moody's Investor's Service.

Refunding. Selling a new issue and using the proceeds to pay off the old one, probably to gain more favorable terms such as a lower interest rate or a later maturity date.

Registration. The act of registering the securities with the registrar or with the Securities and Exchange Commission (generally, municipal bonds are exempt from registration with the SEC).

Revenue Bonds. Bonds which are guaranteed by the revenues of an operation rather than the tax base.

Serial Bonds. Bonds which are scheduled to mature annually over a number of years.

Tax Increment Financing. Using the increase in taxes, the tax "increment," to repay bonds or other debt incurred to build facilities.

Term Bonds. Bonds which mature on a single date.

Underwriter. The broker or the bank that agrees to market the bonds for a fee or to buy the bonds through a sale agreement.

Zero Coupon Bonds. Bonds that bear no interest but that are issued at a substantial discount, producing the effective gain at sale.

System development charges have become an increasingly important part of overall capital financing strategies, since they provide a way to isolate the cost to serve a particular segment of a system, and to levy charges for it. In effect, they allow new users to "buy into" an existing system by paying their fair share of it. As a simple example, consider the community that has a water supply system already built, complete with adequate capacity for new developments. When the new development comes in, the fair cost of serving it is calculated, and it will be charged a system development fee to pay for its share of the system. This fee would, of course, be passed on to the purchasers of developed property in the form of higher costs for their land, or they would be required to pay the fee themselves. Ultimately, the cost of the infrastructure is passed on to the property owner.

In discussing the approach Fort Collins uses to levy user charges for operating costs, some examples were given, including the transportation and drainage utility fees. Fort Collins also uses the principle of "growth paying its own way" to justify the use of user charges for new developments. These user charges, or system development fees, are mostly used for capital expenses. The ones in use are:

• Water plant investment fee
• Water rights acquisition charge

- Sewer plant investment charge
- Storm drainage fee
- Street oversizing fee
- Off-site street improvements
- Electric off-site and on-site fees
- Parkland fees

The total of these fees in 1982 for a $75,000 house on a 7200-square-foot lot was $7025, a figure that is about average for the region. Fees were slightly higher in the Denver metropolitan region, with a high of $9694 being registered by Lakewood, Colorado, a suburban city incorporated only in the late 1960s. This use of fees such as these to finance growth is common in the western United States and is becoming more accepted in other areas as well. Obviously charges of the magnitude shown are of great concern to home buyers and home builders.

Opposition to system development fees, a form of user charges, will certainly appear when the fees begin to increase. Impact fees, a particular type of system development charge which is levied on new development, attracts opposition from developers. An example of this occurred in Miami in 1986 (17). In this case new fees were being levied on developers to pay for growth since tax revenues have been capped. The article reporting the situation in Miami told of several other locations in the East where the development fees so common in California and Colorado are beginning to appear.

A variation of debt financing that also involves public-private cooperation is "tax increment financing," defined as an approach that uses the increase in taxes that occurs after a development is finished to repay debt. An example of this occurred in Fort Collins in 1986 when voters approved, by a substantial margin, a proposal to build downtown redevelopment facilities using funds raised by the Downtown Development Authority (DDA). The DDA was to sell tax-exempt bonds to reimburse developers for some of their expense for a senior citizens' housing facility to be built in conjunction with office and retail space. The increase in taxes, from $14,600 to $162,000 per year, will be used to retire the bonds.

Grants have been an important part of the overall strategy of paying for infrastructure systems. The wastewater construction grants program, for example, has financed some $40 billion in treatment facilities over the past 10 to 15 years. This program, along with most others, is in decline now, and it appears that the emphasis will be on the enterprise concept and self-finance for a long time. Nevertheless, "intergovernmental revenue," as grants are sometimes called, is an important part of the financing of local infrastructure. In the ICMA survey (13), grants from both the federal and state governments were reported to be important parts of the financing picture. The services reported, along with the percentages of local governments reporting the importance of grants to them, were as follows:

Service	Percent Reporting	
	Federal	State
Water supply	19%	17%
Waste/stormwater management	46	26
Solid-waste management	23	16
Public buildings	25	16
Public schools	8	20
Streets, bridges	37	38
Traffic controls	31	29
Public transit	67	38

It is interesting to review some conclusions regarding the direction of capital financing for infrastructure. Of course, it is such a wide field with such high levels of expenditures that generalizations are hazardous, but the ICMA survey article reported some tentative conclusions to consider.

In spite of the emergence of many alternative ways to raise capital, the traditional approaches (current revenues, GO and revenue bonds, and special assessments) are still the favorites. Among public-private approaches, the use of tax-exempt lease purchases is popular, as well as developer financing. None of the "creative" bonding approaches was used by more than 5 percent of those reporting in the survey. Even though nontraditional techniques are not now in much use, they should be understood due to the changing structure of the capital markets. The early 1980s were times of rapidly changing financial management, and more stability seems at hand, but the volatility in capital finances may return. Since the problems of financing infrastructure will not go away, the need for innovation in financing will remain.

6.5. ALLOCATION OF COSTS

Regardless of how revenues are developed to build and operate facilities, costs must be allocated fairly to repay and to generate the needed revenues. The allocation of costs requires attention to principles of equity that always will attract controversy due to the inherent nature of the problem. Cost allocation goes beyond the concept of setting the rate, and extends to political questions between levels of government and between the government and private parties about how to allocate and share costs. In recent years this has become a very important topic as the level of government subsidies has continued to fall for all services.

Cost allocation means to find ways to assess costs in a fair way in proportion to how different parties benefit from a project or a service. This idea was discussed earlier under the topic of user charges. Most projects and services have costs that are necessary to run the service in general, sometimes called "joint costs," and costs that are clearly identifiable with beneficiaries, sometimes called "separable costs." In the previous sections those services that lend themselves to "utility management" can often directly focus their costs on the public using the service and levy charges accordingly, but they still must exercise "cost allocation" between classes of customers. Other services are not even able to distinguish who their customers are.

In multipurpose water resources projects, the need for cost allocation involves the use of a method called the "separable costs–remaining benefits method" of cost allocation for projects. Basically the method presents a way to separate joint and separable costs, and allocate the separable costs according to benefits received. Usually the parties are distinctly identifiable levels of government or industries. This method is useful in that it illustrates the principle of joint and separable benefits which applies to all kinds of infrastructure, not just water.

The case of cost allocation to water ratepayers is different in the sense that so many different parties are involved. To overcome this difficulty, users are divided into "customer classes" for the assessment of costs, both on a one-time basis and for recurring expenses.

There are many examples of cost allocation. Three that are often encountered in urban water management are presented next. These illustrate the general principles involved. For infrastructure services other than water, the same principles often apply, but most services are easier to allocate costs for than water.

The first example is the case of allocation of costs among levels of government to pay for a multipurpose water project. Take, for example, a Corps of Engineers multipurpose reservoir located near some urban areas in the eastern part of the United States. The project might have, for example, three purposes: water supply, flood control, and hydropower. The federal government has been debating its policies for cost sharing of these purposes for several years, and the debate is not settled, so the example will be hypothetical in terms of policies. We might say that the hydropower will be produced by the government and sold to utilities on a wholesale basis, so the separable costs of this purpose are entirely financed by user fees. The flood control might be jointly financed between the federal and state governments, with appropriate allocation by negotiation. The water supplies might be financed through sale of the water to local governments through long-term contracts. In this example, then, the allocation of costs is done mostly through the political and negotiation process.

In the next example, the project might be a drainage and flood control project that is necessary to develop a particular part of an urban area. Some land developers will benefit through the improvements to their property, but some of the benefit will also accrue to the public at large. The city will decide on the allocation of costs through negotiation with the developers and with reference to the policies and goals of the city administration. This situation can benefit from more analysis of costs and benefits than it usually receives. The state of the art of analyzing problems of this kind has been improving through the technique of financial impact analysis. This approach to cost allocation is frequently used in growth management, and lends itself to public-private cooperation. The next chapter presents more detail on this.

In a final example, the allocation will be according to customer classes, say, for a water and wastewater utility. The water cost allocation would be according to principles such as those found in the AWWA manual disussed earlier, and the wastewater allocation would have to consider carefully the impact of industries. A variation of this that has not been used very much is that of zonal allocation of costs. In other words, if it is more expensive to serve some zones of a city than others, the appropriate rates would be assessed. There are, however, variations in charges between central cities and suburban areas, and this is often the source of distress in water management. When the local considerations of rate needs are added to the local political situation, the result is often complex total rate structures and rules.

It would be nice if cost allocation could be organized so that no negotiations were ever necessary; that would greatly simplify infrastructure management. It will probably never happen, though, because too many actors and profit margins are involved. This is why it is so important that the infrastructure manager be familiar with all of the techniques available.

6.6. EXAMPLES OF REVENUE SOURCES FOR INFRASTRUCTURE CATEGORIES

Principal revenue sources for different categories of infrastructure are explained in the following text.

Roads, Streets, and Bridges

For the most part, roads, streets, and bridges are financed from dedicated road funds. These funds depend on which of the three levels of government is responsible for the infrastructure. The federal-aid system utilizes the Highway Trust Fund to provide the federal share of the funds, and the state and local shares are derived from their sources of funds. In the case of state governments, most are now utilizing some form of gas tax to assist in financing. In the case of local governments, most are relying on property taxes.

Of funds used for construction and maintenance, the federal government provides 28 percent, state governments 50 percent, and local governments 22 percent. The state portion is 34 percent from motor fuel taxes, 30 percent from federal grants, and 17 percent from motor carrier taxes. Bond issues pay for only 4 percent of state contributions. Toll roads are normally operated as independent enterprises, with revenues dedicated to the operation and maintenance of the tollway itself. In the ICMA survey, most respondents reported that they used traditional techniques for streets, sidewalks, and bridges, with current revenues (61 percent of reports), GO bonds (40 percent), and special assessments

(37 percent) leading the way. In the Northeast, communities were most likely to use GO bonds and current revenues, and in the West, the use of current revenues and special assessments was popular, with GO bonds almost never used. In the case of traffic controls, current revenues are the mechanism of choice.

Transit, Rail, and Airport Systems

Transit and rail should be candidates for relying on user charges with attempts to remove subsidies. This has been difficult in the past few years due to the rise of the automobile and the related demise of rail travel, except in some cities such as New York with older transit systems. Railroads have received substantial operating subsidies since about 1970 when the National Railroad Passenger Corporation (AMTRAK) was formed. Since that time AMTRAK has needed an average annual subsidy of about $350 million (18). Mass transit has benefited from subsidies which pay about half the operating costs, with user fees paying the other half. Continued subsidies to transit are a controversial political subject with the need to reduce overall government debt and obligations. Cities have ambitious plans for expansion at the same time that they need continuing operating subsidies and at the same time that the federal government is trying to get out of the subsidy business (19). Airports in the United States are mostly owned by local governments, with revenues coming from a variety of sources. At large airports, income from concessions accounts for about 45 percent of total revenues, while income from landing fees accounts for about 25 percent (18). From 1970 to 1980 the federal government spent some $15.3 billion, or 38 percent, of airport capital expenses in the United States (20).

Water Systems

Water supply, wastewater, and stormwater systems are moving toward self-finance and reliance on user charges, and away from reliance on tax subsidies. For these infrastructure systems almost all of the costs are borne by local governments, and the subsidies that do exist, such as the wastewater construction grants program, are diminishing.

Water supply utilities have led the way in the setting of rates and user charges. Their model is generally reflected in the publications of the American Water Works Association. The procedures for setting charges for wastewater are not as well established, and have been driven by the requirements of the EPA for user charge systems that have to be in place prior to the awarding of a federal grant. Stormwater systems are the newest water service to use user charges as a financing vehicle, and they are just getting started in a few locations through the stormwater utility concept, such as that previously mentioned for Fort Collins.

According to AWWA procedures, the rate-setting process consists of the determination of revenue requirements, the determination of the cost of service by customer classes, and the design of the rate structure itself (21). These procedures are appropriate for the other water services as well, and will work for other infrastructure categories in the absence of specific guidelines.

In determining the cost of service, different methods exist. The AWWA manual specifies two basic approaches: the commodity-demand method and the base–extra-capacity method (21). The difference between these two methods is essentially the way to classify the costs. Studying these procedures can aid in cost allocation for all kinds of infrastructure.

In the case of wastewater systems, procedures for collecting user charges are not so well worked out as in water supply systems. The major recent influence has been federal regulations, but in prior years procedures were being worked out on a city-by-city basis. A report prepared in 1973 by a joint committee of three professional associations described the state of the practice at that time (22). In effect, the practice envisioned in this report is a split of costs between property taxes and user fees.

In the case of the stormwater service, rate making is in its infancy and is mostly based on parameters such as lot size and runoff coefficient. In that sense we might consider the charges to be somewhat related to the property value, and so the charge is still somewhat like a property tax. The future of stormwater user charges is yet to be worked out. A good reference is by Cyre (23).

Waste Management Systems

Solid-waste management is another service that is exploring the possibility of using user charges along with tax revenue. The widespread trend toward private collection of solid waste also portends more emphasis on user charges. The ICMA survey found that current revenues and GO bonds were popular for the construction of landfills and resource recovery plants. The South and the West rely on current revenues, while the Northeast relies on GO bonds.

Buildings and Outdoor Recreation

Buildings are in both the private and public sectors. Buildings that are involved in public infrastructure, such as municipal buildings, are usually financed from current revenues and taxes. GO bonds are used in the Northeast heavily, with some use also in the rest of the country. For buildings that are private or quasi-private, such as in the case of the buildings owned by a private power utility, the revenues will be derived from the user charges. These charges are used to repay debt raised from the capital market in general, with these private companies having the same flexibility as other private businesses.

Energy Production and Distribution Facilities

These facilities are almost all financed from user charges. Energy is perhaps the easiest of the infrastructure services to measure so that user charges can be levied, and it is almost always provided by utilities. The revenue from user charges can then be used either to pay operating expenses or to retire debt raised from the bond market, or in some cases, raised by the issuance of stock certificates.

6.7. Infrastructure Banks and Development Banks

In many countries the development bank is a principal source of funds for infrastructure development and financing. Most engineers and planners have heard of or worked with the World Bank, for example, but there are many other development banks in operation as well. One of the principal uses of these banks is to finance infrastructure projects.

In the United States, a response to the problem of financing infrastructure has been to propose "infrastructure banks." Their purposes are generally the same as those for development banks, except that the infrastructure banks will not be focused on economic development so much as they strive to provide needed funds for infrastructure.

Basically, a development bank is an institution created for the purpose of making loans to assist in economic development projects, and infrastructure projects are one of the most important of projects that are assisted. For example, in 1984, of the combined total of some $15.5 billion lent by the World Bank, $2.6 billion was for transportation projects, $0.6 billion for water supply and sewerage, $3.5 billion for energy projects, and $0.5 billion for urban development. Another $3.5 billion was for agriculture and rural development, much of which was for water management through infrastructure systems.

The concept of the development bank is illustrated in Figure 6.5, where both regular loans and subsidized loans are made to project activities. A regular loan would be one that repaid at market interest rates, for example, an energy project. The subsidized loan would be one that repaid at less than market rates, perhaps even with no interest, as, for example, in a long-term rural development

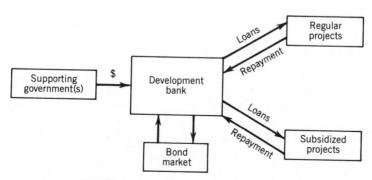

FIGURE 6.5. Operation of development bank.

TABLE 6.7. List of Development Banks

Bank	1985 Lending Plans ($Billions)
World Banks	
International Bank for Reconstruction and Development	11.00
International Development Association	2.98
Regional Development Banks	
African Development Bank	0.54
African Development Fund	0.41
Asian Development Bank	1.82
Asian Development Fund	0.65
Inter-American Development Bank	3.52
Inter-American Development Bank (special fund)	0.40
Subregional Development Banks	
Bank Quest-Africaine de Development	0.03
Caribbean Development Bank	0.04
Caribbean Development Fund	0.03
Central American Bank for Economic Integration	0.33
East African Development Bank	0.02
Arab Development Banks	
Abu Dhabi Fund for Economic Development	0.02
Arab Bank for Economic Development in Africa	0.09
Arab Fund for Economic and Social Development	0.40
Iraqi Fund for External Development	0.00
Islamic Development Bank	0.87
Kuwait Fund for Arab Economic Development	0.30
OPEC Fund for International Development	0.15
Saudi Fund for Development	0.10
European and Japanese Development Banks	
European Development Fund	0.90
European Investment Bank	0.60
Overseas Economic Cooperation Fund, Japan	2.97
International Fund for Agricultural Development	0.15

project. In times of inflation, a long-term no-interest loan is essentially the same as a grant where the borrower never has to repay a significant sum.

Since the development bank may not always make money, depending on the degree of subsidy, it is necessary to have makeup funds from the supporting governments. The bank will also be free to borrow additional funds from the bond market, these being repaid according to usual practices of bond financing.

Many local, regional, and national-level development banks are in operation around the world. Any loan fund can be considered a development bank. However, the formal development banks are more active and visible on a worldwide scale, and constitute an important source of infrastructure financing for the developing countries. Table 6.7 provides a list of 25 of these international development banks as listed in 1985 by *ENR* magazine (24).

ENR also pointed out that many of the lending plans relate to construction, and particularly to categories of infrastructure. For example, agriculture and energy, the two largest categories, include water systems and power plants. Transportation and telecommunications are next in size, both being infrastructure systems. Urban and water supply projects are third in size, and social-sector projects include items such as hospitals, housing, drainage and flood control, sewage and solid-waste management, and other urban projects.

The operation of development banks functions around the "project cycle." According to World Bank practice, the cycle consists of six stages: identification, preparation, appraisal, negotiation and approval, implementation and supervision, and ex post facto evaluation (25).

The development bank concept is an attractive way to solve infrastructure problems since it offers a combination of two concepts: self-finance and subsidy. This is well illustrated by the World Bank with its hard window, IBRD, and soft window, IDA. When the United States was studying ways to improve its infrastructure systems in the early 1980s, the concept of an infrastructure bank surfaced many times. Such a bank would be, in effect, a development bank in the same ways as those already discussed. One specific proposal was contained in a study for the Joint Economic Committee of Congress, where the principles of operation were outlined (26). The principles generally followed the concept shown in Figure 6.6.

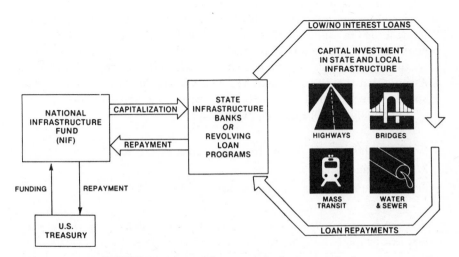

FIGURE 6.6. Proposal for a national infrastructure fund.

The concept in Figure 6.6 proposes a national-level development bank that would provide funds for state-level banks or revolving loan programs, with funds then being lent to specific projects in different infrastructure categories. The initial source of funding would be the Treasury.

Although by 1987 this national infrastructure fund has not yet been implemented, some of the principles may endure. For example, the proposal calls for the loan principals to be fully repaid by the states, with interest subsidies provided by the Treasury. The fund would provide predictable amounts of the loans on a multiyear basis; in this way local and state governments could prepare realistic capital budgets. Compliance would be monitored by the General Accounting Office or another auditing bureau. Funds would be managed by the states, but the operation of the overall fund would be reported in a national capital budget.

The United States has a number of state initiatives in place as well as proposals for a national infrastructure fund (27). Three programs are reviewed in the article cited: New Jersey's program, Massachusetts's "Mass Bank," and the Oklahoma program. All have similar functions, and a state-level infrastructure bank can offer advantages for local governments that need to borrow money for infrastructure.

EXERCISE

In this exercise you are to prepare a cash budget, a balance sheet, and an income statement for a very simple water management enterprise. As you see from the example given in Table 6.1, the enterprise has a capital account, financed with debt, and an operations account. The cash flows are shown as projected over a 20-year period.

You are required to revise this cash budget for the scenario where the interest for the capital debt account is 9 percent and the interest on the operating account debt is 12 percent. You will need to show depreciation on the capital items purchased with the amounts shown in column 2. Assume that the items are acquired at the beginning of the years shown and that the lifetime is 30 years, with straight-line (linear) depreciation.

You should prepare the following items:

1. The cash budget with the revised interest rates
2. The balance sheet after year 15
3. The income/expense statement for year 15.

You can use the balance sheet and the income statement shown in the text as examples, but you are allowed variations from these formats.

REFERENCES

1. Bahl, Roy W., and Johannes F. Linn, "Urban finances in developing countries: Research findings and issues," *Research News*, World Bank, Washington, D.C., Spring 1984.

2. Gitajn, Arthur, Creating and Financing Public Enterprises, Government Finance Research Center, Washington, D.C., 1984.

3. Government Finance Research Center, Financial Management Assistance Program, *Planning for Clean Water Programs, the Role of Financial Analysis*, U.S. Government Printing Office, Washington, D.C., 1981.

4. Block, Stanley B., and Geoffrey A. Hirt, *Foundations of Financial Management*, Irwin, Homewood, Ill., 1981.

5. Aronson, J. Richard, and Eli Schwarz, Management Policies in Local Government Finance, International City Management Association, Washington, D.C., 1975.

6. Grinnell, D. Jacque, and Richard F. Kochanek, Water Utility Accounting, American Water Works Association, Denver, 1980.

7. Graven, Lyndell, Reporting and Control Procedures for Financial Management, in AWWA Seminar Proceedings on Financial Planning and the Use of Financial Information for General Management Personnel, May 16, 1982.

8. U.S. General Accounting Office, Comptroller General of the U.S. Standards for Audit of Governmental Organizations, Programs, Activities and Functions, Washington, D.C., 1972.

9. Mushkin, Selma, ed., Public Prices for Private Goods, The Urban Institute, Washington, D.C., 1972.

10. Congressional Budget Office, Toll Financing of U.S. Highways, Washington, D.C., 1985.

11. Vaughan, Roger J., *Rebuilding America*, Vol. 2, *Financing Public Works in the 1980's*, Council of State Planning Agencies, 1983, Washington, D.C.

12. Morse, Charles, "In quest of higher water and sewage rates," *Newsletter*, U.S. Section, Inter-American Association of Sanitary Engineering, June 1985.

13. Valente, Maureen G., "Local Government Capital Spending: Options and Decisions," in *Municipal Yearbook*, International City Management Association, Washington, D.C., 1986.

14. Shubnell, Lawrence, and W. W. Cobbs, Creative Capital Financing: A Primer for State and Local Governments, Resources in Review, Government Finance Research Center, Washington, D.C., May 1982.

15. Touche Ross & Co., Financing Infrastructure in America, Chicago, 1985.

16. Leigland, James, "Questions that need answers before we go 'whoops' again," *Wall Street Journal*, July 10, 1986.

17. "Fairness of impact fees debated," *ENR*, December 18, 1986.

18. Paquette, Radnor I., Norman J. Ashford, and Paul H. Wright, *Transportation Engineering*, Wiley, New York, 1982.

19. "Mass transit: The expensive dream," *BusinessWeek*, August 27, 1984.

20. Congressional Budget Office, Public Works Infrastructure: Policy Considerations for the 1980's, Washington, D.C., 1983.

21. American Water Works Association, "Water rates," *AWWA Manual M1*, Denver, 1972.

22. APWA, ASCE, and WPCF, Financing and Charges for Wastewater Systems, 1973.

23. Cyre, Hector J., Stormwater Management Financing, APWA Congress, September 1982, Houston.

24. "Funds for development growing," *ENR*, May 2, 1985.

25. World Bank, The World Bank and International Finance Corporation, Washington, D.C., undated.

26. University of Colorado, Hard Choices: A Report on the Increasing Gap between America's Infrastructure Needs and Our Ability to Pay for Them, Report for the Joint Economic Committee of Congress, 1984.

27. Atkinson, Jeff, "Infrastructure banks: Has their time come?" *American City and County*, February 1985.

CHAPTER SEVEN

PUBLIC–PRIVATE COOPERATION AND PRIVATIZATION

Emerging new public–private cooperative techniques for the financing and management of infrastructure will be reviewed in this chapter. The discussion is intended to be of interest both to public officials desiring to explore the alternatives available through these techniques and to potential investors.

"Privatization" is the term that has attracted the most attention in past years, since the return of conservative governments in the United States in 1981, as well as in some other countries, notably Britain. Interest in privatization is not limited to these countries, however.

Other concepts warrant attention also, including leasing and developer financing. Leasing is treated in some discussions of privatization, as it will be here. Developer financing, sometimes called "exactions," involves several techniques such as up-front financing, tax increment financing, and development fees. These have been discussed in the previous chapter and will not be covered here.

Privatization simply means for public entities to turn over the financing and/ or operation of all or some part of an enterprise to private companies. It is of interest to financial managers since it represents both a way to hold costs down for the infrastructure manager and an opportunity for business enterprises.

Of course, the attraction of privatization is the same as that for any private enterprise: greater production at lower cost through competition. Walker (1), writing about privatization in England, quoted a British official who said, "Competition is an extra-ordinarily efficient mechanism. It ensures that goods and services preferred by the consumer are delivered at the lowest economic cost. It responds constantly to changes in consumer preferences. It does not require politicians or civil servants to make it work."

Walker also traces privatization back to Adam Smith, who stated: "It is of the highest impertinence and presumption therefore, in kings and ministers, to pretend to watch over the economy of private people, and to restrain their expense, either by sumptuary laws. . . ."

The basic philosophical question behind the interest in privatization is, Should the government or the private sector provide a certain service? In the United States of the 1980s, the popularity of Ronald Reagan suggests that the nation is convinced there should be less government in general. The same feeling exists at the level of local governments, and the resulting interest in privatization seems destined to continue.

The most visible examples are the privatization of industries at the national level, such as the sell-off in Britain in the 1980s of numerous state-owned enterprises. Margaret Thatcher's government has identified the sale of public-owned companies as one of the highest economic priorities of her government in the mid-1980s. The companies were said to account for more than 10% of the gross domestic product, and to have a return on capital invested of zero (2). They had consumed over $60 billion in capital writeoffs and grants since 1945 and had damaged British competitiveness, according to the report. An example of one of the enterprises that was a drag on competitiveness was the National Coal Board. It has been a high-cost producer itself, and its major customer has been the national electricity industry which buys high-cost local coal and passes the cost on in the form of high energy costs.

In 1981 the Thatcher government began to privatize some of the companies, beginning with some profitable ones. By 1983 the following had been sold wholly or in part to the private sector: British Aerospace, Cable and Wireless, Amersham International, Britoil, and Associated British Ports. Some of these are, of course, businesses that would seem far out of bounds for state enterprises in the United States. Future targets for privatization in Britain include the Electricity Council, British Telecom, British Gas, British Steel, BL, British Railways, British Airways, Rolls-Royce, British Shipbuilders, National Bus, Royal Ordnance Factories, and British Airports Authority. At the time of this writing British Telecom had been sold, and British Gas was scheduled for sale by 1988.

Not even mentioned in most of the press is the effort to return the British Water Industry to private operation. This move is under way at the time of this writing also, but seems to be stalled.

At the local level, privatization is the same, the taking over of public functions by private concerns. Privatization means the process of going private, but there are also many enterprises that are already private. For example, in the United States we are quite accustomed to privately owned telephone, cable television, and electricity companies, examples of regulated public utilities.

There are many apparent advantages to privatization, and with financial assistance from the federal government diminishing, privatization looks better all the time. On the other hand, there are some pitfalls also. These will be examined later in the chapter.

In the case of public infrastructure systems, some private involvement has been traditional, as in the case of private toll roads or private water companies. Savas cites a list of services that are offered by one local government or another on a private basis. The list is topped by refuse collection, followed by street lighting, electricity service, utility billing, water supply, street construction and maintenance, hospitals, and about 30 other miscellaneous major and minor services (3).

There is much interest in privatization today, but we must still understand that the cost must be borne by someone, and the real advantage of privatization is to shift some of the burden of capitalization to the private sector. The implied efficiency savings that some suggest comes with privatization is still controversial. In the remainder of the chapter we will explore some principles of and experiences with privatization.

7.1. GENERAL CONCEPTS OF PRIVATIZATION

In discussing the philosophical underpinnings of privatization, Savas (3) classifies services according to the degree to which they are for individuals or for joint use, and the extent to which access can be limited or that people can be excluded from the service. On the basis of these criteria, he came up with four categories of goods and services: private goods, toll services, common pool services, and collective goods. Examples of these four are automobiles, electric power, clean air, and police protection.

Savas lists the theoretical ways that services can be offered as follows:

- Government service
- Intergovernmental agreement
- Contract
- Franchise
- Grant
- Voucher
- Free market
- Voluntary service
- Self-service

Privatization of services can be implemented in several ways, and it can be classified according to how facilities are financed and how they are operated. The following classification is a simple way to present the basic alternatives:

1. *Complete private ownership and management.* In this arrangement the private company or consortium would build or buy the facility and operate it under a service contract with the city.

2. *Construction privately financed and then leased back to the city.* In this arrangement, the capitalization is by the private investor, and the operation is by the city.
3. *Contract operations by the private firm.* In this situation, the complete responsibility for operations is assumed by the private firm.

In addition, there are the various arrangements for lease-purchases, sale and leasebacks, and cooperative deals. The varieties of privatization arrangements are limited only by the imagination of the private sector.

7.2. EXAMPLES OF PRIVATIZATION

One of the best ways to see the details of how privatization works is to examine a few examples.

Roads and Streets

The use of private funds to construct roads and bridges goes back a long time in the nation's history. Toll roads could theoretcially be constructed by either a private or a public entity. In Colorado there is a current rumor that a private group will construct a high-speed superhighway along the Front Range, with the possibility that other needed services, such as water supply, can be taken along in the right-of-way. No one knows just now whether this will, in fact, occur.

An innovation was reported in 1986 in Texas where a developer was given permission to create a road utility district to construct 7.7 miles of road. This has been carried out under a new Texas law that specifies road utility districts. Under this arrangement the developer uses its funds to construct the roads and then sells tax-exempt bonds to repay the costs. The advantages cited are that this arrangement costs citizens nothing to build the facilities, it puts the whole area under an integrated plan, and the use of tax-exempt financing saves money. How the bonds are to be repaid was not clear in the report (4).

Transit

Transit, and the related services of rail, airport, and port transportation, have traditions of high levels of private involvement. For this reason little has been reported about privatization. Of course, transit facilities would be good candidates for lease-purchase arrangements. Also, more bus companies could go back to the private sector if financial incentives were right. After most of the previously private bus companies were brought out due to financial distress, most transit operations have gone to either municipal or regional operations, with heavy emphasis on federal subsidy. The implications of these problems have been discussed elsewhere in this book.

Water Resources

More publicity has been given to privatization of water facilities in recent years than other infrastructure services, perhaps because, with the exception of the well-founded concept of private water supply companies, the concepts are considered new. During the early 1980s much of the new discussion has been of wastewater treatment applications. The reason is the phase-out of the construction grants program at a time when there are still over $100 billion in needs outstanding.

The use of private firms for water supply has been a common approach for many years. Like electric companies, the private water company is essentially a regulated public utility. The National Association of Water Companies reports 86 private water companies with revenues in excess of $1 million. It has been reported that during the Great Depression the stocks of water companies held up better than most and were regarded as among the safest investments of that time. In 1983 water company stocks were rating higher price-earnings ratios than electric companies. The reasons, in a time of financial turbulence, are reported to be stability and the exemption from taxation of earnings if the company is bought out by the public sector (5). The premiums offered for these companies, whether the sale is of individual stocks or the entire companies, are in spite of reported problems of private water companies: low profitability, regulatory hassles, resistance to rate increases, and local politics. In fact, in 1981 one writer called the water utilities in the public sector "crisis ridden" and suggested they go private (6). This writer's reasons were twofold: the need for capital and the need for repair and renovation. Capital generation with the sales would be logical since the market values of the systems are usually below book value; with a sale, a system in trouble would generate funds but avoid having to deal with problems by raising capital.

The use of the private-sector approach for water supply is well known in France, where some large water companies compete well in the marketplace. The largest of these, Compagnie Generale des Eaux, is penetrating the marketplace in the United States with acquisition of water companies and related businesses. This company is one of three operating nationwide in France, and serves some 4.5 million customers. The firms have subsidiaries that operate in the following businesses: project management, civil engineering, and operation and maintenance of utility companies (7). These private water companies operate cooperatively at times. In Paris it was announced in 1985 that the water service would be split as follows: the city would furnish the treated water, which would then be distributed on the bank of the Seine by Compagnie Generale des Eaux and on the left bank by Societe Lyonnaise des Eaux, another large water company with 2.2 million customers nationwide (8).

Of course, there are many ways to privatize a water supply. The city of College Station, Texas, reported a small step that worked well in 1982. The city contracted with a local company to drill and operate new wells, with the city agreeing to buy the raw water. The term was 12 years and provided for a minimum guaranteed purchase of 3 million gallons per day at 17 cents per thousand gallons.

More has been written lately about the privatization of wastewater management, a service that has become a more important and expected part of municipal responsibilities in recent years with the passage of all the environmental legislation. The need for the Clean Water Act and the construction grants program in the United States was caused by the neglect that the wastewater service experienced until 1972. This neglect still exists in many countries, but in the United States wastewater management is well on its way to becoming a recognized utility service.

By 1986 there were some 30 firms that offered full-contract operations and maintenance services at over 200 facilities. For the most part, these services are contrast operations rather than full-ownership arrangements. Private-sector advocates report substantial savings and satisfaction with these approaches. Twin Falls, Idaho, for example, reported electrical costs dropping 50 percent when a private firm was hired to run the wastewater treatment plant. Also the sludge dewatering costs dropped from $45 per ton to $25 by a careful selection of polymers and close attention to dosing rates. The cities of Gilroy and Morgan Hill, California, were able to develop a regional approach with privatization, with the contractor returning 75 percent of budget underruns to the cities. Pampa, Texas, contracted out both the water and wastewater facilities operation. Lower operations costs allowed the city to begin to recover some depreciation to make improvements in the systems (9).

Chandler, Arizona, is one of the first places to have privatization of wastewater treatment. Chandler, a suburb of Phoenix, has been using the Parsons Corporation to build and operate its wastewater treatment facility. Financing of $22.9 million is by industrial development bonds at an interest rate of 7.2 percent, much lower than would have been required from revenue bonds. Chandler is expected to save about $1.1 million per year, which will allow monthly sewer bills to remain in the range of $7–9 instead of rising to $18–19. The city retains the role of customer billing. There is some discussion that the Parsons venture may have to become a regulated public utility (10).

There is no lack of interest in the concept of privatization of wastewater plants. A call for expressions of interest brought 19 replies from design firms, contractors, and financial concerns to Camden County, New Jersey. If the county goes with the private approach, construction could be completed in about 3 years, whereas it is looking at more than 15 years by continuing to rely on federal grants (11).

Since most of the press is about success stories, we have to be cautious about privatization, however. One utility director, writing in response to "success stories," stated that performance has been less than expected with the operations contractor (12).

There is no reason, of course, that other water services cannot participate in privatization. A stormwater system could contract out maintenance, as some do, or full operation, including construction of capital facilities, or the operation of a "stormwater utility." The Imperial Irrigation District (IID) of California has contracted with Parsons Corporation to develop and finance a $450 million water conservation and transfer program that provides for water savings and the transfer of the saved water to other uses. Although Parsons is not buying facilities from the IID, it is becoming an operations arm in this conservation and renewal effort (13).

Waste Management

In the solid-waste field, privatization is a well-known concept since private trash collection firms predominate. In fact, one of the industry's magazines recently labeled privatization, "a bureaucratic word for competition" (14). The attraction of the solid-waste problem is one reason that companies have been flocking to this newly attractive market. Resource recovery and the use of solid waste to generate energy is one of the most popular and logical private business applications in public works privatization.

There seems to be a tendency for the trash collection business to consolidate with the purchase of smaller firms by larger ones such as Waste Management Inc. and Browning-Ferris Industries (BFI). Waste Management recently signed a $115 million contract with San Jose, California, to provide for the collection of solid waste from 177,000 residences, with other special services as well (15). The company was greeted with a surprise when it assumed service in that it had to start service without knowing who the customers were; it had to identify them, a real challenge!

The literature is rich with accounts of either the private sector being better at trash collection or the public sector. In any event, the private sector is well established in this field. The new part of it is waste disposal, particularly the new emphasis on trash-to-energy plants.

As discussed in Chapter 2, solving the waste disposal problem has become a major new business area (16). It is predicted that capital investment in new plants could be $20 billion in the next 20 years, with some 75 incinerators coming on-line with annual revenues of about $4 billion. The total solid-waste disposal market is said to be a $100 billion market (17). There is controversy over which disposal technology to use since many communities are running out of landfill sites. One of the controversies is the extent to which the United States should copy Europe and go to mass burning and incineration for refuse-to-energy projects. There are complications both with incineration, including air pollution, and with recycling, which suffers from impracticalities.

The Signal Corporation has been developing and building refuse-to-energy plants for about 10 years. In 1985 it was operating plants in Saugus, Massachusetts; Pinellas County, Florida; Westchester County, New York; and Baltimore, Maryland. Other companies are joining in. Waste Management Inc. was building a plant in Tampa in 1985. There are many other potential sites, with industrial plants being customers as well as cities. See Chapter 2 for a more detailed discussion of the solid-waste field.

Buildings

Buildings are another field of infrastructure with a strong tradition of private involvement. There are plenty of buildings that are used for public purposes that have been built with private money, and some that are operated under lease arrangements or other private ventures.

Buildings illustrate one of the clearest applications of the lease-purchase approach to privatization. Lakewood, Colorado, built a new city hall for $11 million through this approach without adding to its long-term debt. Anaheim, California, built a $54 million parking facility, and Jefferson County, Colorado, built a $30 million jail (18). San Jose and Atlanta had their city halls for sale in 1983; Oakland was selling its museum and auditorium; and Berkeley was considering selling its civic center, refuse facility, libraries, parking garage, and senior citizens center (19).

In recent years the privatization of jails has attracted attention due to the need for jails on the one hand and the difficulty of financing them on the other. Because of the increasing prison population, there has been a boom in prison construction in the mid-1980s.

In the example of jail privatization reported in Jefferson County, Colorado, a suburb of Denver, the broker firm E. F. Hutton arranged a financing of $30 million through "certificates of participation" and arranged for a lease-purchase deal (20). In Panama City, Florida, the Bay County jail was privatized by turning it over to Corrections Corporation of America. The county budgeted $700,000 less after turning the jail over to the firm. There are, of course, numerous political problems to be solved, and as with all recent actions, this one will have to be judged by performance. The $700,000 savings is bringing many visitors to see how the system works (21).

Energy Production and Distribution

The energy field is well represented by private firms in generation and distribution. Many of the electric companies are publicly regulated private utilities. Competition between public and private utilities is keen. We may see some takeovers of utility firms and systems later in the 1980s and the 1990s. See Chapter 2 for a more detailed discussion of this industry.

There is some privatization of public companies going on today. The city of Fairbanks, Alaska, distributed this ad in November 1986:

Request for letter of interest, potential utility purchaser, October 29, 1986—The City of Fairbanks requests "letters of interest" from firms wishing to purchase its electric utility, which includes an electric and steam production facility and electrical distribution facilities. The package as currently conceived in the sale currently serves a combination of over 130 district heat and 6500 electrical users with annual revenues of over $13.8 million and assets valued at over $17 million. Firms desiring to be considered for the potential purchase of the described utilities should send their letter of interest accompanied by a brief statement of qualifications detailing their background in the ownership and management of similar utilities.

Another innovation in privatization in the electric industry is the formation of a firm, in Fort Collins, that proposes to develop and manage pumped storage. The firm would forge an alliance between water and electric utilities that would result both in increases in water supplies and in the storage of electric energy. This firm proposes to privatize, in effect, the kinds of work formerly done by the Bureau of Reclamation in the development of regional power systems (22). Again, the jury will remain out on this proposal for some years to come.

Other Applications

Pure services may be the easiest route to privatization. There is almost no limit to the different items which can be contracted out. Newton, Massachusetts, recently contracted out ambulance service, for example. Service improved, but the fee increased some $10 per trip. A number of communities contract garbage collection. Street cleaning, tree removal, and cemetery maintenance were contracted out in Watertown, Massachusetts, with the result being a drop in public works jobs from 150 to 55. Grants Pass, Oregon, allows competition between fire departments, with favorable results being reported. Customers can subscribe, or pay a direct fee when they use the service (19).

7.3. PRIVATIZATION IN OTHER NATIONS

Although the examples given in the previous sections have been from the United States, France, and Britain, there exist opportunities for privatization to succeed in developing countries as well.

The U.S. Agency for International Development reported in 1986 that privatization was "gaining global momentum" (23). This conclusion, coming from an official aid agency, must be verified further, however, since it is a stated goal of the administration to promote privatization. Nevertheless, the reports are encouraging.

Interest in privatization in developing countries is to provide an alternative to the state company. Many developing countries have organized extensive, networks of state enterprises to provide services. This has been necessary due to the lack of sufficient private-sector capacity to provide necessary services. State companies, however, do not have a good record for efficient and effective delivery of services, due to problems with bureaucracy and corruption. These are exactly the problems that provide incentives to consider privatization.

The World Bank is encouraging privatization of services through its loan and technical assistance programs. It has witnessed a willingness in developing countries to pay for telecommunications and electricity, but not the same willingness to pay for water. The problem with water, as discussed in the previous chapter, has to do with the prevailing notion that it should be free. This is one of the obstacles to the completion of effective systems for water and sanitation.

AID provides examples of a number of different approaches to privatization in developing countries. These include development of tube wells in Pakistan and Bangladesh; transportation in Argentina, Kenya, and the Philippines; a port in Tampico, Mexico; air services in New Guinea; light industrial facilities in Mozambique; and agricultural privatization in Malawi.

Other reports of privatization in developing countries abound. American Samoa has experienced reduced revenues due to U.S. budget constraints. The response has been to move to privatization of services. The experience in Samoa has been positive so far, and includes the Marine Railway, the American Samoa Power Authority, solid-waste management, motor pool and real property maintenance, and management of the hotel and hospital management function (24). In the Philippines it is the policy of the Aquino government to move to privatization, and announced targets include the Philippine Airlines and the Manila Hotel, but progress has been slow (25). The National Center for Policy Analysis reports that the United States lags behind other countries, and cites the following as examples of moves in developing countries: telecommunications in Bangladesh, Mexico, Thailand, South Korea, and Malaysia; airlines in Thailand, Singapore, Turkey, and South Korea; bus service in Sri Lanka and Thailand; highways in India and Malaysia; public housing in Cuba and China; and social security in Chile (26).

Since the economic needs in these countries cut across the spectrum, the list of sectors needing assistance with privatization covers the entire economy. It is no surprise that many examples can be found.

7.4. ANALYSIS OF PRIVATIZATION AS A MANAGEMENT TECHNIQUE

Privatization as an attractive alternative to government ownership and/or operation of public service facilities is attractive due to the perception of savings and increased service levels offered by the private sector. The general argument for savings must basically come from increased effectiveness since subsidies from tax savings are not really savings but transfers. From the standpoint of the individual community, the tax savings can be substantial, however. Tax treatment of privatization deals has changed rapidly, however, and it is not certain that advantages such as tax exemptions and investment tax credits will remain.

The principal advantages that have been reported are as follows:

- Financial savings
- Faster implementation
- Avoidance of hassle—unions, politicization, and interest groups
- Transfer of risk to the private sector
- Private financing
- Enhanced tax base
- Better use of smaller public staff and lower pension obligations

- Effective public control through regulation and oversight
- Lower fire insurance rates through improved service
- Innovations and bias for action in the private sector
- Better training of workers

These perceived advantages still must be studied and evaluated.
  Reported disadvantages of privatization are:

- Not sensitive to the needs of the poor
- Less accountable to the public by insulation from politics
- Potential poor service and neglect
- More expensive
- Slower due to complexity of selection, decision making, and transfer of risk

All in all, there are still many factors to consider, and the jury must remain out until we have more experience with privatization. Some systems are obviously appropriate for privatization as they have worked well, as, for example, waste collection. Others are simply financial matters, such as the lease-purchase of a public building. If lease-purchase is really long-term debt, it may have to be counted that way in the future.

The city of Phoenix, Arizona, has presented material to show the other side of privatization during the last 2 years. Phoenix decided to privatize garbage collection, with the city bidding against the private sector. The result was some serious problems. Collection was disrupted twice by labor and equipment problems. One of the contractors almost took bankruptcy. City employees report low morale and sloppy work by the private contractor. The privatization has turned out to be very complex, with hidden costs, such as the need for additional city staff to monitor the private contractor. There are also legal problems (27).

Obviously privatization is not a panacea for all the problems of infrastructure capitalization and management. It also does not always cause serious problems like those that occurred in Phoenix. The raising of capital for public infrastructure and the operation of all the services desired by the public remains a challenge, and public-private cooperation needs to be given every chance to succeed in doing its part. Every case has to be considered on its own merits, and careful analysis with full consideration of all alternatives and all possible outcomes is necessary.

EXERCISE: PRIVATIZATION

In this exercise you should prepare a proposal to privatize the storm drainage system of Fort Collins. Even though there are no privatized storm drainage systems, there seems to be no legal or theoretical reason that there could not be. The request for proposals that follows provides information about the type of proposal desired. Basically it is to be a business proposal that shows the city how you can provide better service at lower cost through private ownership and operation.

The detailed information you would need to completely analyze the system has not been provided. However, some insight into the Fort Collins approach to storm drainage is provided in the budget documents in Appendix D; it is best if you just make estimates of the information needed so that you can focus on the important concepts. Fort Collins has gone to a storm drainage utility concept and charges a monthly fee for operations and another for capital. Each fee is about $1 per house per month.

REQUEST FOR PROPOSALS

The City of Fort Collins solicits proposals from qualified firms for purchasing and operating the storm drainage system of the city. The services that will be included are maintenance, repair, operation, and billing.

Proposals should be approximately five pages in length. They should include the following information: concept for the privatization; estimates of the total cost to residential and business property owners or users; estimates of the costs for key items of operation, repair, and maintenance; proposed methods of financing the service; and qualifications of the firm.

Proposals are due in the offices of the contracting officer no later than 5:00 P.M. on November 3, 19__.

_____

Contract Officer

_____

REFERENCES

1. Walker, D. L., The Economics of Privatisation, IWPC Symposium on Privatisation and the Water Industry, March 1985.
2. Brown, Andrew C., "For sale: Pieces of the public sector," *Fortune*, October 31, 1983.
3. Savas, E. S., *Privatizing the Public Sector*, Chatham House, Chatham, N.J., 1982.
4. "Texas tries 'no-tax' roads," *ENR*, October 23, 1986.
5. Blyskal, Jeff, "Water money," *Forbes*, February 14, 1983.
6. Hanke, Steve H., "Crisis-ridden water systems should go private," *Wall Street Journal*, September 3, 1981.
7. Deschamps, Jean-Dominique, "Privatization of water systems in France," *Journal AWWA*, February 1986.

8. "Paris water distribution goes private," *World Water*, March 1985.

9. Giachino, John A., "Private-sector treatment programs tailored to utility needs," *Waterworld News*, March/April 1986.

10. "The fiscal threat to public works, *Business Week*, April 9, 1984.

11. "Lining up for 'public' work," *ENR*, June 9, 1983.

12. Wallner, Michael J., Utility Director of Fort Dodge, Iowa, letter to editor, *Waterworld News*, May/June 1986.

13. "Parsons leaps into irrigation," *ENR*, April 25, 1985.

14. Editorial, *World Wastes*, May 1986.

15. "Private hauler mobilizes to meet San Jose's demands," *World Wastes*, May 1986.

16. Leinster, Colin, "The sweet smell of profits from trash," *Fortune*, April 1, 1985.

17. Morris, David, and Neil Seldman, "New ways to keep a lid on America's garbage problem," *Wall Street Journal*, April 15, 1986.

18. Bernstein, Aaron, "Lease-a-jail," *Forbes*, September 12, 1983.

19. "Want to buy a fire department?" *Newsweek*, April 25, 1983.

20. "Privatization spreads to prisons," *ENR*, April 5, 1984.

21. Bean, Ed, "Private jail in Bay County, Florida, makes inroads for corrections firms, but the jury is still out," *Wall Street Journal*, August 29, 1986.

22. "Privateers seek water projects," *ENR*, August 14, 1986.

23. Scriabine, Raisa, Privatization Gaining Global Momentum, Front Lines, USAID, February 1986.

24. Dudek, Donna, "Privatization is American Samoa's answer to US budget constraints," *Wall Street Journal*, July 7, 1986.

25. Spaeth, Anthony, "Sale of Philippine state firms is sputtering," *Wall Street Journal*, October 30, 1986.

26. Young, Peter, and John C. Goodman, "US lags behind in going private," *Wall Street Journal*, February 30, 1986.

27. Neikirk, Bill, "Phoenix shows some bruises after plunge into privatization," *Chicago Tribune*, March 30, 1986.

CHAPTER EIGHT

PROJECT ENGINEERING AND MANAGEMENT

The construction project is an essential vehicle for completing and placing public works facilities into service. Unless projects are completed with quality results and within budget, there can be no solutions to the problems of developing and managing infrastructure. This chapter is about the process of managing and developing projects to ensure the highest quality and greatest value of the completed facilities.

The development of projects goes beyond the ordinary operations and maintenance function of public works organizations, and is often handled with a special engineering staff, using outside consultants and contractors. The role of the engineering staff in this process is described later in this chapter. After the project is completed, it is turned over to the operating staff. The process involved is illustrated in Figure 8.1.

The project engineering and management process is part of what we call "implementation." This sometimes takes a back seat to the more esoteric and quasi-political aspects of planning and management, but anyone who has ever been involved in a difficult project development task, with cost and schedule overrun problems, or with lawsuits, knows how difficult the problems can be to solve.

There is a massive construction industry ready to design, build, and sometimes operate entire projects. Making this industry work for the benefit of infrastructure is a challenge to construction managers. The task of management of construction is sometimes regarded as an engineering function, but there are many skilled construction managers who are not engineers, and in fact, there are some very effective academic programs in place to train such managers. One of them is at Colorado State University. Some of the faculty are engineers, but the students

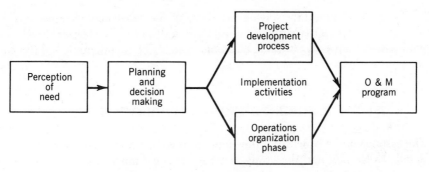

FIGURE 8.1. Project development in perspective.

are graduates in industrial construction management. There has been a high demand for this major.

The construction industry is large. In the United States it consists of 1,200,000 firms, with 720,000 of them being so small they have no payrolls. There are 70 labor organizations and regulatory agencies to contend with. The industry does more than $300 billion in work every year, and employs some 5.5 million workers. Construction is the industry that adds the most to the nation's capital investment (1).

The industry also includes the suppliers of equipment and components, as well as the consulting engineering profession. These add substantially to the work force, making construction's total share of the work force some 17 percent of the total.

The U.S. construction business has been slipping as a percentage of the gross national product, dropping from the 9–12 percent range in 1975 to about 6–8 percent by 1985. Some other countries devote more of a percentage to construction, such as Japan with 20 percent.

The industry has been afflicted with problems. Studies over the past few years show that the problems can be traced to environmentalism, preservation forces, growth management, union activities, tax and regulatory policies, and lagging technology. These problems are seen as creating a drag on infrastructure productivity on the one hand, but the infrastructure rebuilding and rehabilitation challenge is also seen as an opportunity to make strides with infrastructure on the other hand. The problems of the industry are featured weekly in *Engineering News-Record*, McGraw-Hill's journal of the construction industry, which is now called *ENR*. Information from this magazine has been helpful in compiling this book.

Solving problems of the construction industry is seen as critical to solving the infrastructure problems (and the competitiveness problems) of the United States. Areas where new technologies and innovations are possible are seen to be construction technologies, robotics and remote control, knowledge engineering, advanced materials, electrochemistry, and management innovation.

The place to begin for solving problems of the construction industry is the planning-design-construction process. Making this process work effectively and with cost-effectiveness is a real challenge due to the fragmentation of the construction industry.

8.1 THE PLANNING-DESIGN-CONSTRUCTION PROCESS

The essence of the process for developing projects is a sequence of increasingly detailed planning and designing activities that culminate in the construction and completion of a project. Thus we speak of conceptual planning, preliminary planning, preliminary design, final design, preparation of construction documents, contracting, construction, and inspection as tasks that lie along this continuum of design-construct activities.

Due to the tremendous experience in the construction industry with the construction process, the process takes on both the traditional and the modified forms. The traditional process is one where the actors are the owner, the general contractor and subcontractors, the architect, the engineer, the surveyors, and any other team members such as the attorney. In recent years, more attention has been given to fast-track approaches that alter the traditional approach in the name of speed, economy, and control. These processes involve different organizational plans for the design-construct team and different financial and legal arrangements (2).

Regardless of the type of design-construct process used, the needs in planning, designing, and constructing are the same. In planning, facts must be determined, sites must be selected, feasibility studies must be carried out, and financing must be arranged. In design, final details must be set for all aspects of construction. Design itself can be characterized as schematic, preliminary, and final. The initiation of construction involves numerous legal and procedural steps which must be maintained.

In general, these activities are managed by the engineering staff of the public works organization. This staff undertakes a number of related functions ranging from initial surveys and plans to construction management and, finally, record keeping. This is discussed in somewhat more detail in a later section of this chapter.

Planning

Planning for projects is the first stage of the project development process. It covers several activities, each extending over a period of time and leading to a convergence of concepts to the final and fixed concept for construction.

Planning studies and reports are classified according to the level of detail and certainty of the project characteristics. Common types of plans are reconnaissance, feasibility, definite project, and final plans. The content of these different types of plans varies with the application, and there is a semantic problem relating to the content of the plan to overcome when specifying the needed plan detail.

The terminology for planning varies with the practice of different groups of engineers and planners. Water projects will seem different from road projects due to these differences in terminology, but in reality the processes are about the same, with only minor procedural differences that have to be observed.

It is common to refer to project planning in the following phases or variations thereof: reconnaissance, feasibility, and definite project. These plans can be transitioned directly into the phases of design, beginning with conceptual design, so that the difference between the final stages of planning and the initial stages of design becomes blurred.

The World Bank illustrates these phases of project planning. It refers to the "project cycle," which consists of six stages: identification, preparation, appraisal, negotiation and approval, implementation and supervision, and ex post facto evaluation (3).

The purpose of the reconnaissance phase is to identify those possible projects that meet goals established in the overall planning and development process. The phase typically will lead to recommendations for further studies rather than to definite plans. For this reason the results from the reconnaissance stage need to be presented clearly to prevent decision-makers from stating that no more studies are needed.

The purpose of the feasibility phase is to establish definite feasibility, including financial, technological, environmental, and political. This is a very substantive phase, and may result in documents that are costly to prepare, depending on the complexity of the project.

The definite project phase results in plans, specifications, and operating agreements, all the guidance needed to construct and begin to operate the project.

In transportation some of the terms used to describe the processes just mentioned will include "route survey," "preliminary location," and "final location." These terms point up the fact that finding the route for a roadway is one of the most complex parts of the planning process.

Design and Value Engineering

In design the purpose is to prepare the actual construction drawings and details. With so much emphasis on liability and safety today, the design process has taken on new constraints. The use of computers is increasing at the same time, adding to the complexity.

The design process involves creative decision making about the configuration and details of projects. There are many decisions to make that require experience and consultation. The results of design will be the documents and plans necessary to initiate the construction process.

Value engineering (VE) is a "scientific method of analyzing a product or service so that its function can be achieved at the lowest overall cost" (4). It has the attraction that if applied early in the design of a construction project, substantial savings may be realized. The GAO estimated that net savings of 3 to 5 percent could be realized for VE program costs ranging from 0.1 to 0.3 percent of total project costs.

Value engineering is one of several different cost reduction methods, but it does its job by analyzing functions and asking whether methods, processes, and materials that have been in use for years could not be replaced by more economical means. It asks the following questions: What is it, what does it do, what must it do, what does it cost, what other material or method could do the same job, and what would the substitute method cost?

The VE process is implemented by a multidisciplinary team with a specific plan. It goes through five phases:

- Information phase, where the team becomes familiar with the design and performs the function analysis
- Speculation phase, where the team develops alternative ideas to perform the same function through different methods
- Analytical phase, where the team screens ideas and selects the best ones
- Proposal phase, where written recommendations for cost reductions are prepared
- Report phase, where results of the study are reported with requests for implementing action by the appropriate officials

The VE process sounds like it would be a panacea for reducing costs of projects, but like other reform methods, it meets resistance from many quarters. For example, the Department of Transportation responded to the GAO report cited earlier that it did not consider VE requirements essential, since VE is only one of several cost-reduction techniques. Engineers do not like to be constrained in their designs by such techniques, so the actual results may not measure up to the promise.

Construction

The construction process involves bidding, review, award, organization, construction, inspection, and acceptance. There is a formally recognized process for these steps developed over many years as a requirement to control costs, the quality of construction, and the quality of the final product.

The construction phase begins with the preparation of the contract documents. These are discussed later in the chapter. The actual construction involves complex operations which must be designed to fit the infrastructure category involved. An important step in the construction process is the quality control–quality assurance process. It culminates with the final inspection and acceptance activity.

Keeping all of these phases going in the proper direction and order is the task of the project management process.

8.2. THE PROJECT MANAGEMENT PROCESS

The actual management of multifaceted projects is a complex undertaking, and there is no direct and easy "cookbook" method that leads to success. This conclusion was reached by a study team in its report (5):

> Project management is a complex mechanism containing numerous variables of significance to project success. There is no simple approach to insure project effectiveness. Many factors contribute to project success.

This conclusion refers to all kinds of "projects." An example of a project that is even more complex than most construction tasks is the Manhattan Project, which resulted in the production of the first nuclear weapon, or the Apollo Project, which put the first man on the moon. The construction project is thus a microcosm of the larger concept of a "project."

Construction project management has been studied as a necessary component for the solution of the infrastructure problems of the country. At a workshop in 1984, the organizers advocated the adoption of a "project management system," and offered the following definitions to explain it (6):

> A "project management system" (PMS) is a networking system that utilizes an integrated approach to successfully control and direct a project.

> A "project" is a definable concept which employs the functions of planning, design, finance, construction and control to achieve an end.

> "Management" is the catalyst which directs and guides the functional operations to complete the project on time, within budget and at an acceptable level of quality.

> A "system" is an information network, integrating all functional requirements through the various levels of management for the successful direction and guidance of the project to an efficient end.

The importance of project management on the one hand, and its complexity on the other, has led many engineers who become project managers to consider the special requirements for succeeding in managing projects. There has even been organized a Project Management Institute, located in Drexel Hill, Pennsylvania.

At the workshop noted previously, the participants identified some 13 areas of project effort that needed attention:

- Preliminary feasibility
- Land acquisition
- Master planning
- Schematic design
- Financing (preliminary)

- Zoning
- Design development
- Construction documents
- Financing (final)
- Bidding phase
- Contract award
- Construction phase
- Operation and maintenance

From these steps the process identified by the participants looks very similar to the general process already presented. They also identified project management "tools" that can be used to improve overall effectiveness:

- Project scope definition
- Project team responsibility definitions
- Design and finance documents
- Estimates
- Activity-based schedules
- Cost Control systems
- QA/QC systems
- Information-handling systems
- Change-order-handling systems

They also identified tools to aid in planning. These included economic analysis, value engineering, and life-cycle costing. All of these "tools" are techniques that are already available; they just need to be used better.

At the conference, participants focused on a familiar list of constraints that face the construction process: government regulation and interference, public apathy about infrastructure, and the need for better construction management systems. Recommendations included the need for strategic planning for infrastructure, more understanding of the project management system, public education about infrastructure, political attention to the infrastructure problem, implementation of project management standards and systems, and development of data bases of infrastructure data. These recommendations and observations are similar to those that came out of the Business Roundtable study of the construction industry in the early 1980s.

Fort Collins, Colorado, as a rapidly growing community, found it necessary to furnish special training to its project managers. The city has a special system for managing capital projects which includes a project management manual, special project financing and tracking processes, and training sessions (7). The system includes the following features: planning, administration, evaluation, project tracking, and reporting. These are described in the manual, which has a special process for updating and revisions.

The process for planning projects involves the conceptual design, the preliminary design, and the final design phases. These are variations of the terms described in the previous section. Each phase contains different challenges for the project manager.

As shown in Figure 8.2, the conceptual phase is the one where the project manager is assigned. The input to the phase is the identification of the project, and the output is the authorization to proceed to preliminary design.

As shown in Figure 8.3, the preliminary design phase involves considerable coordination, and concludes with authorization to proceed with final design. Since final design is often quite costly, this is a significant decision.

Figure 8.4 shows the activities necessary during the final design stage. The output of this phase is authorization to go to the construction phase.

Project administration itself is broken down into the preconstruction and construction phases. As shown in Figure 8.5, the preconstruction phase is the most complex and involves considerable additional coordination. Items involved include checking for fund availability, getting land acquisition contracts, requisitioning the project, assembling contract documents, evaluating bids, obtaining contractor signatures on contract documents, and issuing the notice to proceed.

The construction phase (shown in Figure 8.6) involves reviewing contract documents, holding the preconstruction conference, assisting in obtaining permits, receiving and reviewing contractor documents such as work schedules and financial information, processing requests for payment, managing change orders, and handling all reporting.

Project evaluation and closeout (Figure 8.7) involves inspection, preparation of final pay estimates, final settlement, and preparation of the closeout report.

A summary of these phases with emphasis on approvals and finance is shown in Figure 8.8.

The project tracking system is an information system for tracking the progress of the project and the cost control factors. The city has a separate capital projects fund to manage projects and keep their finances from being managed in the regular operating accounts of the services involved.

The land acquisition system specifies the activities necessary, by planning phase, to make sure the land needed is available when needed. It involves close collaboration between the consultant, the project manager, and the right-of-way office.

The contract formulation and administration system allows for the selection of consultants and contractors, the use of standard city contracts for the majority of capital projects, bid document preparation and procedures, and change-order procedures.

The success of project management requires special management skills. Often engineers or managers will assume that the principal requirement is a good scheduling or evaluation system, such as CPM/PERT (critical path method/

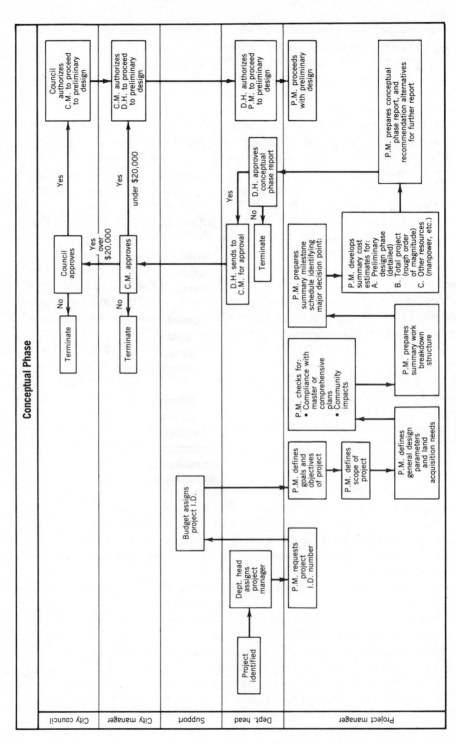

FIGURE 8.2. Conceptual phase.

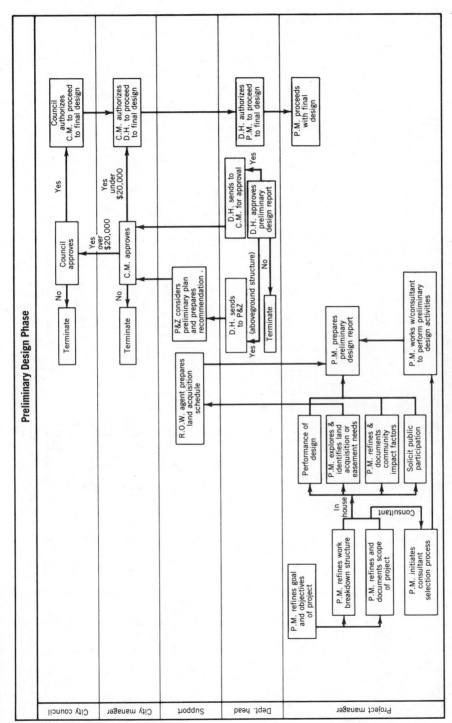

FIGURE 8.3. Preliminary design phase.

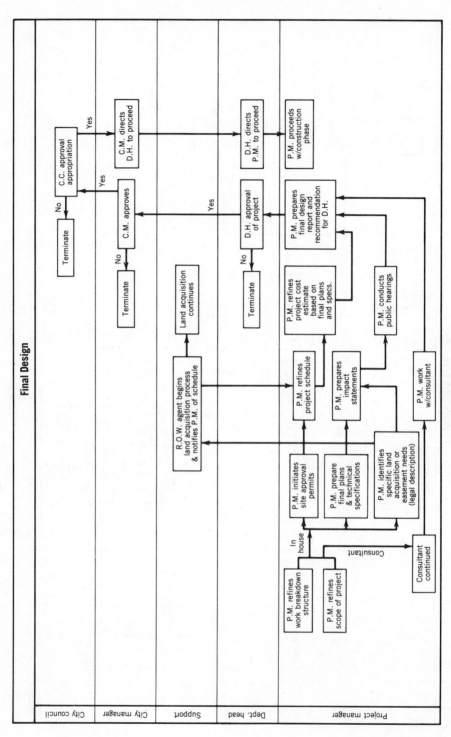

FIGURE 8.4. Final design.

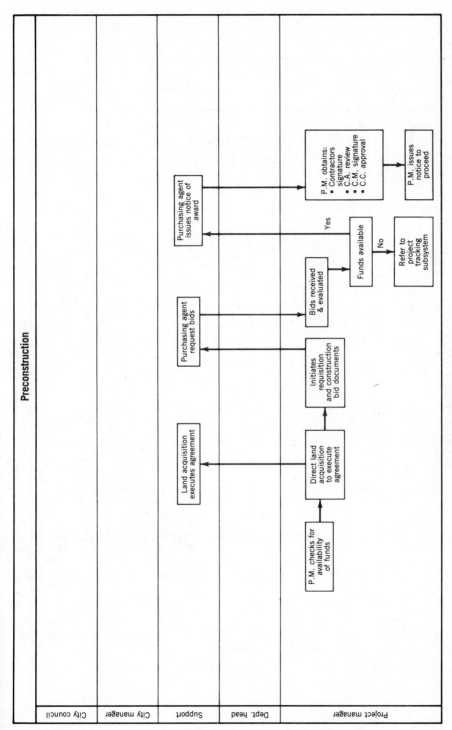

FIGURE 8.5. Preconstruction.

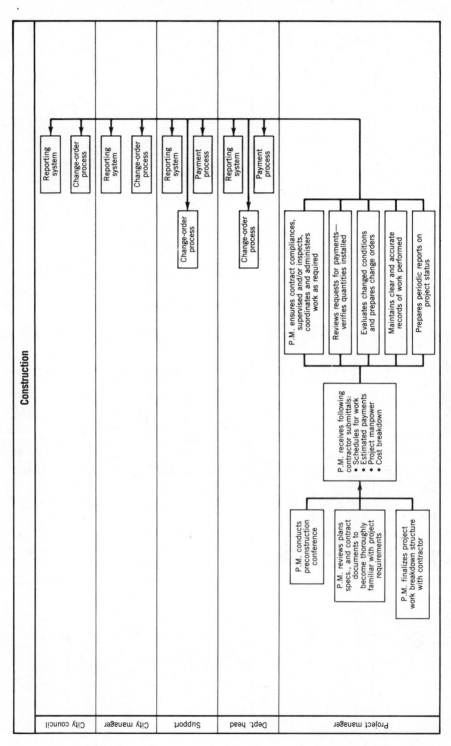

FIGURE 8.6. Construction.

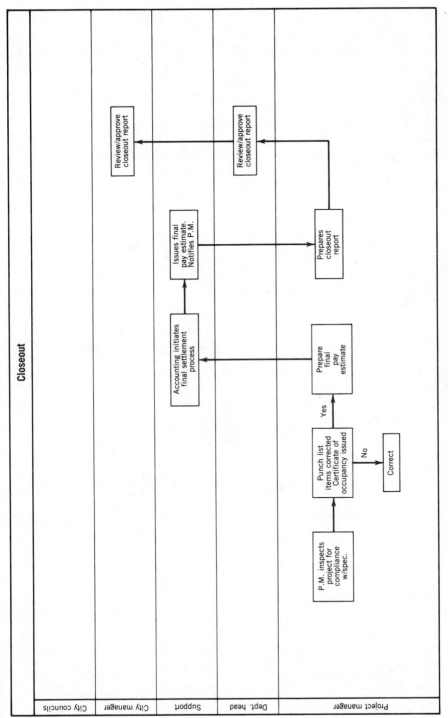

FIGURE 8.7. Close-out.

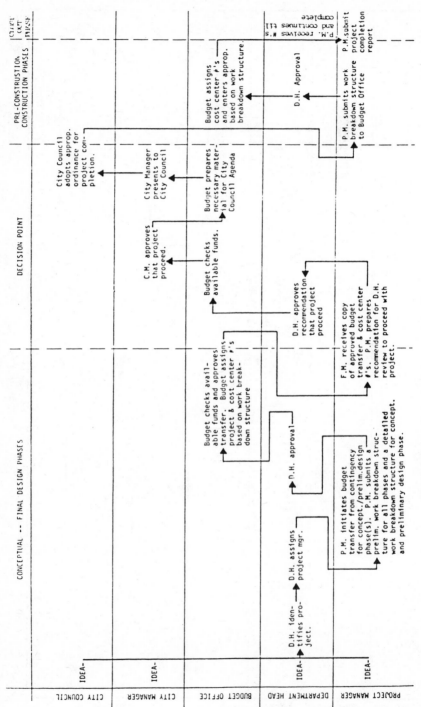

FIGURE 8.8. Approvals in project management process.

216

program evaluation and review technique). While useful and interesting, such techniques are not the most important ingredients to success. Project management is too complex to be governed by simple formulations.

In the publication previously cited reporting on the factors necessary for project success (5), Boston College tried to relate the complexity of project management to the factors explaining success. The report concluded that the factors could be grouped into three categories: those that were linearly related to success or failure, those that tended to improve the chances for success, and those that tended to cause failure. It found that the presence of negative factors would tend to cause failure, but their absence would not guarantee success. Neither would the presence of positive factors guarantee that failure would not occur. As a result, the team concluded that it was necessary both to encourage success and to prevent failure.

As examples of the factors the team examined, major groups included the project manager and the project team, the parent organization, the client organization, the managerial techniques used, and the preconditions. The project manager variables included commitment to goals, authority, skill, and others. The project team variables included sense of mission and commitment to goals. There were many other logical factors. Because of the importance of these factors, they are shown in Table 8.1.

Implications for the project organization, the parent organization, and the client organization are given in Table 8.2. These allow the manager to look at some of the changes that could be considered in his or her organization.

TABLE 8.1. Major Variables Affecting Success of Projects

Project manager
  Commitment to project goals
  Authority and influence
  Task orientation
  Administrative skill
  Human skill
  Technical skill
  Early and continued involvement
  Participation in goal setting and criteria specification

Project team
  Capabilities
  Commitment to goals
  Participation in
    Goal setting
    Setting budgets and schedules
    Major decision-making
    Problem solving
  Early and continued involvement

(Table continues on p. 218)

TABLE 8.1. (Continued)

Project team (continued)
"Sense of mission"
Structural flexibility

Parent organization
Coordinative efforts
Structural flexibility
Effective strategic planning
Rapport maintenance
Adaptability to change
Past experience
External buffering
Prompt and accurate communications
Enthusiasm
Project contributes to parent capabilities

Client Organization
Coordinative efforts
Rapport maintenance
Establishment of reasonable and specific goals and criteria
Change procedures
Prompt and accurate communication
Commitment
Lack of red tape
Prompt decisionmaking
Influence and authority of contact

Managerial Techniques
Judicious, and adequate but not excessive use of planning, control, and communication systems

Preconditions
Clearly established specifications and design
Realistic schedules
Realistic cost estimates
Avoidance of buy-ins
Avoidance of over-optimism
Favorable interface with legal-political environment
Conceptual clarity

From Reference 5.

TABLE 8.2. How Organizations Affect Project Success

Project Organization/Project Manager
Insist upon the right to select his own key project team members.
Select key project team members with proven track records in their area of expertise.
Develop commitment and a sense of mission from the outset among project team members.

TABLE 8.2. *(Continued)*

Seek sufficient authority and a projectized form of organizational structure.

Coordinate frequently and constantly reinforce good relationships with the client, the parent, and the team.

Seek to enhance the public's image of the project.

Call upon key project team members to assist in decisionmaking and problem solving.

Develop realistic cost, schedule, and technical performance estimates and goals.

Develop back-up strategies and systems in anticipation of potential problems.

Develop an appropriate, yet flexible and flat, project team organizaion structure.

Seek to maximize influence over people and key decisions even though formal authority may not be sufficient.

Employ a workable and candid set of project planning and control tools.

Avoid preoccupation with, or overreliance upon, one type of project control tool.

Constantly stress the importance of meeting cost, schedule, and technical performance goals.

Generally, give highest priority to achieving the technical performance mission or function to be performed by the project end-item.

Keep changes under control

Seek to find ways of assuring the job security of effective project team members.

Plan for an orderly phase-out of the project.

Client Organization/Client Contact

Encourage openness and honesty from the start from all participants.

Create an atmosphere that encourages healthy, but not cutthroat, competition or "liars" contests.

Plan for adequate funding to complete the entire project.

Develop clear understandings of the relative importance of cost, schedule, and technical performance goals.

Seek to minimize direct public participation and involvement.

Develop short and informal lines of communication and flat organizational structures.

Delegate sufficient authority to the principal client contact and let him promptly approve or reject important project decisions.

Reject "buy-ins."

Make prompt decisions regarding contract award or go-ahead.

Develop close, but not meddling, working relationships with project participants.

Avoid arm's-length relationships.

Avoid excessive reporting schemes.

Make prompt decisions regarding changes.

Parent Organization/Principal Contact

Select, at an early point, a project manager with a proven track record of technical skills, human skills, and administrative skills (in that order) to lead the project team.

Develop clear and workable guidelines for the project manager.

Delegate sufficient authority to the project manager and let him make important decisions in conjunction with his key project team members.

Demonstrate enthusiasm for the commitment to the project and the project team.

Develop and maintain short and informal lines of communication with the project manager.

(Table continues on p. 220)

TABLE 8.2. (*Continued*)

Parent Organization/Principal Contact (continued)

Avoid excessive pressure on the project manager to win the contract.

Avoid arbitrarily slashing or ballooning the project team's cost estimates.

Avoid "buy-ins."

Develop close, but not meddling, working relationships with the principal client contact and the project manager.

From Reference 5.

8.3. THE ENGINEERING FUNCTION

Most of the organization charts presented earlier in the text show an engineering department as one of the staff functions. Not much has been said about the roles of that department; yet everyone is familiar with the engineering function as it is carried out in, for example, the city engineer's office, or, in the military, the post engineer's office. Actually these terms are more or less synonyms for what we understand to be the roles of public works directors; the roles that are reserved for the engineering staff function are more distinct.

Korbitz, writing in the 1976 ICMA "green book" about public works management, refers to an "engineering function." The activities described are surveys, studies, and investigations; capital improvement program development; field survey work; planning, design, and cost estimating for construction; construction contracting and contract administration; construction inspection and supervision; preparation of maps, records, construction records and reports, and critical path method and PERT charts; and assistance in maintenance, repair, and reconstruction work (8).

When the engineering function was reviewed in the successor volume to the green book, Martin listed five processes that fall into the category of engineering and contract management:

- The planning and design process
- Construction management, including inspection
- Surveys, maps, and records
- Engineering management and private activity
- Retention and use of consultants

"Private activity" in this context means interfacing with developers, consultants, and other private-sector participants in the plan-design-build process (9).

From these two delineations of the engineering function, the picture is clear: there is a well-defined set of engineering activities that are necessary to support infrastructure management, and they revolve around managing the construction process.

Regarding infrastructure management, there seem to be three principal roles of the engineering function: keeping the standards for infrastructure development, maintaining the quality of construction, and keeping records. Each of these tasks, while simply stated, is critical in infrastructure management.

Not only is keeping standards for development important to initiate at least the chance for quality development of facilities, but it is one of the greatest determinants of cost of infrastructure. The city engineer has not only the obligation to make sure the quality is there, but also the responsibility to make sure that the cost is kept down. Political heat from the private sector is usually, but not always, sufficient to ensure that the cost minimization aspect is maintained.

Maintaining the quality of construction is, of course, critical to making sure that investments in infrastructure pay off. It is very difficult to imagine a more serious breach of the public trust than for a responsible public works official to accept shoddy construction work or to engage in corrupt practices; yet this is one of the real problems facing the infrastructure field.

The final task, keeping records, is important to the development of an effective decision support system, as discussed in Chapter 4. The geo-data base described there, one where common mapping is used for all public utilities, would be the responsibility of the engineering office. All of the as-built drawings, the official standards, the surveys, the reports, the plans, and the related data would be located in this office.

8.4. CONSULTING ENGINEERING SERVICES

One of the tasks of the engineering function is to retain and supervise consulting engineers. Of course, some engineering design work is done in-house, but a great deal of it is contracted out, especially capital facilities design.

The consulting engineering profession is quick to point out that engineering costs less than 1 percent of the life cycle cost of projects. This statement is intended to underline the assertion that it pays to get good engineering. One way to do that is to use the best consulting engineers.

There are advantages both to doing work in-house and to using consultants. With in-house work you can maintain better control over details and sometimes reduce costs. With consultants you can get the best engineers you can afford, and use them only when needed. Sometimes you can save money by using consultants rather than in-house staff. This has to be evaluated on a case-by-case basis.

The Consulting Profession

There are over 10,000 consulting engineering firms in the United States. On the state level, they are organized into consulting engineer councils; nationally they are organized through the American Consulting Engineers Council (ACEC), with headquarters in Washington, D.C. However, when speaking of consultants, there are far more professionals involved than only these consulting engineers—there are also management consultants, financial consultants, independent practitioners, lawyers, and others. They are all available to provide consulting services to infrastructure organizations.

In the case of infrastructure, however, the main group involved is the consulting engineering profession. This group is largely responsible for the planning, design, and supervision of construction of the nation's infrastructure.

The role of engineering consultants is to assist client organizations in all the tasks needed to manage the infrastructure. This can include everything from design of facilities to troubleshooting. The American Society of Civil Engineers, in its manual for the practice of consulting engineering, spells out the following typical services: doing feasibility studies, performing field investigations and data collection, assessing environmental impact, preparing reports and impact statements, providing design services, preparing specifications, securing bids, observing construction, testing and evaluating, and making appraisals (10).

The use of consultants involves selection, contracting, management, and compensation. These are responsibilities of the infrastructure owner, normally an infrastructure management organization.

Selection of consultants is usually accomplished through what is known as "competitive negotiation." This procedure, advocated by ACEC and in compliance with the restraint of trade requirements of the federal government, provides an alternative to the lowest-bid process. This is desirable since the lowest-bid process is not seen to lead to the highest-quality work or the best arrangement for either client or engineer. The process of competitive negotiation has superseded the earlier practice of merely selecting firms without a structured decision process.

Competitive negotiation involves the following process. The client asks engineering firms to submit qualifications and performance records for evaluation. Factors to be considered in reducing the list to a "short list" are technical qualifications, experience in similar projects, reputation, timeliness, mobility and workload, and financial references. Those firms making the short list are asked to make brief presentations explaining their concepts of the work to be done. This allows the firms to express their creativity in meeting the client's needs. On the basis of these presentations the client ranks the firms and begins a negotiation with the top one. The negotiation involves the scope of work and other contract provisions, and finally, the compensation. If the negotiations are successful, the contract is drawn. If not, the next firm on the list can be asked to begin negotiations (11).

The request for proposals (RFP) used in the selection of consultants is a work of art. The client uses the RFP development process to clarify what is wanted, and the request provides a clear statement to the engineer and all others involved as to the scope and objectives of the project.

The preparation of proposals for the engineering work is also a work of art. The engineer uses the proposal development process as a way to express creative ideas about the solution of the client's problem, as well as a way to present credentials.

The management of consultant activities begins with the preparation of the contract that specifies the scope of work and all items that are required for delivery. Also, regular reports are required from the consultant. Frequent meetings are needed to maintain coordination. The consultant should be viewed as an extension of the client's staff in one sense, and as an independent contractor needing direction in another sense.

8.5. CONSTRUCTION CONTRACTING, INSPECTION, AND QUALITY CONTROL

Once a project has been designed and the construction phase is entered, the legal aspects of construction take on a high level of importance. The legal instruments of construction contracting are well known in the profession, generally consisting of the following elements:

- Bid advertisement
- Information for bidders
- General and special provisions
- Measurement and payment information
- Proposal form
- Notice of award
- Notice to proceed
- Change-order information
- Form of contract
- Detailed specifications
- Contract plans and drawings
- Bonds, insurance certificates, and other certifications

The adversarial environment of construction today demands that all parties be as careful as possible not to get into a situation requiring litigation, especially where liability is concerned. The high cost and problems of getting liability insurance today has greatly complicated the design-construction process.

The role of the infrastructure manager and the engineer in inspection of constructed work is obviously important in determining the final quality of work. Inspection involves determining that the work is completed according to the plans and specifications, and is a very responsible activity. The American Society of Civil Engineers has begun to emphasize the maintenance of quality in construction as part of the society's leadership charge in the construction industry. The president in 1986, Daniel Barge, a consultant from Tennessee, continued the emphasis his predecessor placed on quality in the constructed environment. This will result in the production of an ASCE manual, *Manual of Professional Practice for Quality in the Constructed Project.* This manual was in the final stages of review at the beginning of 1987.

EXERCISE

This exercise is to prepare a request for proposal to conduct a study of the street system for the Fort Collins city government.

As the public works manager, you are very concerned about the condition of the streets. This has been a political issue, and you want to get ahead of anticipated problems by getting an effective management system implemented.

The following are some details of what the city needs. You can use your discretion to add items to the job as you see fit.

The city of Fort Collins desires to have a complete assessment of the condition of its street system. Proposals will be sought from qualified firms to collect data; analyze condition; estimate costs for repair, replacement, and rehabilitation; and prepare a report for the use of the Transportation Department, the City Manager, and the Fort Collins City Council. The report will be, in effect, a "needs assessment" for the Fort Collins street system. The firm chosen will also be required to design and furnish a computerized data base management system for the streets inventory and condition.

In preparing proposals each firm will be expected to prepare preliminary estimates of the number and length of streets in the city with different classifications, and determine the procedure and level of effort needed to prepare an inventory of location, dimensions, and condition of the existing network of streets.

The following final work products are expected from the consulting firm that is selected: a plan drawing of the street network; a report showing the typical cross sections, the quantity of streets with different classifications, and condition indexes; estimates of the cost and optimal sequence for repair, rehabilitation, and replacement of the street system; and a computerized data base of the street system formatted using a software and hardware system compatible with the city's existing computer facilities and acceptable to the city.

Proposals will be due no later than 5 P.M. on December 31, 19XX. They must be delivered to the office of the public works director in City Hall. They should contain the following information: background and understanding of the work, procedure to be followed in conducting of the work, procedure to be followed in conducting the study, time and effort required, project schedule, special problems expected, qualifications of the firm, and estimated cost. It is expected that a fixed-cost contract will be negotiated with the successful firm.

REFERENCES

1. Moavenzadeh, Fred, "Construction's high-technology revolution," *Technology Review*, October 1985.

2. Tenah, Kwaki, A., *The Construction Management Process*, Reston Publishing Co., Reston, Va., 1985.

3. World Bank and International Finance Corporation, descriptive brochure, Washington, D.C., undated.

4. U.S. General Accounting Office, Greater Use of Value Engineering Has the Potential to Save the Department of Transportation Millions in Construction Costs, Washington, D.C., November 2, 1984.

5. Murphy, David C., Bruce N. Baker, and Dalmar Fisher, Determinants of Project Success, Boston College, School of Management, Report for NASA, NTIS # N74-30392, 1974.

6. Colorado State University, A Summary Report of the Infrastructure Rebuilding Management Challenge Conference, held in Colorado Springs, February 1984, Scott Condreay and Timothy McCune, codirectors

7. City of Fort Collins, *Capital Project Management Control System Manual*, January 1981.

8. Korbitz, William E., ed., Urban Public Works Administration, International City Management Association, Washington, D.C., 1976.

9. Martin, James L., in *Management of Local Public Works*, Sam M. Cristofano and William S. Foster, eds., International City Management Association, Washington, D.C., 1986.

10. American Society of Civil Engineers, Consulting Engineering, New York, 1981.

11. American Consulting Engineers Council, The Bridge Is Ours!, Washington, D.C., 1984.

CHAPTER NINE

OPERATION AND MAINTENANCE STRATEGIES

Focusing on the needed operational strategy of any business or organization helps to provide the right perspective on the purpose of the organization and to clarify objectives. In effect, when the organization is operating, it is fulfilling its basic mission. In public service organizations this is an important observation due to the need to constantly guard against straying from fundamental purpose and becoming ossified with bureaucracy.

More emphasis on operations and maintenance of infrastructure is necessary if the infrastructure problem is to be overcome. While it is true that the financial problems are severe, they will always be, since there is never enough money to fulfill all investment needs. The way to overcome the problem is through improved operations, both by getting the most out of existing facilities and by calling attention to the *real* need for new and continuous investment. The latter capability arises from the introduction of improved information systems and accounting practices that result from improved operations.

The infrastructure categories identified in Chapter 1 all need similar operational and maintenance activities. This is true from the *functional* viewpoint; that is, the basic functions required of operations and of maintenance are the same. This can be seen from the organizational chart shown in Figure 9.1, featuring operations and maintenance. Operations is the basic function of the organization, and maintenance supports operations.

Operations management in an organization is, in effect, the last and final phase of problem solving and planning. The planning process is concerned with deciding what to do, and operations is concerned with doing it. Figure 9.2 illustrates this. The planning phase proceeds from problem identification through the planning process (see Chapter 3), through implementation, to the final and

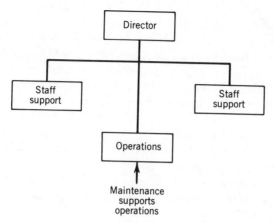

FIGURE 9.1. Simple organization showing role of maintenance to support operations.

permanent operations phase. Although it is called "final," that does not mean that operations is not dynamic and changing; on the contrary, continuous monitoring and improvement are necessary.

Success in operations is critical to overall success in the purpose of the service involved, whether it is transportation, water, waste management, energy, or building systems. The purpose of entire disciplines such as industrial engineering is largely to improve operations. The introduction of the field of "operations research" was intended to improve operations, initially in the military area, but later in industry as well.

9.1. MODEL OF OPERATIONS MANAGEMENT

Competent managers have in their minds a general model of operations (including maintenance). They ask if the system and the staff are organized properly; whether the work, all of it, is planned thoroughly, at all levels; and whether the operation is adequately controlled. To ensure that it is, two checks need to be continuously made. The first is a check to see whether the product or the service is being adequately delivered, including timing, quantity, and quality of service. The second is a check to see whether the condition of the facilities is acceptable. All of these topics are discussed in this chapter.

One way to classify operations management would be to use an industrial classification: production management, facilities management, maintenance

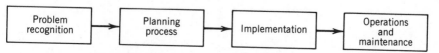

FIGURE 9.2. Problem-solving/planning process.

management, and information management. Classifications such as these, and specific studies of operations as a science, are available from business texts such as the one cited in Reference 1. These activities would then be keyed to the organization chart. The concept of operations management, as understood in this chapter, includes all of these. Two generic management systems, operations management and maintenance management, are used to organize the concepts. In this section, the operations management system is described. Maintenance management follows in the next section. Facilities management is considered as a higher-level term that includes infrastructure operations and maintenance. Information management was discussed in Chapter 4.

Operations management is concerned with the work activities necessary to achieve the purpose of the organization. These activities depend on the specific service involved, the design of the system to supply the service, and the unique features of the management organization.

But operations involves more than performance checking and assessment of facility condition; it involves the functioning of the entire organization. The following seem to be the most important areas needing attention for a well-functioning organization:

1. A clearly stated organizational purpose
2. A valid and effective organizational structure, with good communications and information flow
3. Operational missions and objectives for the subunits of the organization
4. Job descriptions for the jobs down through the hierarchy of the organization
5. Plans and production targets for the subunits of the organization
6. A work management system
7. A method for checking performance including all of the appropriate parameters for the system at hand
8. Procedures for making changes when necessary

These features are part of the "operations management system," and are illustrated in Figure 9.3.

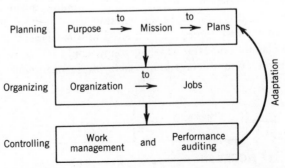

FIGURE 9.3. Elements of operations management system.

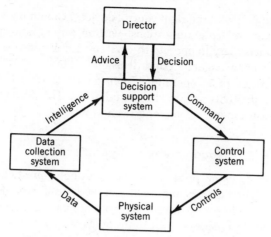

FIGURE 9.4. Operations control system with C³I.

The compilation of items in the operations management system is important, as may be seen from the following:

- The purpose establishes the reason for the operation.
- The organization establishes the capability to perform.
- The mission sets the stage for specific performance.
- The jobs structure ensures that the human resource is ready.
- The plans organize the individual and subunit work.
- The work management system provides for getting the most out of the system.
- The performance audits allow for continuous checking of the output of the organization.
- The adaptation capability enables changes when needed.

Control of Operations

The control of operations can be viewed as a generalized process such as is shown in Figure 9.4. In this figure we see that there is a system to be operated with certain objectives. Examples could be a transportation system, a water system, a building system, or a solid-waste management system. The system is controlled by the control system and monitored by the data collection system, and decisions are made in the headquarters, with the aid of the decision support system.

The essence of the items shown in Figure 9.4 is captured in the military term, "command, control, communications, and intelligence," or C³I. Each of these crucial elements of the operations system is shown in Figure 9.4. Command provides for decision making and the issuance of control orders. Control means the capability to actually control the system, such as through a functioning organization equipped with the right control devices. Communications includes all of the data flow, telecommunications, written orders, and other forms of communications necessary to operate the system. Intelligence is the collection of data necessary for management and decision making.

The whole purpose of an operations management system is to provide for the maximum productivity within the organization. This leads to concepts of performance measurement, effectiveness, and efficiency.

Productivity of Operations

Operations has its focus on production. The pertinent questions are: What is produced, what is the quantity and quality of the output, what is the cost, and what are the external impacts? These questions are easier to identify when the operation is a private business and the products are sold in the marketplace; but when the product is a public service, it has to be analyzed using different approaches that center on defining the service levels needed and supplied. This is one of the most important skills in public works management: to be able to discern and deliver the right levels of service within the allowable budget.

Production management activities depend on the product of the organization. In the case of water or wastewater treatment, the parallel with industrial production is clear: there is a product of treated water. In the case of transportation, the product is not so easy to see, but it is still there: travel and person-trips. In the case of buildings, the product is to provide the space needed for other operations. Whatever the service, there is a product which can be identified and measured.

It is helpful to think of the output of an organization in terms of production. What is the product of all the work? Water foremen have said proudly, "We make water." A road crew could say it provides safe and effective roads. But what about the staff workers? Do they have a clear idea of what they produce? Are there workers in the organization that have no clear purpose? These questions need to be asked.

Production management is still a matter of measuring the output of an organization as a function of the input. Scientific management can be applied to infrastructure organizations as well as to manufacturing. The challenge of measuring the output becomes the difficult part to achieve, and for this reason measuring the output of public organizations has received attention from management researchers.

The "productivity function" comes from economics and illustrates the concept of measuring outputs as functions of inputs. It shows how the output varies with inputs and represents a tool for analysis of productivity. The function, illustrated in Figure 9.5, represents the highest output for a particular input, or the "technological frontier" for a given technology. As an example, for solid-waste collection, the best that could be done with certain kinds of collection trucks and techniques might follow a certain production function. If the technol-

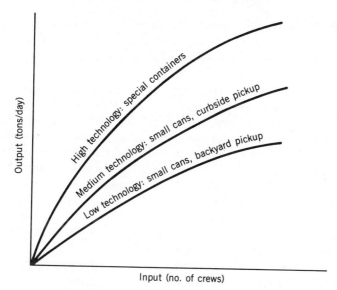

FIGURE 9.5. Illustration of production function.

ogy was improved, as with a larger storage device and some lifting equipment on the trucks, then the production function would increase.

The concept of "productivity measurement" is used to refer to the need to make sure we achieve the greatest effectiveness as a result of the investments we make in a particular service. This means we must know how to measure "effectiveness." Effectiveness is a self-explanatory term which includes, but is not the same as, the term "efficiency." Effectiveness refers to doing the right thing well, while efficiency refers to the ratio of output to input. Unless the outputs are geared toward the right objective, an efficiency measure is not helpful. The difference is illustrated by the story of two truck drivers. One wakes from a nap and asks, "Where are we?" The other responds, "I have good news and bad news. The good news is, we're making great time. The bad news is, we're lost!"

Productivity measurement for infrastructure categories would generally make use of parameters such as cost per 1000 gallons of water delivered, tons of solid waste collected per work-hour expended, cost per mile of street cleaned, cost to maintain a certain amount of the street network, and related parameters.

In operations management the measurement of productivity is appropriate due to the need for operations to be as effective as possible. However, it is often the planning and organization of the service that determines the effectiveness of operations rather than the direct work itself. For this reason the subject of "effectiveness measurement" has been discussed in the chapter on planning and performance evaluation rather than this chapter covering operations.

Concerning operations, the same questions apply as in planning and evaluation. What are the goals of the operation? How can the success of the enterprise be measured? What are the numerical parameters? These are certainly appropriate questions, but they cannot be easily applied to infrastructure programs for many of the same reasons that they are resisted in private industry.

The concept of measuring productivity arose as part of "scientific management," brought into the industrial world in the late nineteenth and early twentieth century by persons such as Frederick Taylor and Frank and Lillian Gilbreth. They were the early developers of the discipline, which led to industrial engineering, the branch of engineering concerned with measuring work and making it more efficient. The discipline of industrial psychology is concerned with many of the same concepts since so many human factors are involved.

The potential attractiveness of being able to measure productivity outweighs the difficulties and resistance that are certain to be encountered, so we continue examining the concept. The discussion in Chapter 3 concerned with planning and evaluation covers the relevant parameters, and Appendix A contains suggested parameters for certain infrastructure categories.

In Appendix A the details of effectiveness measurement for several categories of infrastructure are described. These include solid-waste collection, solid-waste disposal, public transit, general transportation, water supply service, wastewater treatment and sewerage, storm drainage, and water quality management (2). The approach taken recognizes the multiple objective character of effectiveness measurement, and begins for each service with an overall objective. Then it proceeds to a list of objectives, each objective of which has a quality characteristic, specific measure, and data collection procedures.

An example of this process can be seen from Appendix A, as in the case of public transit. The overall objective is to "maintain a public transit system that provides *access* to places where citizens want to go in a *safe, quick, comfortable, pleasant, convenient* and *reliable* manner, and that helps minimize pollution, congestion, and energy consumption in the community." Each of the emphasized characteristics becomes an objective, with, for example, quickness being measured by rapid movement as an objective. The main quality characteristic of this is travel times, measured by actual travel times from the schedules. To keep track of the times requires data of actual schedule compliance.

Each of the services can be described in a similar manner as shown in Appendix A, and as can be worked out by planners.

Measuring productivity is one of the main bones of contention between management and labor. In the beginning days of scientific management the contention was between owners and labor, and this led to the rise of some of the labor movements, to provide for greater quality of work for laborers and less exploitation by the owners. In a book by Vladimir Lenin, one of the fathers of Soviet communism, Lenin referred to the measurement of work in the scientific sense as inhuman, treating workers as animals. These facts bear on the reasons that we still see resistance in implementing programs such as effectiveness measurement in local government.

However we approach production management, we must get back to the concept of providing the required levels of service for the least cost to the public. This introduces the concept of productivity management as a tool for measuring how well the organization is doing. Productivity as a concept arises from the word "production," and really means the quality of "being productive." The production function is a concept from economics that is central to measuring productivity. It measures the output resulting from the factors of input such as work units, materials, energy, and cost, and is defined for each level of technical achievement or knowledge. For example, if you have small solid-waste collection trucks, you can achieve a certain production function which relates work-hours to tons collected. With a higher level of technology represented by larger trucks with a transfer station, you will have a different relationship.

Quality Control

"Quality control" (QC) is a term that is really becoming important to U.S. industry, since we are learning that high product quality is not only the best way to be competitive; it is essential. Industry in the United States is learning that the best way to have high quality is to do things right the first time. There is a lot of discussion about quality control today, and there will continue to be emphasis on it in urban water organizations as well.

Quality control is an operational concern. It means to assure that the quality of the product, whatever it is, is within acceptable limits, as defined for that particular product. Sometimes the words "quality assurance" are used in place of QC.

Again, the concept of production operations offers a place to find ideas about quality control. In Reference 1, Greene devotes most of two chapters to the subject, with one of them covering the statistical aspects of QC alone. His discussion of the internal organization for quality control offers a test as to whether our organizations are adequate to make the checks. The parts of the organization Greene identifies are inspection, administration and record keeping, quality control engineering, and the gauge room.

QC functions have familiar rings relative to the water or wastewater treatment functions, since they have become necessary to meet regulatory requirements. The principles can be applied even more vigorously than the regulations require, however, and there are also other opportunities for the application of the principles. As an example, if the goal of the water utility is to deliver service that involves water of a certain quality, with certain pressures, during certain time periods, how can it make sure that it does? It would need an inspection program, a quality control sampling effort, laboratory work, and record keeping.

Another example of QC concerns would have to do with the stormwater department. If the goal is to prevent a certain level of flooding, how do we know we are being successful? The normal indicator might be the absence of complaints, but the organization could plan and execute an inspection program.

There are many aspects to QC programs that can be considered by the managers of water organizations. Instituting quality control can be considered as taking the offensive, rather than always being on the defensive.

Operations Audits

It is necessary to have continuous audits of the performance of the infrastructure system. To gain a perspective on how to improve operations in complex operating environments, a technique called "diagnostic analysis," or "diagnostic evaluation," has been effective in different settings. It represents a general approach to studying performance improvement. In a sense, it is a comprehensive performance audit.

An EPA report recommends a diagnostic analysis of the performance of entire wastewater utilities to be carried out in four phases (3). This procedure is applicable to other infrastructure categories as well.

The first phase is a preliminary investigation which identifies problems and sets the stage for the remainder of the study. In effect, this is the problem identification phase of the planning and management process.

The second phase consists of an on-site evaluation of the general management, the support services, and the operations and maintenance activities of the utility. The evaluation of the adequacy of the general management would consider how the utility was organized, directed, and operated at the overall level. The support services that would be evaluated would consist of the finance, engineering, purchasing, personnel, and information services. The operations and maintenance, or facilities function, would be studied for adequacy in the following areas: policies and procedures, organization, staffing and training, planning, and management controls.

The third phase is the one in which the individual findings are compiled into an overall utility evaluation, and evaluations are made of problems and potential solutions. The final phase is the one in which the solutions that were identified are reviewed with the management of the utility, and implementation plans are developed.

The general applicability of the diagnostic analysis approach can be verified by its use in other approaches. Colorado State University has developed a "diagnostic analysis" approach to improving operations in the complex social-political arena of irrigation systems in developing countries (4). The developers stress the importance of interdisciplinary teams and the involvement of the farmer in the analysis. Again this is a specialized approach to the performance audit.

9.2. MODEL OF MAINTENANCE MANAGEMENT

Maintenance is such an important topic that it ordinarily receives equal billing with operations—"operations and maintenance," or O&M. In recent years managers have been saying that O&M should stand for more than operations and maintenance and be extended to the broader concept of operations and management. This is a valid concern since management should be all-encompassing, and not stop with "operations and maintenance."

Maintenance must be supplied at different levels, and providing the proper levels has implications for both the operating and capital budgets. Preventive maintenance is intended to head off problems. This is the most common maintenance operation in organizations. Corrective maintenance has both the minor and major aspects, depending on the extent of the correction needed. Corrective maintenance involves repair, replacement, and rehabilitation of facilities, sometimes called the "three R's."

Operations and maintenance need to be coordinated activities. It is true that maintenance is a subordinate activity, intended to support operations; but if maintenance is not successfully carried out, then operations will eventually fail or at least be less than fully successful.

Maintenance is linked with operations in the way shown in Figure 9.6, where operations involves continuous checking to ascertain whether maintenance is needed. Also, scheduled maintenance proceeds at all times.

Operations requires a continuing check to determine whether the system is working as it should. Another check is built into the maintenance function to enable the scheduling of repair work. The definition of maintenance should be expanded to include condition assessment, inventory, and maintenance management.

In effect, there are four separate maintenance-related functions: condition assessment, inventory, preventive maintenance, and corrective maintenance. The latter is sometimes called "major and corrective maintenance" to stress the major nature of some of the corrective actions. The condition assessment activity is a linkage between the operation and the maintenance function, and illustrates why the two functions must be unified. If the condition starts to worsen, the operation will be affected, and it will be time to schedule repairs and maintenance.

The result of the inventory and condition assessment functions is a continuous determination of the location and condition of the system component of interest,

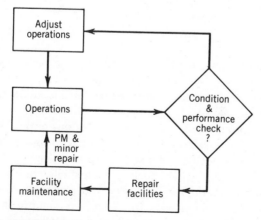

FIGURE 9.6. Linkage of operations and maintenance.

these two pieces of information being taken together. There should always be an answer to the question, "Is the system OK?" If the answer is yes, the operations and surveillance continues. If not, we must enter the corrective and major maintenance activity. The need for an inventory seems obvious for valuable equipment, but we are just now starting to think about the need for inventories of infrastructure systems.

Corrective maintenance requires a decision: is the deficiency serious enough to warrant entering the planning- programming-budgeting activity, leading to a capital request, or is it minor enough to go ahead and take care of? If the problem is major, the PPB activity incorporates information about new standards and growth forecasts to lead to decisions about rehabilitation and/or replacement. The planning part of PPB also yields information to be used in the needs assessment process, which is the linkage between the major maintenance program and the capital budgeting program. Due to this linkage, it seems appropriate to have the same planning staff do the planning work for rehabilitation work as well as new facilities.

The sequence of activities that leads to a decision about minor or major corrective actions also explains the differences between the three R's: repair, rehabilitation, and replacement. These activities are part of a spectrum that covers the range from routine operating budget activities to major capital budget activities. This is an important distinction for management, since the operating budget should have enough funds for routine and important repairs, and there should be sufficient funds in the capital budget for major rehabilitation, without excessive deferral. The dividing point is somewhere between repair and re-habilitation, but each manager and organization must decide this individually.

The concept of the "maintenance management system" (MMS) has arisen in recent years as an attempt to bring together the disparate concepts of maintenance activities into a holistic approach to caring for a system. In effect, it is the "systems approach" applied to maintenance. There are some consulting firms that specialize in maintenance management, and conventional consulting firms have also gained recent experience in the concept.

An MMS is, in effect, a program for making sure that overall maintenance is managed adequately. It involves all the tasks of management: planning, organizing, and controlling, and it requires an effective decision support system. The MMS will include condition assessment, preventive maintenance, and corrective and major maintenance, and the decision support system will provide the information and data needed for these activities.

In studying maintenance, we find many variations of the MMS. There are not many comprehensive references, but those that do appear are usually based on maintenance in a specified industry. References are found again in the literature of industrial production, such as the text cited in Reference 5, which is based on experience in the steel industry. Generally, references such as this contain the same management principles that are found in infrastructure ex-periences: information systems, work orders, preventive and corrective main-tenance, and management of maintenance as a significant support activity of production. The same principles have been found in several references published in current journals. One that specifies procedures for vehicle maintenance refers to the importance of the maintenance management information system (6). Another refers to the need to have valid condition assessment data to develop a management system for roof maintenance (7). Another discusses the advantages of contracting out highway maintenance (8). All of these are current references, published to report interesting and new information to the public works profession.

The principles of developing maintenance systems are no secret in industrial and public works organizations. Rather, the lack of application of known principles has been the problem. This is the general conclusion of a study by the Urban Institute, in which 62 cities were surveyed about their practices and experiences in capital stock management and maintenance (9). One of the most significant findings of the study related to maintenance management: that large improvements could be made by paying more attention to selecting effective maintenance strategies. The selection of these strategies involves systematic identification and analysis of the strategies that are available. These include the following, as well as combinations of them:

- Do crisis maintenance only.
- Maintain the worst facilities first.
- Perform opportunistic maintenance, when related work is scheduled.
- Use prespecified maintenance cycles.
- Repair those components with the highest risk of failure.
- Use preventive maintenance.
- Reduce the demand for wear and tear on the facility.
- Compare the economic advantages of maintenance strategies.

The generalized aspects of maintenance management systems are reflected in the apparently growing market for professional services in developing computerized MMSs. One consultant, Roy Jorgensen Associates, has literature that suggests the need to develop comprehensive MMSs that start with the basic operating procedures, and work toward a complete system that includes work activities, documentation of system inventory, establishment of service levels, development of performance standards, and calculations of work programs and budgets. The American Public Works Association has felt the need for and has written a set of guidelines for developing maintenance management systems (10). The Urban Institute study just cited found that when evaluation of maintenance strategies was done, it was usually by an outside consultant (9).

The MMS should constitute an integral part of the overall organizational management control system. As a minimum, it will have an inventory control system, with numbering and identification for all equipment and components, and a record system for maintenance scheduling and completions. This record system will include equipment data, the preventive maintenance (PM) record, the repair record, and a spare parts stock card.

Inventory and Condition Assessment

The inventory and condition assessment processes are critical to planning, maintenance management, and needs assessment. Although these processes make a lot of common sense in infrastructure management, they are often neglected in the haste of everyday operations.

The inventory activity is necessary to know where facilities are, what their initial characteristics were, and when they should receive attention. It is a combination of mapping and data about facilities as they were installed, along with the maintenance history. The inventory is the centerpiece of the information system used for all other records and for work scheduling and budgeting.

Condition assessment is necessary to know when something needs to be done in repair or replacement. It refers to periodic checks on performance and facility condition. An automobile shop that checks out a used car prior to sale is making a condition assessment. Most infrastructure management organizations do not have systematic condition assessment programs. For a very sensitive maintenance program such as for aircraft, it would be mandatory to have such a system. For infrastructure systems, failures are usually managed through redundant facilities, such as a parallel water pipe, and condition is noted more by the observance of failure or obvious deterioration.

To have an effective inventory requires a base map system and access to data about the components of the infrastructure. The condition assessment provides data on current condition ratings and other information that is needed to plan for maintenance activities. Table 9.1 shows some elements of the information system needed to support these activities (9).

The inventory, beginning with a map-based information system, is the organizing vehicle to get all information together into one place. Information professionals immediately see the advantages of having all information coordinated and in one system, and with current hardware and software it is becoming possible to achieve this goal. In fact, a professional society, the Urban and Regional Information Systems Association, based in Washington, D.C., is devoted to the development of information systems of this kind. The association's 1986 annual meeting featured sessions on geographic information systems, facilities

TABLE 9.1. Basic Elements of an Information System

Inventory	Contition/Performance
Unit, e.g., street segment, bridge, pipe	Current condition rating and date
Type of material	Percentage of capacity in use on average
Location	Repair history
Physical dimensions	Type of repair
Initial value/cost	Cost
Responsible department	Date
Funding source/eligibility	Trends in performance of key variables

From Reference 9.

management and mapping, land records, public works and utilities, and many related topics.

The inventory can be done at different levels of accuracy and sophistication. The beginning point is to have files with some maps and basic data so that the manager has some idea of where facilities are and how many there are. Some organizations lack even this basic information. The next level up is to have some sort of master file for information that allows the coordination of different data sets.

It is natural to think of computer-based inventory systems. The fact is, however, that a good manual system is needed before computers can be employed, and in many locations a manual system is all that will ever be needed.

When automated geographic inventories are possible, a new world is entered, and many larger and well-financed infrastructure management agencies are taking that step now. Two levels of geo-based inventories seem to be emerging. One is based on Census bureau mapping using the GBF-DIME map files. This stands for "geographic base file, dual independent map encoding technique" (11). This system provides census block maps for the 256 Standard Metropolitan Statistical Areas in the United States. It provides detail sufficient to make inventories, but not to locate facilities in the field. In one of the volumes of the Urban Institute study devoted to the assessment of capital stock condition, the writers include inventory as one of the requirements of condition assessment, and discuss applications to roads and streets, bridges, water, and sewer facilities. They report that Kansas City has utilized the DIME system of the U.S. Census Bureau to define the location of streets (12).

The second level is more accurate mapping at a local scale. When accuracy for locating facilities in the field is needed, then base maps using appropriate control are required. As an example, Houston has implemented a system called METROCOM, which provides detail at a map scale of 1 inch = 100 feet (13). In this system, which required over 300 work-years to develop, two stages were used. In the first, the GBF-DIME file was used for an initial inventory, and in the second, the mapping based on a scale of 1 inch = 100 feet was used to establish accuracy (within 2.5 feet for well-defined points).

The practical aspects of the inventory requirement can be seen emerging in the literature as it applies to the different infrastructure applications. In the case of water distribution systems, for example, Batts describes the system of mapping and distribution system records for Kalamazoo, Michigan (14).

Kalamazoo's manual system begins with the wall map which shows the entire system. It is available for different offices at a reduced size of 6 by 8 feet. Working maps at a scale of 1 inch = 50 feet show the details of each area and are available at legal size to be bound into books. These show material and size of main, work order numbers and dates of installation, distances from property lines, fire hydrant data, valves, service lines larger than 1¼ inch in diameter, and all locational data. These are updated annually.

Data on system components are maintained on old asset files and ledger cards showing data on initial installation. Valve and hydrant cards are now also maintained for recent installations. Service line information is recorded in the field when connections are made. Main break records are kept.

Kalamazoo's inventory system is over 100 years old. The city is considering a future computerized system, but no decisions have been made yet.

In the case of pavement inventories the same general approach is followed. The computerized pavement management system, "Paver," has demonstrated a practical approach to classifying and recording pavement systems for maintenance and repair (15).

In Paver, the inventory function is handled by breaking the pavement network into successive subdivisions of branches, sections, and sample units. The branch would be a separate, identifiable pavement unit such as an individual street. A section would be a division of a branch with a consistent history, such as common construction date and materials. A sample unit would be the smallest unit identified for the purpose of inspection. For asphalt it would be in the neighborhood of 2500 square feet, or about 100 feet for a 25-foot pavement. For concrete it would be about 20 slabs or a variation.

The information system for the pavement system can be set up manually or on a computer. The manual system, easiest to understand, is based on eight cards. The first lists all branches in the pavement network, the second each pavement section, the third the structural record of the pavement, the fourth the material properties of the section, the fifth the traffic record, the sixth the condition record, the seventh the branch maintenance and repair requirements, and the eighth the section maintenance and repair records.

Table 9.2 illustrates some aspects of inventory for four categories of infrastructure, as suggested by the Urban Institute team (9).

In effect, condition assessment is a process of measuring the physical condition of system components using objective criteria. According to O'Day and Neumann, the process should include such parameters as safety and structural integrity, capacity, quality of service, role, and age (16).

A good example of condition assessment can be seen in the Paver program, which helps in pavement management by scheduling maintenance according to optimally planned schedules, based on inspections and the assessment of condition. Another example of condition assessment is the current attention being paid in water utilities to unaccounted-for water and to breakages. Another would be the infiltration and inflow program applied to sewer systems. The National Bridge Inspection Program and the National Dam Safety Program are examples of condition assessment activities that were mandated nationally since safety became such an important factor.

Two aspects of condition assessment stand out in the management process. First, condition assessment is unique for each facility type, because each one has to be monitored in the way that it is configured and operates. Second, the condition assessment activity requires good record keeping, or an effective information system.

The Paver system relies on a pavement condition survey conducted by visual inspection. It recognizes that pavement condition is dependent on several factors: structural integrity and capacity, roughness and skid resistance, and rate of deterioration. A pavement condition index (PCI) has been developed to measure these parameters. On the basis of a scale of 0 to 100, the ratings for pavement are as follows:

PCI	Rating
85–100	Excellent
70–85	Very good
55–70	Good
40–55	Fair
25–40	Poor
10–25	Very poor
0–10	Failed

Procedures for calculating the PCI for both asphalt and concrete pavements are presented in Reference 15, and similar systems have been implemented by others. Commercially available pavement management systems are being implemented, and the APWA has offered assistance in pavement management to local governments.

The American Association of State Highway Transportation Officials (AASHTO) has developed a "present serviceability rating" (PSR) which allows for the correlation of condition index with the ability to provide service. The verbal ratings are shown correlated to the numerical ratings (12) in Table 9.3. To illustrate how America's highways rank on these scales, Figure 9.7 presents the shifts in condition from 1970 to 1978.

In the case of water systems, less formalized condition assessment procedures are in place. El Haj (17) found that while many papers have been written about the condition of water mains, little has been done to develop actual indexes of condition. He proposed that condition of water mains could be measured by three parametric groups: capacity, safety and structural integrity, and water quality. He analyzed the data available from the work by the Denver Water Department and concluded that the implementation of an information system for managing water mains would be cost-effective.

Other infrastructure categories are still evolving condition assessment techniques. This is one of the most important aspects of improving infrastructure management, since valid condition assessments will be the key to developing good planning and programming for maintenance and replacement.

Needs Assessments

One of the most difficult parts of planning and budgeting is knowing how much of a system to build. The problem is to determine what the "need" is. The

TABLE 9.2. Elements of a Condition Assessment System: Examples of Inventory Characteristics

	Streets	Bridges	Water	Sewer
Unit/location	Block segment or DIME^a coordinates	Bridge number and/or DIME coordinates or street termini	Pipe, hydrant, or valve and/or DIME coordinates or street address	Code for pipe, joint, or manhole and/or DIME coordinates or street address
Material	Flexible or rigid, and base characteristics	Material in deck, wearing surface, substructure and superstructure	Ductile or cast iron, or plastic. Type of lining, if present	Clay, brick or cast iron and type of lining, if present
Dimensions	Number and width of lanes, pavement depth, sq. yd., length	Number and width of spans, number and width of lanes, wearing surface thickness	Pipe diameter and length; valve size	Pipe diameter and length
Date of installation	Day/month/year	Day/month/year	Day/month/year	Day/month/year
Responsible agency	List	List	List	List
Funding eligibility	Eligibility for state or federal funding, and type eligible for $	Eligibility for state or federal funding, and type eligible for $	Eligibility for state or federal funding, and type eligible for $	Eligibility for state or federal funding, and type eligible for $
Initial cost				
Condition rating	Present serviceability or pounds per square inch	Sufficiency rating for deck, superstructure, and substructure	TV monitoring reports	TV monitoring reports

Performance indicators	—	—	Breaks per 1,000 ft., leaks per 1,000 ft., Hazen–Williams Coefficient	Breaks per 1,000 ft., stoppages, flooding, peak flow, average flow
Capacity/demand	Volume/capacity ratio, average daily traffic, % traffic heavy vehicles	Design loading, average daily traffic, % traffic heavy vehicles	Design/capacity/average capacity	Manning coefficient/average flow
Repair history (for each occasion)	Date of resurfacing or rehabilitation; seal coat, and type of material	Date of deck resurfacing, and type of material; date of major repainting; date and type of rehabilitation	Date of break leak, repair, relining; type of repair and material used	Date of patching, grouting, sealing; type of repair and material used
Repair cost	$	$	$	$
Other key variables	Type of bedding drainage; individual components of present serviceability rating	Condition of drainage system, joints, etc. Detour length to alternative bridge.	Type of soil and whether corrosive; proximity to other service lines, underground tunnels, etc.	Slope, bearing load characteristics, proximity to underground systems, depth underground, etc.

aDIME = Dual Independent Map Encoding, which provides a geographic base file with detail at the block, census tract, and metropolitanwide levels. From Reference 9.

TABLE 9.3. Pavement Condition Rating

PSR	Verbal Rating	Description
5	Very good:	Only new (or nearly new) pavements are likely to be smooth enough and sufficiently free of cracks and patches to qualify for this category. All pavements constructed or resurfaced during the last year should be rated very good.
4	Good:	Pavements in this category, although not quite as smooth as those described above, give a first-class ride and exhibit few, if any, visible signs of surface deterioration. Flexible pavements may be beginning to show evidence of rutting and fine random cracks. Rigid pavements may be beginning to show evidence of slight surface deterioration, such as minor cracks and spalling.
3	Fair:	The riding qualities of pavements in this category are noticeably inferior to those of new pavements, and may be barely tolerable for high-speed traffic. Surface defects of flexible pavements may include rutting, map cracking, and more or less extensive patching. Rigid pavements in this group may have a few joint failures, faulting and cracking, and some pumping.
2	Poor:	Pavements that have deteriorated to such an extent that they are in need of resurfacing.
1	Very poor:	Pavements which are in an extremely deteriorated condition and may even need complete reconstruction.
0		

Source: Federal Highway Administration, Highway Performance Monitoring System, Field Manual, U.S. Department of Transportation, January 1979.

From Reference 12.

needs assessment process is the part of the PPB process that leads to a workable definition of "needs" as distinct from "wishes" or some other expression of demand for facilities. This is important because the needs statements must be credible, or they will be ignored. Opinions that are not based on objective data are not worth that much, even when they are somewhat informed. This is an important issue for public works managers.

Needs assessments are part of both the maintenance management and capital improvement processes. In effect, it is the needs assessment that links these two processes together. It is natural to ask, How do we make the decision between rehabilitation and new facilities? The answer comes from the needs assessment and other evaluations, and must be an input into the budgeting process. Growth forecasts and new standards will come into the equation as well. Maintenance decisions, and strategies, need planning. These are presently not much used by local governments for a number of reasons, and they need attention through the planning process. Valid needs assessments will be a product of improvements in this process.

The needs assessment process depends on the inventory, the condition assessment, and an identification of desired levels of improvement and main-

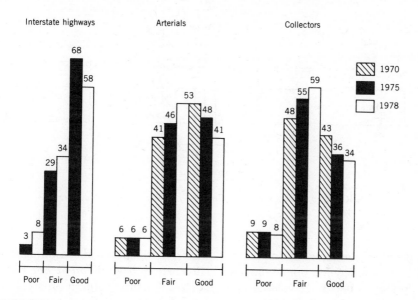

FIGURE 9.7. Urban pavement condition (percentage of miles classified as poor, fair, and good). *Source: The Status of the Nation's Highways,* Federal Highway Administration.

tenance. These must be viewed in the light of present and expected future conditions.

The item most lacking in present practices of compiling needs assessments is *analysis*. The purpose of analysis is to answer the question, "Why are these facilities needed?" Analysis should include projections of demand, exploration of alternative ways to meet demands, evaluation of rates of deterioration and obsolescence, cost-benefit and impact studies, and recommendations. Sensitivity analysis will improve the credibility of the recommendations, since the decision makers will make their own implicit analysis of sensitivity if it is not supplied with the report and recommendations. In effect, the needs assessment requires the full power of planning technologies and essentially as much emphasis on presentation and approval as that required for new projects.

Many improvements must be made in the needs assessment process. Many decision makers have seen so many poorly done needs assessments and plans that they consider a needs assessment as hardly more than a "wish list." This is a debilitating problem for public works managers, one that needs attention to improve the management of all kinds of public facilities.

9.3. INFORMATION SYSTEMS FOR OPERATIONS AND MAINTENANCE

There is not a general norm or set of guidelines for developing computerized information systems for operations and/or maintenance. Instead, varied systems

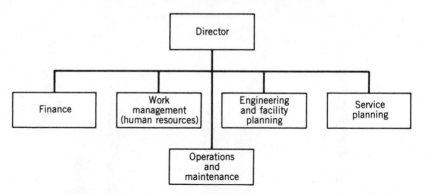

FIGURE 9.8. Organizational elements needing information systems.

have been developed by commercial software developers and consulting firms. The two functions, operations and maintenance, have different but related information needs. Development of effective systems is still in progress, and great strides are expected in the years ahead, bringing with them improvements in O&M and in solving the infrastructure "problem."

Although different infrastructure systems have unique management needs, they tend to converge toward similar or generic organizational approaches, with definable information needs. Figure 9.8 presents an approach to this generic organization, with operations and maintenance shown, facilities management, and the following staff functions: finance, engineering, planning for service, and a function called "work management," which is normally part of the personnel function, at least the planning of it. Figure 9.8 is the same as that presented earlier in chapter 4 as a generic organization.

Operations Information Systems

Information related to operations subdivides into that part of operations dealing with facilities (hardware) and that part of operations dealing with workers (software). In some cases, such as totally automated systems like the "automatic factory," the operations management system (OMS) would be devoted to the hardware alone. In other cases, such as a labor-intensive operation like solid-waste collection, the OMS would be oriented toward the performance of the workers. Most cases would be mixtures, such as the treatment plant which has performance that depends on the results of human operation of facilities.

Depending on the capital intensity of the particular infrastructure category, the OMS would tend toward emphasis on facility instrumentation and data collection, or toward some sort of "work management" information system. An example of the former would be the load management operation of an electric utility, and an example of the latter would be a bus transit operation, such as that in the first case study at the end of this chapter.

Operations managers need information and reports on how well the systems are doing. The information needed is unique to each facility. For example, in a water supply organization, the operations of source of supply, treatment, and distribution facilities are separate and unique. Operational objectives are functions of the purposes of the facilities: to supply raw water, to provide treatment, and to distribute water according to predetermined performance standards. Probably treatment plants have received the most attention due to regulatory reporting requirements and to the trend to automatic monitoring and control of operations. Pumping has received attention also due to the large energy cost involved. Operations data management systems are coming on-line for source of supply systems, treatment plants, and distribution systems. They furnish information for operators and generate environmental reporting information. There are a number of examples of firms that are marketing information systems for these applications, and innovative plant managers are installing their own systems.

The experience with other infrastructure categories is the same: attention has been given to the processing plants, such as nuclear power plants, wastewater plants, and waste-to-energy plants, but little to the *operation* (as distinguished from maintenance) of distributed plants, such as water distribution systems, roads, and buildings.

The logical extension of operational information systems is movement toward automatic control. The stages of movement toward automatic control are data logging, supervisory control, and full automatic control with software providing the logic based on preprogrammed control programs. Applications have reached the second stage of supervisory control in processing plants, and will evolve continuously toward more automation for specific cases. Electric power probably leads in automation among infrastructure categories.

Maintenance Information Systems

Maintenance management is a necessary support activity for operations, and information management should reflect that relationship. The "maintenance management systems" should provide condition information for maintenance and repair needs and for budgeting. The MMS is a concept whereby traditional maintenance functions are converted to computerization. These include an inventory of equipment and a scheduling system for maintenance activities and record keeping. The record keeping will include at least the following: equipment data, preventive maintenance records, repair records, and a spare parts stock card. These are concepts that have been developed through the maintenance needs of industrial equipment.

A number of viable commercial software packages are available for maintenance management. Beginning with standard equipment maintenance approaches, they extend to the specific applications found in facility systems.

For all facilities the beginning point for maintenance information is the *inventory* data base for locating and recording data on system components. All physical capital should be included in a data base such as this. The inventory data base can connect to financial management through some variation of the continuing property record (CPR) system, which is described by AWWA for water supply utilities (18). This system provides for maintaining a record of the nature and cost of each separable unit of property, either individually or in groups. The purpose is financial management, but the CPR system forms the core of the fixed-asset control system for the water utility, and should be understood in conjunction with the inventory concept that is now becoming a reality with computer information systems.

The normal practice in a utility would be to have a property record system consisting of cards or other financial records of property. This would normally not be used as part of the maintenance management system, nor would it be used to update condition of facilities on a realistic basis. This is changing with improvements in data management, however, and constitutes one of the best opportunities to provide an interface between the financial and management information systems.

Normal inventories of centralized and self-contained facilities such as processing plants and buildings are usually in place. There is now an increased recognition of the need for inventories of distributed facilities, such as collection and distribution facilities and roads, however simple. The problem is being approached comprehensively in some areas by developing integrated geographic-based systems. The one previously referred to in Houston, called "METROCOM," contains a planimetric map of some 600 square miles of the city. About 554,000 parcels of property are located and described, and there is location information on water, sanitary and storm sewers, roads, and bridges (13). As another example, a consulting firm has begun to market a lower-cost system with limited graphics capabilities. Called the "Infrastructure Management System," it relies on Census Bureau maps with information on facilities added by the user organization. The city of St. paul, Minnesota, is planning to have such a system on-line in 1985. St. paul plans to take 2 years to create the data base at a cost of $250,000 excluding hardware (19).

One of the most serious infrastructure problems is deferred maintenance. To study it there is a need to have *system condition* information. This system condition data base can be directly related to the inventory in the sense that inventory is a static record and the condition index would provide for periodic updates of the real condition of the facility. The condition data should be linked with the maintenance function, whereas the inventory, as a generalized data base, can be used by planning, engineering, and operations for many different functions.

Having valid condition information as a basis for scheduling minor and major maintenance, including replacement, is an important need in most infrastructure organizations. One of the problems is the absence of a linkage between fixed-asset financial management and maintenance management. Fixed-asset management, consisting of property records without updated condition data, is a sterile resource to managers looking for valid needs estimates. The records should reflect current value, arrived at by depreciating current replacement costs and deferred maintenance estimated from valid condition data. This differs markedly from a historical "accounting value" which would be derived from an annual depreciation deduction that would be calculated from the original cost and the estimated service life.

Engineering Information Systems

In public works organizations the engineering function is responsible for studies and designs necessary to construct and reconstruct facilities. While duties vary, they normally include design, selection of consultants and contractors, construction supervision, maintenance of standards, project management, and record keeping.

The engineering department would normally be responsible for numerous records, especially as-built drawings of newly constructed or reconstructed facilities. Also, any system maps would be the responsibility of the engineering department. There is an obvious linkage with the information needs of operations and maintenance, and a common data base should be available.

The generalized role of engineering is finding a new term in "facilities management." In early 1985, *ENR* magazine had a cover story on the evolution of facilities management as a business opportunity area (20). The story points out that facilities managers are seeing the following as computer opportunities: access to as-built drawings, space allocation, tenant records, utility information, and long-range planning.

There are not many actual "design" models available, but the engineering department would be a place where they could be productively used. Models of water distribution system operation constitute one example. How such models can be used is illustrated by a network model that was developed for sewer system evaluation and design (21). Implemented for the city of St. Petersburg, Florida, by the firm of Camp, Dresser and McKee, Inc, the system includes several linked models that run on microcomputers. The first model is a sewer system analysis model. It uses the input data about the existing system and potential new developments. The model predicts pipe peak flows and feeds information to the flow measurement analysis program. After an engineering analysis of the predicted flows, the information goes to the preliminary design program. There is also a cost program that provides a summary of the project costs.

Planning Information Systems

Planning is the area of data management that is most adaptable to the concept of decision support systems. The reason is the need in planning to ask questions of "what if." It makes no sense, however, for planning to be separate from operations with data bases; the two need to be connected.

Data bases which will be necessary for effective planning include data on the supply system, the demographics, and the demand parameters. Unless these data bases are organized by the planning staff, they may be ignored.

These data bases should offer management the opportunity to gain a perspective on the entire operation at once, and need attention from the planning staff to be properly organized. Of particular interest in the future will be the compilation of planning data bases that allow the combination of hydrologic and financial studies at the same time.

Planning support for decisions can be "scripted." This allows the examination of alternative scenarios, an approach which is necessary for very complex situations. This is an approach that has been studied in the development of artificial intelligence systems, and one that merits consideration for infrastructure systems in the future, especially for operating systems. After the scenarios are scripted, they can be routinized and data bases can be brought to bear on the analysis. The information systems needed to develop the kind of decision support necessary for planning are still evolving. System models are needed to aid in processing the information and determining what it means.

Integration of Operations and Maintenance Information with Other Management Information

The design of total information systems begins with actual applications which take place within the different parts of organizations such as finance and engineering, but there is also a need to begin to work on integration of all management information. The organizing concept for such integration can be found in decision support systems (see Chapter 4 for a discussion of DSSs). Ideally the manager could sit at a computer terminal and have the information needed for decision making displayed so that integrated information could be produced by special models and "what if" scenarios. Following computer industry advertising, the way this would work would be to have several different "menus" in front of the manager on the screen at all times. Of course, such an idealized situation is not yet possible on a practical basis.

The approach to integration should begin with effective development of the suborganizational information systems, beginning with finance, operations, and maintenance. This is evolving at the present time quite well in response to the demands of the industry and the opportunities available in the marketplace. After these parts are well enough developed, the development of integrated systems will take place naturally.

The mathematical and computer framework for integrated systems is available. Today's spreadsheets provide a way to handle considerable information at once and provide the way for the manager to look at several accounts simultaneously. Modern data bases can handle any collection of well-defined information.

On a realistic basis, the place for the integration of management information is still in the human mind. Integration is the main contribution that a competent and experienced manager makes to the success of an enterprise, and this contribution is not expected to be replaced by a machine soon. We can expect, however, continued trends toward the automation of decision making and the mechanization of work in general.

The needs are to move incrementally toward integrating information systems. Management models can be developed and improved by beginning with the financial management system and making information more revelant and useful for management purposes. Operations can be integrated with improved models of the "metropolitan water intelligence system" type, and research on these systems needs to advance. Facilities information systems, especially those with reports of condition, need to be improved and linked to financial management.

9.4. APPLICATIONS OF OPERATION AND MAINTENANCE MANAGEMENT

The generic aspects of operations and maintenance for infrastructure are clear, but the applications to specific problem areas are different. In this section we will point out some of the unique features of several categories of infrastructure.

Roads

In highway management, much of the "operation" is in maintaining the roads. In urban areas, traffic operations include the operation of traffic signal networks, and in some highly congested areas, there may be facilities such as ramp metering or other arrangements that enable the system to handle more traffic that it would if it were left unattended. Due to the emphasis on maintenance of roads, large shares of operating budgets will actually be for maintenance and the four R's of roads: repair, resurfacing, rehabilitation, and replacement. Operations is, then to a large extent, the management of maintenance forces.

Transit

Transit differs since much of the operations effort must go into the scheduling and operation of the transit system itself. The maintenance effort will go into the stock, such as buses in the case of a bus operation. Also to be operated and maintained are the support facilities, such as garages and parking lots. More detail about the operational needs of a transit system are given in the first exercise at the end of the chapter.

Water Systems

Water systems include diverse types of infrastructure components, but the operational aspects are important in all. In water supply, for example, the emphasis is on delivering water to consumers, much like electric power or other basic commodities. In wastewater management, the emphasis is on the operation of collection, treatment, and disposal systems to handle wastewater, without violating permits or regulations. In stormwater, the emphasis is much the same as in wastewater itself, but there is little treatment involved. Maintenance is the main concern after the systems are in place. Large water systems such as dams and reservoirs are subject to special operating rules such as those for flood control reservoirs. The operation and maintenance considerations for urban water systems are discussed in Grigg (22).

A special case of water systems is the irrigation system, which has received massive attention due to the world food needs. Irrigation systems in developed countries such as the United States can be operated and maintained much the same as other infrastructure systems, with emphasis on operating rules, on maintenance, and on effective organizations. In the developing countries, however, the complexity of the social systems makes the operation and maintenance problem more complex, and attention has been given to the development of basic principles governing them. Approaches suggested include the proposed "development model" (4,23) and the "operations and maintenance learning process" proposed by Skogerboe (24). In the case of the latter, it can be seen that the steps involved in learning how to operate and maintain facilities better are essentially those discussed in this chapter, but extended to apply to the special case of complex irrigation systems in developing countries (see Figure 9.9).

Some detail concerning the MMS for a water supply utility is given at the end of the chapter in the second exercise.

Solid-Waste Management

Solid-waste management is like wastewater management in the sense that there are collection, treatment, and disposal steps to be followed. In the case of wastewater, one agency often, but not always, handles all stages. In the case of solid waste, the collection organization is normally not the treatment and disposal organization, however. Moreover, each of the stages requires a different approach to operations and maintenance. The operation and maintenance of the collection system is similar to that of a transit organization; vehicles and laborers are involved. This normally means the involvement of a union or organized labor activity. In the case of the treatment and disposal activity, the normal situation is the operation of a landfill, usually a local government function, but there are increasing tendencies to go to a "trash-to-energy" plant, a concept that lends itself to privatization and that is discussed in Chapter 7. These plants require the same kind of operation and maintenance as other industrial plants.

Buildings

In the case of buildings the operation and maintenance is dependent on the kind of facility. Most buildings would focus on maintenance and the operation of support services such as heating and ventilating. The operation of these support services could become more complex, as in the case of large facilities like the World Trade Center in New York City, these facilities being practically cities within themselves.

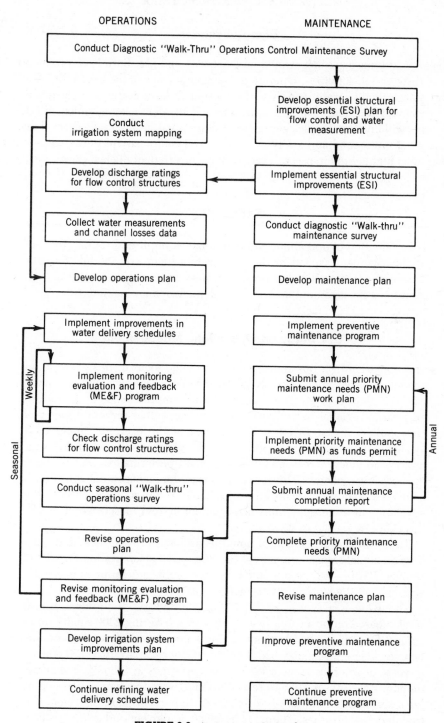

OPERATIONS   MAINTENANCE

Conduct Diagnostic "Walk-Thru" Operations Control Maintenance Survey

FIGURE 9.9. An irrigation O&M plan.

Energy Systems

Energy systems are concentrated on electricity and gas. Both have production and distribution activities. Operation and maintenance of the gas facility would be generically like water supply in the sense that there would be an acquisition and delivery function, including distribution, that would need attention. Electric energy will involve complex generation facilities that must, among other things, meet environmental and safety standards. The complexity of these operations has been highlighted in recent years by the concern over nuclear power plants.

EXERCISES

The evaluation of operations and maintenance requires attention to all of the management aspects of the organization being considered. For this reason two case studies are presented here to provoke thought: one on operations management and one on maintenance management.

Case Study on Operations Management

The operation of a bus transit company is the focus of this exercise on operations management. You are to play the role of a management consultant who is required to prepare a report on the improvement of operations for a large regional bus company such as those that serve a number of metropolitan areas. In effect the product of the exercise should be a management consultant's report to aid the governing board of the organization to analyze reasons for lack of good performance, and to make the necessary changes. This is a common role for management consultants in diverse types of organizations. What is required is essentially the development of an operations management system, described earlier in this chapter.

To aid in the discussion of how the problem can be alleviated, data from an actual transit company—the Regional Transportation District of Denver (RTD)—will be presented, but the problem description is entirely fictional and does not apply to that company.

The RTD is a typical regional transit authority. It provides transit service based on buses to a six-county region covering 2300 square miles around Denver, Colorado, and serving a population of nearly 2 million people. Average weekday boardings in 1985 were more than 150,000, an increase of 15 percent since 1983. Total boardings in 1985 were about 44 million. Revenues in 1985 were $126 million, with the main sources being sales tax (63 percent), fare-box revenues (14 percent), and the remainder from federal subsidies. The RTD has 2200 employees and a 750-bus fleet (24).

The actual organization of the RTD in 1986 is shown in Figure 9.10. Some of the major functions are as follows:

- Bus operations is divided into five division garages, each with a general superintendent. At this level the schedules are coordinated, timeliness is enforced, accidents are tracked, and grievances are handled. Unionization requires voting for routes by seniority and record keeping of union "points."
- The Planning and Development Department handles systems planning, with 20 traffic checkers assisting in tracking bus operations and related parameters; it also handles design, construction, construction management, and service planning.
- The Marketing Department handles customer service information, marketing and communications, and sales and marketing.
- The Administration Department handles all aspects of training and development, as well as labor relations.
- Financial management is handled by the Deputy General Manager, who oversees the controller and other accounting functions.
- Information systems are handled by a unit reporting to the Assistant to the General Manager, but there is some computerization in effect and planned in systems planning and in bus operations.

The problems with the fictitious bus company assumed for this exercise are these: reports of bad service, including late and irregular schedules and inconsiderate employees; high cost of operations; and bad equipment that is noisy and polluting. Your task is to analyze the steps that should be taken to investigate how to overcome these problems and improve operations.

To aid your thinking and preparation of your response to this exercise, you should consider the following items:

1. The purpose of the organization and the general goals of a transit authority
2. The organizational structure and related information systems necessary to achieve those goals
3. The specific missions of each major subunit of the organization
4. The major jobs that should be created to administer and carry out the duties of the subunits
5. The plans that should be formulated for each subunit
6. The schemes that should be formulated to manage work and achieve a production organization
7. Methods to audit the performance of the organization
8. Schemes for adapting to the need for change and improved performance

Regional Transportation District

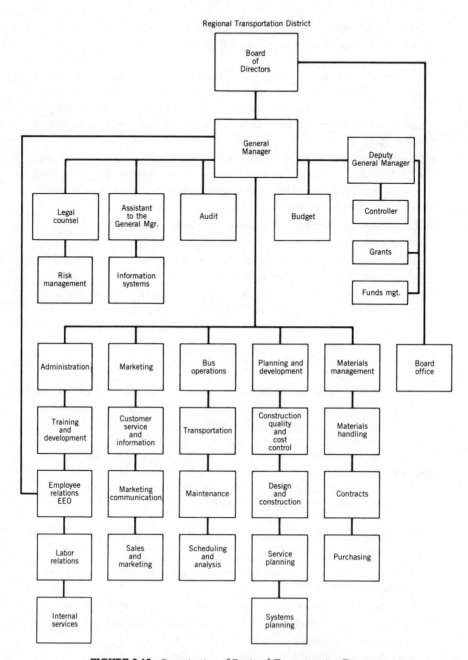

FIGURE 9.10. Organization of Regional Transportation District.

Experienced managers will see quickly that to answer these questions for a complex organization is a major undertaking. The discussion of this exercise has turned out to be a useful classroom activity requiring at least 3 hours to be effective.

Case Study on Maintenance Management

The organization for maintenance management in a water organization is the subject of this case study. Again, you are asked to consider the task of preparing a management consultant's report, this time on how to organize an overall maintenance management system for a water supply utility.

In this case some general information about the Denver Water Department is provided, including the organization chart. The problem would not be to remedy any deficiencies, but to consider how an MMS could be organized for a large complex water organization such as this.

The Denver Water Department (DWD) supplies treated water to a large share of the Denver metropolitan area. Some of the suburban communities have independent supplies, and the DWD supplies water through master meters to others. The supplies are coming mostly from transmountain diversions of surface water supplies, but for the purpose of this exercise you should consider that some of the water is coming from wells, and that in the future, some may come from reclaimed wastewater (Denver has a very promising experiment under way with water reclamation).

The organization chart for the DWD is shown in Figure 9.11. The main activity of operations is shown under "Plant," and it includes source of supply, treatment, and distribution, as well as some support functions. To support operations, there are divisions for engineering, planning, finance, and administration.

The questions that should be answered for the MMS are different than those for the OMS. The major ones are as follows:

1. What facilities will be maintained? A general inventory scheme is required.
2. How are responsibilities for maintaining facilities distributed in the organization?
3. What condition information on these facilities has been collected and is available for use by management?
4. What are the preventive maintenance requirements?
5. What routine minor repairs are required? How should plans be organized to get them done?
6. How should major repairs, rehabilitation, and replacement planning responsibilities be handled?

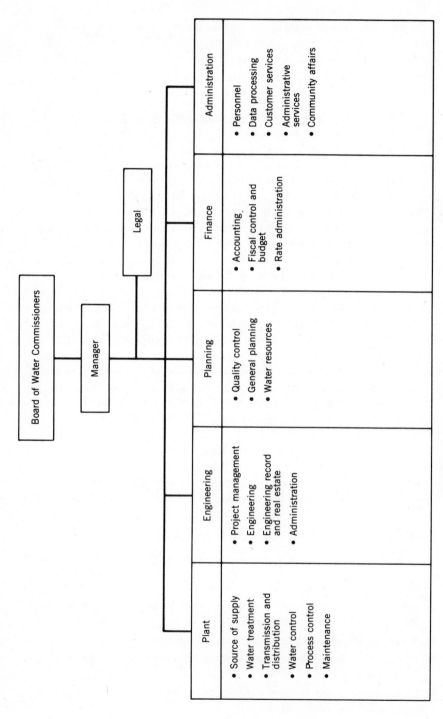

FIGURE 9.11. Organization chart of Denver Water Utility.

7. What kind of overall information system can be developed to maximize the use of routine information in maintenance management, and to mesh the maintenance management with operations management?

Again, the experienced manager will see in these questions a complex undertaking, striking to the heart of the overall management problem in the water utility. Designing of an MMS amounts to designing a system that will function in harmony with the rest of the organization. Since maintenance management (or facilities management) is a principal challenge to infrastructure organizations, it is clear that this kind of problem deserves considerable attention from management.

REFERENCES

1. Greene, James H., *Operations Management: Productivity and Profit*, Reston Publishing Company, Reston, Va., 1984.
2. Urban Institute and International City Management Association, Measuring the Effectiveness of Basic Municipal Services, Washington, D.C., 1974.
3. Government Finance Research Center and Peat Marwick, Mitchell & Co., Wastewater Utility Management Manual (draft), prepared for the EPA, July 1981.
4. Podmore, C. A., ed., *Diagnostic Analysis of Irrigation Systems*, Vol. 1, *Methodology, Water Management Synthesis Project*, Colorado State University, December 1983.
5. Newbrough, E. T., *Effective Maintenance Management*, McGraw-Hill, New York, 1967.
6. Ward, Peter, "The fleet maintenance management cycle," *Public Works*, November 1984.
7. Lindow, Edward S., "Maintenance management for roofing systems," *APWA Reporter*, October 1984.
8. Whitman, John C., "Contracting highway and street maintenance," *APWA Reporter*, March 1984.
9. Hatry, Harry P., and Bruce G. Steinhal, *Guide to Selecting Maintenance Strategies for Capital Facilities*, Urban Institute Press, Washington, D.C., 1984.
10. APWA, Guidelines for Developing a Maintenance Management System, Chicago, 1980.
11. U.S. Department of Commerce, Census Bureau, The Census Bureau's GBF/DIME System: A Tool for Urban Management and Planning, September 1980.
12. Godwin, Stephen R., and George E. Peterson, Guide to Assessing Capital Stock Condition, Urban Institute, Washington, D.C., 1984.
13. Hanigan, Francis L., and Carlos A. Rivera, "METROCOM: An interactive database for managing a modern metropolis," *Journal AWWA*, July 1984.
14. Batts, Leonard R., "Distribution system maps and record keeping," *Journal AWWA*, November 1984.
15. Shalin, M. Y., and S. D. Kohn, Pavement Maintenance Management for Roads and Parking Lots, U.S. Army Construction Engineering Laboratory, Champaign, Ill., October 1981.
16. O'Day, D. Kelly, and L. A. Neumann, *Assessing Infrastructure Needs: The State of the Art*, Hanson, Royce, ed., Perspectives on Urban Infrastructure, National Academy of Sciences Press, Washington, D.C., 1984.
17. El Haj, Riad, Information Systems for Improving Management of Water Supply Mains, Ph.D. dissertation, Colorado State University, December 1985.

18. Grinnell, D., and R. F. Kochanek, Water Utility Accounting, American Water Works Association, Denver, 1980.

19. "Consultants join to market municipal mapping service," *ENR*, December 20, 1984.

20. "Computer maze slows managers seeking answers," *ENR*, April 4, 1985.

21. Calise, John, G. S. Walters, and D. T. Zimmer, "Microcomputers and software provide useful tools for sewer system evaluation," *Public Works*, July 1984.

22. Grigg, Neil S., Urban Water Systems: Planning, Management and Operations, John Wiley & Sons, New York, 1986.

23. Lowdermilk, M. K., W. Clyma, L. Dunn, M. Haider, W. Laitos, L. Nelson, D. Sunada, C. Podmore, and T. Podmore, *Diagnostic Analysis of Irrigation Systems*, Vol. I. *Concepts and Methodology*, Water Management Synthesis Project, Colorado State University, December 1983.

24. Skogerboe, Gaylord V., Operations and Maintenance Learning Process, International Irrigation Center, Utah State University, 1986.

25. Regional Transportation District, *Annual Report*, Denver, 1985.

CHAPTER TEN

MANAGEMENT AND LEADERSHIP IN INFRASTRUCTURE

As the foreword to this book states, "Abundant food is in the fallow ground of the poor, but it is swept away by injustice." This is a quote from the Book of Proverbs and seems to refer to agricultural difficulties, but it applies as well to infrastructure.

As noted earlier, the quality of life is directly dependent on how well government supplies certain basic services. This varies all the way from survival conditions to the provision of the amenities needed for a higher-quality life rich with culture and the arts. Often this is swept away from the citizen by "injustice." In this case, "injustice" can take many forms: corruption, inequitable pricing, or public managers drawing paychecks without rendering a service to the citizens they serve. What is required in the infrastructure field is to have the best possible management and leadership, and to avoid the problems that result from poor management and corruption.

These are the subjects of this chapter: how the manager and others working in the infrastructure field can do a better job of serving. This requires management, leadership, and careful attention to ethics. Additional topics that will be discussed include the political nature of infrastructure, a condition that gives cause to some of the difficulties we face, and some opportunities for innovation in both management problem solving and technological applications.

10.1 POLITICS OF INFRASTRUCTURE

As shown in Chapter 1, the total wealth of the United States is on the order of $12.5 trillion, most of which is related, in one way or another, to infrastructure.

The annual expenditures in large industries such as transportation and water are in the hundreds of billions of dollars. These large sums attract powerful people since they offer the possibility of increasing wealth and gaining influence. It should come as no surprise to anyone that the infrastructure field is highly political. In fact, it is the political nature of the field that makes it so difficult to manage.

Sanders has written a summary of the political nature of the field (1). His points are summarized in this section, and then some additional political issues related to infrastructure are noted.

The value of infrastructure lies in the things it makes possible. This means that urban developers and other business interests will have a strong interest in the development of infrastructure along lines favorable to them, and they will support the candidates for office that make the promises they need. This support may translate into campaign contributions and other forms of financial inducements that will be difficult for officials to turn down. In addition, elected officials make promises to the electorate as a whole. If the promises have to do with providing new facilities that are highly visible, like roads or a sports stadium, everyone will be able to see whether the promises were kept. If, on the other hand, the needed promise is to do a better job of maintenance, that will not seem so glamorous.

Sanders cites the case of Boss Tweed, a nineteenth-century political "boss" who was a politician in New York City. In the years just after the Civil War, Tweed managed to spend the city into considerable debt through street paving. He recognized that the paving increased the value of abutting property and made his friends wealthy. The work generated also provided jobs for newly arrived immigrants and weakened the positions of some of his enemies. All of this was done in the name of improving infrastructure, but was based on corrupt motives. The days of the influence of corrupt bosses have waned, but there is still corruption around in the infrastructure field. The resignation of a U.S. Vice-President in the 1970s was a case of infrastructure-related corruption.

It is not only the elected official who may exercise political influence in the infrastructure decision making. However, many of the appointed or hired officials may work on the fringe areas of politics, and there are some areas of bureaucratic influence that have the same effect.

Agencies and bureaucrats work for outside support for their programs. Sometimes the program becomes the important objective, whether it does any good or not. The idea of the bureaucrats may be to enhance their image and the impression their program makes on their elected bosses and on their constituencies. This translates into enlarging programs and budgets to increase power. These larger programs result in higher employment, more powerful positions, and higher pay. These are the kind of bureaucratic forces that led Parkinson to formulate "Parkinson's law." Parkinson predicted that bureaucracies will grow at a certain rate whether there is any need for them or not. The reason is in human needs for power and influence. A manager finds things to do as he learns about his job. soon the manager needs help. Rather than hiring one assistant to help, the work is subdivided into two parts and two assistants are needed for the manager to supervise. Soon these assistants have made their work grow, partly by writing memos to each other to "coordinate," and they each need two assistants. You get the picture. Parkinson showed that this process will lead to a bureaucracy growing at a certain rate, and his theory has some basis in fact. There is also the old bureaucrat joke where a new manager comes to an agency and finds a note from the previous occupant of the office. The note says, "things get tough in this job from time to time, so I am leaving three envelopes for you; open one every 6 weeks." The new manager opens the first one, and it says, "When you get frustrated, reorganize!" After 6 weeks this first act has created so much attention that he eagerly opens the second envelope, which says, "Ask for more money and positions." This really attracts attention from the higher authorities and gains support from his subordinates as they see new opportunities for themselves, so when the time to open the third envelope arrives, he can hardly wait. The contents of the third envelope? Three more envelopes! That joke is sad but true in the plight of some bureaucracies.

In addition to the political considerations facing elected officials and bureaucracies, some natural forces are at work in the political marketplace that affect infrastructure. One of these is the natural tendency to defer capital needs, especially those that are not visible such as storm sewer repairs, improvements in certain neighborhoods, and improvements in underground facilities. These problems would seem to be more serious in older cities with lower rates of growth than they would in newer cities with growth-induced infrastructure programs.

The problem of standards is political in several ways. Engineering standards provide a rational way to determine the capacities and other characteristics of facilities, and thus the cost, but engineers are not always rational and they do not always determine the best standards; rather the standard-setting process is a political one involving the interests and opinions of engineers and other related interest groups. Take, for example, the familiar problem of determining storm sewer standards. Should the standard be 5 years or 10 years? The city engineer prefers the larger one since it reduces maintenance and local nuisance flooding. The developer prefers the smaller one or none at all since profit is involved. The hydrologist calculates the scientific aspects but recognizes that neither the hydrologic nor the economic data are sufficient to really determine what is "optimum." While the untrained observer would think the arguments were based on fact in this case, the truth is that they are usually based on biased points of view. The result is a politically set standard.

Public works have historically been an area of intense political struggle for the reasons just given, and others. If you wish to delve further into this topic, examine the writings of Robert Moses who had so much influence on the development of New York, and the histories of some leading political figures with roots in local government. There are many of these. Mayor LaGuardia of New York is a colorful figure. Teddy Roosevelt began in city politics. The effort will be rewarding. Moses' life has been chronicled by Caro in a book entitled

The Power Broker, and Moses himself put some of his stories down into a book entitled *Public Works: A Dangerous Trade* (2).

Sanders's analysis of the political aspects of infrastructure results in some logical conclusions: that public administrators have to be very capable and have to be able to understand political trade-offs. These are conclusions of much of this book and are discussed in the remainder of this chapter as well. The need for capable public administration is one of the main themes of the book. Another main theme, the need for good management information, also relates to the political aspects of infrastructure in that a key role of the administrator is to provide decision information to the elected officials; this requires good decision support, the subject of Chapter 4.

10.2. MANAGEMENT AND LEADERSHIP SKILLS IN PUBLIC WORKS

Management and leadership skills on the part of public administrators and public works managers are the most critical prerequisities for success. This is one of the recurring themes in all of the studies of needed actions to overcome the infrastructure problem. Of course, the field of public administration is devoted to providing the kinds of managers needed. The need for improved management in public works has been one of the areas of emphasis of the professional associations. This section is intended to highlight some of the most important areas needing emphasis.

Studies of management identify planning, organizing, directing, and controlling as the most important processes. Three aspects of these processes are of principal concern to the infrastructure manager: managing the organization (organizational management), building physical systems (project management), and operating the systems after they are built (operational management). Sometimes these scenarios are confused in discussions of management. We will focus on management of organizations in this section. The other aspects have been covered elsewhere in this book.

The manager in an infrastructure organization must have skills in three generic roles: leader, supervisor, and technical manager. These require certain personal skills, some by cause of habit and training and some by virtue of the knowledge gained through education, training, and experience. Personal skills needed include time management, interpersonal relations, and good work habits. Knowledge-based skills include financial management, public relations techniques, and numerous technical skills, as, for example, those involved in working with computers. Integrity is not a skill, but it is the most important personal characteristic of infrastructure managers. Talk of improving management or productivity is meaningless when integrity is absent in management systems.

The difference between leadership and management is generally understood, but the terms are often blurred. "Management" is a general term meaning to handle all of the decision making, planning, organizing, and administrative aspects of an enterprise. Leadership means providing inspiration and extraordinary inputs to the enterprise.

Leadership is not really a topic that can be taught or even analyzed very well. People recognize leadership qualities, however, and studying these qualities and leadership styles can help the manager make a leadership "self-assessment." A list of qualities that has been given to cadets at the U.S. Military Academy includes integrity, knowledge, courage, decisiveness, dependability, initiative, tact, justice, enthusiasm, bearing, endurance, and unselfishness. Other qualities include fluency of speech, dominance, emotional balance, creativity, self-confidence, achievement drive, drive for responsibility, interest in work, and sociability. All of these are important for the public works manager. The qualities that seem particularly critical in infrastructure organizations are, in order of priority, integrity, knowledge, dependability, and emotional balance.

Managers must be able to make effective and timely decisions. When decision making is effective, the organization knows it can depend on quick and effective action. When decision making is not effective, morale may suffer, and rumors feed on the uncertainty. Decision making is really an art and science mixed together, especially the unstructured decision making that accompanies the political aspects of infrastructure. The use of science in decision making, utilizing such techniques as decision theory, statistics, and operations research, is at a low level, with most of the decision making being done at a political level or based on heuristics and judgment.

The management of infrastructure organizations requires effective supervisory skills. Supervision is a "control" responsibility of management with strong leadership requirements. After the work of the organization is planned and organized, it must be controlled. This requires effective information systems. Supervisory management involves work planning, direction, coaching, and performance review. A good organization will work symbiotically, with the different levels and functional units working smoothly together. Techniques such as management by objectives are designed to help achieve this, but as today's management literature will attest, the organization and management of work is a topic that needs constant attention. This is discussed in Chapter 9.

The manager should be able to command respect on the basis of a solid foundation of knowledge, the ability to learn, and the ability to listen to experts and learn from them. This latter ability requires that the manager be able to distinguish between good advice and bad advice.

The financial area of knowledge is often missed by engineers who migrate to positions of management without management training. Chapters 5 and 6 provide summaries of the main points needed by the manager. Debt financing, tax rollback initiatives, capital budgeting, utility fees, financial impact statements, and infrastructure banks are just a few of the terms encountered. It helps to keep up with the business press, especially the *Wall Street Journal*, which carries daily news about infrastructure problems.

The manager must have a good understanding of the technological area unique to the particular category of infrastructure. In today's complex "high-tech" and heavily regulated world, management must be a process of calling on various experts, and so the technological knowledge needed must be of the overview variety. This is one of the reasons that the percentage of engineers involved in public administration is falling, since the need is for generalists, not specialists. However, probably the best way to become a generalist manager is to begin with a strong specialty, such as engineering.

The scenarios where effective management is needed include a wide variety of situations. One deals with employees, especially in the labor-intensive areas of infrastructure such as transit and solid-waste management. Here, effective supervisory skills are needed, as well as the wisdom of Solomon!

Dealing with an irate public is a tough problem, since some people will be unreasonable no matter how well they are treated. People respect credibility and honesty, however, and if management gives straight answers and if the people perceive that management has their interests in mind, they will usually cooperate. The problem of dealing with the public has led APWA to give attention to how communications can be improved in public works agencies. This has resulted in some recent reports on the subject, one which is distributed in short popularized form (3). The subjects covered are:

- Listening: the neglected communication skill
- Nonverbal communication
- Public speaking
- Appearing on television
- Improving your annual and special report
- Equipment/facilities for communication
- Understanding the media
- The press release
- The feature story
- The photo story
- How to work with reporters
- Radio and television
- The press conference
- Using media files
- Maximizing media gains
- Releasing critical and complex documents
- Crisis preparedness
- Communicating with the public
- Public hearings
- Communicating with specific groups
- The effect of feelings in communications
- Feedback: an interpersonal skill
- Small-group communication
- Internal communications

- Communication between departments
- Intergovernmental communication

Just a glance at this long list of topics should convince anyone of the importance of communications in public works and the many aspects to consider. This is a key management topic all the way through organizations.

Solving regional problems requires enlightened leadership highlighted by cooperation. Many complex public works problems require this today more than they require the "push-it-through" style of a Robert Moses.

Management must be competent in dealing with technical problems, such as acquiring new technologies. Managing the design and construction of a complex treatment plant or waste-to-energy plant is an area requiring real technical skill, and experience. Obviously the problem of supervising the operation of a nuclear power plant is one that requires the utmost in technical skill. Another example is rate-setting, with all the attendant financial and economic considerations involved.

10.3. INNOVATION IN INFRASTRUCTURE ORGANIZATIONS

This section is included in this chapter to respond to the critics who claim that infrastructure problems are only based on politics and that there is no need for innovation to find better ways to solve them. There is always a way to do something better, and this applies to infrastructure organizations as well, in spite of all the political, financial, and human constraints facing them.

The two general areas where innovations are necessary are in regard to management and the use of technology. This section first describes in general what an innovation is as it applies to infrastructure management, and then lists some that seem promising.

"Innovation" means doing something with a new or better method. This word has been used many times, often meaninglessly, in the past few years in conjunction with the infrastructure situation. EPA even had a program where local governments could quality for extra grant funds if they used "innovative and alternative technologies" for wastewater treatment. This was almost a contradiction in terms since what was considered "innovative" was essentially spelled out in the regulations. It shows how futile it is to try to spur innovation with regulations.

Recognizing that technology, computers, and systems analysis have a lot to offer, there have been deliberate attempts to improve public works management with them for over 20 years. The use of systems analysis goes back to the mid-1960s with the introduction of program budgeting and other tools of systems analysis into the public sector. The impact of these tools has been limited. In the 1970s there were attempts to apply space technology to the problems of cities. The saying that "if we can land a man on the moon we can certainly pick up the garbage in New York" was heard, but as we now know, due to human problems it may be more difficult to pick up the garbage in New York than to land on the moon. This is stated with tongue in cheek, of course, but it underlines the difficulty of public works in some settings.

In the 1970s there were a number of government efforts to improve productivity in local governments. All kinds of "innovations" were tried, many with the use of systems analysis. "Public technology" programs were attempted, and cities were able to get "technology agents" with the job of finding applicable technologies and applying them to the problems of the cities. The firm Public Technology Inc. (PTI) was formed to apply technology to cities, and a PTI report is summarized later in this section. With all of this background it seems that great progress would have been made. Not that much progress has been made, however, because infrastructure problems are more complex than the ordinary problems that give way to technological solutions. Still, technology has a lot to offer to infrastructure, and innovations will lead to advances.

One study in the 1970s of the effectiveness of innovations in public works organizations led to the conclusion that public agencies were not so slow as some think to adopt innovations (4). This study evaluated 43 innovations in the fields of air pollution control, firefighting, traffic control, and solid-waste management. Most of the innovations were what we would consider technological rather than management-oriented. The cities studied included all sizes in all regions of the United States, covering 551 as a maximum response in the firefighting area. The types of innovations considered were continuous SO_2 monitoring in air pollution, lightweight hoses in firefighting, optically programmed traffic signals, and transfer stations in solid waste.

In the case of firefighting, innovations were implemented when they improved the performance of systems as measured by insurance ratings. Changes tended to be incremental, as would be expected. Decisions on solid waste tended to be based on efficiency and productivity. There has apparently been little federal government influence in this area. Opposition to improvements was cited as due to fear of impact on morale, fear for public safety, union opposition, uncertainty about the magnitude of cost savings, and satisfaction with the status quo. For both traffic and air pollution control, the need to increase performance was cited as the incentive to innovate, with cost as a secondary factor.

Officials rated the following as important to the stimulation of innovations: fiscal resources, the need to improve productivity, prestige that results from being an innovator, attitudes and skills of staff, legislative incentives, and availability of information. The importance of these parameters varied. The availability of technical assistance from other levels of government was considered to be the least important of the parameters.

The fragmentation of the infrastructure field was evident in the findings. One conclusion was that "our study emphasizes that municipal responsiveness to new technologies is organized along functional rather than city lines, and that functional areas differ in the manner in which problems are defined, information disseminated and resources distributed (4)."

Discussions today of innovations sin the public works field cover a broad range of topics. APWA held a seminar on innovations in public works management in 1985. The topics selected were:

- Managing the movement of people in the future
- Waivers for regulatory requirements
- Innovative financing
- Labor management under unique collective bargaining rules
- Minimizing disruptions during infrastructure rehabilitation
- Automatic control of water systems operations
- Public works management innovations: case studies

These illustrate the range of innovation topics that some professionals consider worthy of discussion.

Next, some of the promising innovations reported in studies in the literature are presented. The studies relate to finding better ways to manage and to use technology for infrastructure management.

The first study is a paper by a manager who summarizes some of the innovations he sees to have promise (5). These innovations are:

- Planning and budgeting applications
    Capital project planning
    Life cycle costing
    Fiscal impact analysis
- Financial management
    Increased user fees
    City facility charges
    Creative capital finance
    Privatization of capital projects
    Contracting to private sector
    State and federal assistance
- Operations and maintenance
    Energy conservation
    Safety awareness
    Fuel management
    Microcomputer usage
    Street pavement management
    Computerized sewer management
    Growth-retardant chemicals
    Snow and ice removal with new technologies

    Equipment maintenance management
    Street light modernization
    Planned maintenance of capital assets
- Management
    Public works education
    Excess government property
    Community service workers
    Shared purchasing
    Equipment and machinery sharing
    Part-time employees
    Contract administration

The list of these innovations reveals how many of them fall into the category of simply good management.

Another set of studies reviewed are those by Public Technology Inc. that relate to innovations (6). In these studies, PTI reports on the innovations that were submitted on one-page summaries for consideration as ideas that held the most promise for improving local government performance. These innovations can be studied on their one-page formats on an on-line data base, the LOGIN system, managed by Control Data Corporation; or information can be obtained by contacting the local governments directly. The following data will present only the title of the concept and the local government involved to demonstrate the kinds of innovations that promise to help in the infrastructure management field. These are selected topics from the 1982, 1983, and 1984 reports; there are many more, of course.

Innovation	Local Government
Recycling of asphalt for smaller jobs	Madison, Wis.
Faded documents enhancement	Philadelphia
Consolidated construction schedule	Phoenix, Ariz.
Automated fuel dispensing	Wichita, Kans.
Automated ridership	Colorado Springs, Col.
Traffic accident analysis	Hennipin Co., Minn.
Refurbished buses	Madison, Wis.
Energy audit program	St. Petersburg, Fla.
Public power	Rochester, N.Y.
Hydropower generation	Rochester, N.Y.
Computerized records	Atlanta
Automated meter reading CATV	Dallas
Waste to energy	Madison, Wis.
Aquaculture	San Diego, Cal.
Energy management tracking	San Jose, Cal.

Treated water reuse St. Petersburg, Fla.
Capital plant assessment Alexandria, Va.
Computerized preventive maintenance Evanston, Ill.
Storm drainage utility Fort Collins, Col.
Local materials purchase Dallas
Needs assessment for capital planning Pasadena, Cal.
Robotic vehicle painting New York
Leaf collection Burbank, Cal.
Maintenance management Fort Worth, Tex.

The interesting thing about all these innovations is that they mostly involve good management and application of resources, rather than any new application of technologies or computers. It shows that the challenge in public works is mostly making the best use of what is available, rather than developing new approaches that are not already available to business and industry. After all, public works is a business too. With good business practices and innovations, there is obviously a lot of room to save money and provide better service in the infrastructure field.

10.4. ETHICS IN INFRASTRUCTURE MANAGEMENT

There is much discussion of ethics in the United States today. In the 1970s we had a President and a Vice-President both resign over political and ethical questions. In the case of the Vice-President, the resignation was over payoffs related to construction industry matters, one of the most common situations in infrastructure management, where corruption can creep in. We have had bid-rigging convictions, some where the principals did not even know they were doing wrong. In one case, a case with which the author of this book was personally familiar) the contractor involved was an upstanding citizen, but fell into the trap of inheriting business practices with the family business. He probably did not realize that bid-rigging cheats the public.

Ethics deals with defining right conduct. Nowhere in the public service is ethics more critical than in managing infrastructure systems, since so much money is being spent on behalf of basic human needs. If every public official was ethical and honest, there would be little human misery in the world today, but they are not. The results? Obvious problems with hunger, public health, lack of basic needs, and lowered standards of living in many parts of the world.

There is a passage in the Book of Proverbs that states "When the righteous are in authority the people rejoice; but when the wicked rule, the people groan" (7). This ancient piece of wisdom states the case for ethics in public works.

This section concludes with the code of ethics for the American Public Works Association. It is not the only code that applies to infrastructure, but it has the main points (8).

AMERICAN PUBLIC WORKS ASSOCIATION CODE OF ETHICS

Recognizing their responsibilities to the people, desiring to inspire public confidence and respect for government, and believing that honesty, integrity, loyalty, justice, and courtesy form the basis of ethical conduct, members of the American Public Works Association:

- Uphold the Constitution, laws and regulations of their country and all other applicable units of government.
- Put public interest above individual, group, or special interest and consider their occupation an opportunity to serve society.
- Recognize that government service is a public trust that imposes responsibility to conserve public resources, funds, and materials.
- Recognize that political (policy) decisions are the responsibility of the people's elected representatives but that identification and communication of technical and administrative alternatives and recommendations as a basis for decision making are the responsibility of public works officials, professional engineers, or other administrators.
- Never offer, give, nor accept any gifts, favors, or service that might tend to influence them in the discharge of their duties.
- Never use their position to secure advantage or favor for themselves, their family, or friends.
- Never disclose confidential information gained by reason of their position, nor use such information for personal gain.
- Never make recommendations, while empoyed by a public agency, on any matter that involves a business in which they have a direct or indirect financial interest.
- Never engage in supplemental employment, business, or professional activity which impairs the efficiency of their services; or while employed by a public agency become involved in work which could come before their agency for review or inspection.
- Recognize that it is not in the public interest for officials of public agencies to select and retain professional engineering services on the basis of price alone and that consideration must be given to experience, technical expertise, availability, and other qualifications.
- Do not attempt either falsely or maliciously to injure the reputation, business, or employment status of any individual.

EXERCISE: TECHNOLOGY OR MANAGEMENT INNOVATIONS TO IMPROVE INFRASTRUCTURE MANAGEMENT

In this exercise you should find and evaluate a new technology or a new management procedure that promises to improve infrastructure management by introducing an "innovation." You should search for the innovation until you find one you think might either form the basis for a new business you would organize or add a product or a service to an existing business. Your report is to be a brief exposition (five pages or less) of why you think you can make a profit with the innovation while at the same time improve some part of infrastructure management. In this you are following the admonition that says, to be successful in business, "find a need and fill it." Your report should be like a "business plan" you might show an investor.

The items you should cover in your report are as follows: the problem and the opportunity to be addressed by the innovation; the technology or management improvement that makes up the innovation; the way the innovation would be developed into a business product or service; the type of customers and the way they would use the service; and your financial plan to sell the innovation. In the financial plan, you should present some analysis of your cost factors to offer the product, and estimate what would constitute a good pricing level for the product.

Examples of the kinds of innovations you might consider are these: for technology, you could propose a new instrument that would detect weakening beams in bridges without detailed inspection; for management, you could develop new software for something like a maintenance management system. There are many others. You can use magazine articles or your own experience and imagination to identify possibilities.

REFERENCES

1. Sanders, Heywood T., Politics and Urban Public Facilities, in *Perspectives on Urban Infrastructure*, Hanson, Royce, ed., National Academy Press, Washington, D.C., 1984.
2. Moses, Robert, *Public Works: A Dangerous Trade*, McGraw-Hill, New York, 1970.
3. American Public Works Association, Better Communication: The Key to Public Works Progress, Chicago, 1984.
4. Feller, Irwin, Donald C. Menzel, and Lee Ann Kozak, Diffusion of Innovations in Municipal Governments, Pennsylvania State University, June 1976.
5. Kemp, Roger L., "Public works productivity: Beyond cutback to creativity," *Public Works*, December 1986.
6. Public Technology Inc., Solutions/Innovations for Technology-Sharing Networks, Washington, D.C., 1982, 1983, 1984.
7. Proverbs 29:2, Revised Standard Version.
8. American Public Works Association, Code of Ethics.

CHAPTER ELEVEN

FUTURE ISSUES IN INFRASTRUCTURE MANAGEMENT

The first chapter of the book focused on the importance of infrastructure to the quality of life of the human race. The chapter stated that this book was about the engineering and management techniques that can help solve infrastructure problems, and that although many aspects of the infrastructure "crisis" could be debated, the technologies and funds to solve the problem are available if good management techniques are employed. It is the business of public works engineers, managers, and policymakers, in both the public and private sectors, to solve the infrastructure problem. The importance of the problem will continue, and we can look for future attention to the issues we have discussed all through the book. But what are the trends to watch? What are the really difficult questions? What are the needs for research? These are the subjects of this final chapter.

A workshop was held during 1984 in Vermont to explore the trends and the needs for the future for infrastructure. The participants concluded that (1):

> Technological opportunities are so boundless that there is little we cannot do to improve or create a socially sound infrastructure for the decades ahead. Little will be done until we act upon the realization that the social, institutional, political, and organizational infrastructure is central to repair or construction of durable, financially and socially sound public physical facilities. This means that we will need to apply our research and development capabilities to the innovative questions associated with alternative infrastructure technologies.

In a nutshell this collection of experts focused on the social, institutional, political, and organizational questions, and confirmed again that they are the keys to solving our infrastructure problems. At the same time these people recognized that the future will demand research into technological alternatives. Their conclusions are interesting mostly in that they attempted to look into the future to forecast what it will hold for infrastructure.

They examined six infrastructure systems: communications, transportation, waste disposal, energy, water supply, and urban drainage and flood control. Conclusions reached about some of the trends were as follows.

In the communications area we have the combined technologies of telecommunications and computers. This combination produces the new word "telematics," which means the application of automation and telecommunications to improving the processes of life; these processes include everything from ordering groceries over cable TV to working at home with a computer modem, as some are now doing. Workshop participants concluded that the potential impacts of telematics on the remaining categories of infrastructure constituted one of the most important issues for the future of public works needs. These impacts include the following: there will be trade-offs between transportation and communication (if more people work and shop at home, less transportation will be needed); energy requirements will be altered; water supplies and waste management systems will be different; and the new infrastructure system of telematics will have to be guarded against failure due to natural disasters. What happens in this area will affect every other category of infrastructure, and in fact, every aspect of economic and social life itself.

In the field of transportation we are dealing with the most expensive and spatially obvious infrastructure system. At the same time that telematics is affecting the future of transportation needs, the technologies of transportation management and hardware are advancing. Electronics will be a big factor in providing new sensing and automation opportunities for planning and control of systems, and the availability of new technologies for rapid transit will provide cost-effective alternatives for some applications. At the same time, the old problems of expensive and labor-intensive systems will continue and must be dealt with.

Waste disposal is in the news more every day. The problems with hazardous wastes, including industrial and agricultural categories, and nuclear waste are difficult to resolve. In addition there is the problem of scarce landfill space that will continue to drive interest in waste-to-energy plants. Waste disposal will be a high-priority infrastructure area for the future. Financially it is not as difficult as transportation, but technologically it is perhaps the most challenging category.

Energy has not been thought of as an infrastructure problem so much as it has been considered a problem of national competitiveness. Again there is a trade-off between energy and telematics; but, as pointed out in Chapter 2 in discussing systems, some believe that the electronics revolution will drive demand for electricity up, not down. In any event, this is not expected to be a major problem for urban governments, but it will affect the capital markets and the national infrastructure picture. The problems with nuclear power plants, with finding new hydro sites, with regulatory agencies and the utilities, and with external effects centered on air pollution are expected to dominate the picture. Alternative energy sources will receive more attention.

Water supplies involve several areas of technology. Those mentioned at the workshop include telecommunications, computers, instrumentation, construction techniques, new materials, energy systems, fluid flow technologies, water treatment and waste disposal technologies, and various systems control technologies. There will be no absolute shortages of water in the future, but there will be relative shortages and difficulties associated with poor management and with contamination. There will also be large-scale water quantity problems in the field of agriculture, such as running out of water in aquifers that have been mismanaged.

Urban drainage and flood control is an area that has received little attention from the infrastructure community in the past, but it has a large influence on natural disaster protection, on the quality of life, and on pollution control. It will attract more attention in the future, especially in the supercities that need to provide better living conditions for their people at the same time as they need to overcome the problems of poor planning during the stages of rapid urbanization.

These six categories are interesting to consider due to the thought the participants in the workshop put into defining future conditions, and they set the stage to understand what some of the most important policy needs, development needs, and research needs will be in the future. The only category included as a main one in this book that was not mentioned in the workshop is the buildings category. It seems clear that this will be an interesting area to watch also, with new supertall buildings possibly coming on-line, with the need to guard against natural disasters, and with the trends to the "integrated building" as discussed in Chapter 2.

The workshop concluded that "innovation is needed not only in technology but also in information delivery, better planning and more effective management associated with the long duration of the public policy process" (1). Here again we have a statement of the combined needs of technology and management.

Other workshops and studies have also pointed at what should be done to deal with the infrastructure crisis in the future. The report "Hard Choices" that was reviewed in Chapter 1 received a lot of attention since it was associated with the Joint Economic Committee of Congress. It came up with four recommendations (2):

- Congress should establish a national infrastructure fund to supplement resources available under existing federal, state, and local capital infrastructure programs.
- Congress should mandate the creation of a coordinated national infrastructure needs assessment program, and within the unified budget, require that capital expenditures be presented and highlighted in a clear, comprehensive way.

- Congress should initiate a review of technical standards now governing construction of the nation's roads, bridges, transit systems, water, and wastewater facilities.
- Congress should carefully reevaluate the statutory and administrative rules that govern the use of existing federal infrastructure assistance programs.

Another study and workshop assessed research needs in four categories (3):

- The development of standards and criteria for the design and performance of urban public facilities, against which national and local needs for investment can be measured.
- The identification of the effects of technology on urban infrastructure, including the potential for using new technologies to improve the performance and reduce the costs of existing systems and facilities and the need for developing new systems, materials, and devices to support the functions of the private sector in the cities of tomorrow.
- Financing techniques for public facilities systems.
- Analysis of institutional problems of planning and management of facilities and the processes of decision making.

Martin concluded his year as president of APWA in 1984 with the following observations (4):

- Maintenance analysis and programming capabilities need to be developed and improved.
- We need better communications, especially with the public.
- Emergency response should be improved.
- Productivity needs to be raised.
- Workers should experience better safety on the job.
- We need mechanisms to assess the emerging technologies available to us.
- We need better access to information resources.

After studying as many statements as could be found about research needs in infrastructure, it was concluded that five categories of them seem to need interdisciplinary attention (5). There are, of course, thousands of research needs in all of the problem areas such as transportation, water, and structures. The five interdisciplinary categories are:

1. *Improve the processes of public works management.* In this category four elements of the research problem appear: to improve the effectiveness of public works managers, to improve the processes of management, to use computer-based tools, and to encourage innovation in management.

2. *Utilize new technologies and materials in infrastructure management.* This field of technology contains many opportunities for improving the cost-effectiveness of services, including instruments to measure performance and predict failures, materials for construction and repair, use of information systems and models to locate problems, and making in-situ repairs and tests.

3. *Reduce constraints caused by codes, standards, and incentive structures.* The "Hard Choices" report identified this as one of the major areas of need. The specific studies needed, according to that report, were an inventory of federal standards; an analysis of relationships between key federal standards and the related state, local, and professional standard areas; an evaluation of the likely impact of federal standards on the overall cost of infrastructure; and an analysis of the opportunity costs and environmental risks associated with reducing or amending standards. Helpful additions to this list would be a study to identify "norms of practice" in use by the engineering profession that constrain cost reduction, an analysis of why the engineering profession is so "risk-averse" when it comes to design, the development of new techniques to analyze the conflicts between standards, and a study of the standards-setting process to identify flaws and conflicts of interest.

4. *Improve the financial capacity for infrastructure management.* Four elements to this question include managing finances to make services self-supporting, determining the best roles of the three levels of government, evaluating tax and regulatory policies, and evaluating the results of privatization.

5. *Adjust infrastructure management of future patterns of living.* The elements of this question are evaluating communications-transportation trade-offs, evaluating the social forces inducing demand for infrastructure, increasing the affordability of existing infrastructure, and finding how to make the social adjustments needed to mitigate infrastructure problems.

All of these statements lead to the conclusion that there are six main categories of needs to improve our response as a nation to the infrastructure "crisis." These are broad and general, but they seem the most important. They involve roles for all the actors—government, the professions, the universities, and individuals.

- Apply the best management techniques to infrastructure management.
- Get rid of corruption wherever it exists in the infrastructure field.
- Improve the processes of education for infrastructure managers.
- Use the best skills of the private sector.
- Work on reducing built-in industry structure problems such as fragmentation and harmful duplication and competition.
- Consider trade-offs, and where a level of infrastructure service cannot be maintained, bite the bullet and reduce it.

Most of these have to do with improving the skills of the public administrator. One of the ways to improve those skills is to use technology better. Thus the solutions do involve joint use of technology and management. The other main direction of these needs is to avoid waste, whether it comes from bad management or corruption.

These issues constitute a challenge for our public administrators and for all of the others working in the infrastructure field. It is indeed a manageable problem, but one with many challenges for engineers and managers.

REFERENCES

1. Eberhard, John P., and Abram Bernstein, eds., Technological Alternatives for Urban Infrastructure, National Research Council, Washington D.C., 1984.

2. University of Colorado, Hard Choices: A Report on the Increasing Gap between America's Infrastructure Needs and Our Ability to Pay for Them. Report for the Joint Economic Committee of Congress, 1984.

3. Hanson Royce, ed., *Perspectives on Urban Infrastructure*, National Academy Press, Washington D.C., 1984.

4. Martin, James L., "The challenges facing public works today and tomorrow," *APWA Reporter*, November 1984.

5. Grigg, Neil S., "Interdisciplinary research needs related to physical infrastructure," *Journal of the Urban Planning and Development Division, ASCE*, November 1985.

MEASURES OF EFFECTIVENESS FOR BASIC MUNICIPAL SERVICES

Source: Urban Institute and International City Management Association, "Measuring the Effectiveness of Basic Municipal Services," February 1974.

OVERALL OBJECTIVE: Promote the <u>health</u>, <u>safety</u> and <u>aesthetic</u> values of the community by providing an environment free from the <u>hazards</u> and <u>unpleasantness</u> of uncollected refuse with the least possible <u>citizen inconvenience</u>.

Objective	Quality Characteristic	Specific Measure	Data Collection Procedure
HEALTH AND SAFETY	Health Hazards	1. Percentage of blocks with/without one or more health hazards.	Systematic visual inspection of a representative sample of city streets.[1]
	Fire Hazards	2. Percentage of blocks with/without one or more fire hazards.	Same as above
	Fires Involving Uncollected Waste	3. Number of fires involving uncollected solid waste.	Fire Department records.
	Rodent Hazard	4. Percentage of households reporting having seen/not seen one or more rats on their block.	Citizen survey of a representative set of city households. (See Question #22, Chapter IV).[2]
	Rodent Bites	5. Number of rodent bites reported per 1,000 individuals.	City-county health records along with the latest planning department population estimates.
	Injuries to Solid Waste Collectors	6. Number of man-days lost due to injuries per 1,000 days paid.	Sanitation Department records.
PLEASING AESTHETICS	Street and Neighborhood Cleanliness	7. Percentage of blocks whose appearance is rated satisfactory/ unsatisfactory (fairly dirty or very dirty--2.5 or worse) on visual rating scale.[3]	Systematic visual inspection of a representative sample of city streets using a photographic rating guide.[1]
PLEASING AESTHETICS (Cont'd.)	Street and Neighborhood Cleanliness (Cont'd.)	8. Average block cleanliness rating.	Systematic visual inspection of a representative sample of city streets using a photographic rating guide.[1]
	Offensive Odors	9. Percentage of households reporting/ not reporting offensive odors.	Citizen survey of a representative set of city households. (No sample question included).
	Objectionable Noise Incidents	10. Percentage of households reporting/ not reporting objectionable noise during solid waste collection periods.	Citizen survey of a representative set of city households. (See Question #21, Chapter IV).[2]
	Unsightly Appearance	11. Percentage of blocks with/without abandoned automobiles.	Systematic visual inspection of a representative sample of city streets.[1]
MINIMUM CITIZEN INCONVENIENCE	Missed Collections	12. Percentage of collection routes completed/not completed on schedule.	Sanitation Department records.
		13. Percentage of households reporting/ not reporting missed collections.	Citizen survey of a representative set of city households. (See Question #19, Chapter IV).[2]
	Spillage of Trash and Garbage During Collections	14. Percentage of households reporting /not reporting spillage by collection crews.	Same as above (See Question #20, Chapter IV).[2]
	Damage to Private Property by Collection Crews	15. Percentage of households reporting /not reporting damage to personal property by collection crews.	Same as above (No sample question included)
GENERAL SATISFACTION	Overall Citizen Neighborhood Cleanliness Rating	16. Percentage of households rating overall neighborhood cleanliness as satisfactory/unsatisfactory.	Citizen survey of a representative set of city households. (See Question #18, Chapter IV).[2]
	Citizen Complaints	17. Number of valid citizen complaints, by type, per 1,000 households served.	Sanitation Department records.

[1] For a detailed description of the procedures and results of previous testing of the systematic visual inspection system see <u>How Clean is Our City</u>?, The Urban Institute, 1972.

[2] Examples of questions that might be included on an annual multi-service citizen survey to collect these data are included in Chapter IV. A government may also wish to collect similar information on commercial service using a special commercial users survey. An illustrative questionnaire is under development.

[3] A local government might prefer different threshold values than those illustrated here.

SUMMARY OF PRINCIPAL MEASURES OF EFFECTIVENESS FOR SOLID WASTE DISPOSAL SERVICE

OVERALL OBJECTIVE: Provide for solid waste disposal in a safe, sanitary, and aesthetically acceptable manner.

Objective	Quality Characteristic	Specific Measure	Data Collection Procedure
ENVIRONMENTAL SOUNDNESS	Impact on Water[1]	1. Number of days per year that last test for leaching from landfill did/didn't show leaching. (Measured at each landfill site, with any corrective actions taken noted separately.)	Testing (perhaps quarterly) of wells around landfill; regular tests by qualified chemists for water quality characteristics affected by leaching. Number of days based on compilation of periods between first test showing leaching at some well and first test showing no leaching at any well. Some sites currently have periodic testing at test wells, but the testing is usually under state or federal auspices and there is generally no regular reporting in terms of evidence of leaching.[2]
		2. Number of instances of untreated runoff water from landfill being released to nearby bodies of water.	Observations by landfill supervisors or trained observers during and just after storms. This is an untested measure.[3]
ENVIRONMENTAL SOUNDNESS	Impact on Water (Cont'd.)	3. Number of days per year that last test of ground or surface water at points of water use near landfill showed contamination, with any corrective actions taken noted separately.	Tests of groundwater and surface water for contamination at points where some usage is possible, where the direction of flow from the landfill places the points in the path of moving water, and where the distance to the landfill is minimized. Number of days would be based on compilation of periods between first test showing contamination and time of correction. Procedures will be the same as those in #1 and those for measuring water quality in bodies of water.
	Impact on Air[4]	4. Number of days per year that last test of stack emissions from incinerators satisfied/ exceeded federal or state standards.[5]	Daily monitoring or periodic inspections to obtain the data, depending on the size of the operation. Standards exist for particulates and sulfur oxides, and should be developed for other substances in the near future. Number of days would be based on compilation of periods between test showing excessive emissions and tests showing acceptable emissions.

282

Objective	Quality Characteristic	Specific Measure	Data Collection Procedure
ENVIRONMENTAL SOUNDNESS (Cont'd.)	Recycling	5. Percentage of all waste, by weight, reused for productive purposes.	Records should be available for sites with recycling operations.
AESTHETICS	Appearance, Odors, and Noise In and Around Disposal Sites	6. Number of trained observer site inspections that detect aesthetic problems in surrounding area attributable to site.	Obtained from inspections by trained observers, using specified guidelines for inspection. Procedures for conducting these measurements are currently being developed.
SAFETY	Safety Hazards and Pest Control	7. Number of trained observer site inspections that detect no/some hazardous conditions, with separate listing of inspection dates and conditions of sites that have hazards.	Obtained from same inspections as #6 by trained observers, using specified guidelines for inspection. Procedures for conducting these measurements are currently being developed.
	Safety Incidents	8. Number of incidents of citizen injury and damage, requiring repair or replacement, to citizen property.	Tabulation of reports of such incidents to department.

Footnotes

[1] For operations involving disposal on land.

[2] Standards do not exist to permit local governments to determine whether leaching is indicated, based on a given chemical analysis; determinations are currently made by state officials on the basis of judgment and experience with the area in question.

[3] If the landfill site is properly graded and has proper provision for drainage, there should be no instances during light and moderate rains. During heavy rains, this measure reflects the adequacy of the drainage provisions.

[4] For operations involving controlled burning.

[5] At present, the technology required for continuous monitoring of particulates is only in the developmental stage. The only generally available equipment must be attached to the incinerator stacks and requires several days and several thousand dollars to perform. An alternative procedure would be to measure the ambient air quality in the vicinity of the incinerator, using the concentration of particulates per cubic meter as the measure and the EPA ambient air quality standards for reference.

OVERALL OBJECTIVE: Maintain a public transit system that provides _access_ to places where citizens want to go in citizens want to go in a _safe_, _quick_, _comfortable_, _pleasant_, _convenient_ and _reliable_ manner, and that helps minimize pollution, congestion, and energy consumption in the community.

Objective	Quality Characteristics	Specific Measure	Data Collection Procedure
RAPID MOVEMENT	Travel Times	1. Travel times between selected key origins and destinations.	Available from transit schedules; validated using trained observer for a sample of runs. Key origin-destination (O-D) pairs should include major O-D's for persons without ready access to autos and cover major residential, commercial and recreational areas within the jurisdiction. Peak times normally would be used. Since the emphasis here is on area-to-area, rather than point-to-point travel, door-to-door times are not needed, only in-vehicle times. Transit travel times can be evaluated relative to auto travel times for some O-D's (See Measure 1 in the General Transportation Table).
	User Satisfaction	2. Percentage of users rating travel time as satisfactory/ unsatisfactory.	Survey of a representative sample of citizens. A special purpose survey of users only might be used as a supplement (See Chapter IV, Question 3c).
	Non-User Satisfaction	3. Percentage of non-users giving travel time as a reason for non-use.	Same as above. (See Chapter IV, Question 5 (3) and 6).
CONVENIENCE	Accessibility of Service	4. Percentage of citizens within x feet of a transit stop.[2]	Can be estimated by overlaying a map of transit stops on a map of population density, and computing the percent of population living within circles of radius x drawn around the stops, taking into account barriers to direct paths to stops. The radius should represent an appropriate walking time such as ten minutes. Procedure in development.
CONVENIENCE AND RELIABILITY	User Satisfaction	5. Percentage of users rating reliability and convenience (e.g. location of stops, frequency, difficulty in getting schedule information, need for transferring) as satisfactory/ unsatisfactory.	Survey of a representative sample of users.[1] (See Chapter IV, Questions 3a, 3b, 3d, 3f, and 7a.)
	Non-User Satisfaction	6. Percentage of non-users giving lack of convenience or reliability as a reason for non-use.	Survey of a representative sample of citizens.[1] (See Chapter IV, Questions 5(1), 5(2), 5(5), 5(9), and 6.)
	Reliability[3]	7. Percentage of sample runs that vary from schedule by more than "x" minutes.	Observations by transit inspector or independent trained observer for a sample of runs.
COMFORT AND PLEASANTNESS	Seating Availability	8. Percentage of runs with more than x riders standing during any portion of the route.	Data noted by driver at the end of each run (perhaps only for a sample of runs). Could be supplemented by ratings by trained observers for a sample of peak period runs.

Objective	Quality Characteristics	Specific Measure	Data Collection Procedure
COMFORT AND PLEASANTNESS	User Satisfaction	9. Percentage of citizens who feel transit ride is comfortable and pleasant (e.g. in terms of temperature, noise, crowdedness, odors, waiting conditions, driver helpfulness and courtesy, interior cleanliness and attractiveness, ease in boarding and exiting, bumpiness/jerkiness of ride, seat width and cushioning).	Survey of representative sample of citizens.[1] This might be supplemented by ratings by trained observers for a sample of runs. (See Chapter IV, Questions 3e and 4.)
	Non-User Satisfaction	10. Percentage of non-users giving comfort or pleasantness factors as reasons for non-use.	Survey of representative sample of citizens.[1] (See Chapter IV, Questions 5 (7) and 6.)
SAFETY	Frequency of Traffic Accidents	11. Number of accidents per 1,000 transit vehicle miles.	Statistics usually kept by transit department.
	Casualties from Traffic Accidents	12. Number of deaths and number of injuries per 1,000 passenger trips (and per 1,000 passenger miles).	Data on number of passenger trips are usually available. Data on passenger-miles usually requires special study of sampled passengers (or trips) to determine average trip lengths. ("Average trip length" times "number of trips" yields passenger-miles.)
	Crime	13. Number of crimes on-board and at stops per 1,000 passenger trips.	Police and transit employee incident reports on transit-related crimes. Categorization by location of incidents (e.g. on-board vs. at stops) and by type of crime are likely to be useful.
SAFETY	Non-User Fear	14. Percentage of non-users giving fear of crime on-board or at stops as a reason for non-use.	Survey of representative sample of citizens.[1] (See Chapter IV, Question 5 (8) and 6.)
ENVIRONMENTAL SOUNDNESS	Air Pollution	15. Percentage of transit vehicles meeting/not meeting local air pollutant standards (or preferably, the percentage of vehicle-days in/out of standard).[3]	Periodic testing of vehicles -- using device for analyzing pollutants in vehicle exhaust for conditions simulating various operating modes. Visual rating of vehicle exhaust using a Ringelman Chart may also be used. (Vehicle-days out-of-standard might be roughly estimated based on average time to repair and average time between tests.)
	Noise Pollution	16. Percentage of transit vehicles meeting/not meeting local noise standards (or preferably, the percentage of vehicle-days out-of-standard).	Periodic testing of all vehicles using noise meters to measure noise from various operating modes (e.g. acceleration, idling, cruising).
OVERALL CITIZEN SATISFACTION/ USEFULNESS	Usage-Persons	17. Percentage of population using/not using service more than x times per month.	Survey of representative sample of citizens.[1] The percentage of citizens not using service for reasons relatively controllable by the government (e.g., lack of access to a bus stop, frequency and reliability of runs) should also be estimated using data obtained by the survey. (See Chapter IV, Question 2.)

Objective	Quality Characteristics	Specific Measure	Data Collection Procedure
OVERALL CITIZEN SATISFACTION/ USEFULNESS	Usage-Trips	18. Total and per capita number of passenger-trips.[4]	Statistics usually available. Data might be reported separately for peak and off-peak usage, to indicate commuter vs. other usage.
	Usage-Mileage	19. Total and per capita number of passenger-miles.[4]	Same as measure #12.
	Mode Choice	20. Percentage of all motor vehicle passenger trips made by public transit.[4]	Survey of representative sample of citizens, such as in O-D studies, coupled with usually available transit data on passenger-trips.
	Citizen Satisfaction	21. Percentage of citizens generally satisfied with transit service.	Survey of representative sample of citizens, with data for users and non-users reported separately.[1] Reasons for dissatisfaction should also be reported, especially for non-usage on commuter trips. A systematic survey of transit riders only would provide a larger sample of users than the multi-purpose citizen survey, but "on-board" surveys have difficulties with the length of the survey and the representativesness of the sample. (See Chapter IV, Question 8.)

[1] An annual multi-service citizen survey that could be used to collect this data is described in Chapter IV of this report.

[2] A measure of the accessibility to destinations might be the "percent of selected key destinations within y feet of a transit stop." If worker distributions are known, the "percent of workers with accessibility to transit stops at their place of work" would also be a desirable measure. More complex measures considering accessibility of selected origins to selected destinations might also be desirable for indepth analysis.

[3] Air pollution from transit vehicles needs to be considered by a community in the light of the pollution that would result from alternative modes such as the automobile.

[4] Measures 18-20 should be used with particular caution. A goal of maximizing their values can become perverse at some point. For example, at some time, local conditions might make increasing public transit usage less attractive than, say encouraging walking, bicycling, private para-transit or car pooling; therefore a goal of "increasing passengers" cannot always be stated as an overall objective for a local transportation system taken as a whole.

SUMMARY OF PRINCIPAL MEASURES OF EFFECTIVENESS FOR GENERAL TRANSPORTATION (VEHICULAR AND PEDESTRIAN)[1]

OVERALL OBJECTIVE: Provide and maintain a street and sidewalk network that will promote convenient, safe, quick, and comfortable vehicular and pedestrian travel, with minimum harmful effects on the environment.

Objective	Quality Characteristic	Specific Measure	Data Collection Procedure
VEHICULAR TRAVEL			
RAPID MOVEMENT	Travel Times	1. Peak and off-peak travel times between key representative origins and destinations.	Timed runs on selected routes, preferably several times a year to reflect seasonal fluctuations.
	Severity of Congestion	2. Ratio of peak travel time to off-peak travel time (between selected pairs of points).	Timed runs (off-peak and peak) between selected points in congested areas or on major routes. Off-peak time may be defined as the time to travel between the points at the legal speed limit, obeying all traffic laws.
	Duration of Congestion	3. Length of time that peak travel times are "x" percent above off-peak times.	Same as above
SAFETY	Frequency of Accidents	4. Number of traffic accidents and the rate per 1,000 population.	Available from police and insurance company records. Other versions of interest for analysis include: the accident rate per thousand drivers, per 1000 vehicle-miles, and per 1000 passenger-miles. Also the rate per 1000 daily average pop. (including non-resident workers and visitors) if available would better reflect the population.
SAFETY (cont'd)	Casualties from Accidents	5. Number of deaths and number of injuries from traffic accidents per 1,000 population.	Same as above.
	Property Losses from Accidents	6. Dollar property loss from traffic accidents, and loss per capita.	Same as above. Constant dollars should preferably be used for comparisons over time.
	Preventability of Accidents	7. Percentage of accidents involving a contributing factor influenceable by a specific city agency (e.g., potholes, signal malfunction, view obstruction) -- classified by city agency of concern.	Analysis of data from accident reports. May require improved reports or trained investigators at sample of accidents.[2] (Procedure remains to be tested.)
	Feeling of Security in Driving	8. Percentage of drivers who feel driving conditions are generally safe/unsafe.	Survey of representative sample of drivers.[3] Factors of most concern to those feeling unsafe should also be solicited as well as information on the geographical areas where concern is felt.
SAFETY (ALSO CONVENIENCE AND FAIRNESS)	Traffic Law Enforcement Adequacy	9. Percentage of citizens who feel, based on their personal experience, that traffic law enforcement is too strict/about right/ too lax.	Citizen survey of a representative sample of drivers or citizens in general.[3] (See Chapter IV, Question 35.)
COMFORT	Street Surface Condition- Government Ratings	10. Percentage of streets with surface rated as excellent/good/ fair/poor/dangerous.[4]	Systematic visual inspection of a representative sample of streets, perhaps supplemented by a "bumpiness" measuring instrument such as a roughometer. Measures for several seasons are desirable.

Objective	Quality Characteristic	Specific Measure	Data Collection Procedure
COMFORT (cont'd)	Street Surface Condition-Citizen Ratings	11. Percentage of citizens rating street surfaces in their neighborhood as satisfactory/unsatisfactory.	General citizen survey of a representative sample of drivers/passengers.[3] (See Chapter IV, Question 48.)
CONVENIENCE [5]	Parking Convenience	12. Percentage of drivers who feel that finding a parking space is usually/sometimes/infrequently a problem.	Survey of a representative sample of drivers.[3] (See Chapter IV, Question 9a.) Detail by area, time of day, day of week, type of parking could also be obtained.
	Understandability of Traffic Controls and Signs	13. Percentage of drivers rating the understandability and visibility of (a) traffic signs (regulatory and advisory), (b) street markings, and (c) street name signs, as satisfactory/unsatisfactory.[6]	Survey of a representative sample of drivers (as can be obtained from a general citizen survey).[3] A survey of visitor driver perceptions may also be of interest. Note that "visibility" includes obstructions to signs, and convenience of placement, as well as adequacy of the graphics. (See Chapter IV, Question 9c for signs; markings question remains to be tested.)
	Lane Blockages -- Driver Perceptions	14. Percentage of drivers who feel they are frequently/infrequently inconvenienced by blocked lanes.	Survey of a representative sample of drivers.[3] Could be supplemented by data collected from agencies on "number of blocked lane-days due to construction or repair work."
ENVIRONMENTAL QUALITY	Air Pollution	15. Air pollutant levels attributable to transportation sources and number of persons possibly exposed to hazardous levels.	Can be estimated using systematically gathered air samples throughout the city, combined with population density maps, e.g., based on census data.
ENVIRONMENTAL QUALITY (cont'd)	Air Pollution (cont'd)	16. Percentage of citizens bothered by polluted air in their neighborhood frequently/occasionally/rarely.	Survey of a representative sample of citizens.[3] Where problems are reported, air sampling may be needed to determine the source (transportation or stationary sources). (See Chapter IV, Question 11.)
ENVIRONMENTAL SOUNDNESS	Noise Pollution	17. Percentage of street miles with traffic noise above/not above "x" decibels -- by residential/non-residential areas, and by type of street.	Measured using A-weighted noise meter along the more heavily traveled streets by time of day and day of week, and reason. Alternatively, can be estimated using approach outlined in HUD's Noise Assessment Guidelines, T. J. Schultz and N. M. McMahan, U.S. Government Printing Office, 1971.
		18. Percentage of citizens bothered by traffic noise in their neighborhood frequently/occasionally/rarely.	Survey of a representative sample of citizens.[3] (See Chapter IV, Question 10.)
PEDESTRIAN TRAVEL			
CONVENIENCE/SAFETY	Sidewalk Availability	19. Percentage of residents who feel there are adequate/inadequate sidewalks (a) on their block, (b) in their neighborhood.	Same as above. (See Chapter IV, Question 13.)
	Sidewalk Condition	20. Percentage of blocks in satisfactory/unsatisfactory condition.	Inspection by a trained observer using a photographic or other well-defined rating system. An alternative or supplementary rating of sidewalk conditions might be obtained by citizen survey.[3] (See Chapter IV, Question 13.)

Objective	Quality Characteristic	Specific Measure	Data Collection Procedure
CONVENIENCE/ SAFETY (cont'd)	Adequacy of Street Lighting	21. Percentage of residents who feel street lighting in their neighborhood is insufficient/about right/too bright.[7]	Survey of representative sample of citizens.[3] (See Chapter IV, Question 12.)
	Adequacy of Traffic Controls	22. Percentage of citizens who, as pedestrians, feel that there are too many/ too few/ about right amount of walk/don't walk controls at intersections.	Survey of representative sample of citizens.[3] (Remains to be tested.)
SAFETY	Pedestrian Casualties	23. Number of traffic accidents involving pedestrian casualties per 1,000 population.	Statistics kept by most police departments. Accidents at controlled intersections, uncontrolled intersections, and mid-street or road should be reported separately. The rate per 1,000 average daily population should be considered. (See Measure #4.)
	Feeling of Safety	24. Percentage of citizens who feel there is relatively low/high danger to pedestrians (especially children or the elderly) from traffic in their neighborhood.	Survey of representative sample of citizens.[3] (Remains to be tested.)

[1] This table covers only intracity transportation, other than public transit (which is included in another table).

[2] This measure presents potential problems in interpretation and legal involvement of the city, unless ground rules and definitions for making the necessary classifications are carefully worked out.

[3] An annual multi-service citizen survey that could be used to collect this data is described in Chapter IV of this report.

[4] The street surface rating levels might be defined as follows: Dangerous - Street surface with a major safety hazard to drivers going at speed limit (e.g., wide, deep pothole); Poor - Surface with minor safety hazard, potentially damaging to some vehicles, or with extremely bumpy, poorly shaped surface causing major discomfort; Fair - No safety hazard, but considerably uncomfortable to ride over in spots or all over; Good - Only minor bumps or cracks, good configuration, no significant discomfort to ride on; Excellent - Perfect surface condition, no repairs needed, no discomfort. The ratings might also be defined using a photographic rating system. Note that engineering ratings commonly used in many communities emphasize the magnitude and priority of ratings needed; they may or may not give the same impression as the user-oriented rating above. For example, a street with a dangerous pothole is often not rated "poor" on engineering ratings if a simple patch will suffice.

[5] The measures listed attempt to reflect various specific aspects of driver convenience. But a satisfactory measure of the overall convenience in driving about the jurisdiction remains to be identified.

[6] Trained observer rating of the understandability and visibility of traffic signs and signals markings may be a useful additional or substitute measure if the ratings are based on well-defined criteria that have been correlated with citizen perceptions. The trained observers might then conduct surveys of all or a sample of streets by day and by night at least once a year.

[7] If after study, these citizen ratings appear highly correlated with standard measurements of light intensity, the latter could be substituted as the measure.

OVERALL OBJECTIVE: Provide an adequate supply of water that is free of health hazards, aesthetically acceptable, and adequate for household, commercial, and industrial use. Provide prompt, courteous, reliable service in support of the system and minimize injuries and damage associated with the system.

Objective	Quality Characteristic	Specific Measure	Data Collection Procedure
HEALTH HAZARDS	Presence of Substances Linked to Health Risks	1. Number of days per year that the last test of some/no water quality characteristic was outside its standard for the following characteristics: total coliform, residual chlorine,[1] carbon chloroform extract, lead, barium, cadmium, hexavalent chromium, selenium, silver, arsenic, cyanide, zinc, gross beta activity, radium, strontium, fluoride, nitrate, sodium. Number of days for a particular test should be reported only if the number is not zero. Provide breakdowns for each treatment plant and points along the distribution system.[2]	Regular testing[3] done by a qualified chemist in accordance with tests contained in the American Public Health Association's Standard Methods for the Examination of Water and Wastewater. Standards are available from the U.S. Public Health Service and the American Water Works Association. Most states require such tests to be conducted annually. All tests should be performed at the treatment plant; coliform and chlorine tests should be performed at points throughout the distribution system (also fluoride, if fluoridation is provided). Tests for lead or other chemicals may be made in part of the distribution system if problems are suspected. Other tests may be added if tests become technically feasible (e.g., viruses) or if standards are developed (e.g., asbestos, mercury).
HEALTH HAZARDS	Presence of Substances Linked to Health Risks (Cont'd.)	1. (Cont'd.)	"Number of days" would be obtained from compilation of periods between the first test of the characteristic that shows it above standard (or start of year if characteristic ended the previous year over standard) and first test showing characteristic within standard (or the current date if the characteristic has not yet been brought within standard). Actions taken to correct the situation should probably also be noted.
	Evidence of Water-Borne Diseases	2. Number of confirmed cases, if any, of water-borne disease among city population, with those due to public water supply and those due to other water supplies separated and cause of contamination, if known, identified for each case.	Reports from county and state Public Health Departments, which are required to collect such data and report them to the National Center for Disease Control.
AESTHETIC QUALITY	Presence of Substances with Adverse Effects on Appearance, Taste, or Odors	3. Number of days that the last test of some/none of the following substances was outside its standard: turbidity (appearance), color (appearance), odor, taste, chlorides (taste), sulfates (taste), copper (taste), and methylene-blue-active substances (taste, appearance). Optional additional tests for aluminum (appearance) and uranyl ion (taste, appearance) may be added.	Same as 1.(a).
	Citizen Perception of Water Quality	4. Percentage of persons that rate their drinking water as satisfactory/unsatisfactory in appearance, taste, and odor, with breakdowns provided by type of complaint for those who rate water unsatisfactory.[4]	Obtained from citizen survey.[5] (See Chapter IV, Question 40.)
HOUSEHOLD USE QUALITY	Levels of Water Qualities with Effects on Household Use	5. Same measure as 1.(a), but qualities to be checked are hardness and pH (cleaning effectiveness), and iron and manganese (staining). Optional additional test for alkalinity and the coupon test for corrosion may be added.	Same as 1.(a). Federal and state criteria for hardness and pH do not generally exist, but guidelines can be set up, based on recommendations from other sources, such as the American Water Works Association and the U.S. Environmental Protection Agency's standards for bodies of surface water used as drinking water sources.

Objective	Quality Characteristic	Specific Measure	Data Collection Procedure
FLOW ADEQUACY	Citizen Perception	6. Percentage of persons reporting no/some problems with water pressure or flow	Obtained from citizen survey.5 (See Chapter IV, Question 43.)
	Restrictions on Household or Commercial Usage	7. Number of days of restrictions on water use, by type of restriction	City and department records
	General Flow Adequacy	8. Percentage of fire hydrants surveyed that do/don't meet static water pressure standard of, say, 40 pounds per square inch.6	Annual inspections of the fire hydrants to assure their operational readiness for firefighting. The data may be taken from these inspections.
SERVICE ADEQUACY	Rate of Validated Complaints	9. Number of valid requests per 1000 clients for non-routine service (not shown to be private responsibility), with breakdowns provided by type of request (e.g., billing overcharge, water quality, broken or leaking pipe or meter).	Cities should have standard forms for recording and coding the nature of external requests for service. Those to be included here are those that are not shown to be due to citizen negligence and that do not refer solely to tasks that are the citizens' responsibility.7
	Citizen Perception	10. Percentage of persons requesting service who were satisfied/dissatisfied with response.	Obtained from a follow-up survey of persons requesting service.8 Each citizen surveyed would be asked whether he was satisfied or dissatisfied with the overall handling of his request and with each aspect of the response, such as satisfactoriness of completion of work required, speed of response, courtesy, etc.
SERVICE ADEQUACY (Cont'd.)	Injuries and Damage	11. Number of valid reported incidents of citizen injury and of damage, requiring repair or replacement, to citizen property.	Based on department records
	Traffic Disruption	12. Number of blocked lane-days due to construction or repair. 9	Can be collected as part of job logs or permits for tearing up streets. Number calculated as number of lanes blocked during job times the number of days required to do the job, totalled over all jobs.
	Firefighting Support	13. Percentage of fires at which water supply was adequate/inadequate.	Tabulated by fire department, based on data to be included in fire incident report and screened to remove cases where fire department procedures were at fault.10

[1]The measure of residual chlorine is a proxy measure for bacterial decontamination. The standards for residual chlorine are not as widely accepted as those for other measures on this list (e.g., no standards are available from the Public Health Service). There are criteria available from the Environmental Protection Agency, but these are not considered to be on a par with the Public Health Service standards for other water properties. Since ozone can be used as an alternative to chlorine for treatment and since unacceptably high levels of chlorine are needed to affect viruses, this measure may be more readily dropped by localities than the other measures of water quality.

[2]A separate measure with the same form may be used if the local government monitors water quality at private wells. The measure could be "Number of well-days per year that last test showed some/no problems", based on adding up the "number of days" for each well and then obtaining the total for all wells.

[3]The frequency of testing required to assure a safe water supply will vary from place to place, depending upon the natural protection of the water-source (e.g., groundwater under rock) and the presence of various potential contaminants in the area, from natural or industrial sources. Many tests will be performed less than once a year in some areas, because there is no source of exposure to that substance anywhere in the area. Also, the fact that a measure exceeds its standard does not mean that an imminent health threat exists; all Public Health Service standards include substantial safety margins.

[4]An alternate measure would be the number of valid (confirmed) complaints on water aesthetics, a measure which is already available under #9. However, the complaints may not be representative of overall public perceptions, so this measure is less reliable than the citizen survey measure.

[5]An annual multi-service citizen survey that could be used to collect this data is described in Chapter IV of this report.

[6]General flow adequacy is measured by firefighting standards because firefighting places the highest demand on flow. A reference target of, say, thirty pounds per square inch might be used for domestic uses only. For general flow adequacy, again based on fire requirements, the American Insurance Association has standards on flow in gallons per minute, sustainable over a ten hour period, based on population. Also, the AIA provides a comprehensive rating of the water supply system about once every ten years.

[7]It may also be useful to keep track of the number of valid (in the sense that the facts are as stated) complaints that are shown to be citizen responsibility. This may provide indications that the public needs better information regarding the extent of public responsibilities. It may also indicate that the agency personnel are unclear as to the extent of public responsibility or that they are misclassifying complaints. It is desirable to see to it that areas of responsibility are understood by all parties.

[8]The citizen survey referred to in footnote #3 would be unlikely to provide a large enough sample of households requesting these services to obtain reliable data.

[9]Note that there is a measure in the General Transportation Service section on traffic disruption from all causes combined.

[10]Pressure and flow can be affected by the number and size of hoses used and the lines to which they are attached. This often changes over time for a particular fire. Distinction between inadequacy upon initial attach and inadequacy later in the fire might be made. Also, a system might perform as designed but still be inadequate.

SUMMARY OF PRINCIPAL MEASURES OF EFFECTIVENESS FOR WASTEWATER TREATMENT AND SEWERAGE

OVERALL OBJECTIVE: Assure that the city's wastewater[1] does not adversely affect the <u>environment</u>, assure
the <u>aesthetic acceptability</u> of all facilities, provide <u>prompt, courteous, reliable service</u> in support
of the system, and <u>minimize injuries and damages</u> associated with the system.

Objective	Quality Characteristic	Specific Measure	Data Collection Procedure
ENVIRONMENTAL SOUNDNESS	Public System Adequacy	1. Amount and percentage of total wastewater influent treated/ not treated, by type of treatment (primary, secondary, etc.), total and by treatment plant.[2]	Should be obtainable from meters at the treatment plants.
	Private System Adequacy	2. Number of households without an environmentally acceptable system for wastewater removal (e.g., septic tanks in saturated land areas).	Obtained by an initial survey of the unsewered population and updated in accordance with replacement and construction activities. Some local governments have this information by area as part of ongoing programs to replace septic tank systems in overloaded areas with sewer connections.
	Adequacy of Removal and Level of Pollution in Effluent	3. Number of days per year (based on standards that may be daily, weekly, monthly, or annual) that each of the following characteristics exceeded its standard: fecal coliform, BOD (percentage removed and concentration), suspended solids (percentage removed and concentration), pH, phosphates, nitrates, oil and grease--total and by treatment plant.[3]	Regular testing by a qualified chemist in accordance with tests contained in the American Public Health Association's <u>Standard Methods for the Examination of Water and Wastewater</u>. Some states provide standards for some or all of these characteristics; many states do not. Recommended federal guidelines are available for some of them. Many municipalities collect weekly, biweekly, or daily readings on all these characteristics.
AESTHETIC QUALITY	Presence of Objectionable Appearance, Odors, or Noise Near Sites	4. Number of inspections by trained observers that find some/no objectionable appearance, odors, or noise near pumping and treatment sites--in total and by site.[4]	Obtained by inspections conducted according to detailed guidelines so that standardized readings are produced. Procedures for these measures have not yet been tested. Inspections should take into account the weather, the season, and the time of day.
SERVICE ADEQUACY	Rate of Validated Complaints	5. Number of valid complaints per 1000 clients (not shown to be private responsibility)-- with breakdowns provided by type of complaint (e.g., sanitary sewer backup, billing overcharge, raised manhole cover damaged car, flooded basement).	Tabulation of department records of complaints and requests for service. Those to be included are those not shown to be due to citizen negligence or solely the responsibility of the citizen.[5]
	Citizen Satisfaction with Responses to Service Calls	6. Percentage of persons who had contacted agency and who indicate that response was satisfactory/unsatisfactory--and classified by reason for dissatisfaction.	Obtained from a follow-up survey of persons making contacts. Those who are not satisfied would be asked to give reasons for dissatisfaction (such as: work not done, took too long, discourteous, etc.) to provide statistics by reason.

Objective	Quality Characteristic	Specific Measure	Data Collection Procedure
SERVICE ADEQUACY (Cont'd.)	Rate of Incidents Requiring Repair	7. Total number of breaks, leaks, or other incidents requiring repair or replacement of sewerage facilities per mile of pipes--with those that stop flow distinguished from those that don't.[6]	Obtained from tabulation of job logs and job orders.
	Time to Provide Service	8. Average time to repair breaks, leaks and other damage needing repair or replacement--with those that stop flow distinguished from those that do not.	Obtained from tabulation of job logs and job orders.
	Injuries and Damage	9. Number of valid reported incidents of citizen injury and of damage, requiring repair or replacement, to citizen property (e.g., flooded basements).	Based on department records.
	Traffic Disruption	10. Number of blocked lane-days due to construction or repair.[7]	Can be collected as part of job logs or permits for tearing up streets. Number calculated as number of lanes blocked during job times the number of days required to do the job, totalled over all jobs.

FOOTNOTES

[1]The disposal of sewage sludge may be handled jointly with the solid waste disposal service in some local jurisdictions. The objectives and measures relating to disposal of all solid wastes, including sludge, are included under the Solid Waste Disposal Service section.

[2]Wastewater will include some storm water from infiltration, and if an area uses combined sewers, the combined flow may be mostly storm water. (If wastewater is bypassed at pumping stations or treatment sites, without meters to measure the amount of untreated water released, two additional measures of "the number of hours and the number of instances of bypassing, total and by site, by dry vs wet flows" might be used.) Analogous measures to these could be used for private treatment plants if monitoring is carried out.

[3]Standards for effluent characteristics are generally stated in terms of weeks and months. Some characteristics will have both a weekly standard (e.g., a weekly average of 45 parts per million of BOD) and a more restrictive monthly standard (e.g., a monthly average of 30 parts per million of BOD). Violations, then, can be expressed in terms of which weeks and which months showed violations of standards. Then, this list of weeks and months can be converted to a list of violation days and the total number of days can be computed from the list. Analogous figures for private treatments could be provided if monitoring is carried out.

[4]An alternate measure would be the number of valid complaints about sewerage and treatment sites, already available under #5. But complaint data may not be representative of community opinion in general.

[5]It may also be desirable to keep figures on the number of valid (i.e., facts are correct) complaints that are citizen responsibility, to check on whether the areas of public and private responsibility are understood by agency personnel and citizens.

[6]This measure reflects, to a certain extent, the reliability of repairs (since a second break will increase the total), and the optimality of the trade-off among periodic maintenance, periodic replacement, and repair and replacement in response to breaks.

[7]Note that there is a measure in the General Transportation Service section on traffic disruption from all causes combined.

OVERALL OBJECTIVE: Provide prompt removal of storm water from streets, eliminate spillage of storm water onto
private property from adjoining properties and streets, minimize injuries and damages associated with the
storm drainage system. Assure that the city's storm water runoff does not adversely affect the environment.[1]

Objective	Quality Characteristic	Specific Measure	Data Collection Procedure
STORM WATER REMOVAL ADEQUACY	Standing Rainwater in Streets and Intersections	1. Percentage of streets and intersections, on the average, that have standing water in them, during or just after storms.	Obtained from trained observer measurements, based on inspection of a representative sample of intersections. Procedures for performing measurements have not yet been tested.[2]
	Drainage Problems	2. Percentage of city street blocks and intersections subject to chronic drainage problems.	Identified by experienced judgment of street officials and confirmed by trained observer inspection, possibly of a sample of blocks and intersections identified.
	Storm Inlet Obstructions	3. Percentage of storm sewer inlets, on the average, that are obstructed/unobstructed.	Obtained from trained observer measurements, based on inspection of a representative sub-sample of storm sewer inlets. This inspection may be readily carried out as part of the street inspections carried out for the Solid Waste Collection Service.
STORM WATER REMOVAL ADEQUACY (Cont'd.)	Citizen Perception of Standing Rainwater Inconvenience	4. Percentage of citizens who have/have not been seriously inconvenienced by standing water in their neighborhood during and after storms, classified by intensity of storm required to cause problems.	Obtained from citizen survey.[3] (See Chapter IV, Question 44.)
ENVIRONMENTAL PROTECTION	Runoff Effects on Environment	5. Average and maximum values of runoff water quality characteristics (BOD, suspended solids, and fecal coliforms) as a percentage of weekly standards for wastewater effluent, for each major point of runoff discharge into nearby bodies of water.[2]	Based on water quality measurement at principal runoff discharge points by city pollution control agency, county health department, city sewer department, or other competent agency. These measurements have been conducted in a few cities, but only as part of special studies, not on a regular basis.
SERVICE ADEQUACY	Injuries and Damage to Citizens	6. Number of valid reported incidents of citizen injury and of damage, requiring repair or replacement, to citizen property (e.g., flooded basements, if they are a public responsibility).	Based on department records.
	Traffic Disruption	7. Number of blocked lane-days due to construction or repair.[4]	Can be collected as part of job logs or permits for tearing up streets. Number calculated as number of lanes blocked during job times number of days required to do the job, totalled over all jobs.

Footnote

[1]This last objective does not currently seem to exist explicitly in most cities. It is emerging as
an objective as awareness of the importance of storm water pollution increases. Where combined (waste water
and storm water) sewer systems are used, some measures listed under the Wastewater Treatment Service section
will be relevant (e.g., measures #1, 3, and 4).

[2]It will be necessary to determine what intensity of storm for what period of time will be required
to trigger an inspection, what points should be sampled, and when, before or after the storm ended, the
sampling should be done.

[3]An annual multi-service citizen survey that could be used to collect this data is described in a
separate section of this report. An alternative measure would be the number of valid complaints, but
complaint data may not be representative of community opinions in general.

[4]Note that a measure of traffic disruption due to all causes is contained in the General Transportation
Service section.

OVERALL OBJECTIVE: Provide information to city officials and citizens on _safety_ of nearby bodies of water. Take equitable measures to assure that the _viability_ and _recreational usability_ of nearby bodies of water is not reduced by _water pollution_ from the city.[1]

Objective	Quality Characteristic	Specific Measure	Data Collection Procedure
WATER QUALITY	Health Effects	1. Number of injuries and infections reported to the Public Health department and traceable to the quality of bodies of water near the city.	State Public Health department records. These records are known to be incomplete; it may be desirable to encourage doctors and hospitals to report possible cases for investigation.
	Violations of Water Safety Standards at Nearby Bodies of Water	2. Number of days per year that bodies of water within the jurisdiction satisfied/violated the State quality standards for waters of their class (drinking water supply, fishing, industrial source, contact recreation, non-contact recreation, navigation, etc.) during the past year, for each body of water. Include number of days from time that violation was discovered to date of first measurement within standards, if that has occurred, and length of time water area was closed or restricted, if applicable.	Periodic measurement by a qualified chemist will generate the data on water quality. City records will provide details on actions taken in response. These measurements have generally been carried out by state agencies in the past.
WATER QUALITY (Cont'd.)	Other Restrictions	3. Number of beaches that are closed due to water pollution, total and number closed during past year.	City records.
		4. Number of days of restrictions on recreational and commercial fishing due to pollution, for each water area.	City records should provide data. Decisions and records of county and state may be involved.
		5. Number of species of flora and fauna inhabiting the water, total and with "quality" (high-oxygen, low turbidity) fish separated from "trash" (low-oxygen, high turbidity) fish.	Analysis by qualified biologist. Methods are given in the American Public Health Association's _Standard Methods for Examination of Water and Wastewater_. These measurements have been collected by ecologists as parts of studies, but not as part of regular monitoring.
		6. Number of fish kills attributed to man-made pollution from the city (number of separate incidents reported to the city, total number of fish killed).	Analysis by qualified staff. Positive identification of source of pollution may require county or state intervention. Has been collected for studies but not generally for regular reporting.

Footnote

[1]In many local governments, these are emerging rather than existing objectives. Authority may be shared among city, county, state, and federal agencies. There are several possible levels of local government responsibility; for example, (1) monitoring of water quality; (2) prohibition of public access to areas with dangerous water characteristics; (3) enforcement of laws governing discharges into waters, with responses on a case-by-case basis as alleged violations are pointed out; (4) regular auditing of periodic monitoring by all dischargers of their discharges, using established targets on individual discharges. All of these stages need to be interpreted in light of the intended uses of the water discharges outside of local control.

If regular monitoring of private dischargers is authorized, the local government may want to add other measures, such as "Number of violations cited per year"; "Percentage of audits that discovered violations"; and "Number of discharge-days in violation", based on summing over all discharges the number of days that that discharger was in violation.

SELF-ANALYSIS GUIDE: RATE YOUR ORGANIZATION'S APPROACH TO ASSESSING, PLANNING, SELECTING, AND CONTROLLING ITS PHYSICAL CAPITAL

Source: General Accounting Office, "Effective Planning and Budgeting Practices Can Help Arrest the Nation's Deteriorating Public Infrastructure," November 18, 1982.

ASSESSMENT

Assessing the condition of an organization's physical capital yields important information that is needed to determine the requirements for repair, renovation, and replacement.

1. Your organization collects information on the condition of specific capital investments (e.g., buildings, major equipment, utilities).

    (a) annually

    (b) every 2 to 3 years

    (c) every 5 years

    (d) at more than 5 year intervals

    (e) different items, different schedules, most items annually

    (f) different items on different schedules, most items every 2 to 3 years and none less often than every 5 years

    (g) not done   your choice /____/

2. Information gathered from periodic physical capital assessments is used to (1) identify needs and projects that are included in capital plans and budgets and (2) identify maintenance needs and items that are included in operating plans and budgets.

    (a) 1 and 2

    (b) 1 only

    (c) 2 only

    (d) not done   your choice /____/

3. Your organization has and uses formal or informal standards or guidelines to periodically assess the condition of its physical capital. (It does not matter if the standards are generated internally or externally.)

    (a) formal standards or guidelines are used regularly for most physical capital

    (b) formal standards or guidelines are used periodically for most physical capital

    (d) inventory not up to date

    (e) partial inventory not up to date

    (f) no inventory   your choice /____/

PLANNING

Planning what your organization's future physical capital needs allows careful consideration of trends and desires. This helps prevent the long-term being traded off for short-term advantages.

1. Your organization annually or biannually prepares capital
   budgets and capital plans that cover planned capital
   acquisitions for

   (a) the current year

   (b) 2 future years

   (c) 3 to 5 future years

   (d) 5 or more future years

   (e) not prepared   your choice ╱___╱

2. Your organization coordinates the current operating budgets
   and plans with capital budgets and plans.

   (a) in all relevant areas

   (b) in over half the areas

   (c) in a few areas

   (d) not at all   your choice ╱___╱

3. Your organization reviews both operating and capital budgets
   regularly (coordinates day-to-day activities with short-
   and long-term plans) and updates them as conditions change.

   (a) always

   (b) usually

   (c) sometimes

   (d) never   your choice ╱___╱

9. Do capital projects in your organization tie into the
   budget process and does the budget process reflect project planning?

   (a) always

   (b) usually

   (c) occasionally

   (d) never   your choice ╱___╱

SELECTION

Various analyses can be performed on potential capital investment projects. Each project should also be considered as part of
a broader planning framework.

1. Your organization uses life cycle costing, rate of return,
   or other capital budgeting techniques (where applicable)
   as a basis for project selection.

   (a) always

   (b) at least half the time

   (c) occasionally

   (d) never   your choice ╱___╱

298

2. Your organization considers alternative methods for meeting
    the objective before it selects a specific capital project.

    (a)   occasionally

    (b)   at least half the time

    (c)   always

    (d)   never   your choice /___/

3. Your organization considers long-term operation and main-
    tenance costs before selecting capital projects.

    (a)   always

    (b)   at least half the time

    (c)   occasionally

    (d)   never   your choice /___/

CONTROLS

Control of funds and time used on capital acquisition projects
helps prevent sloppy management practices and inefficiencies.

1. Your organization has funds that can only be used for
    capital investment.

    (a)   yes

    (b)   no   your choice /___/

2. Your organization reviews ongoing physical capital project
    status to ensure that established time and money targets
    are being met. Reviews take place

    (a)   monthly

    (b)   quarterly

    (c)   semiannually

    (d)   annually

    (e)   other (more frequently than 4 times a year)

    (f)   other (less frequently than 4 times a year)

    (g)   never   your choice /___/

3. Your organization has and uses a reporting system to in-
    form top management when project targets are not being
    met or cannot be met.

    (a)   always

    (b)   usually

    (c)   sometimes

    (d)   never   your choice /___/

ASSESSMENT

		Points	Your Points				Your Points	Points
Q.1:	a	10		Q.4:	a	3		
	b	8			b	5		
	c	4			c	0		
	d	2						___
	e	8						
	f	6		Q.5:	a	5		
	g	0			b	4		
					c	4		
			___		d	4		
Q.2:	a	25			e	3		
	b	15			f	0		
	c	15						___
	d	0		Q.6:	a	15		
			___		b	10		
Q.3:	a	15			c	8		
	b	8			d	5		
	c	12			e	3		
	d	6			f	0		
	e	0						___
			___					

<u>SELECTION</u>

		Points	Your Points			Points	Your Points
Q.1:	a	20		Q.5:	a	20	
	b	10			b	10	
	c	5			c	5	
	d	0			d	0	
			_____				_____
Q.2:	a	3		Q.6:	a	10	
	b	8			b	5	
	c	15			c	3	
	d	0			d	0	
			_____				_____
Q.3:	a	25		Q.7:	a	20	
	b	15			b	10	
	c	10			c	5	
	d	0			d	0	
			_____				_____
Q.4:	a	10		Q.8:	a	15	
	b	5			b	8	
	c	3			c	4	
	d	0			d	0	
			_____				

			_____				_____
Q.2:	a	20		Q.6:	a	15	
	b	15			b	10	
	c	10			c	5	
	d	5			d	0	
	e	18	_____				_____
	f	10		Q.7:	a	10	
	g	0			b	0	
			_____				_____
Q.3:	a	15		Q.8:	a	10	
	b	10			b	0	
	c	5					
	d	0					_____

	VERY GOOD System	420 – 500 points
	GOOD System	350 – 419 "
Q.4: a 20	AVERAGE System	290 – 349 "
b 13	WEAK System	240 – 289 "
c 8	POOR System	Below 240
d 0		

PARTIAL LIST OF PUBLIC WORKS AND INFRASTRUCTURE ORGANIZATIONS

American Association of State Highway and Transportation Officials, Washington
American Concrete Institute, Detroit
American Concrete Paving Association, Washington, D.C.
American Concrete Pipe Association, Washington, D.C.
American Consulting Engineers Council, Washington, D.C.
American Iron and Steel Institute, Washington, D.C.
American National Standards Institute, New York
American Public Health Association, Washington, D.C.
American Public Power Association, Washington, D.C.
American Public Transit Association, Washington, D.C.
American Public Works Association, Chicago
American Road and Transportation Builders Association, Washington, D.C.
American Society of Civil Engineers, New York
American Society of Testing Materials, Philadelphia
American Water Works Association, Denver
Asphalt Emulsion Manufacturers' Association, Washington, D.C.
Asphalt Institute, College Park, Md.
Associated General Contractors of America, Washington, D.C.
Associated Public Works Contractors, Milwaukee

Association of State and Interstate Water Pollution Control Administrators, Washington, D.C.

Chemical Manufacturers' Association, Washington, D.C.

Construction Industry Manufacturers' Association, Milwaukee

Ductile Iron Pipe Association, Birmingham

Government Finance Officer's Association, Chicago

Governmental Refuse Collection and Disposal Association, Silver Spring, Md.

Institute of Electrical and Electronics Engineers, New York

Institute of Transportation Engineers, Washington, D.C.

International Bridge, Tunnel and Turnpike Association, Washington, D.C.

International City Management Association—Washington, D.C.

International Road Federation, Washington, D.C.

Interstate Conference of Water Problems, Washington, D.C.

National Asphalt Pavement Association, Riverdale, Md.

National Association of Counties, Washington, D.C.

National Association of Urban Flood Management Agencies, Washington, D.C.

National Association of Water Companies, Washington, D.C.

National Clay Pipe Institute, Crystal Lake, Ill.

National Corrugated Steel Pipe Association, Washington, D.C.

National Crushed Stone Association, Washington, D.C.

National Sanitation Foundation, Ann Arbor, Mich.

National Utility Contractor's Association, Arlington, Va.

National Water Well Association, Worthington, Oh.

Portland Cement Association, Skokie, Ill.

Prestressed Concrete Institute, Chicago

Transportation Research Board, Washington, D.C.

Water and Wastewater Equipment Manufacturer's Association, Washington, D.C.

Water Pollution Control Federation, Washington, D.C.

BUDGET DATA FROM THE CITY OF FORT COLLINS, COLORADO

Letter of Transmittal
City Manager's Budget Message
City Facts
Budget Process and Philosophy
How to Use the Budget Document
Budget Summary
Economic Assumptions
Balance Sheet
Expenditures by Fund
Property Tax Data
Personnel Summary
Organization Chart
General Fund Data
Capital Improvement Program
Cost Control Budget
Glossary
Development Fees
Debt and Capital Improvement Policies
Fund Explanations

CITY OF FORT COLLINS

August 27, 1985

The Honorable Mayor and Members of City Council
City of Fort Collins
Fort Collins, Colorado 80522

Councilmembers:

Transmitted herewith is the Recommended Budget for 1986. It represents numerous hours of analysis and difficult decision making by departments, the Budget and Research Office and managerial staff.

Both the Operation and Maintenance and Capital Budgets are soundly constructed and reflect direction provided by Council. The Inflator segment of the City's Cost Control Budget is recommended to be initiated during 1986, and additional funding requests will be submitted to Council early next year, when the uncertainties relating to federal budget actions and economic conditions are better known.

The 1986 Recommended Budget document incorporates several new sections, which we hope will be informative and useful to all its readers. The "Introduction" section contains four new sections: "Fort Collins Facts", to familiarize our many non-local readers with general information about our community; "How to Use the Budget Document" and "Key to Understanding Financial Statements" explain what this document contains; and "Budget Process and Philosophy" describes how we develop the Budget, how we amend it, and how we control it. The Appendices section includes a summary of Development Fees, to assist interested readers. A Combined Balance Sheet is another innovation for the reader of private financial documents. It shows that the City is "big business."

A great deal of credit goes to the staff of the Budget & Research Office for the quality of the document. The GFOA Budget Award recognizes that quality. Departments and staff of the entire City deserve credit also for doing long range thinking and for meeting the community's needs within targets.

The 1986 Recommended Budget provides a solid basis from which City Council can direct the progress of the City of Fort Collins in the upcoming year.

Respectfully submitted,

John E. Arnold
City Manager

CITY MANAGER'S BUDGET MESSAGE

The 1986 Recommended Budget has been built on the conservative financial and management principles embraced by staff and City Council, and reflects the commitment of both to maintaining necessary services to the City's residents, improving the quality of operation of the City, and keeping expenditures and taxpayer load to a minimum.

OVERVIEW

The 1986 Recommended Budget totals $148,736,893. When internal transfers are excluded, the 1986 Net Budget totals $103,312,053 for a decrease of 14.5% from the 1985 Net Revised Budget of $120,856,161.

City-wide, we will be able to maintain service levels in 1986 with a net expenditure of $76,457,100, an increase of 6.6% in Operation and Maintenance costs over 1985 levels. Net capital expenditures in the Capital Improvement Program, and Light and Power Utility, will amount to $22,211,784, a decrease of 51.4% from 1985. Expenditures for Debt Service will total $4,643,169, an increase of 32.8% over 1985.

The General Fund provides for 1986 gross expenditures of $24,876,939 (an increase of 7.8% over 1985 adopted Budget) and a projected year-end balance of $522,698.

DRIVING FORCES

The City of Fort Collins 1986 Recommended Budget is a financial plan which provides the necessary resources to respond to needs identified by three basic "driving forces" within the City:

     I. Council Goals
    II. Citizen Input
  III. Managers' Expertise

I. COUNCIL GOALS

A number of major goals were identified by Council at its retreat in April 1985. Several of these goals require direct financial support, and are appropriately reflected in the Budget.

    a.   Basic Municipal Services and Infrastructures

        The basic responsibilities of local government continue to be a high priority, and have been funded to the extent that projected resources allow. Services such as police, fire, utilities, and streets have retained their funding priority standing in the 1986

Recommended Budget, as they are crucial elements of Council's commitment to the residents of our community. Protection and maintenance of these services is of paramount importance, and 1986 funding has been dedicated to:

- enhance police, fire and ambulance response through a computer-aided dispatch system,

- replace fire equipment,

- improve and maintain excellent streets,

- provide smooth and steady traffic flows, and

- improve handicapped accessibility on City sidewalks and at facilities.

b.   Natural Resources

The evolution of the Department of Natural Resources will continue, with the designation of the department in the "Maintenance of Effort" category of City services.

c.   Air Quality

Protecting and improving air quality for our residents continues to be a Council goal and existing 1985 funding is available to move forward with a formal program of research and action, to protect this precious resource in our community. Additional funding for this program will be considered, as a Supplemental Request, during 1986.

d.   Corridor

Preservation of a corridor area between Fort Collins and Loveland is an important Council goal. A Corridor Task Force is investigating options and financing mechanisms to secure the area, which would help fulfill the open space needs essential to the quality of life in our communities.

e.   Railroad

Methods of dealing with safety and transportation issues affected by the presence of railroad traffic through the center of the City are being studied. In addition, resources to accomplish railroad crossing improvements have been provided for in 1986.

f.   Intergovernmental Relations

The City is committed to maintaining a close working relationship with Larimer County Commissioners, administrators and staff, to promote cooperation in areas of mutual need and concern. Although no new funding is provided in the 1986 Recommended Budget for joint projects, a number of cooperative financing efforts are underway or have been recently completed, such as Block 31 acquisition, Prospect Bridge, Timberline-Prospect to Harmony, and Spaulding Lane. Mutual cooperation is a continuing City goal.

g. Colorado State University

City Council has indicated a goal of nurturing Colorado State University, one of our best citizens and our largest employer. Both direct and indirect City support of CSU enhances the interaction between the City and University, which--developing as a center of educational excellence--will benefit the entire city. Our relationship with CSU has always been cooperative and mutually supportive.

This listing of goals specified by Council in April is not all-encompassing. Many other Council goals, such as assistance to our City's lower income residents, are considered to be on-going, and funding toward the accomplishment of such goals is included in the 1986 Recommended Budget. A full description of Council's Financial and Management Policies, which form the foundation of the 1986 Budget are included in this document.

II. CITIZEN INPUT

Assuring that the City is providing its residents with services which are desired and needed requires a significant amount of citizen input. Through the normal channels of communication available to our residents--telephone calls and letters to Council and the staff, public participation at Council meetings and public hearings, membership on Boards and Commissions--the City actively solicits maximum public input. During the 1986 Budget process, for example, there will be a cable TV call-in show (simulcast on radio) to respond to residents' inquiries and comments, several community meetings, as well as two formal public hearings on the Budget.

During the past several years, two additional major efforts were conducted to obtain direction from our residents: Project RECAP (REevaluation of Capital Projects) was a citizens' committee which provided Council with a recommended capital plan, which forms the basis for the 1986 Capital Projects Fund budget; and the Quality of Life Survey, which sampled City residents' views on a multitude of aspects of life in the City of Fort Collins.

The "Quality of Life" was rated in 1984 as "good" or "extremely good" by 86% of respondents. Compared to the past, the current (1984) situation is rated as equal to or better than five years ago by 74% of respondents. Looking to the next 5 years, 33% expect the quality of life to improve, while 39% believe it will deteriorate.

These responses indicate that our efforts to provide City services have been successful in maintaining a good quality of life for our residents. Some problems were identified by the survey, and the 1986 Recommended Budget provides resources to address the major problems.

The category of things "liked least" about living in Fort Collins include, as we might expect, problems relating to the fast-paced growth of the community: traffic congestion, rapid growth, air quality and poor roads. Respondents also expected these to be the major problems in the next five years, and expect that the best things to happen in the coming five years will be (a bit of an apparent contradiction, but perhaps a vote of confidence in the City's ability to manage growth): industrial growth, controlled growth, Anheuser-Busch brewery, a growing economy, and downtown development.

Under the category of growth, which is seen as both good and bad by survey respondents, the City will pursue its philosophy of "growth paying its own way", with developers being required to pay various development fees to the City, as well as to provide necessary improvements associated with their projects.

Since traffic congestion and poor roads can have an impact on the City's air quality, the City is pursuing an aggressive program of improvement. We are presently working to improve traffic flow by building a "one-way couplet" on Mason/Howes to assist north-south traffic movement in the central business district. The City also now has 82 of its 91 traffic signals computerized, and has implemented the "people friendly" Go Button/Blue Light special to help motorists understand the computerized system. Traffic signal timing is being updated, as well, for better traffic flow.

Road improvements are also underway, with 22 miles of local streets being rehabilitated in 1984-5 through revenues generated by our Transportation Utility Fee. A "Pothole Patrol", initiated in 1984, has repaired 9,000 potholes to date, and will soon be equipped to receive reports on potholes 24 hours a day. Crack sealing and patching programs have also improved the condition of City streets.

The 1986 Recommended Budget continues the City's commitment to an aggressive street improvement program, dedicating over $900,000 for street maintenance (major, minor, pedestrian access ramps, and railroad crossing improvements), and almost $800,000 in new street capital expenditures. The five year Capital Improvement Program includes over $12 million for major street improvements.

III. MANAGERS' EXPERTISE

Completing the triad of driving forces in the City is the professional expertise and judgment of our managers, who must respond to direction from the Council and from citizens, and provide services within the reality of financial constraints.

BUDGET STRATEGY

In an ideal situation, the City could simply respond to the "driving forces" described above, and forge ahead with a spending plan for the coming year. However, significant outside forces have come into play in the 1986 Budget process, requiring a level of conservatism which is more intense than in recent years. Following are descriptions of unique characteristics of the 1986 Budget process, and the strategy we recommend.

UNCERTAINTIES

Federal Budget

The Federal budget for 1986 is not yet final, and will likely not be formally adopted before the time at which our City Charter mandates our budget must be adopted. We have assumed that a compromise will be reached between the houses of Congress, and that Revenue Sharing will be available to us through 9/30/86, at 90% of current levels.

Tax Reform

President Reagan's Tax Reform proposal is currently before Congress. Although it is impossible to know which elements of the proposal will be enacted into law, we believe the 1986 Recommended Budget will not be materially impacted by any of the proposed changes which might be made to present tax law.

FLSA

Under a Supreme Court ruling made earlier this year, the City appears to be subject to the provisions of the Fair Labor Standards Act (FLSA), and an interpretation of this ruling is expected from the Department of Labor sometime this year.

We have initiated administrative actions to reduce the City's potential liability under FLSA, but have not included any additional funding related to compliance with FLSA. Instead, we recommend waiting until early 1986, when specific applicability of FLSA to the City will be known, and to allocate funding, if necessary, at that time. The listing of Supplemental Requests to be considered for 1986 presently includes $532,200 related to FLSA. As more specific information becomes available later this year, the amount may be modified.

City Sales and Use Taxes

The 1986 Recommended Budget anticipates that 1985 growth in Sales and Use Taxes will reach 8% by year end. However, actual collections in the first half of this year have been below this 8% growth. We expect that the situation will improve as the year progresses, and project that 1986 growth will increase to 10%. Because of the uncertainty in this revenue source, particular care is needed in authorizing 1986 expenditures.

Other key "Basic Assumptions" regarding Economic Indicators are summarized on page C-2 of this document.

COST CONTROL BUDGET-INFLATOR

The 1986 Budget provides us with an opportunity to implement the "Inflator" segment of our Cost Control Budget in 1986. The budget process began with development of "Target" budgets for each department, based upon conservatively projected resources. Many departments limited their base budget requests to stay within Target Budget guidelines, but needed to submit Supplemental Requests (Inflators) designated as "Essential", that is, necessary to maintain current service levels.

In past years, such Supplementals would have been approved by the City Manager's Office and incorporated into the Recommended Budget, as projected resources permitted. However, the resources we currently project will be available for 1986 expenditures are barely adequate to cover base budgets in the General Fund. Because of this fact and the uncertainties listed earlier, it would not be prudent fiscal management to approve 1986 Supplementals in the General Fund at this time. In the interest of equity, no Supplementals have been incorporated for any City department.

Instead, we plan to implement the "Inflator" segment of the 1986 Budget during 1986. After the first quarter of 1986 has ended, we will examine actual 1985 revenues and expenditures, as well as updated 1986 revenue projections, and determine if some 1986 Supplementals can be funded. (Based on past experience of annual departmental savings, we expect to be able to fund approximately $500,000 in Supplementals.)

UNFINANCED NEEDS

OPERATION AND MAINTENANCE COSTS

The current listing of Supplemental Requests which will be considered as 1986 Inflators does not include all departmental requests, which totalled $4.3 million. The City Manager's Office reviewed each request, and has reduced that list to $1.3 million to be considered for funding during 1986. (This amount is in addition to $532,200 currently estimated to be needed for FLSA compliance.)

Many of the 1986 Supplemental Requests (which were detailed for Council in the 1986 Budget Issues Memo) are deemed "essential." Pending additional funding approval, departments will need to utilize their basic 1986 appropriations to cover such needs which cannot be deferred, effectively cutting back on some currently non-essential activities. Included in the 1986 Supplemental Requests are 8.5 positions, at a cost of $175,000.

CAPITAL COSTS

Funding for the following capital projects has not been included in the 1986 Recommended Budget. The primary funding source for these projects is the 1985 and 1986 Contingency shown in the 5-year Capital Improvement Program--General City "Essential" Capital Projects. Available amounts total $214,224. The projects are:

Recycling	$ 175,000 to 250,000
Air Quality Program	100,000 to 200,000
North Lemay Preliminary Design	60,000
Annual Sidewalk Improvement Program	60,000
Airport Capital Requests	33,333
Lincoln Center - Performance Hall Expansion Feasibility Study	25,000

REVENUES

TAXES

The 1986 Recommended Budget maintains tax rates at existing levels:

Property Tax at 12.86 mills (a mill is one-tenth of a penny, or $1.00 revenue for each $1,000 assessed valuation)

Sales and Use Tax at 2.75%:

On all Sales and Uses	2.25%
On all Sales & Uses, excluding grocery food	0.50%

USER FEE INCREASES

Minor increases are included in the 1986 Recommended Budget for Parking, Golf, Cemeteries, Lincoln Center, and Recreation.

UTILITY RATE CHANGES

The 1986 Recommended Budget reflects the following changes to utility rates:

- Electric   0%

- Water   9%

- Sewer   4%

- Storm Drainage   15%

- Transportation Utility Fee   0%

DEVELOPMENT FEE CHANGES

The 1986 Recommended Budget incorporates the following changes in development fees (DU = Dwelling Unit):

	1985	1986
Parkland	$ 625/DU	$ 655/DU
Storm Drainage	4,521/acre (average)	4,319/acre* (average)
Sewer Plant Investment Fee		
-Residential Single Family	1,600/DU	No change
-Non-residential 3/4"	1,600/unit	No change
Water Plant Investment Fee		
-Residential Single Family	300/DU + 0.22/sf of lot area	No change
-Non-residential 3/4"	2,000/unit	No change
Street Oversizing		
-Residential	248/DU	255/DU
-Commercial	4,528/acre	5,041/acre
-Industrial	1,514/acre	2,020/acre

*There has been no change in existing basin fees. The decrease in the average basin fee is due to the addition of one new basin with lower than average fees.

EXPENDITURES

The "highlights" sections, appearing at the beginning of each grouping of funds in this document, provide specific information relating to 1986 expenditures in each fund. An overview of 1986 Recommended Budget expenditures follows:

INFLATOR IN 1986

As described earlier, additional 1986 funding requests will be considered by Council during 1986, when more reliable projections of resources will be available.

SPECIAL CONTINGENCIES

The 1986 Recommended Budget provides allocations for the following special contingencies:

Venture Capital

The City Manager's contingency account will contain $50,000 for "Venture Capital". This amount will be made available, on a competitive basis, to City departments to assist them in developing entrepreneurial, cost-saving, or profit-making innovations. Departments must demonstrate that the innovation will have a positive pay-back, and enhance basic City services, before funding allocations would be made from this account.

City Council Contingency

The City Council's budget will contain a $100,000 contingency account for the first time in 1986. The purpose of the contingency is to provide Council a direct source of funding for projects which surface during the year. Examples would include: more neighborhood planning, increased or new forms of citizen participation (such as "direct dial democracy"), seed money for research on a new idea that Council supports, etc.

Economic Development

Beginning in 1986, the General Fund will contain an appropriation specifically for "Economic Development"--shown as a Special Item in this fund. Expenditures are not earmarked in the 1986 Recommended Budget, pending the establishment of guidelines for its use by Council.

Funding for Economic Development will total $423,000 in 1986, with $163,000 being provided by 1986 revenues from the City's Lodging Tax, and $260,000 from amounts which have been collected from IDRB issuance fees.

TRANSPORTATION AND OTHER SUBSIDIES

The 1986 Recommended Budget includes a continuation of this City's commitment to the Transfort and Care-A-Van services. A potential General Fund subsidy of $709,617 is expected to be partially offset by incoming Federal revenues of $383,990, resulting in reduced City subsidies of $315,127 for Transfort and $10,500 for Care-A-Van, in addition to a subsidy of $140,344 for Streets and Traffic. Council policies include a goal of continuing to improve Transfort ridership and decreasing the needed City subsidy accordingly.

Other major functions subsidized from General Fund resources include $806,732 to Recreation, $526,665 to Cultural Services, $480,817 to Communications, and $128,037 to Cemeteries.

In addition, we recommend allocating funds to outside agencies in 1986 as follows: $4,350,257 to Poudre Fire Authority for operations, $275,000 to the Housing Authority for an Affordable Housing Program, $152,100 to Community Service Agencies, and $137,890 to the Fort Collins/Loveland Airport Authority for debt service payments.

PERSONNEL ISSUES

Changes in employee pay and benefits are reflected in the following items incorporated into the 1986 Recommended Budget:

- The implementation of a new pay-for-performance system has been budgeted at increases of 4.5% for pay and 0.5% for associated benefits. These increases total $1,150,000, consisting of $560,000 in the General Fund and $590,000 for all other City funds.

  The allocation of these amounts simply provides this maximum amount in the 1986 Recommended Budget. If pay increases needed, and approved by Council later this year, are shown to be lower based on competitive market increases, the full amounts shown here would not be used. Budgeted amounts in excess of Council-approved levels would be "frozen" and would not be available for expenditure.

- The first year amount budgeted for a three-year program to reconcile comparable worth is $98,000 City-wide.

- The cafeteria benefits design, including addition of dental coverage, is budgeted at $262,500 City-wide. The cafeteria plan will also provide for an additional holiday for employees, Martin Luther King Day, at a value of $92,000, as well as Medical Insurance for disabled and early retiree employees, to be funded by $150,000 from the City's General Pension Fund.

- An increase in salaries paid to year-round hourly employees has been budgeted at a cost of $81,000.

The rulings on Fair Labor Standards Act legislation may also create a budget impact in 1986. Because of outside legislative and regulations changes, and our own work schedule restructuring, the actual dollar impact of this legislation is not certain at this time, but is estimated at $532,200. Any increase needed in the 1986 Budget to accommodate FLSA impacts will be presented to Council as our "number-one" priority on the 1986 Supplemental Request list, to be considered in early 1986.

ADDITIONS TO STAFF

The 1986 Recommended Budget provides for a net increase of 7.25 positions to be added to existing staff levels. Seven of the new positions are for the Indoor Pool/Ice Rink, and will begin in mid-1986.

CAPITAL PROGRAMS

The 1986 Recommended Budget provides for $22,376,656 of new capital expenditures in the City's Capital Improvement Program and Light and Power capital, a significant (51.4%) drop from 1985 Budget Capital appropriations. This decrease in funding levels does not indicate a reduction in the City's commitment to capital needs, but rather is a reflection of the major allocation of funding to capital in 1985, and a return to normal spending patterns in 1986, as well as of legal and accounting mechanisms. Since capital appropriations do not legally lapse at year-end, it is not necessary to reappropriate in 1986 any unspent capital funds authorized by Council in prior years.

As with the Operation and Maintenance budget, supplemental requests for General City Capital projects' funding will be presented to Council for consideration during 1986.

REVENUE SHARING

Although the Federal budget for 1986 has not yet been approved, the 1986 Recommended Budget assumes that when it is, Revenue Sharing will be available to the City through September 30, 1986, at 90% of current levels. We are dedicating resources from what is expected to be the final year of Federal Revenue Sharing to programs which will have the greatest direct benefit to our City's residents, as follows:

Capital Projects	$ 300,000
Affordable Housing	275,000
Rebate Programs	200,000
Community Service Contracts	152,100
Handicapped Accessibility	33,330
Volunteer Program	· 30,943
Total	$ 991,373

Existing programs which are being funded by Revenue Sharing in 1985, but have not been included in the 1986 Recommended Budget, are Air Quality and Energy Conservation. Each of these programs will appear on the Supplemental Request listing for consideration during 1986.

*   *   *   *   *   *   *   *   *

In conclusion, the 1986 Recommended Budget allocates such resources as are fiscally prudent to provide services to the City's residents, and to undertake capital projects which will enhance the City, and utilizes the Inflator segment of the Cost Control Budget, providing an opportunity for additional funding, should economic conditions indicate that it is appropriate, during the year of 1986. With the exception of enhancing the City's existing performance-based pay system, and initiating a program to

317

reconcile the issue of comparable worth, the 1986 Recommended Budget neither includes, nor suggests, any major policy shifts. Rather it is designed to continue those policies and practices which have proven successful in the past, and to encourage the identification of those which may benefit from improvement.

By not increasing either the Sales and Use Tax or Property Tax rates in the 1986 Recommended Budget, the City's managers welcome the opportunity and challenge to exercise their professional expertise by continuing to provide excellent service levels to the City's residents while keeping taxpayer burdens to a minimum. City staff continues its commitment to retaining Fort Collins' designation as the "Choice City."

SUMMARY

The 1986 Recommended Budget:

- EMPHASIZES A COST CONTROL BUDGET WITH 5-YEAR PROJECTIONS

- MAINTAINS A SOUNDLY-FINANCED CITY WITH CONSERVATIVE REVENUE ESTIMATES AND A POSITIVE GENERAL FUND BALANCE

- PROVIDES FOR INFLATORS TO BE CONSIDERED IN 1986

- CONTINUES PRIORITY FUNDING FOR BASIC SERVICES AND INFRASTRUCTURE NEEDS

- BUILDS CAPITAL PROJECTS USING PROJECT RECAP RECOMMENDATIONS

- UTILIZES FINAL YEAR OF REVENUE SHARING FUNDS FOR CAPITAL PROJECTS AND PROGRAMS OF DIRECT BENEFIT TO RESIDENTS

- PROVIDES LOW-INCOME HOUSING ASSISTANCE

- PROVIDES REBATE PROGRAMS ON PROPERTY TAXES, UTILITY BILLS AND SALES TAX ON FOOD

- ADDS 7 EMPLOYEES TO STAFF

- INTRODUCES AN IMPROVED PAY-FOR-PERFORMANCE SYSTEM

- INITIATES A THREE-YEAR PROGRAM TO RECONCILE THE ISSUE OF COMPARABLE WORTH

- MAINTAINS A PHILOSOPHY OF DEVELOPMENT PAYING ITS OWN WAY

- DOES NOT INCREASE TAXES

FORT COLLINS, COLORADO "FACTS"

The City of Fort Collins is located at the eastern base of the "Front Range" of the Rocky Mountains, 65 miles north of Denver. As such, it is an integral part of the Colorado Front Range Urban Corridor, and serves as a regional trade center for Northern Colorado, Southern Wyoming and Western Nebraska. Originally an agricultural community, the city has recently acquired the name "Silicon Mountain", as it is home to a growing number of national electronics firms spearheading the computer revolution. Fort Collins is also home to Colorado State University, the land-grant educational institution of Colorado.

From its humble beginnings to the present "Choice City" of some 80,000 residents, Fort Collins has enjoyed a rich history. The city had its beginnings in 1836 when a party of French trappers, proceeding north along the Rocky Mountain foothills, found it necessary to lighten their loads before pushing on through a heavy snowstorm. Planning to reclaim this part of their cargo later, they buried the excess supplies, principally gunpowder. The river which flows through Fort Collins, the Cache La Poudre ("hide the powder"), owes its name to these events. This part of Colorado was exclaimed to be the "loveliest spot on earth" by Antoine Janis, a member of the trapping party. In 1844, eight years after originally passing through the area, Janis returned and became the first white settler in what is today Larimer County.

One of the ironies in the history of Fort Collins is that there is actually no military outpost in the city. The name Fort Collins originated during the Civil War period when soldiers under the command of Col. William Collins were sent from Fort Laramie, Wyoming to guard the Overland Stage Route. The original "Camp Collins" was located in what is now the town of LaPorte. A devastating flood in 1864 destroyed the camp and a new location for "Fort Collins" (a subtle name change) was chosen near what is the present downtown area of the city. For almost two years Fort Collins remained a military post until the last soldiers were evacuated in 1866. The fort was abandoned in 1867, but the town remained and prospered. The only remaining building from the old fort has been preserved as part of the Fort Collins Museum.

Much of the history of Fort Collins has to do with the natural beauty of the area, its bountiful agricultural and mineral resources, and its panoramic view of the Rocky Mountains. Part of that panorama is seen on the front cover of this document. One of the most familiar sights in Fort Collins is Horsetooth Mountain, so named for a rock formation which bears resemblance to a horse's molar. Also familiar in the Fort Collins scene are the more than 60,000 Canadian geese which winter in the mild climate.

These are but a few of the facts which make Fort Collins unique - a potpourri of Fort Collins information follows:

FORT COLLINS, COLORADO "FACTS"

* **POPULATION:**   82,150 (as of April, 1985)

    Average Age: 24.7
    Average Educational Level: For people over 25-average 14.1 years
                                  36% of residents have college degrees
    Average Household Income: $27,130

* **ELEVATION:**   5,004 feet above sea level

* **GROWTH:**   In 1984, the 4th fastest growing metropolitan area in the nation, as identified by the U.S. Bureau of the Census.

* **ECONOMY:**   Strong, growing - rated #48 out of 329 Standard Metropolitan Statistical Areas (SMSA's) in the nation under the category of economics in the Rand-McNally "1985 Places Rated Almanac", which also predicts a 24.5% growth in jobs between 1985-1990.

* **EMPLOYMENT:**   Consistently lower rate of unemployment than national average. In 1984, the unemployment rate was 4.5% as compared to the national rate of 7.5%.

* **MAJOR EMPLOYERS:**

	EMPLOYEES
Colorado State University	6,425
Kodak	3,000
Hewlett-Packard	2,360
Poudre R-1 Schools	1,800
Woodward Governor	1,006
Teledyne Water Pik	800
Larimer County	772
Poudre Valley Hospital	740
City of Fort Collins	718
NCR	460

* **COLORADO STATE UNIVERSITY:**

    - operates 11 research centers statewide.
    - has four campuses (over 38,000 acres) in and around Fort Collins.
    - enrolled students over 18,000
    - utilizes a Control Data Cyber 205 "supercomputer". CSU was the first university in the country to have a supercomputer and the first university with a graduate program in large-scale computational research.
    - national leader in fields of agricultural sciences, forestry, and veterinary science.

* **COUNTY SEAT** of Larimer County government since 1873.

FORT COLLINS, COLORADO "FACTS"

* **AIRPORTS:**

    - Community "airpark", 5 minutes from downtown (serves small aircraft)
    - Fort Collins/Loveland Airport, 15 minutes from downtown serves
      commuter aircraft, small airlines, and charters.
    - Stapleton International Airport - Denver, the nation's seventh
      busiest airport, 65 minutes from downtown, serves over 900 domestic
      and international flights per day.
    - Cheyenne Municipal Airport - 45 minutes from downtown, serves
      three airlines.

* **CULTURAL AMENITIES:**

    - Lincoln Center, presents performances by nationally acclaimed artists
    - Fort Collins Symphony
    - Foothills Civic Theatre
    - CSU Art Series

* **IDEAL CLIMATE:**

- Average annual sunny days	296
- Average annual snowfall	46 inches
- Average annual precipitation	14 inches
- Average relative humidity	43% - winter
	30% - summer
- Average temperatures	27 degrees - January
	71 degrees - July
	49 degrees - October

* **RECREATION**

    - Fort Collins is a very recreation oriented city. It ranked #4
      in the 1985 Places Rated Almanac under this category - the
      smallest city in the Top 10.
    - Skiing - Colorado's world-famous ski areas are within several
      hours' easy drive on major highways.
    - Boating - many lakes are close by and easily accessible.
      Horsetooth Reservoir, just outside the city limits is 6.5 miles
      long and provides many water sport opportunities.
    - Fishing - Colorado's "Trout Route" starts nine miles northwest
      of Fort Collins in the Poudre Canyon.
    - Hunting - opportunities abound in the immediately surrounding
      area for antelope, bear, deer, elk, mountain lion, and
      small game hunting.
    - Hiking/Biking - the City maintains a trail system 12.5 miles
      long. Hiking opportunities in the foothills, state parks, and
      Rocky Mountain National Park are unlimited.
    - Camping - state and national campgrounds and forests are within
      short, easy driving distances.
    - Golf - the City owns one nine-hole and two 18-hole courses.
    - Parks - the City maintains 380 acres of developed parkland.
      Citizens can take advantage of softball, volleyball, racquetball,
      and tennis at City facilities. The City also manages 234 acres
      of undeveloped parkland and 828 acres of open space.

BUDGET PROCESS AND PHILOSOPHY

Charter Requirements

The Fort Collins City Charter provides that "on or before the first Monday in September of each year, the City Manager shall submit to the Council a proposed budget for the next ensuing budget year with an explanatory message. The proposed budget shall provide a complete financial plan for each fund of the City and shall include appropriate financial statements for each type of fund." The Charter also requires a budget to be adopted for the ensuing fiscal year "before the last day of October of each year."

Funds Included

A single appropriation ordinance is presented to Council at the first meeting in October of each year, containing the appropriations for all City funds for the ensuing year.

Basis of Accounting

The accounts of the City are organized on the basis of funds and account groups, each of which is considered a separate accounting entity. The operations of each fund are accounted for with a separate set of self-balancing accounts that comprise its assets, liabilities, fund equity, revenues, and expenditures or expenses.

In Governmental Funds (General Fund, Special Revenue and Debt Service Funds,and Capital Projects Funds), the modified accrual basis of accounting is used. Revenues are recognized in the accounting period in which they become available and measurable. Expenditures are recognized in the accounting period in which the liability is incurred.

In Proprietary Funds (Enterprise Funds and Internal Service Funds), the accrual basis of accounting is used. Revenues are recognized in the accounting period in which they are earned and become measurable. Expenses are recognized in the accounting period incurred.

Although classified as Special Revenue Funds for budgetary purposes, the City's three Pension Funds are classified as Trust and Agency Funds for accounting purposes. Trust and Agency Funds are used to account for assets held by the City in a trustee capacity, or as an agent for others. Revenues and expenditures in these funds are recognized on the basis consistent with the fund's accounting measurement objective. For Pension Funds, the accrual method of accounting is used.

Adoption Process

The annual budget process is based upon Charter requirements and City Council adopted financial and management policies. In March, departments develop 5-year REVENUE PROJECTIONS and submit them to the Budget and Research Office, which develops "TARGET BUDGETS" for each department, based upon projected available resources.

Departments begin their BUDGET DEVELOPMENT in April, based upon Targets and a Budget Manual compiled by Budget and Research, which provides detailed instructions. Budget proposals are turned into Budget and Research in May, along with policy analysis relating to matters involving policy decisions that must be made by Council prior to development of the Recommended Budget.

All funds are expected to stay within their Targets. Requests for funds above Target amounts must be submitted in the form of Supplemental Requests. These requests are reviewed by the City Manager, and those having the greatest merit are incorporated into the Recommended Budget, if adequate resources are available.

Each department meets with the City Manager in May, to justify its budget submittal and Supplemental Requests.

In June, the Budget and Research Office prepares a Budget Issues Memo for Council, containing summary information on the upcoming budget and policy analyses for review. This memo forms the basis for discussion at two COUNCIL WORKSESSIONS, which provide staff with direction in developing the RECOMMENDED BUDGET.

The Recommended Budget is submitted to Council in late August and is made available to the public at the same time. During September, two additional COUNCIL WORKSESSIONS are held; public input is solicited at two PUBLIC HEARINGS, and at COMMUNITY MEETINGS held at various locations throughout the City.

The budget for the upcoming year is ADOPTED in October per Charter requirements, and a final adopted budget document is then printed.

Changes to the Adopted Budget

Budget Increases

Funds are expected to confine spending to amounts appropriated during the Budget process. In certain cases, however, appropriations may be increased during the budget year in the following circumstances:

1. **Carryover Encumbrances** - If a department has open purchase orders at year end, related appropriations are encumbered and carried over into the next year to cover the actual expense when it occurs.

2. **Unanticipated Revenue** - If a fund receives revenue during the year from a source that was not anticipated or projected in the Budget, such as a grant or a bond issue, such revenue may be appropriated by Council for expenditure in the year received.

3. **Prior Year Reserves** - In cases where a fund's reserves are greater than required by policies, the inflator portion of the cost control budget may be implemented, with Council appropriating amounts from reserves to fund Supplemental Requests which were not included in the adopted budget. Council may also appropriate reserves in cases of emergency or unusual circumstances, if it determines that such appropriations are in the best interests of the City.

Budget Decreases

When economic developments dictate, budgets may be decreased during the year to levels below adopted appropriations by the deflator portion of the Cost Control Budget. As part of the Budget Process, departments are required to submit Cost Curtailments, detailing, in order of preference, which appropriations they would relinquish should such action become necessary. If this action becomes necessary in the opinion of the City Manager, Budget and Research moves these appropriations to a line item called "Frozen Appropriations." While this does not lower the appropriations within a fund, it prevents them from being spent. If the economic situation should later change, the appropriations may be returned to other line items for expenditure.

Level of Control and Budget Transfers

Control of expenditures is exercised at the fund level. Fund managers are responsible for all expenditures made against appropriations within their fund, and can allocate available resources as they deem appropriate.

There are two general types of budget transfers:

1. **Within Fund** - This is a transfer between line items and/or departments within a fund, and requires approval of the fund manager.

2. **Between Funds** - This type of transfer requires the recommendation of the City Manager and formal action by the City Council.

In order to provide City Council with information and control over capital improvements taking place within the City, Council approval is also required to transfer appropriations between Capital Projects. This is normally done in cases where a project is completed under budget and Council wishes to use the unused appropriations to enlarge the scope of another project.

Lapsing of Appropriations

Per the City Charter, any appropriations which are unspent at the end of the year lapse into fund balance, where they cannot be spent unless appropriated by Council with the following exceptions:

1. **Capital Projects** - Appropriations for Capital Projects do not lapse until the project is completed and closed out.

2. **Grant Funds** - Appropriations funded by federal or state grants do not lapse until the grant expires, or the project for which the grant was received is completed and closed out.

HOW TO USE THE BUDGET DOCUMENT

This section is intended to assist those readers not familiar with the City of Fort Collins, budget documents or local government organizations, in gaining an understanding of how the budget is organized and what information is presented. The preceding section, which details the City of Fort Collins' "Budget Process and Philosophy", will also benefit such readers.

The Fort Collins adopted Budget is divided into two volumes. The first document spells out the Financial and Management Policies upon which the budget has been built. These policies are reviewed, updated, and adopted each year by the Council in order to ensure that any changes in Council priorities and philosophy are reflected in the Budget. The second document, containing the actual budget, is the focus of the remainder of this section.

The first section of the Budget is devoted to the City Manager's Budget Message. This section, in addition to providing an overview of the entire budget, highlights where we are as a city, and how we are respondng to the City Council's policy direction.

The third section is devoted to Summaries which provide a quick reference to basic information in a capsulized form. A Net City Budget, Economic Assumptions, City Balance Sheet, City Resources, City Expenditures, Expenditures by Fund, City Property Tax, Personnel Distribution, and an Organization Chart are contained in this section, which depicts the Budget in a "big picture" format without the detail found in later sections.

The following sections of the document are devoted to the Budgets of the City's various funds. Funds are included in each section based upon the type of activities performed by the funds and requirements to account for different monies coming into the City in different ways. The first part of each fund section is devoted to listing the activities performed within the funds, detailing any changes that have occurred since last year in the programs and service levels provided, and enumerating the revenue and rate changes that will take place. The remainder of the fund sections contains financial statements and projections for each fund. Readers not familiar with financial data in statement form are referred to the immediately following "Key to Understanding Financial Statements". The various fund types contained in the Budget and a description of each are as follows:

General Fund: Is used to account for all activities associated with the general government of the City.

Enterprise Funds: Are used to account for various services for which there exists a significant potential for financing through user charges.

Internal Service
Funds: Are used to account for certain centralized activities benefitting all City departments.

**Special Revenue and
Debt Service Funds:**   Are used to account for the proceeds of specific
revenue sources which are legally restricted to
expenditure for specified purposes.

**Other Governmental
Units:**   Are entities which, although not a part of the
City government, work with the City in order to
provide services to the citizens of Fort
Collins.

**Capital Projects
Funds:**   Are used to account for revenue that is used to
finance capital improvements in the City.

A complete listing of the funds included in each section can be found in
the Table of Contents.

The final section of the Budget is the Appendices; outlining the Fort
Collins Cost Control Budget, which details how the City provides a
soundly-financed plan for operations and capital improvements; a Glossary
of terms important to the understanding of the budget; and a listing of
each position, by fund, included in the budget.

KEY TO UNDERSTANDING FINANCIAL STATEMENTS

Two main types of financial statements will be found in this document, the "Comparative Statement of Income" and the "Comparative Statement of Changes in Financial Position". Both reports provide actual data for 1984; the 1985 Budget and a revised projection for 1985; the proposed Budget for 1986; and projections for the next four years , 1987 through 1990. The "Comparative Statement of Income" shows the profit or loss for each year and the "Comparative Statement of Changes in Financial Position" shows changes in the resources available.

A sample of each type of statement appears on the following pages.

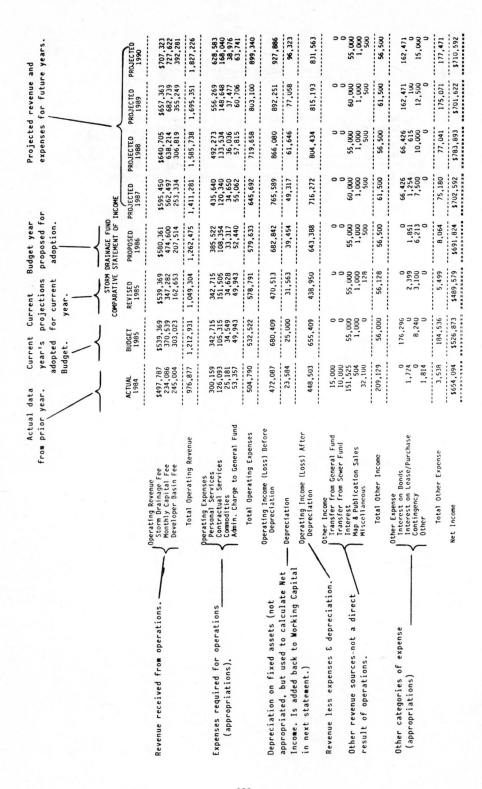

STORM DRAINAGE FUND
COMPARATIVE STATEMENT OF INCOME

Annotations (top):
- Actual data from prior year.
- Current year's adopted Budget.
- Current year's projections for current year.
- Budget year proposed for adoption.
- Projected revenue and expenses for future years.

Annotations (left):
- Revenue received from operations.
- Expenses required for operations (appropriations).
- Depreciation on fixed assets (not appropriated, but used to calculate Net Income. Is added back to Working Capital in next statement.)
- Revenue less expenses & depreciation.
- Other revenue sources--not a direct result of operations.
- Other categories of expense (appropriations)

	ACTUAL 1984	BUDGET 1985	REVISED 1985	PROPOSED 1986	PROJECTED 1987	PROJECTED 1988	PROJECTED 1989	PROJECTED 1990
Operating Revenue								
Storm Drainage Fee	$497,787	$539,369	$539,369	$580,361	$595,450	$640,705	$657,363	$707,323
Monthly Capital Fee	234,086	370,539	347,282	474,600	562,497	638,214	682,739	727,622
Developer Basin Fee	245,004	303,023	162,653	207,514	253,334	306,819	355,249	392,281
Total Operating Revenue	976,877	1,212,931	1,049,304	1,262,475	1,411,281	1,585,738	1,695,351	1,827,226
Operating Expenses								
Personal Services	300,159	342,715	342,715	385,522	435,640	492,273	556,269	628,583
Contractual Services	126,093	105,315	151,505	108,354	120,340	133,534	148,648	168,040
Commodities	25,181	34,549	34,628	33,317	34,650	36,036	37,477	38,976
Admin. Charge to General Fund	53,357	49,943	49,943	52,440	55,062	57,815	60,706	63,741
Total Operating Expenses	504,790	532,522	578,791	579,633	645,692	719,658	803,100	899,340
Operating Income (Loss) Before Depreciation	472,087	680,409	470,513	682,842	765,589	866,080	892,251	927,886
Depreciation	23,584	25,000	31,563	39,454	49,317	61,646	77,058	96,323
Operating Income (Loss) After Depreciation	448,503	655,409	438,950	643,388	716,272	804,434	815,193	831,563
Other Income								
Transfer from General Fund	15,000	0	0	0	0	0	0	0
Transfer from Sewer Fund	10,000	0	0	0	0	0	0	0
Interest	151,525	55,000	55,000	55,000	60,000	55,000	60,000	55,000
Map & Publication Sales	504	1,000	1,000	1,000	1,000	1,000	1,000	1,000
Miscellaneous	32,100	0	128	500	500	500	500	500
Total Other Income	209,129	56,000	56,128	56,500	61,500	56,500	61,500	56,500
Other Expense								
Interest on Bonds	0	176,296	0	1,851	66,426	66,426	162,471	162,471
Interest on Lease/Purchase	1,724	0	2,399	6,213	1,254	615	100	100
Contingency	0	8,240	3,100	0	7,500	10,000	12,500	15,000
Other	1,814	0	0	0	0	0	0	0
Total Other Expense	3,538	184,536	5,499	8,064	75,180	77,041	175,071	177,471
Net Income	$654,094	$526,873	$489,579	$691,824	$702,592	$783,893	$701,622	$710,592

STORM DRAINAGE FUND
COMPARATIVE STATEMENT OF CHANGES IN FINANCIAL POSITION

	ACTUAL 1984	BUDGET 1985	REVISED 1985	PROPOSED 1986	PROJECTED 1987	PROJECTED 1988	PROJECTED 1989	PROJECTED 1990
Beginning Net Working Capital	$1,162,459	$1,796,931	$1,201,656	$445,004	$619,040	$72,358	$629,769	$40,792
Additions								
Net Income	654,094	526,873	489,579	691,824	702,592	783,893	701,622	710,592
Depreciation	23,584	25,000	31,563	39,454	49,317	61,646	77,058	96,323
Contributions in Aid	0	5,000	0	0	0	0	0	0
Bond Proceeds	0	0	0	797,425	0	1,153,010	0	758,684
Total Additions	677,678	556,873	521,142	1,528,703	751,909	1,998,549	778,680	1,565,599
Deductions								
Transfer to Capital Projects	629,513	1,857,565	1,251,625	1,341,152	1,256,462	1,399,108	1,288,977	1,347,889
Capital Outlay	0	12,351	20,062	6,863	7,206	7,566	7,945	8,342
Principal Reduction	0	73,460	0	0	27,671	27,671	67,680	67,680
Reduction in Lease Obligation	8,968	0	6,107	6,652	7,252	6,793	3,055	0
Total Deductions	638,481	1,943,376	1,277,794	1,354,667	1,298,591	1,441,138	1,367,657	1,423,911
Ending Working Capital	$1,201,656	$410,428	$445,004	$619,040	$72,358	$629,769	$40,792	$182,480
Reserves								
Revenue Reserve	$24,259	$24,259	$25,250	$28,226	$25,310	$33,907	$30,792	$39,103
Capital Reserve	1,126,156	284,392	419,754	590,814	0	548,814	0	28,301
Debt Reserve		101,777	0	0	47,048	47,048	10,000	115,076
Reserve for Encumbrances	51,241	0	0	0	0	0	0	0
Total Reserves	$1,201,656	$410,428	$445,004	$619,040	$72,358	$629,769	$40,792	$182,480

Money available as of January 1st. —— Beginning Net Working Capital

Items which increase money available. —— Additions

Items which decrease money available (appropriations). —— Deductions

Money available as of December 31st. —— Ending Working Capital

Reserved uses of money available as of December 31st. —— Reserves

NET CITY BUDGET

FUND	1986 BUDGET	LESS: TRANSFERS =	NET 1986 BUDGET	NET 1985 REVISED BUDGET	% CHANGE
General	$24,876,939	$2,742,374	$22,134,565	$22,400,825	-1.19
Cemeteries (E)	366,419	0	366,419	346,303	5.81
Golf (E)	595,493	52,637	542,856	547,306	-0.81
Light & Power - O & M (E)	28,989,501	2,364,657	26,624,844	25,161,135	5.82
Sewer (E)	9,776,303	3,490,530	6,285,773	6,072,272	3.52
Storm Drainage (E)	1,941,819	1,393,592	548,227	563,377	-2.69
Water (E)	17,123,278	7,878,006	9,245,272	7,487,453	23.48
Benefits (I)	1,748,976	1,423,888	325,088	223,797	45.26
Communications (I)	1,181,333	688,286	493,047	407,847	20.89
Energy (I)	588,674	588,674	0	100,000	-100.00
Equipment (I)	2,271,544	2,081,549	189,995	162,493	16.93
Community Services (S)	658,043	0	658,043	657,247	0.12
Cultural Serv. & Fac. (S)	975,736	8,000	967,736	884,802	9.37
Fire Pension (S)	200,800	0	200,800	190,000	5.68
Gen. Employees' Retirement (S)	155,000	0	155,000	150,000	3.33
Perpetual Care (S)	61,203	61,203	0	0	0.00
Police Pension (S)	72,700	0	72,700	70,000	3.86
Recreation (S)	1,491,722	0	1,491,722	1,288,690	15.75
Revenue Sharing (S)	991,373	991,373	0	0	0.00
Rockwell Ranch (S)	1,600	800	800	800	0.00
Sales & Use Tax (S)	21,591,427	21,453,537	137,890	137,890	0.00
Southridge Greens (S)	313,500	0	313,500	313,500	0.00
Street Oversizing (S)	1,559,000	0	1,559,000	909,000	71.51
Transportation Services (S)	4,184,685	40,862	4,143,823	3,628,432	14.20
Sub-Total Operating	121,717,068	45,259,968	76,457,100	71,703,169	6.63
Capital Projects	14,297,662	96,373	14,201,289	36,675,186	-61.28
Conservation Trust	210,000	0	210,000	464,000	-54.74
Light & Power Capital	6,494,090	0	6,494,090	7,422,269	-12.51
Parkland	1,374,904	68,499	1,306,405	1,094,879	19.32
Sub-Total Capital	22,376,656	164,872	22,211,784	45,656,334	-51.35
Debt Service	4,643,169	0	4,643,169	3,496,658	32.79
TOTAL CITY	$148,736,893	$45,424,840	$103,312,053	$120,856,161	-14.52

(E) = Enterprise Funds
(I) = Internal Service Funds
(S) = Special Revenue Funds

NET CITY BUDGET TRANSFERS

The Net City Budget is computed as follows: the total budget or appropriations for each fund are reduced by the duplicate appropriations (for interfund transfers), which results in a net budget for each fund.

Duplicate appropriations are necessary because the City Charter states that no amount can be transferred to another fund or expended without an existing appropriation. For example, for control purposes, all city telephone bills are paid by the Communications Fund. Each fund transfers money to the Communications Fund for their telephone expense and must include this amount in their budget for transfer to the Communications Fund. The actual telephone bills are then paid by the Communications Fund, which must include this expense in their budget. Although each telephone bill is paid only once, under the City's financial structure it must be budgeted twice in compliance with the City Charter. Other examples of transfers are Capital Projects, employee insurance, General Fund administrative charges and utility billing charges. Thus the total City Budget is the amount that must legally be appropriated and the Net City Budget is the amount that can legally be spent.

ECONOMIC ASSUMPTIONS IN THE 1986 BUDGET

1. Population will increase by 1,975 (2.3%) to 86,675.

2. Dwelling units will increase by 800.

3. City limits will increase by .75 square miles.

4. Developed area within the city will increase by .45 square miles.

5. Inflation will be 5%.

6. The City's mill levy will remain at 12.86, generating $3,722,262. A homeowner with a house worth $80,000 will pay $124.45 in City property taxes.

7. The City's Sales and Use Tax rate will remain at 2.75%, composed of the base tax of 2.25% and 0.25% (excluding grocery food) for General City "Necessary" Capital and 0.25% (excluding grocery food) for the Pool/Ice Rink, as approved by the voters in 1984.

8. Sales and Use Tax growth will be 10% above Revised 1985 projections, generating $17,512,268 from the base 2.25% and $1,670,881 from each of the 0.25% taxes.

CITY OF FORT COLLINS
COMBINED BALANCE SHEET
AT 12/31/84

ASSETS

Current Assets	$138,921,872
Restricted Assets	405,079
Net Plant, Property & Equipment	164,141,360 *
Other	38,972,183
Total Assets	$342,440,494

LIABILITIES

Current Liabilities	$40,026,092
Current Liabilities Payable from Restricted Assets	30,079
Total Current Liabilities	40,056,171
Long Term Liabilities	86,489,115
Total Liabilities	126,545,286

EQUITY

Investment in General Fixed Assets	55,316,382 *
Net Contributions	53,731,375
Retained Earnings	70,079,208
Fund Balances	36,768,243
Total Equity	215,895,208
Total Liabilities & Equity	$342,440,494

This balance sheet demonstrates that, at 12/31/84, the City's Equity (the amount by which Assets exceed Liabilities) is almost $216 million. Based upon a population of 81,000 at that date, this means that equity per resident equals $2,665.

*In accordance with generally accepted accounting principles, these amounts do not include "Public Domain Assets", which consists of roads, bridges, curbs and gutters, and streets and sidewalks. If these items were included, the equity per resident would be close to $6,000.

TOTAL EXPENDITURES BY FUND

	ACTUAL 1984	BUDGET 1985	REVISED 1985	PROPOSED 1986
GENERAL FUND	$21,589,259	$23,076,728	$25,709,627	$24,876,939
ENTERPRISE FUNDS				
Cemeteries	315,624	345,992	346,303	366,419
Golf	502,921	546,240	598,790	595,493
Light & Power	28,518,720	35,643,119	34,836,690	35,483,591
Sewer	6,815,574	9,379,489	11,917,470	9,776,303
Storm Drainage	1,137,841	2,660,434	1,864,945	1,941,819
Water	8,547,114	19,956,674	27,097,740	17,123,278
TOTAL ENTERPRISE FUNDS	$45,837,794	$68,531,948	$76,661,938	$65,286,903
INTERNAL SERVICE FUNDS				
Benefits	1,083,934	1,565,551	1,563,699	1,748,976
Communications	729,351	1,017,684	1,005,050	1,181,333
Energy	493,987	651,346	657,446	588,674
Equipment	1,894,260	2,053,005	2,023,158	2,271,544
TOTAL INTERNAL SERVICE FUNDS	$4,201,532	$5,287,586	$5,249,353	$5,790,527
SPECIAL REVENUE & DEBT SERVICE				
Community Services	211,210	654,217	657,247	658,043
Cultural Services & Facilities	754,799	885,785	884,802	975,736
Debt Service	2,232,996	3,048,528	3,370,853	4,643,169
Fire Pension	172,594	190,000	190,000	200,800
General Employees' Retirement	190,606	135,000	150,000	155,000
Perpetual Care	49,956	51,759	57,203	61,203
Police Pension	66,478	70,000	70,000	72,700
Recreation	1,161,816	1,282,187	1,288,690	1,491,722
Revenue Sharing	1,099,510	1,724,749	1,944,691	991,373
Rockwell Ranch	1,580	1,600	1,600	1,600
Sales & Use Tax	14,551,568	17,808,494	20,343,071	21,591,427
Southridge Greens	911,161	0	313,500	313,500
Street Oversizing	461,181	1,593,333	1,349,000	1,559,000
Transportation Services	2,936,996	3,352,349	3,670,356	4,184,685
TOTAL SPECIAL REVENUE & DEBT SERVICE	$24,802,451	$30,798,001	$34,291,013	$36,899,958
CAPITAL IMPROVEMENT FUNDS				
Capital Projects	17,185,665	30,263,565	36,675,186	14,297,662
Conservation Trust	170,234	50,000	464,000	210,000
Parkland	665,560	890,493	1,167,256	1,374,904
TOTAL CAPITAL IMPROVEMENT	$18,021,459	$31,204,058	$38,306,442	$15,882,566
TOTAL ALL FUNDS	$114,452,495	$158,898,321	$180,218,373	$148,736,893

NET BUDGETED EXPENDITURES PER CAPITA
IN 1986 DOLLARS
(1984 & 1985 Adjusted for Inflation)

OPERATIONS	1984	1985	1986
Utilities	$488	$469	$493
Special Revenue & Debt Service	91	111	137
Public Safety	109	106	106
General Government	84	95	100
Parks & Recreation	54	52	53
Public Works	27	28	24
Internal Services	10	11	12
Cultural Services & Facilities	10	11	11
Sub-Total Operations	873	883	936
Capital Improvements	209	482	256
Total	$1,082	$1,365	$1,192
Net City Budget (In Millions of 1986 Dollars)	$87.6	$115.6	$103.3

WHAT DOES A CITY PROPERTY OWNER PAY?
TAX LEVIES BASED ON YEAR OF ASSESSMENT 1981 - 1986

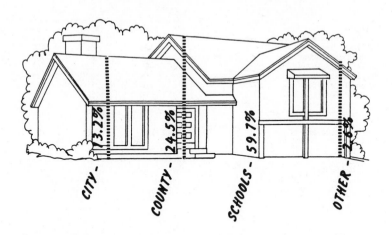

	CITY	COUNTY	POUDRE R-1 SCHOOL DISTRICT	OTHER	TOTAL
YEAR			MILL LEVY		
1981	9.1	19.019	48.63	10.7	87.449
1982	10.7	20.527	49.88	10.7	91.807
1983	10.7	21.548	52.97	10.7	95.918
1984	13.5	23.438	61.46	10.77	109.168
1985	12.86	23.818	58.17	2.55	97.398
1986	12.86	*	*	*	*

*Has not been determined.

To illustrate City property tax payable by an individual owning a home currently worth $80,000:

- Based on 1983 Colorado Statutes, Larimer County assesses residential property at 21% of its 1977 actual value. A home with a current value of $80,000 has a 1977 actual value of $46,083.

ACTUAL VALUE		21%		ASSESSED VALUE
$46,083	X	.21	=	$9,677

- In 1986, the City's mill levy is 12.86 mills (a mill is one tenth of a penny, or $1.00 revenue for each $1,000 assessed valuation).

ASSESSED VALUE		MILL LEVY		PROPERTY TAXES
$9,677	X	.01286	=	$124.45

PERSONNEL DISTRIBUTION

TOTAL CITY EMPLOYEES 718.275

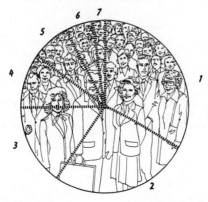

1.UTILITIES-32.7%

2.GENERAL GOVERNMENT-26.6%

3.PUBLIC SAFETY-15.7%

4.PARKS & RECREATION-10.7%

5.PUBLIC WORKS-6.6%

6.INTERNAL SERVICES-5.5%

7.CULTURAL SERVICES &
  FACILITIES-2.2%

PERSONNEL SUMMARY BY FUND

	ACTUAL 1981	ACTUAL 1982	ACTUAL 1983	ACTUAL 1984	BUDGET 1985	REVISED 1985	PROPOSED 1986
GENERAL FUND:							
City Attorney	6	6	6	5	5	6	6
City Clerk	6.75	6.625	6.625	6.625	6.625	6.625	6.625
City Manager							
Administration	6.9	6.726	6.126	7.126	7.126	7	7
Budget & Research	0	0	0	4	4	4	4
Information & Communication Systems	0	0	0	15	14	14.5	14.5
Management Information Systems	12.5	0	0	0	0	0	0
Performing & Visual Arts	0	0.5	0.5	0	0	0	0
TOTAL	19.4	7.226	6.626	26.126	25.126	25.5	25.5
Community Development							
Administration	1.5	1.5	3	3	3	3	3
Building Inspection	20	14.5	15	15	16	16	16
Development Center	0	0	4	7.5	7.5	11	11
Planning	10	8	3	2.5	2.5	0	0
TOTAL	31.5	24	25	28	29	30	30
Cultural Services & Facilities	6	4.5	0	0	0	0	0
Employee Development	8.25	7	7	7	7	7	7
Finance							
Administration	2.75	2.75	2.75	2	2	5	5
Accounting	13	13	13	13.5	13.5	14	14
Budget & Research	3.25	3.25	3.25	0	0	0	0
Management Information Systems	0	11.5	11.5	0	0	0	0
Purchasing	6	6	6	6	6	7	7
Revenue	25	23.5	15.5	15.5	15.5	15.5	16
TOTAL	50	60	52	37	37	41.5	42
Library	20	25.6	25.75	25.25	26.25	26.25	26.25
Municipal Court	3.5	3.5	3.5	3.5	3.5	4	4
Natural Resources	0	0	0	3	3	3.75	3.75
Parks and Recreation							
Administration	3	3	4	4	4	4	4
Forestry	5	5	5	5	5	5	5
Parks, Maintenance & Construction	17	19.5	20.5	24	25	25	25
Planning & Open Space	3	3	3	3	3	3	3
Recreation	15.25	19	0	0	0	0	0
TOTAL	43.25	49.5	32.5	36	37	37	37

PERSONNEL SUMMARY BY FUND

	ACTUAL 1981	ACTUAL 1982	ACTUAL 1983	ACTUAL 1984	BUDGET 1985	REVISED 1985	PROPOSED 1986
Police							
Office of the Chief	4	4	4	4	4	4	4
Investigative Services & Support	22	23	23	23	23	23	23
Staff Services	33	33	20	20	20	16	16
Uniformed Services	67.5	64	63	63	63	70	70
TOTAL	126.5	124	110	110	110	113	113
Public Works							
Administration	3.4	3	3	2	2	2	2
Engineering Services	19.75	13.3	13.12	23.5	23.5	23.5	23.5
General Services	21.5	21.1	18.1	18.1	18.1	21.6	21.6
Transportation Services	36.5	32	0	0	0	0	0
TOTAL	81.15	69.4	34.22	43.6	43.6	47.1	47.1
TOTAL GENERAL FUND	402.3	387.351	309.221	331.101	333.101	347.725	348.225
Benefits	0	0	0	0	0	1	1
Capital Projects	1.75	8.2	9.7	0	0	0	0
Cemeteries	5.5	5.5	5.5	5.5	5.5	5.5	5.5
Communications	0	0	13	13	15	15	15
Community Services	0.5	0.5	0.5	0.75	1.25	1.45	1.45
Cultural Services & Facilities	8	11.5	16	16.5	16.5	16	16
Equipment	18.6	17	17	22.6	22.6	23.6	23.6
Golf	7.5	7.5	5.5	5.5	5.5	5.5	5.5
Light & Power	108	106	113	115	115	116	116
Parkland	1	1	1	1	1	1	1
Recreation	0	0	18	18.75	19.25	20.75	27.75
Sewer	44	47.5	48.5	50	50	53	54
Storm Drainage	4.5	7.5	7.5	10	10	10	10
Transportation Services	9.5	6	38	38	38	39.5	38.75
Water	52.5	54	54	55.5	55.5	55.5	54.5
TOTAL OTHER FUNDS	261.35	272.2	347.2	352.1	355.1	363.8	370.05
TOTAL CITY EMPLOYEES	663.65	659.551	656.421	683.201	688.201	711.525	718.275
Population	73,450	76,000	78,300	81,000	83,900	84,700	86,675
Employees Per 1,000	9.04	8.68	8.38	8.43	8.2	8.4	8.29

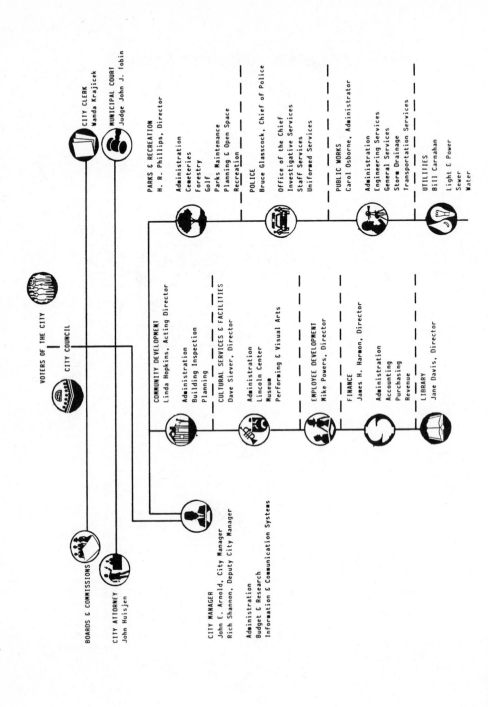

VOTERS OF THE CITY

CITY CLERK
Wanda Krajicek

MUNICIPAL COURT
Judge John J. Tobin

CITY COUNCIL

BOARDS & COMMISSIONS

CITY ATTORNEY
John Huisjen

CITY MANAGER
John E. Arnold, City Manager
Rich Shannon, Deputy City Manager

Administration
Budget & Research
Information & Communication Systems

COMMUNITY DEVELOPMENT
Linda Hopkins, Acting Director

Administration
Building Inspection
Planning

CULTURAL SERVICES & FACILITIES
Dave Siever, Director

Administration
Lincoln Center
Museum
Performing & Visual Arts

EMPLOYEE DEVELOPMENT
Mike Powers, Director

FINANCE
James H. Harmon, Director

Administration
Accounting
Purchasing
Revenue

LIBRARY
Jane Davis, Director

PARKS & RECREATION
H. R. Phillips, Director

Administration
Cemeteries
Forestry
Golf
Parks Maintenance
Planning & Open Space
Recreation

POLICE
Bruce Glasscock, Chief of Police

Office of the Chief
Investigative Services
Staff Services
Uniformed Services

PUBLIC WORKS
Carol Osborne, Administrator

Administration
Engineering Services
General Services
Storm Drainage
Transportation Services

UTILITIES
Bill Carnahan

Light & Power
Sewer
Water

GENERAL FUND RESOURCES

	ACTUAL 1984	BUDGET 1985	REVISED 1985	PROPOSED 1986
Taxes				
Ad Valorem Tax	$2,774,975	$2,965,150	$2,962,389	$3,042,320
Delinquent Ad Valorem Tax	922	2,000	1,000	1,000
Lodging Tax	39,901	100,000	100,000	163,000
Beer & Liquor Occupation Tax	160,480	146,400	149,250	151,500
Franchise Tax - Telephone	250,148	257,621	257,920	265,657
Franchise Tax - Gas	353,742	350,492	367,230	341,392
Franchise Tax - Cable TV	64,744	65,560	74,456	0
Penalties on Ad Valorem Tax	10,814	5,000	10,000	10,000
Total Taxes	$3,655,726	$3,892,223	$3,922,245	$3,974,869
Licenses & Permits				
Beer & Liquor License	$5,098	$4,549	$4,846	$4,879
Contractor License	43,768	40,000	41,000	41,500
Electrician License	750	0	0	0
Plumber License	450	0	0	0
ROW Contractor License	850	0	375	0
Mechanical Contractor License	50	0	0	0
Sheet Metal Contractor License	250	0	0	0
Gas Fitter License	300	0	0	0
Home Occupation License	2,415	2,500	2,500	2,700
Business License	3,484	3,500	3,500	3,500
Business License-Class II	36,890	40,000	31,515	31,515
Building Permits	593,400	420,000	504,000	352,800
Alarm Compliance Certificate	225	0	50	50
Dog License	10,066	0	0	0
Miscellaneous Permits	119	0	0	0
Bicycle License	6,095	7,000	7,000	7,000
Miscellaneous License	50	0	0	0
Concealed Weapons Permit	25	120	0	0
Total Licenses & Permits	$704,285	$517,669	$594,786	$443,944
Intergovernmental				
Senior Transportation Grant	$6,000	$0	$0	$0
State Drunk Driving Grant	28,046	0	0	0
Severance Tax	1,602	0	0	0
Tobacco Tax	434,276	430,000	430,000	430,000
County Shared Court Fines	65,008	50,000	60,000	60,000
Library Contribution-County	77,952	93,950	92,580	99,061
County Office on Aging-SAINT	0	0	3,500	0
PILOT - Light & Power	799,479	798,820	834,033	873,233
PILOT - Water	307,141	343,943	346,413	387,902
PILOT - Sewer	210,861	212,567	216,501	231,278
Total Intergovernmental	$1,930,365	$1,929,280	$1,983,027	$2,081,474

GENERAL FUND RESOURCES

Charges for Services

Court Costs, Fees, Charges	$2,922	$2,700	$3,000	$3,100
PUD, Subdivision & Zoning Fees	9,420	9,300	9,500	10,000
Plan Checking Fees	210,002	140,000	168,000	117,600
Sales of Maps & Publications	14,797	10,500	12,000	12,000
Beverage Application Fees	20,423	13,000	14,905	16,865
Miscellaneous Fees	588	500	500	500
Administrative Fee	490	0	175	0
Computer Charges to Departments	19,832	0	9,283	0
Library Xerox Charges	9,416	9,600	9,600	9,700
Library Borrower Fee-County	18	0	0	0
Total Charges for Services	$287,908	$185,600	$226,963	$169,765

Fines and Forfeitures

Court Fines	$192,363	$204,000	$200,000	$205,000
Library Fines	16,476	15,000	20,000	22,500
Total Fines and Forfeitures	$208,839	$219,000	$220,000	$227,500

Miscellaneous

Interest on Investments	$656,223	$126,510	$250,000	$250,000
Interest from Lease/Purchase	391	0	0	0
Sale of Equipment	171	0	4,790	0
Other Miscellaneous Revenue	37,625	50,000	35,000	35,000
Auction & Miscellaneous Sales	4,356	0	540	0
Utility Billing-Light & Power	221,432	261,952	261,952	279,689
Utility Billing-Water	160,000	125,376	125,376	136,357
Utility Billing-Sewer	63,845	62,686	62,686	68,180
Administrative Charge-Light & Power	405,894	461,675	461,675	484,759
Administrative Charges-Water	333,573	369,073	369,073	387,527
Administrative Charges-Sewer	210,662	242,729	242,729	254,865
Administrative Charges-Equipment	68,175	82,495	82,495	86,620
Administrative Charges-Golf	20,338	23,038	23,038	24,190
Administrative Charge-Storm Drain.	53,357	49,943	49,943	52,440
Administrative Charges-Parking	6,277	15,161	15,161	15,919
Administrative Charges-Parkland	6,905	17,837	17,837	18,729
Cable TV	143	0	270	0
Admin. Charges-Street Repayments	147	0	0	0
Computer Rental-Library	718	6,500	2,600	2,750
Robot Rentals	290	0	0	0
Training Center	23,903	0	9,505	7,000
Recycle Something Refunds	0	0	25	0
Lease/Purchase Proceeds	173,398	0	809,710	0
Contribution-City of Loveland	13,730	21,742	22,600	23,400
Loan Repayment - Parking	28,585	26,763	26,763	24,943
IDRB Issuance Fees	0	0	0	260,000
Total Miscellaneous	$2,490,138	$1,943,480	$2,873,768	$2,412,368
Total General Fund Revenue	$9,277,261	$8,687,252	$9,820,789	$9,309,920

GENERAL FUND RESOURCES

Transfers In

Work for Other Funds	$41,955	$117,129	$54,785	$43,000
Transfer from CDBG	0	0	15,820	0
Transfer from Revenue Sharing	479,725	734,497	734,497	33,330
Transfer from Capital Projects	50,000	0	0	0
Transfer from Sales & Use Tax	12,029,128	11,583,289	12,550,632	13,899,173
Transfer from Street Oversizing	0	183,333	0	0
Total Transfers In	$12,600,808	$12,618,248	$13,355,734	$13,975,503
TOTAL GENERAL FUND RESOURCES	$21,878,069	$21,305,500	$23,176,523	$23,285,423

GENERAL FUND REVENUE USES

REVENUE USE	PERCENT OF EXPENDITURES	PERCENT OF REVENUE
Departments		
Boards & Commissions	0.02%	0.03%
City Attorney	1.04	1.11
City Clerk	0.95	1.02
City Council	0.80	0.86
City Manager		
Administration	1.82	1.94
Budget & Research	0.67	0.71
Information & Communication Sys.	3.85	4.12
Community Development		
Administration	0.64	0.69
Planning	1.78	1.90
Building Inspection	2.35	2.51
Employee Development	1.41	1.51
Finance		
Administration	0.77	0.82
Accounting	1.51	1.61
Purchasing	0.98	1.05
Revenue	2.08	2.23
Library	3.00	3.20
Municipal Court	0.57	0.60
Natural Resources	0.78	0.83
Parks & Recreation		
Administration	0.67	0.71
Forestry	1.16	1.24
Parks Maintenance	6.55	7.00
Planning & Open Space	0.50	0.54
Police		
Office of the Chief	0.89	0.95
Investigative Services	3.51	3.75
Staff Services	3.07	3.28
Uniformed Services	12.08	12.91
Public Works		
Administration	0.38	0.40
Engineering	3.51	3.75
Facilities	4.29	4.58
Total Department Use	61.63%	65.85%

GENERAL FUND REVENUE USES

Subsidies and Contributions

Cemeteries Fund	0.52%	0.55%
Communications Fund	1.93	2.07
Cultural Services Fund	2.12	2.26
Recreation Fund	3.24	3.46
Transportation Services Fund	1.87	2.00
Poudre Fire Authority	17.49	18.68
General Employees Retirement Fund	0.66	0.70
Fire Pension Fund	0.50	0.54
Police Pension Fund	0.18	0.20
	---------	---------
Total Subsidies & Contributions Use	28.51%	30.46%
	=========	=========
Contingency & Other Miscellaneous Use	9.86%	10.53%
	=========	=========
TOTAL USE	100.00%	106.84% *
	=========	=========

*This percentage reflects the fact that current revenues are
 inadequate to fund expenditures. The additional 6.84% is funded
 by reserves.

ENTERPRISE FUNDS
BUDGET HIGHLIGHTS

ACTIVITIES

The City of Fort Collins provides Cemetery, Golf and Storm Drainage
services, as well as Light and Power (electric), Sewer and Water utilities.
Specific operations are:

Cemeteries - directs, coordinates, and maintains the activities,
buildings, grounds, and records at Grandview and Roselawn Cemeteries.

Golf - provides for the operation and maintenance of Collindale and
City Park Nine Golf Courses through cooperative efforts of City staff,
contractual golf professionals, and contractual snack
bar concessionaires, and the Golf Board.

Storm Drainage - provides the administration of the Storm Drainage
Utility, including drainage ways, bridge and drainage crossings, storm
sewer mains, catch basins, and detention ponds; construction management
of storm drainage facilities; and the review of storm drainage plans
for new development.

Utilities

Light and Power - provides the management, operation, maintenance, and
installation of electric utility lines, meters, substations, and
substation tie circuits; coordination of energy conservation
opportunities within the community, and general administration,
material control, and customer service programs.

Sewer - operates and maintains the facilities which provide for the
proper treatment and disposal of domestic, commercial, and industrial
waste waters to meet state and federal regulations.

Water - provides the management, operation and maintenance of water
mains, valves, fire hydrants, and meters; processes water received from
the Cache La Poudre River and Horsetooth Reservoir to meet federal and
state drinking water standards; monitors, operates, and maintains high
mountain raw water supplies to meet present and future water
requirements.

REVENUE SOURCES AND USES

Enterprise Funds

Enterprise Funds are used to account for operations that are financed and operated in a manner similar to a private business in order to provide goods or services to the public on a continuing basis.

Fund	Revenue Sources	Revenue Uses
Cemeteries	Sale of Lots Cemetery Fees Transfers from General Fund & Perpetual Care	Maintenance of buildings, grounds, and records of cemeteries
Golf	User Fees	O & M of Golf Courses
Light & Power	Billings to Customers	Purchase of Power Warehouse Operation Transmission & Distribution Billing & Collection
Sewer	Service Charges	Wastewater Treatment Plant Operation Laboratory Collection of Wastewater
Storm Drainage	Monthly Fees Developer Basin Fees Capital Fees	Storm Sewer Mains Bridge & Drainage Crossings Detention Ponds Catch Basins
Water	Billings to Customers Tap Fees	Water Treatment Plants Operation Quality Control Transmission & Distribution

1986 RECOMMENDED EXPENDITURES

The 1986 Recommended Budget provides for net expenditures which are lower, or significantly higher, than the 1985 Revised Budget amounts for the following funds:

- Golf: -0.8%; due to capital purchase in 1985.
- Storm Drainage: -2.7%; due to 1984 Carryover encumbrances in 1985.
- Water: +23.5%; due to interest expense in 1986 on 1985 bond issue.

PROGRAM/SERVICE LEVEL ADJUSTMENTS

Utilities

In 1986 the Light and Power Utility will act as a contractor for the City Traffic Department in the installation of the City-owned communication system. This will reduce the installation cost by using the existing Light and Power conduit capacity. All costs will be reimbursed to Light and Power by the Traffic Department.

The Water Utility's 1986 budget reflects its 1985 loan of $1,200,000 to the Capital Projects Fund for the Block 31 project, and the repayment of the loan, including interest, during 1985.

REVENUE/RATE ADJUSTMENTS

The preliminary 1986-1990 Budget/Long Range Plan for the Light and Power Utility projects the generation of $5.9 million (3.3% of revenues) in excess of that required to operate, maintain, and capitalize the Utility over the next 5 years. Approximately $2.0 of the $5.9 million will be accumulated by year end 1986. Several options for the disposition of these funds, together with information regarding the possibility of future increases in purchased power cost due to potential Federal legislation, were presented to City Council. Council consensus was to accumulate the $2.0 million in a "restricted reserve" through 1986 to partially offset potential purchased power increases. Funds in excess of those needed for meeting purchased power requirements would be "rebated" to the individual rate payers who contributed to the surplus.

To maintain current service levels and provide for system expansions, the following utility rate increases are budgeted for 1986 and projected through 1990:

	1986	1987	1988	1989	1990
Light & Power	0%	0%	0%	0%	0%
Sewer	4%	4%	3%	3%	3%
Storm Drainage	15%	8%	8%	6%	6%
Water	9%	5%	5%	4%	4%

These rate increases have changed from the rates projected for 1985-1989 due to:

- no increase in the cost of purchased power;
- an increase in the historical growth rate of utility customers; and
- a readjustment of the Five-Year Capital Improvement Program.

The impact of the 1986 utility rate increases on the average residence varies, depending upon whether the home is all electric. The estimated monthly utility bill for a single family home is:

	1986	1987	1988	1989	1990
Light and Power					
Gas Heat	$31.60	$32.52	$32.97	$33.46	$35.30
All Electric*	62.49	62.49	62.49	62.49	62.49
Sewer	10.83	11.26	11.60	11.95	12.30
Storm Drainage	1.76	1.90	2.05	2.18	2.31
Transportation					
Utility Fee	1.00	1.00	1.00	1.00	1.00
Water	18.15	19.05	20.01	20.81	21.64
TOTAL					
Gas Heat	$63.34	$65.73	$67.63	$69.40	$72.55
All Electric	$94.23	$95.70	$97.15	$98.43	$99.74

*Residential demand rate

To satisfy cost recovery policies set by City Council, Cemetery user fees are being increased by 10% in 1986. A 5% increase for annual passes and greens fees is budgeted in 1986 for Golf Fund. Fee increases proposed for 1986 and projected through 1990 are:

	1986	1987	1988	1989	1990
Cemeteries	10%	10%	10%	10%	10%
Golf	5%	5%	5%	5%	5%

POLICIES

The adopted financial and management policies are reflected in the five-year financial plans for the Light and Power, Sewer, Storm Drainage, and Water funds and include:

- administrative charges;
- payment-in-lieu-of-taxes;
- reserve policies;
- debt policy; and
- financing policies.

The City's Enterprise Fund policy requires Cemeteries, Golf, Light and Power, Sewer, Storm Drainage, and Water to recover a minimum of 50% of expenditures, and to work toward a 100% recovery rate. Except for Cemeteries, all are recovering 100% of their costs in 1986-90, and the Cemeteries' recovery rate (including the Perpetual Care contribution) is:

1986	1987	1988	1989	1990
70%	71%	71%	72%	73%

ASSOCIATED CAPITAL

Capital improvements associated with the Sewer, Storm Drainage, and Water Utilities are in the Capital Projects Fund and are found in the Capital Improvement section of this document. The Light and Power Utility conducts ongoing capital programs based upon the need to replace depreciated plant and to add to plant for satisfaction of new customers and to meet demand added by existing customers. The following capital projects are included in the 1986 Budget for the Light and Power Utility's Five-Year Capital Improvements Program:

LIGHT & POWER CAPITAL PROGRAMS

		PROPOSED 1986	PROJECTED 1987	PROJECTED 1988	PROJECTED 1989	PROJECTED 1990
2611	Substation Sites	$0	$0	$0	$142,370	$0
2612	Harmony Station	171,580	0	0	0	0
2613	Richard's Lake Station	443,559	0	0	0	0
2615	Linden Tech Station	0	3,009,805	465,742	0	0
2617	Station Landscaping	25,000	10,008	10,008	10,008	10,008
2618	Substation Dist. Capacitors	0	70,433	56,682	0	0
2630	Major Duct Banks & Circuits	501,773	530,897	578,749	630,924	687,812
2651	Autom'td Dist. & Load CNT	543,696	88,488	105,084	97,919	115,006
2680	Subdivision Construction	840,290	938,607	1,024,614	1,118,525	1,221,069
2681	System Purchases	491,715	206,876	222,654	239,639	254,572
2800	Conversions 4kU-13kU	77,465	82,026	86,427	91,067	95,959
2801	Replacement of EPR Cable	27,568	0	0	0	0
2820	Street Light Conversions	40,031	40,031	40,031	40,031	40,031
2840	Meters & Related Devices	182,921	201,867	220,031	239,833	261,420
2860	Services	96,020	108,185	118,225	129,200	141,196
2890	Dist. Blanket Work Orders	731,641	707,257	790,041	844,996	925,089
2895	Transformer Purchases	294,771	324,056	356,251	391,645	430,555
2921	Load Research	103,560	27,769	64,620	30,614	32,147
2931	Computer Applications	137,975	93,765	31,500	33,075	34,729
2990	Gen. Plant Blanket W.O.'s	309,150	156,404	170,169	185,146	201,440
2991	Power Equip. & Vehicles	375,375	370,037	255,835	261,332	289,460
2992	Southside Service Center	0	500,000	800,000	0	0
2993	Wood Street Service Center	1,100,000	1,000,000	500,000	0	0
	Total Capital	$6,494,090	$8,466,511	$5,896,663	$4,486,324	$4,740,493

1986-1990 PROJECTIONS

Significant factors which impact the current utilities projections are:

- horizontal growth (increase in the number and type of customers); and vertical growth (increased consumption by current customers);
- purchased power from Platte River Power Authority; and
- changes in federal and state regulations regarding standards.

Assumptions used to develop the utilities' projections are:

	1986	1987	1988	1989	1990
Water					
Horizontal Growth	3%	4%	4%	4%	4%
Vertical Growth	--	--	--	--	--
Sewer					
Horizontal Growth	3%	4%	4%	4%	4%
Vertical Growth	--	--	--	--	--
Light & Power					
Purchased Power	--	--	--	--	--
Horizontal Growth	3.62%	3.62%	3.62%	3.62%	3.62%
Vertical Growth	1.08%%	1.08%	1.08%	1.08%	1.08%

In 1986, purchased power comprises 62% of the Light & Power budget.

LIGHT & POWER FUND
COMPARATIVE STATEMENT OF INCOME

	ACTUAL 1984	BUDGET 1985	REVISED 1985	PROPOSED 1986	PROJECTED 1987	PROJECTED 1988	PROJECTED 1989	PROJECTED 1990
Operating Revenue								
Sale of Electricity-Residential	$10,852,007	$11,553,601	$11,362,904	$11,902,181	$12,415,528	$12,989,595	$13,595,878	$14,242,394
Commercial and Industrial	17,147,457	17,980,235	17,941,886	18,779,935	22,283,725	24,077,852	25,688,189	26,773,060
Street & Traffic Lighting	627,219	770,108	716,276	749,941	785,187	822,092	860,730	901,184
Total Operating Revenue	28,626,683	30,303,944	30,021,066	31,432,057	35,484,440	37,889,539	40,144,797	41,916,638
Operating Expenses								
Distribution	2,258,745	2,278,163	2,371,222	2,828,212	3,030,337	3,318,002	3,633,047	3,978,085
Billing & Collections (1)	221,432	264,952	267,952	286,217	311,407	338,814	368,633	401,076
Administration	1,292,274	1,376,570	1,494,896	1,293,969	1,488,099	1,615,343	1,751,043	1,898,885
Purchased Power	19,229,372	20,788,070	21,013,628	22,073,404	24,890,658	26,699,890	28,366,201	29,599,721
Payment in Lieu of Taxes (2)	1,431,334	1,515,197	1,501,053	1,571,603	1,814,389	1,948,033	2,070,714	2,160,496
Material Control	152,570	193,023	189,185	192,311	216,571	258,130	273,125	288,995
General Fund for Administration	405,894	461,675	461,675	484,759	508,997	534,447	561,169	589,228
Contingency	0	118,254	114,810	120,551	126,578	132,907	139,552	146,530
Communications	0	0	0	138,475	7,215	74,650	7,936	8,357
Total Operating Expenses	24,991,621	26,995,904	27,414,421	28,989,501	32,394,251	34,920,216	37,171,420	39,071,373
Operating Income (Loss) Before Depreciation	3,635,062	3,308,040	2,606,645	2,442,556	3,090,189	2,969,323	2,973,377	2,845,265
Depreciation	1,552,382	1,700,000	1,608,578	1,666,810	1,727,147	1,789,670	1,854,456	1,921,587
Operating Income (Loss) After Depreciation	2,082,680	1,608,040	998,067	775,746	1,363,042	1,179,653	1,118,921	923,678
Other Income								
Investment Earnings	681,320	260,000	564,195	636,895	527,175	480,015	631,080	764,100
Miscellaneous	1,179,921	747,105	846,848	1,093,194	944,595	1,083,343	1,039,074	1,089,876
Total Other Income	1,861,241	1,007,105	1,411,043	1,730,089	1,471,770	1,563,358	1,670,154	1,853,976
Net Income (Loss)	$3,943,921	$2,615,145	$2,409,110	$2,505,835	$2,834,812	$2,743,011	$2,789,075	$2,777,654

(1) Includes other contractual of $6,528 in 1986.

(2) Includes streetlight charges of $698,370 in 1986.

WATER FUND
ARATIVE STATEMENT OF INCOME

	ACTUAL 1984	BUDGET 1985	REVISED 1985	PROPOSED 1986	PROJECTED 1987	PROJECTED 1988	PROJECTED 1989	PROJECTED 1990
Operating Revenue								
Flat Rate Sales	$3,254,382	$3,639,722	$3,687,215	$4,139,636	$4,520,483	$4,936,367	$5,339,175	$5,774,851
City Metered Sales	2,214,388	2,545,024	2,508,902	2,816,744	3,075,884	3,358,866	3,632,949	3,929,398
Rural Metered Sales	542,175	542,504	596,392	650,068	682,571	716,700	745,368	775,182
Irrigation Sales	100,869	100,000	100,000	100,000	105,000	110,000	115,000	120,000
Sales to City	28,750	44,500	28,750	44,500	46,725	49,061	51,024	53,065
Standpipe Sales	2,106	2,100	2,000	2,100	2,200	2,300	2,400	2,500
Miscellaneous	153	5,000	5,000	5,000	5,000	5,000	5,000	5,000
Total Operating Revenue	6,142,823	6,878,850	6,928,259	7,758,048	8,437,863	9,178,294	9,890,916	10,659,996
Operating Expenses								
Operation & Maintenance	1,140,538	1,699,267	1,699,267	1,797,879	1,887,773	1,982,162	2,081,270	2,185,333
Labor	1,790,879	1,815,653	1,815,653	2,020,033	2,171,535	2,334,401	2,509,481	2,697,692
Less Labor to Capital	(211,515)	(200,000)	(200,000)	(200,000)	(200,000)	(200,000)	(200,000)	(200,000)
Meter Reading Expense	52,310	49,905	49,905	52,401	57,641	63,405	69,746	76,720
Admin. Charges-General Fund	333,573	369,073	369,073	387,527	418,160	459,975	505,973	556,570
Payment in Lieu of Taxes	307,141	343,943	346,413	387,902	421,893	458,915	494,546	533,000
Utility Billing Expense	160,000	125,376	125,376	136,357	143,175	150,334	157,850	165,743
Contingency	0	100,000	100,000	100,000	100,000	100,000	100,000	100,000
Total Operating Expenses	3,572,926	4,303,217	4,305,687	4,682,099	5,000,177	5,349,192	5,718,866	6,115,058
Operating Income (Loss) Before Depreciation	2,569,897	2,575,633	2,622,572	3,075,949	3,437,686	3,829,102	4,172,050	4,544,938
Depreciation	962,178	950,000	950,000	1,000,000	1,050,000	1,100,000	1,200,000	1,300,000
Operating Income (Loss) After Depreciation	1,607,719	1,625,633	1,672,572	2,075,949	2,387,686	2,729,102	2,972,050	3,244,938
Other Income								
Investment Earnings	1,239,453	650,000	600,000	1,150,000	650,000	500,000	500,000	600,000
A-B Master Agreement	0	0	815,065	752,368	752,368	752,368	742,618	732,155
Total Other Income	1,239,453	650,000	1,415,065	1,902,368	1,402,368	1,252,368	1,242,618	1,332,155
Other Expense								
Loan Interest	690,500	1,576,025	1,536,090	2,958,144	2,868,268	2,977,019	2,917,518	2,855,606
Miscellaneous Expense	61,237	0	0	0	0	0	0	0
Total Other Expense	751,737	1,576,025	1,536,090	2,958,144	2,868,268	2,977,019	2,917,518	2,855,606
Net Income	$2,095,435	$699,608	$1,551,547	$1,020,173	$921,786	$1,004,451	$1,297,150	$1,721,487

STREET AND TRAFFIC COMPARATIVE BUDGET STATEMENT

	ACTUAL 1984	BUDGET 1985	REVISED 1985	PROPOSED 1986	PROJECTED 1987	PROJECTED 1988	PROJECTED 1989	PROJECTED 1990
Beginning Working Capital	$93,007	$122,491	$433,386	$277,093	$288,850	$272,924	$260,585	$231,093
Revenue								
Taxes	301,076	271,185	281,858	295,951	310,749	326,286	342,601	359,731
Charges for Services	302,222	434,700	483,000	497,500	512,432	527,808	543,644	559,951
Intergovernmental	1,512,722	1,443,202	1,506,638	1,544,309	1,595,965	1,639,724	1,684,647	1,740,826
Interest Earnings	10,692	6,000	6,000	6,500	7,000	7,500	8,000	8,500
Miscellaneous Revenue	83,956	61,670	61,670	484,378	500,704	517,595	535,010	553,112
Total Revenue	2,210,668	2,216,757	2,339,166	2,828,638	2,926,850	3,018,913	3,113,902	3,222,120
Expenditures								
Personal Services	968,242	1,020,486	1,020,486	1,101,425	1,156,496	1,214,321	1,275,037	1,338,789
Contractual Services	813,287	936,269	955,219	949,916	1,027,412	1,111,676	1,119,647	1,160,122
Commodities	197,302	221,928	216,302	632,456	664,079	697,283	732,147	768,754
Total Expenditures	1,978,831	2,178,683	2,192,007	2,683,797	2,847,987	3,023,280	3,126,831	3,267,665
Excess of Revenue Over (Under) Expenditures	231,837	38,074	147,159	144,841	78,863	(4,367)	(12,929)	(45,545)
Other Financing Sources (Uses)								
Other	(1,142)	(40,772)	(90,453)	(40,385)	(42,404)	(44,524)	(46,750)	(49,088)
Transfer from General Fund	149,917	114,457	114,157	140,344	140,000	120,000	100,000	80,000
Capital Purchases	(40,684)	(95,049)	(327,156)	(233,043)	(192,385)	(83,448)	(69,813)	(20,884)
Reorganization of Prior Year Fund	451	0	0	0	0	0	0	0
Total Other Financing Sources (Uses)	108,542	(21,364)	(303,452)	(133,084)	(94,789)	(7,972)	(16,563)	10,028
Excess of Revenue and Other Sources Over (Under) Expenditures and Other Uses	340,379	16,710	(156,293)	11,757	(15,926)	(12,339)	(29,492)	(35,517)
Ending Working Capital	$433,386	$139,201	$277,093	$288,850	$272,924	$260,585	$231,093	$195,576
Reserves								
Revenue Reserve	$44,335	$44,335	$56,573	$58,537	$60,378	$62,278	$64,442	$66,375
Capital Reserve	276,581	43,538	0	0	0	0	0	0
Undesignated Reserve	12,036	51,328	135,728	121,121	108,222	102,491	90,835	58,878
Snow Reserve	25,000	0	0	0	0	0	0	0
Transportation Utility Fee Reserve	0	0	84,792	109,192	104,324	95,816	75,816	70,323
Reserve for Encumbrances	75,434	0	0	0	0	0	0	0
Total Reserves	$433,386	$139,201	$277,093	$288,850	$272,924	$260,585	$231,093	$195,576

CAPITAL IMPROVEMENT PROGRAM OVERVIEW

The development of the Capital Improvement Program was significantly modified in the City's Budget, commencing with the 1984 Budget, by Resolution No. 83-86, dated May 3, 1983. Council stated its intention "to develop and implement a program for soliciting citizen involvement and participation in formulating a Capital Improvements Program and the funding therefor." This was accomplished with the adoption of Resolution No. 83-94, dated June 7, 1983, creating a Citizens' Advisory Committee on Project RECAP (RE-evaluation of CApital Projects). Council directed the Citizen's Advisory Committee on Project RECAP to make recommendations on the capital improvement needs of the community. The Project RECAP Committee was instrumental in the determination of the General City Capital projects to be accomplished in the 1985-1989 Capital Improvement Program. On February 21, 1984, Council passed Resolution No.84-38, indicating specific General City Capital projects to be incorporated into the 1985-1989 Capital Improvement Program. Appropriations for each year's expenditures will be authorized with the adoption of the City's annual budget for each of these years. The 1986 Recommended Budget incorporates Project RECAP recommendations.

In addition, at the City's May 1, 1984 election, the City's voters approved the imposition of a 0.25 cent increase in the Sales and Use Tax rate (excluding grocery food), effective for a five year period commencing July 1, 1984, to finance "necessary" General City Capital projects, as well as a 0.25 cent increase in the Sales and Use Tax rate (excluding grocery food), effective for a five-year period commencing January 1, 1985, to finance the construction of a Pool/Ice Rink Facility in the City.

POLICIES

With the incorporation of General City Capital Projects into the 1986 budget, the City of Fort Collins will continue to operate under its existing Capital Improvement Policy:

1. The City will develop a multi-year plan for capital improvements and update it annually.

2. The City will make all capital improvements in accordance with the adopted Capital Improvement Program and the Capital Project Management Control System.

3. The City will identify estimated costs and funding sources for each capital project requested before it is submitted to City Council.

4. The City will use intergovernmental assistance to finance only those capital improvements that are consistent with the Capital Improvement Plan and City priorities and whose operating and maintenance costs have been included in the operating budget forecasts.

The policy also includes an overall strategy to give direction on how capital projects should be financed based upon categories of projects as follows:

- **Replacement** - capital expenditures relating to normal replacement of worn or obsolete capital plant.

    In general, capital expenditures relating to the normal replacement of worn or obsolete capital plant will be financed on a pay-as-you-go basis with debt financing considered where appropriate.

- **Expansion** - capital expenditures relating to the construction of new or expanded facilities necessitated by growth.

    Capital expenditures relating to the construction of new or expanded facilities necessitated by growth will be financed primarily on a pay-as-you-go basis, but when the City's share of the new improvements can be determined to benefit the overall population in the future, debt financing may be appropriate.

- **Unusual** - capital expenditures that enhance the quality of life in Fort Collins and are consistent with the City's goals, but cannot be categorized as essential for the provision of basic services or maintenance of life.

    The City looks to the ultimate beneficiary of each unusual capital improvement in order to determine the source of funding.

ORGANIZATION

As stated in the Capital Improvement Policy, all City capital improvements will be made in accordance with the Capital Project Management Control System (CPMCS). The CPMCS was implemented in 1980, to provide a comprehensive system by which the City of Fort Collins capital projects would be designed and built. The system delineates internal control systems and a comprehensive project reporting system.

One of the internal control systems, project tracking, provides that all projects "will be budgeted and accounted for in a capital projects fund, rather than in the fund financing the project." Accordingly, the Capital Projects Fund was created in 1980. By budgeting and accounting for all capital construction projects in one fund,

- project costs are consolidated even though there may be more than one revenue source;

- all capital budgets are clearly distinct from operation and maintenance budgets;

- accounting for capital projects in capital funds is consistent with generally accepted accounting requirements;

- custom reporting is allowed.

Not included in the Capital Projects Fund are Light and Power, neighborhood parks, and Open Space acquisition and development capital projects, which are budgeted and accounted for in the Light and Power, Parkland, and Conservation Trust Funds, respectively.

The CPMCS provides that:

- Appropriations are made by phase for major projects.
- Appropriations are not necessarily tied to the Annual Appropriations Ordinance. (Supplemental appropriations may be made throughout the year as new projects are approved and/or projects are authorized to move to the next phase.)
- Authorization is required to move from one phase to the next.
- Appropriations are required before a project can proceed.

In addition, a City Charter amendment approved in April, 1981, provides that appropriations in capital projects do not lapse until completion of the capital project.

FINANCING

The Capital Improvement Program includes the Capital Projects Fund, the Conservation Trust Fund and the Parkland Fund.

Capital Projects Fund

The major types of capital projects included in the Capital Projects Fund are financed as follows:

1. General City capital improvements (facilities, parks and recreation, streets and traffic, Police and Poudre Fire Authority) are financed by transfers from the financing fund (General, Sales and Use Tax, Transfort) bond proceeds, and/or grant funds deposited directly in the Capital Projects Fund, in accordance with the 2.25 cents Sales Tax Distribution Policy adopted by City Council, 16% of the Sales and Use Tax Revenue after fixed costs (airport contribution, debt reserve, and other reserve requirements) is committed for General City Capital Projects. In addition, the proceeds of the two 0.25 cent Sales and Use taxes (excluding grocery food) are specifically dedicated to "necessary" General City Capital Projects and a Pool/Ice Rink Facility. In 1986, $300,000 of Revenue Sharing Funds has also been allocated for General City Capital projects.

2. Utilities (sewer, storm drainage, and water) capital projects are financed by transfers from the respective financing fund. Sources of funding in the financing funds are bond proceeds and specific fees.

Conservation Trust Fund

Originally established as a trust fund for money received from the state, the Conservation Trust Fund now provides only for the receipt and expenditure of revenue received from the Colorado State Lottery in accordance with state statutes. The Lottery revenue will finance capital projects which relate to the acquisition and development of open space and trails, as per Council direction.

Parkland Fund

In accordance with the Parkland Fund Policy as shown in the Financial and Management Policies section of this document, Parkland Fund monies will be spent in growth areas, specifically for the acquisition and development of neighborhood parks. The Parkland Fund, therefore, includes funds for neighborhood park capital improvements with associated operation and maintenance costs included in the operating budget.

CAPITAL IMPROVEMENT PROGRAM - FUNDING SOURCES

The following table identifies the three major sources for capital projects: the resident or user, the developer, and the City; and identifies the specific type of revenue collected for each type of capital project.

	FUNDING SOURCE		
	Resident/User	Developer	City Generated
Capital Projects Fund General City	Sales & Use Tax	--	Bond Issue Grant Revenue Sharing
Sewer	Sewer Fees	Plant Investment Fee	Bond Issue Grant
Storm Drainage	Basin Fees	Developers Fee	Bond Issue Grant
Water	Water Fees	Plant Investment Fee	Bond Issue Grant
Conservation Trust Fund	--	--	Colorado State Lottery Proceeds
Parkland Fund	--	Parkland Fee	Bond Issue Grant Interest on Invested Balance

OPERATION AND MAINTENANCE COSTS

Operation and Maintenance costs associated with each capital project are budgeted in the appropriate Operating fund, and are noted on the capital project sheets which appear in this section of the document.

1986 CAPITAL IMPROVEMENT PROGRAM (CIP)

The 1986 Capital Improvement Program Appropriation totals $15,882,566 and includes the following:

- Utilities capital improvements totalling $11,216,152;
- Street improvements including rehabilitation and new construction totalling $1,666,373;
- Neighborhood park improvements, contingency, and administrative expenses totalling $1,374,904;
- Computer-aided dispatch totalling $777,137;
- Open space and trails acquisition, development, and improvements totalling $520,000;
- Recreation facilities totalling $150,000;
- Firefighting equipment replacement totalling $128,000; and
- Handicapped Accessibility improvements to City facilities totalling $50,000.

Only projects which would be incorporated in the Capital Project Management Control System are channeled through the Capital Projects Fund; consequently, Light and Power capital programs are not included in the Capital Projects Fund, but are shown in the total Light and Power Fund only. The 1986 Recommended Budget provides for $6,494,090 in Light and Power Capital programs.

SUMMARY

The Capital Improvement Program is developed in accordance with the City of Fort Collins' adopted management and budget policies, prioritization of capital needs and Capital Project Management Control System (CPMCS). Combined with five-year financial plans for all funds, these policies and the CPMCS form the basis for making various annual capital budget decisions and support our continued commitment to sound long-range financial planning and direction.

CAPITAL PROJECTS FUND

	PROPOSED 1986	PROJECTED 1987	PROJECTED 1988	PROJECTED 1989	PROJECTED 1990
Resources					
Beginning Fund Balance	$431,342	$1,093,801	$357,735	$0	$0
Sales and Use Taxes	3,949,705	2,817,408	5,050,249	4,476,703	3,734,593
Revenue Sharing	300,000	0	0	0	0
Investment Income	43,134	415	35,773	0	0
Sub-total General City	4,724,181	3,911,624	5,443,757	4,476,703	3,734,593
Sewer Fees	325,000	0	0	0	0
Plant Investment Fees	2,600,000	945,000	1,715,000	1,400,000	3,430,000
Sub-total Sewer	2,925,000	945,000	1,715,000	1,400,000	3,430,000
Storm Drainage Basin Fees	207,514	253,334	246,781	213,742	392,281
Capital Fees	474,600	562,497	575,822	498,730	727,622
Bond Proceeds	385,289	412,136	576,505	576,505	227,986
Capital Reserves	273,749	28,495	0	0	0
Sub-total Storm Drainage	1,341,152	1,256,462	1,399,108	1,288,977	1,347,889
Water Fees	4,590,000	573,000	425,000	0	0
Plant Investment Fees	2,360,000	105,000	5,459,000	1,274,000	2,722,000
Sub-total Water	6,950,000	678,000	5,884,000	1,274,000	2,722,000
Total Resources	15,940,333	6,791,086	14,441,865	8,439,680	11,234,482
Expenditures					
General City Essential Projects	1,379,173	1,629,089	3,028,482	3,364,732	3,734,593
General City Necessary Projects	2,251,207	1,924,800	2,415,275	1,111,971	0
General City Pool/Ice Rink Facility (see page J-7) (General City See Section J)	0	0	0	0	0
Sub-total General City	3,630,380	3,553,889	5,443,757	4,476,703	3,734,593
Sewer Projects (see page K-3)	2,925,000	945,000	1,715,000	1,400,000	3,430,000
Storm Drainage Projects (see page L-3)	1,341,152	1,256,462	1,399,108	1,288,977	1,347,889
Water Projects (see page M-3)	6,950,000	678,000	5,884,000	1,274,000	2,722,000
Total Expenditures	14,846,532	6,433,351	14,441,865	8,439,680	11,234,482
Ending Fund Balance	$1,093,801	$357,735	$0	$0	$0

Streets Capital

1. Lincoln-Mountain Realignment	$305,000
2. Taft-Hill Horsetooth Intersection	145,000
3. Timberline-Prospect to Summitview-ROW	100,000
4. Prospect-Shields to Taft Hill	100,000
5. Prospect Street Bridge	96,373
	$746,373

Street Maintenance

Major	$760,000
Minor	100,000
Railroad Crossing Improvements	40,000
Pedestrian Access Ramps	20,000
	$920,000

Facilities

6. New Concessions/Bathhouse-Outdoor Pool	$150,000
Handicapped Accessibility	50,000
	$200,000

Poudre Fire Authority

Equipment Replacement	$128,000
	$128,000

Capital Equipment

Computer Aided Dispatch	$777,137
	$777,137

Open Space and Trails

7. Recreation Trails West of Taft Hill	$140,000
Acquisition of Open Space	100,000
8. Spring Park Road & Parking Improvements	45,000
9. Riverbend Ponds	25,000
	$310,000

Sewer

10. WWTP #2 Improvements	$2,600,000
11. WWTP #2 South Improvements	220,000
12. Lake Street Relief Sewer	105,000
	$2,925,000

Storm Drainage

13. Fossil Creek Basin	$ 300,000
14. Canal Importation Basin	282,120
15. Spring Creek Basin	250,240
16. Foothills Basin	144,958
17. McClellands-Mail Creek Basin	100,000
18. Fox Meadows Basin	98,100
19. Evergreen Park-Greenbriar Basin	75,149
20. West Vine Basin	70,585
21. Dry Creek Basin	20,000
	$1,341,152

Water

22. WTP #2 Expansion	$6,600,000
23. Service Center Improvements	300,000
24. Minor Road Waterline	50,000
	$6,950,000

Conservation Trust

25. Strauss Cabin Trail	$100,000
26. Spring Creek-College Avenue Underpass	60,000
27. Poudre Trail	25,000
28. Spring Creek Trail	25,000
	$210,000

Parkland

29. Troutman Park	$ 425,000
New Park Site Acquisition(s)	300,000
30. Parkwood East Detention Pond Park	275,000
Administration/Contingency	94,229
Department Master Plan	75,000
31. Trilby Area Acquisition	60,905
Park Site Equipment and Plantings	60,000
Transfer to Debt Service	49,770
32. Rossborough Park	35,000
	$1,374,904

TOTAL	$15,882,566

NUMBERED ITEMS REFER TO MAP ON FOLLOWING PAGE.

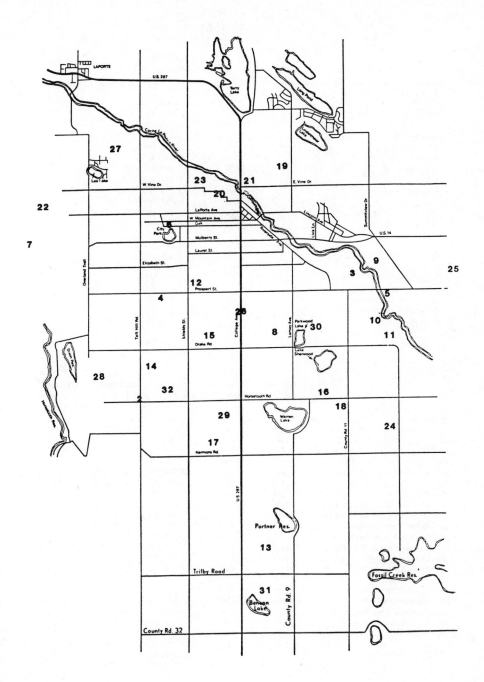

CURRENT PROJECTS WITH
EXISTING APPROPRIATIONS
(as of 6/30/85)

RESOURCES	EXISTING APPROPRIATION
Bank Loan	$2,000,000
BAN's	6,600,000
Bonds - A-B	25,000,000
Bonds - Parks	3,646,500
Bonds - Sewer	1,775,000
Bonds - Streets	13,006,966
Bonds - Water	4,100,000
Contributions	118,014
D.D.A.	807,344
General Fund	2,933,022
Grants	4,913,466
Interest on Investments	133,440
Larimer County	1,545,400
Light & Power	121,444
Revenue Sharing	1,087,885
Sales & Use Tax	6,371,094
Seven-Year Capital	1,401,954
Sewer Fund	14,675,946
Storm Drainage Fund	4,411,973
Street Oversizing Fund	450,200
Transportation Fund	970,593
Water Fund	19,692,385
Total Resources	$115,762,626

FACILITIES	FIRST YEAR BUDGETED	ESTIMATED YEAR OF COMPLETION	EXISTING APPROPRIATION	EXPENDED/ ENCUMBERED TO DATE	AVAILABLE APPROPRIATION
106 Methane Fuel Conversion	1981	1985	$187,885	$189,541	($1,656)
107 Old City Hall Renovation	1983	1986	1,371,206	1,371,206	0
109 Southside Service Center	1982	1985	1,045,700	934,452	111,248
110 Indoor Pool Renovation	1983	1988	80,566	80,020	546
111 Transfort Bus Facility	1982	1985	5,530,970	5,124,997	405,973
113 Block 31 Parking Lot	1982	1985	1,747,800	1,745,662	2,138
117 Aztlan Commun. Ctr. Floor Repair	1984	1985	165,000	0	165,000
119 Lincoln Center Entrance	1984	1985	83,300	77,675	5,625
120 Service Center Building "B"	1984	1985	143,500	30,253	113,247
122 Indoor Pool/Ice Arena	1984	1986	7,360,000	433,194	6,926,806
123 New Concession/Bathhouse	1985	1986	75,000	0	75,000
124 Computer Aided Dispatch	1985	1987	429,000	8,485	420,515
125 Library Remodel	1984	1985	143,000	123,740	19,260
126 Block 31-Phase II	1984	1986	2,400,000	1,461,357	938,643
127 Aztlan Community Center Renovation/Expansion	1985	1986	183,000	0	183,000
128 Asbestos Removal	1985	1986	100,000	0	100,000
129 City Hall West Wing Walls	1985	1985	20,000	0	20,000
130 Avery House Renovation	1985	1985	30,000	0	30,000
131 Canyon West/Columbine Rooms	1985	1986	150,000	8,158	141,842
Total Facilities			21,245,927	11,588,740	9,657,187

	FIRST YEAR BUDGETED	ESTIMATED YEAR OF COMPLETION	EXISTING APPROPRIATION	EXPENDED/ ENCUMBERED TO DATE	AVAILABLE APPROPRIATION
STREETS					
215 Linden Street Bridge Alignment	1980	1985	665,479	652,214	13,265
222 Street Rehabilitation Program	on-going		1,575,478	1,244,742	330,736
229 Timberline-Prospect to Summitview	1981	1988	436,935	299,640	137,295
230 Timberline and Prospect Intersection	1981	1986	1,851,200	375,927	1,475,273
231 Prospect-Shields to Taft Hill	1981	1989	154,900	59,719	95,181
234 S. Lemay-Horsetooth to Harmony	1983	1986	2,084,436	269,024	1,815,412
235 Horsetooth Road-College to Shields SID #76	1981	1985	829,000	792,686	36,314
250 Minor Capital Projects	on-going		200,000	115,479	84,521
252 Harmony Rd. BNRR Crossing	1984	1985	158,800	38,686	120,114
254 Boardwalk & Landings SID #77	1982	1985	900,400	888,042	12,358
258 Lemay and Harmony SID #78	1983	1985	3,942,375	3,603,604	338,771
259 North Lemay Redesign	1983	1985	16,350	0	16,350
260 University Mall Medians	1983	1985	3,463	1,330	2,133
261 Johnson Drive Improvements	1983	1985	30,000	0	30,000
262 Sidewalk Improvements/Pedestrian Ramps	on-going		40,000	18,739	21,261
263 Fairbrooke SID #79	1984	1985	950,000	938,233	11,767
266 Cunningham Corners SID #82	1984	1986	847,550	538,836	308,714
267 West Horsetooth SID #83	1984	1985	1,183,352	680,577	502,775
268 Landmark SID #80	1984	1986	315,000	257,545	57,455
269 Railroad Crossing Improvements	1985	1988	40,000	0	40,000
270 Mountain Ave./Walnut Street	1984	1985	204,344	198,123	6,221
271 Prospect Bridge Over Spring Creek	1984	1985	96,400	0	96,400
272 Provincetown/Portner SID #81	1985	1986	1,770,861	986	1,769,875
273 Hart SID #84			0	117	(117)
274 Timberline Road-Harmony to Prospect	1984	1987	418,000	24,973	393,027
275 Spaulding Lane Improvements	1985	1985	15,000	0	15,000
276 Rossborough SID #85			0	266	(266)
277 South Lemay SID #86			0	281	(281)
Total Streets			18,729,323	10,999,769	7,729,554
TRAFFIC					
313 Mason & Howes One-Way Couplet	1984	1989	1,329,200	941,139	388,061
314 Bikeways	on-going		135,000	6,790	128,210
316 Horsetooth-JFK Signal	1981	1985	31,500	12,200	19,300
317 Horsetooth-McClelland	1981	1985	31,500	31,499	1
318 Jefferson Street Parking	1982	1985	169,353	166,840	2,513
322 Harmony & Boardwalk Traffic Signal	1983	1985	39,500	28,679	10,821
325 Master Signal Plan (7 Year)	1979	1985	68,834	62,800	6,034
Total Traffic			1,804,887	1,249,947	554,940

	FIRST YEAR BUDGETED	ESTIMATED YEAR OF COMPLETION	EXISTING APPROPRIATION	EXPENDED/ ENCUMBERED TO DATE	AVAILABLE APPROPRIATION
PARKS					
404 Lee Martinez Park	1982	1985	760,000	711,689	48,311
406 Rolland Moore Park	1982	1985	2,886,500	2,742,194	144,306
412 Recreation Trail West of Taft Hill	1985	1989	140,000	0	140,000
414 Open Space & Trails (7-Year)	1979	1985	886,908	866,530	20,378
415 City Park Roads & Parking Lots	1985	1985	223,000	13,600	209,400
416 Acquisition of Greenbelt Corridor	1985	1986	100,000	0	100,000
417 Spring Creek Trail Crossing	1985	1985	40,000	0	40,000
418 Outdoor Pool Painting	1985	1985	40,000	0	40,000
Total Parks			5,076,408	4,334,013	742,395
STORM DRAINAGE					
501 Unspecified Drainage	1981	1989	143,737	16,758	126,979
512 McClellands & Mail Creek Basin	on-going		663,944	4,421	659,523
514 Ditch Consolidation	1980	1985	31,500	20,123	11,377
515 Greenbriar Basin	on-going		242,400	0	242,400
516 Spring Creek Basin	on-going		761,373	192,348	569,025
518 Dry Creek Basin	on-going		133,940	8,239	125,701
519 West Vine Drainage Basin	on-going		190,680	0	190,680
520 Fox Meadows Basin	on-going		317,403	53,413	263,990
521 Foothills Basin	on-going		942,412	393,259	549,153
522 Canal Importation Basin	on-going		961,360	535,636	425,724
523 Cooper Slough Basin	on-going		25,000	0	25,000
Total Storm Drainage			4,413,749	1,224,197	3,189,552
WATER					
601 Water Capital Projects	on-going		56,535	0	56,535
609 Minor Road Waterline	1982	1986	265,000	10,195	254,805
610 Foothills Water System	1982	1986	3,034,850	2,355,412	679,438
612 Modifications to WTP #1	1982	1985	700,000	684,877	15,123
614 WTP #2 Improvements	1982	1985	1,395,000	1,176,227	218,773
618 South Lemay Water Line	1983	1985	190,000	23,287	166,713
619 Timberline Water Line	1983	1987	45,000	33	44,967
620 Westside Transmission Line	1983	1985	3,730,000	2,881,856	848,144
621 1982 Water Bonds	1982	1985	100,000	36,874	63,126
622 WTP #2 Expansion	1984	1986	12,500,000	1,677,850	10,822,150
623 Northside Transmission Water Line	1985	1986	550,000	0	550,000
Total Water			22,566,385	8,846,611	13,719,774

		FIRST YEAR BUDGETED	ESTIMATED YEAR OF COMPLETION	EXISTING APPROPRIATION	EXPENDED/ ENCUMBERED TO DATE	AVAILABLE APPROPRIATION
SEWER						
701	Sludge Disposal	1981	1985	9,951,000	9,735,099	215,901
702	Sewer Capital Projects	on-going		317,947	0	317,947
705	WWTP #2	1982	1986	1,330,000	1,542	1,328,458
706	Northwest Trunk Sewer	1982	1985	1,505,000	1,479,050	25,950
710	Harmony Lift Station	1984	1986	300,000	0	300,000
711	Service Center Improvements	1985	1986	1,500,000	0	1,500,000
712	Harmony Farm Trunk Sewer	1985	1985	700,000	0	700,000
713	WWTP #1 Improvements	1985	1986	659,000	18,053	640,947
714	WWTP #2 South Improvements	1985	1987	188,000	0	188,000
	Total Sewer			16,450,947	11,233,744	5,217,203
OTHER						
902	Anheuser-Busch Projects	1983		25,000,000	4,458,412	20,541,588
903	Poudre Fire Authority Equipment Replacement	on-going		475,000	322,500	152,500
	Total Other			25,475,000	4,780,912	20,694,088
TOTAL				$115,762,626	$54,257,933	$61,504,693

COST CONTROL BUDGET

The City of Fort Collins is committed to providing a soundly financed financial plan for operations and capital improvements. To this end, the City utilizes a Cost Control Budget and will:

1. Prepare separate five-year financial plans for operations and capital improvements.

2. Allow staff to manage the operating and capital budgets, with City Council deciding allocations in both.

3. Adopt financial and management policies which establish guidelines for five-year financial plans.

4. Establish target budgets yearly for all funds based upon the adopted policies.

5. Appropriate the next year's annual budget in accordance with City Charter.

6. Adjust the annual budget as required to reflect changes in the local economy, changes in priorities, and the receipt of unbudgeted revenues, through the use of "Inflators" (Supplemental Requests) and "Deflators" (Cost Curtailment Items).

7. Organize the budget so that revenues are related to expenditures wherever possible.

8. Provide department managers with immediate access to revenue and expenditure information for controlling their annual expenditures against appropriations.

9. Provide Council with periodic Budget Outlook Reports, comparing the annual budget with projected revenues and expenditures.

10. Utilize a performance measurement system for all activities in the City.

11. Evaluate recommendations which have a budget impact in light of the annual appropriations and five-year financial plans.

In the 1986 Recommended Budget, the City of Fort Collins anticipates formally implementing the "Inflator" segment of the Cost Control Budget, as described in item #6 above. Because of various uncertainties at the federal (Federal Budget not final at this time) and local (Sales & Use Tax growth currently running at lower than expected rate) levels, the 1986 Recommended Budget provides for appropriations based on conservative estimates. During 1986, when 1985 actual financial results are known and 1986 resources can be better projected, staff may recommend that Council approve additional 1986 appropriations, based on the City's ability to fund additional expenditures.

GLOSSARY OF TERMS

Ad Valorem Tax	Tax based on the Assessed Valuation of property.
Appropriation	Legal authorization granted by City Council to make expenditures and incur obligations.
Assessed Valuation	Basis for determining property taxes. Assessor determines assessed Valuation of Residential Real Property (home and land) at 21% of its actual value or level of value in 1977. (Other property is assessed at 29%).
Bond	Written promise to pay a specified sum of money, called the face value or principal, at a specified date or dates in the future, called the maturity date(s), together with periodic interest at a specified date.
Bond Anticipation Note (BAN)	Short-term interest-bearing note issued by a government in anticipation of bonds to be issued at a later date. The note is retired from proceeds of the bond issue to which it is related.
Budget	Plan of financial operation, embodying an estimate of proposed expenditures for a given period and the proposed means of financing them. Upon approval by Council, the budget appropriation ordinance is the legal basis for expenditures in the budget year.
Contingency	An appropriation of funds to cover unforeseen events which occur during the budget year.
Contributions-in-Aid of New Construction	Funds derived from assessments made on new developments and redeveloped areas to defray the cost of the new or upgraded electrical systems required to serve these areas. Contribution offsets capital installation cost of secondary, primary, and main feeder lines, streetlighting, and supplemental transformer capacity.
Cost Control Budget	System to provide City services at minimum expenditure levels and respond to changes in the economy, through the use of Target Budgets, Inflators and Deflators.

GLOSSARY OF TERMS

Cost Curtailment Items   "Deflators" in Cost Control Budget. Programs and services which could be reduced or eliminated (in priority order) if revenue received is less than anticipated.

Debt Service   Payment of principal and interest related to long term debt.

Deflators   See "Cost Curtailment Items."

Depreciation   Expiration in the service life of fixed assets, attributable to wear and tear, deterioration, action of the physical elements, inadequacy, and obsolescence.

Expenditures   Decreases in net financial resources. Include current operating expenses which require the current or future use of net current assets, debt service, and capital outlays.

Fund   An accounting entity with a self-balancing set of accounts which are segregated for the purpose of carrying on specific activities or attaining certain objectives in accordance with special regulations, restrictions or limitations.

Inflators   See "Supplemental Requests."

Lease-Purchase Agreements   Contractual agreements which are termed "leases," but which in substance amount to purchase contracts, for equipment and machinery.

Mill Levy   Rate applied to Assessed Valuation to determine property taxes. A mill is 1/10 of a penny, or $1.00 of tax for each $1,000 of assessed valuation. The City's maximum mill levy, excluding debt service, is fifteen mills - per City Charter.

Net City Budget   Total City appropriated expenditures, excluding (net of) transfers among funds.

Personal Services   Salaries and related costs of permanent and hourly employees.

Plant Investment Fees   Charges to new developers for connecting to the City's water or sewer system to compensate the City for additional facilities needed to serve the development.

GLOSSARY OF TERMS

Projected

Estimation of revenues and expenditures based on past trends, current economic conditions and future financial forecasts.

Supplemental Requests

"Inflators" in Cost Control Budget. Programs and services which departments would like to have added (in priority order) if revenue received is greater than anticipated.

Target Budgets

Desirable expenditure levels provided to departments in developing the coming year's Recommended Budget. Based upon prior year's adopted budget, excluding one-time expenditures, projected revenues, and reserve requirements.

User Fees

The payment of a fee for direct receipt of a public service by the party benefitting from the service.

DEVELOPMENT FEES

Development fees are paid by the developer before a building permit is issued, and used for the following purposes:

Parkland fees fund the acquisition and development of neighborhood parks in the area contributing the fee;

Sewer plant investment fees are charged for the connection of new customers to the City's sewer system to fund the additional facilities needed to serve the development;

Storm Drainage fees fund the design, right-of-way acquisition, and construction of new drainage facilities within the specific basin;

Street Oversizing fees fund the oversizing of city streets from local street width and structure to collector and arterial widths and structure; and

Water plant investment fees are charged for the connection of new customers to the City's water system to fund the additional facilities needed to serve the development.

Following is a comparison of these fees in the years 1984, 1985, and proposed for 1986 (DU = Dwelling Unit):

	1984	1985	PROPOSED 1986
Parkland	$590/DU	$625/DU	$655/DU
Sewer-Plant Investment Fee			
Residential single family	1,350/DU	1,600/DU	1,600/DU
Non-residential 3/4"	1,350/unit	1,600/unit	1,600/unit
Storm Drainage			
Canal Importation Basin	5,000/acre	5,000/acre	5,000/acre
Cooper Slough Basin	--	--	2,500/acre
Dry Creek Basin	3,800/acre	3,800/acre	3,800/acre
Evergreen Park-Greenbriar Basin	10,000/acre	10,000/acre	10,000/acre
Foothills Basin	4,740/acre	4,740/acre	4,740/acre
Fossil Creek Basin	--	2,115/acre	2,115/acre
Fox Meadows Basin	3,956/acre	3,956/acre	3,956/acre
McClellands-Mail Creek Basin	2,877/acre	2,877/acre	2,877/acre
Spring Creek Basin	1,400/acre	1,400/acre	1,400/acre
West Vine Basin	6,800/acre	6,800/acre	6,800/acre
Street Oversizing			
Residential	247/DU	249/DU	255/DU
Commercial	4,014/acre	4,528/acre	5,041/acre
Industrial	1,007/acre	1,514/acre	2,020/acre
Water-Plant Investment Fee			
Residential single family	240/DU + 0.18/sq.ft. of lot area	300/DU + 0.22/sq.ft. of lot area	300/DU + 0.22/sq.ft. of lot area
Non-residential 3/4"	1,680/unit	2,000/unit	2,000/unit
Light & Power	Fees equal 100% of on-site development costs, plus a pro-rated share of main feeder costs, and thus vary by development.		

VI. DEBT POLICY

The City of Fort Collins will use debt financing when it is appropriate. It will be judged appropriate only when the following conditions exist:

1. When non-continuous capital improvements are desired.

2. When it can be determined that future citizens will receive a benefit from the improvement.

When the City of Fort Collins utilizes long-term debt financing it will ensure that the debt is soundly financed by:

1. Conservatively projecting the revenue sources that will be utilized to pay the debt.

2. Financing the improvement over a period not greater than the useful life of the improvement.

3. Determining that the cost benefit of the improvement, including interest cost, is positive.

Additionally, the City has the following policies in relation to debt financing:

1. Total general obligation debt will not exceed 10% of assessed valuation in accordance with the City Charter.

2. Where possible, the City uses special assessment, revenue, or other self-supporting bonds instead of general obligation bonds.

3. Fort Collins maintains good communications with bond rating agencies about its financial conditions.

Annual budgets include debt service payments and reserve requirements for all debt currently outstanding for all proposed debt issues.

VII. CAPITAL IMPROVEMENT POLICY

Citizen participation

The development of the Capital Improvement Program was significantly modified in the 1984, 1985 and 1986 Budgets by Resolution #83-86, dated May 3, 1983. Council stated its intention "to develop and implement a program for soliciting citizen involvement and participation in formulating a Capital Improvements Program and the funding thereof." This was accomplished with the adoption of Resolution 83-94, dated June 7, 1983, creating a Citizens' Advisory Committee on Project RECAP (REevaluation of CApital Projects). Council directed the Citizens' Advisory Committee on Project RECAP to make recommendations on the capital improvement needs of the community. The Project RECAP Committee was instrumental in the determination of the General City Capital projects to be accomplished in the 1985-1989 Capital Improvement Program. On February 21, 1984, Council passed Resolution #84-38, indicating specific General City Capital projects to be incorporated into the 1985-1989 Capital Improvement Program. Appropriations for each year's expenditures will be authorized with the adoption of the City's annual budget for each of these years.

In addition, at the City's May 1, 1984 election, the City's voters approved the imposition of a 0.25 cent increase in the Sales & Use Tax rate (excluding grocery food), effective for a five-year period commencing July 1, 1984, to finance "necessary" General City Capital projects, as well as a 0.25 cent increase in the Sales & Use Tax rate (excluding grocery food), effective for a five-year period commencing January 1, 1985, to finance the construction of a Pool/Ice Rink Facility in the City.

Capital Improvement Policy

With the above-mentioned modifications to the process of identifying the City's capital needs, the City will continue to operate under its existing Capital Improvement Policy:

1. The City will develop a multi-year plan for capital improvements and update it annually.

2. The City will make all capital improvements in accordance with the adopted Capital Improvement Program and the Capital Project Management Control System.

3. The City will identify estimated costs and funding sources for each capital project requested before it is submitted to City Council.

4. The City will use intergovernmental assistance to finance only those capital improvements that are consistent with the Capital Improvement Plan and City priorities and whose operating and maintenance costs have been included in the operating budget forecasts.

Capital Financing

The financing of capital projects is generally based upon the different types of capital improvements (see Section VIII of these policies for specifics on Water, Sewer, and Light & Power capital policies). Capital Projects are categorized as follows, with financing as noted for each category:

1. REPLACEMENT - capital expenditures relating to normal replacement of worn or obsolete capital plant.

   In general, capital expenditures relating to the normal replacement of worn or obsolete capital plant will be financed on a pay-as-you-go basis, with debt financing considered where appropriate.

2. EXPANSION - capital expenditures relating to the construction of new or expanded facilities necessitated by growth.

   Capital expenditures relating to the construction of new or expanded facilities necessitated by growth will be financed primarily on a pay-as-you-go basis, but when the City's share of the new improvements can be determined to benefit the overall population in the future, debt financing may be appropriate.

3. UNUSUAL - capital expenditures for improvements that enhance the quality of life in Fort Collins and are consistent with the City's goals but cannot be categorized as essential for the provision of basic services or maintenance of life.

   The policy relating to unusual capital expenditures directs the City to look to the ultimate beneficiary of each capital improvement in order to determine the source of funding. As projects are identified, they will be funneled through a decision process in order to:

   a. determine whether projects are acceptable from the point of view of municipal goal achievements or cost benefit analysis,

   b. evaluate each capital project's relevant cash flow in order to determine if a project is financially viable, and

   c. prioritize capital improvements based upon these findings.

Prioritization of General City Capital Projects

With the incorporation of the recommendations of the Citizens' Advisory Committee on Project RECAP into the 1984, 1985 and 1986 Budget processes, a new mechanism for categorizing General City · Capital projects was developed in order to determine priorities for the allocation of available funds to projects.

General City Capital needs are first identified as relating to one of the Council-adopted "categories of service," as detailed in Policy I.3.:

    I.   Basic (or Core)
   II. Maintenance of Effort
  III. Quality of Life

Within each category, projects are then ranked as:

    A. Essential
    B. Necessary
    C. Desirable

The following matrix demonstrates the resulting order of priority in terms of access to available funds:

BASIC SERVICES	MAINTENANCE OF EFFORT	QUALITY OF LIFE
Essential (1)	Essential (2)	Essential (3)
Necessary (4)	Necessary (5)	Necessary (6)
Desirable (7)	Desirable (8)	Desirable (9)

Basic service essential projects are considered top priority and Quality of Life desirable projects last priority.

VARIOUS FUNDS

VIII.1. ENTERPRISE FUNDS

The City currently has six Enterprise Funds: Cemeteries, Golf, Light and Power, Sewer, Storm Drainage, and Water. The Enterprise Fund classification has been used to account for various services for which there exists a significant potential for financing through user charges. In many of these funds, a subsidy from the General Fund has been necessary to cover operating expenses. Historically, services were accounted for in an enterprise fund only if they were financed more than 50% by user charges. In the 1986 Budget, all Enterprise Funds, except for Cemeteries, are recovering 100% of their costs in 1986-1990. Cemeteries Fund anticipates recovery rates of 70 - 73% in the upcoming five-year period.

There has been a nationwide trend toward the regulation of the demand for governmental services through user fee mechanisms. The Fort Collins City Council supports this concept. The long term goal of all enterprise accounts is self-sufficiency. Toward this end, those funds which are not presently self-sustaining shall incrementally adjust their rate structures to achieve a positive income position.

Those operations which cannot achieve a positive income position within a five-year timeframe may be accounted for as subsidized operations and not as Enterprise Funds. In the case of the Cemeteries Fund, efforts will be undertaken to improve recovery rates in 1986, and beyond. Possible reclassification will be considered, if needed.

VIII.2. LIGHT AND POWER UTILITY

The financial policies of the Light and Power Utility are administered in accordance with the City Charter as more specifically defined in Resolution 77-68, as amended from time to time by City Council action.

The 1986 Budget/Five Year Plan was prepared in compliance with the following:

A. FUNDAMENTAL PURPOSE

"To efficiently manage the City of Fort Collins' energy systems and services with sensitivity to the environment, the community, and conservation of resources. To enhance the quality of life for the consumers and the community through provision of sufficient electrical energy, reliably and economically."

B. ELECTRIC RATES

Electric rates will be based upon the cost of service approach to reflect full distribution of costs to appropriate rate classes in order to effect equitable sharing of costs. Rates shall be established and maintained at a level sufficient:

1. To pay the full cost of operation and maintain the electric utility in good repair and working order;

2. To provide an operating reserve equal to eight percent (8%) of budgeted operating expenditures, excluding the cost of purchased power;

3. To provide a future capital improvements reserve in an amount which shall, as nearly as possible, be equal to the average annual cost (excluding debt financing) of the approved five-year capital improvement plan, considering any changes which, from time to time, may be made in such plan provided, however, that the amount in such reserve shall be be permitted to vary from year to year if approved by the Council during the annual budget process for the purposes of achieving stability and predictability in rates and to minimize changes adverse to electric consumers;

4. To pay into the General Fund of the City of Fort Collins in lieu of taxes and franchise permits a percentage of revenue from the sale of electric energy equivalent to five percent (5%) of operating revenues.

C. EXCESS RETAINED EARNINGS

After retained earnings are reserved as specified above, any excess retained earnings shall be added to the future capital improvements reserve.

D. OPERATING RECORDS

1. The Light and Power Utility will maintain a standard system of accounting which shall, at all times, correctly reflect all financial operations of the system and keep other such records and data as are generally used by the electric utility industry.

2. The accounts of the Light and Power Utility shall be kept separate and distinct from all other accounts of the City and shall contain proportionate charges for all services performed by other departments as well as proportionate credits for all services rendered to other departments.

VIII.3. WATER AND SEWER UTILITIES

Formally adopted financial policies are an important factor in planning the financial operations of the Water and Sewer Utilities. Comprehensive financial policies include statements concerning:

    A. Net Income Requirements
    B. Rate Requirements
    C. Reserve Requirements
    D. Capital Cost Financing

Policy statements have been developed for each area listed above and incorporated into the five-year financial plans for the Water and Sewer Utilities as follows:

A. NET INCOME

The net income of the Water and Sewer Utilities shall be at least equal to the annual cost of the following:

1. Principal reductions of outstanding bonds,
2. Loan requirements to Federal or State agencies, and
3. Annual operating reserve increases.

B. RATE REQUIREMENTS

Utility rates shall be set at a level to provide for the net income requirement in each fiscal year. Levelized rate increases are preferred and, when possible, should be achieved through levelized expenditures.

C. RESERVES

The following reserves shall be established and maintained in the applicable utility.

1. Operating Reserve - at least equal to two percent (2%) of the projected annual operating revenue.

2. Plant Investment Fee Reserve - equal to the annual fees less annual cost allocated to System Expansions.

3. Capital Reserve - equal to the amount of bond proceeds available at the end of one fiscal year to be expended in the next fiscal year.

4. Debt Reserve - equal to the amount required by individual bond ordinance.

D. CAPITAL COST FINANCING

Annual capital cost shall be identified as one of three types, and financed as noted:

1. Normal replacement of the existing system.

   Financed on a Pay-As-You-Go basis from a reserve for depreciation funded from current rates.

2. System improvements that benefit the existing and future population.

   Debt financed over the life of the improvement and the annual debt service shall be funded from current rates.

3. System expansions that benefit future populations.

   Debt financed over the life of the expansion, and annual debt service shall be funded from a combination of Plant Investment Fees and Contributions in Aid of Construction.

Federal and/or State grants may be utilized to fund portions of, or all of, capital costs.

VIII.4. STORM DRAINAGE FUND

The primary purpose of the Storm Drainage Fund is to meet the public need for effective stormwater management, including flood control, capital improvements and the operation and maintenance of drainage facilities. Financial policies have been developed for the following categories:

A. Operation and Maintenance Requirements
B. Capital Project Needs
C. Capital Cost Financing
D. Reserves

A. OPERATION AND MAINTENANCE REQUIREMENTS

Utility rates will be set at a level to provide for the operation and maintenance requirement for each fiscal year. The rate is structured on a base rate of $.000384 per square foot per month and on a rate factor compiled at the category of development, such as very light, light, moderate, heavy and very heavy.

B. CAPITAL PROJECT NEEDS

A master plan has been developed for each basin to identify drainage needs, set fees, and determine capital improvement requirements. In the effort to balance storm drainage risk and liability, a 20-year storm drainage capital program has been developed that relates to the system requirements of each basin where a positive cost/benefit ratio exists.

To finance this capital program, a one-time basin fee is collected with new development and a monthly capital fee from property owners.

C. CAPITAL COST FINANCING

The financing of capital improvements will be accomplished through the following:

1. A one-time basin fee that is collected with new development.
2. Monthly capital fee collected from property owners.
3. Bond issues that will be financed over the life of the improvement.

The annual debt service will be provided from the existing monthly capital fees.

D. RESERVES

The following reserves have been established:

1. Capital Reserve - equal to the amount of bond proceeds, monthly capital fees, and one-time new development fees available at the end of one fiscal year to be expended in the next fiscal year.

2. Operating Revenue Reserve - equal to 2% of the projected annual operating revenue.

3. Debt Reserve - equal to the amount required by the individual bond ordinance.

INDEX